COMPUTERIZED

RUNNING TRAINING PROGRAMS

JAMES B. GARDNER and J. GERRY PURDY

Foreword by Payton Jordan
Coach, 1968 U. S. Olympic Track Team

TAFNEWS PRESS, P.O. Box 296, Los Altos, California 94022 U.S.A.

Library of Congress Catalog Card Number: 74-110485

SBN 9115 20-00-7

Printed in the United States of America

Contents

Foreword

This book contains one of the most significant contributions of track training methods in recent years. The tremendous capability of the electronic computer has been put to work to create a valuable aid to the track coach and runner alike. This aid is a set of pacing tables which can be employed to set up custom designed workouts for runners of all abilities.

A continuing problem for the coach is to set up training schedules that are neither too hard nor too easy for the runners. The information given in this book solves this problem by giving workout schedules designed for the individual runner's ability. Most of the established forms of interval and repetition training are contained within these tables as well as less conventional forms of training. This will give the coach and runner a wide choice of workouts for his training program.

Training methods have changed greatly in the past few years. Many have been identified with the coach who developed the method. There are the Lydiard, the Igloi, the Bowerman, the Stampfl methods and many variations of these and others. Each has been successful in its own right. Often, however, an aspiring coach or runner has adapted a particular aspect of one or two of these methods without understanding the total conditioning program and the result often is an athlete who will do *only* marathon training or *only* interval training. This athlete may never reach his fullest potential if he adopts such a narrow training philosophy.

Contemporary successful coaches and athletes alike are coming to the awareness that a single narrow training philosophy is not the answer to achieving the highest levels of performance. Each method has its values and limitations. The best performance is achieved through a combination of the most effective features of each method. The modern training program combines these features in a logical sequence that brings the athlete to supreme fitness at the climax of the competitive season.

This computerized system provides the necessary building blocks to construct such a training program. The various forms of interval training can be combined with continuous running training to build a total program designed for the needs of the individual, whether he be a high school freshman or a world class performer and whether he be a sprinter or long distance runner.

This book should be *as valuable an aid to the coach as the stopwatch itself.* It provides a vast resource of variety workouts that can be extremely effective in bringing the runner to the peak of performance. It also provides a means for the inexperienced coach to evaluate the progress of his runners in each workout. The tables enable the coach to be consistent in the intensity and the quality of the workouts for the runners.

The authors of this book, Mr. Gardner and Mr. Purdy, have combined their respective skills as a systems analyst and computer scientist and their experience and knowledge of track training to create this unique and useful work in the field of running. The result is most impressive and has produced a truly significant contribution to the field of track training.

I fully endorse the contents of this book as an indispensable aid to every coach and every serious competitor in track.

Payton Jordan

About the Book

This book presents a unique development in the field of running training. This development is a set of computerized timetables which indicate the speed (time) at which a runner should perform a given distance for a workout. In addition to the time for each distance, the number of repetitions and the approximate rest interval that should be taken is given. Each of these variables is presented over a wide range of performance abilities, from the world class athlete to jogger or schoolboy runner. This compilation is made possible by using the electronic computer to compute and print the tables.

The reader should be aware that this is not a typical track book in that it does not promote a particular training method or present techniques, such as how a sprinter should get into the starting blocks. What is presented are the raw ingredients from which all running training is based. It is a guide to the amount of workout activity to bring out the best performances in a runner. *This is perhaps the most useful book that has ever been developed for running training since it can be used on a daily basis by runners of all abilities.*

At first glance, the tables may appear to be complex but if the reader will take a few moments to familiarize himself with the meaning of these numbers, they can be an extremely valuable aid to running training for the coach, runner, or student of physical conditioning. It is complete since it covers all ranges of abilities and it is simple since a runner need only to refer to one page of the tables.

The authors firmly believe these tables are an indispensable tool for the coach or runner in building a total training program. However, the tables alone are not enough; for as any tool, they can be used incorrectly. To prevent this as much as possible, a discussion of their proper use and some basic concepts of training are presented in the text which precedes them.

The pacing tables are based on what is termed a "theoretical model" of running performance. A model is that which describes a phenomenon or object either visually or mathematically. In this case, it is a mathematical description which the computer uses to generate the pacing tables. As a model, it may have some minor imperfections which can be corrected as time goes on. Because of this fact, the coach or runner who uses the tables to specify workouts must realize that he cannot always expect the training performance to *exactly* match the charts. Therefore, they should be used as *guidelines* in training rather than rigorous schedules.

The mathematical approach taken in this book has one very important added benefit. In most track literature reference is often made to percentage effort. Effort is an arbitrary reference which varies with the individual. This has been removed and has been replaced by more exact references to percentage of "all out" speed. Effort has its right place relative to how the runner "feels" during a given run, but in an interval workout, the effort for the last run of a set is much greater, due to fatigue, than for the first run of a set. Therefore the reference to percentage speed provides a much more precise method of describing a workout.

The usefulness, practicality and effectiveness of these tables in training have been established over a two year period prior to publication through use by many athletes of widely varying abilities, including the authors. In addition, detailed comparisons have been made with the workouts in the tables and those of champion athletes, as well as by interviews with coaches and athletes. The correlation has been so good that the authors decided to proceed with the publication of these tables for the benefit of all coaches and runners who believe in the value to such a guide.

Much of the track literature presents representative workouts of champion athletes, or a training philosophy of a particular coach. Here, the training schedules of champion athletes can be related to the beginner or the less talented runner by using the relative speed principle of the pacing tables. The book also attempts to present a general review of basic training concepts without promoting one specific philosophy. In contrast to the well known book by Fred Wilt, *How They Train,* this book could well be subtitled, *How You Train,* since it provides the information for you, the runner or coach, to form your own training schedule, patterned after a champion or based on your own ideas of training.

Since this is the first edition of the book, the authors will appreciate any suggestions pertaining to the pacing tables that the reader may have, such as: new ways to use the pacing tables, different or more distances for the intervals, and new areas to which this approach could be applied. The authors are continuing to develop the computerized system. A complete, mathematically based scoring system, age group scoring tables, and advanced pacing tables are under current investigation.

J. Gerry Purdy, San Jose, Calif.
James B. Gardner, Torrance, Calif.
June 1970

Acknowledgments

The authors wish to acknowledge the support and contributions of many people and institutions, without whom this book could not have become a realization. First, acknowledgement is given to the Stanford University Computer Science Department which provided computer time to develop and test the computer program and to generate the tables in the book.

There were a number of people who gave their time to review and constructively criticize the pre-publication version of the text. These people suggested changes that have improved the quality of the book, and their time and talents are greatly appreciated. Many thanks to Bert Nelson, Cordner Nelson, Joe Henderson, Marshall Clark, Dick Reese, Fred Wilt, Chris Stewart, Chuck Menz, F.X. Cretzmeyer, J.Kenneth Doherty; and Alphonse Juilland.

Much needed advice and encouragement were given by Vern Wolfe, Jim Bush, Payton Jordan, Arthur Armstrong, Bob Meyers, Ron Watson, Ernie Bullard, Bryan Springer, Bob Timmons, and Frank Snively.

This book would not be as convincingly successful without the testing of these computer tables by Bill Fitzgerald, Greg Brock, Al Fitzsimmons, Don Snyder, Bill Toole, Bill Rodgers, Tom Keefe, Gene Haynes, John Bunnell, Dave Clearidge, Alan Waterman, and Alan Bell.

The authors wish to acknowledge the patience and understanding given by the families of two "track nuts" who spent many hours running and writing: Carole, Mark, and Matt Gardner; Bunny and Jill Purdy.

Finally, no book ever gets into print without technical support to transform the authors' thoughts into readable type. We thank Rita Jacobus, Norma Edwards, and Joy Custer for their work.

About the Authors

James B. Gardner is presently a spacecraft systems engineer with TRW, Inc. He has been a track and field enthusiast since his high school days. As a prep in a small Iowa town, he competed in the sprints and throwing events and as a collegian ran the 440 and 880 yard runs for the University of Northern Iowa. After getting an M.S. in physics from the University of Iowa in 1963, he came to California and has been employed in the aerospace industry. His interest in running and training was renewed and he turned to long distance running and has been racing at nearly all distances including the marathon. As an officer of the Seniors Track Club, he has advised many of its members on their training program, including W.F. Fitzgerald, National Masters (over 40) Champion at 440, 880 and one mile. In this book, Mr. Gardner has applied the methods of systems engineering to systematizing the training schedules of runners. By combining his talent with that of Mr. Purdy, a computer scientist, the computerized system for training was developed.

J. Gerry Purdy is presently a doctoral candidate in computer science at Stanford University. Mr. Purdy is a track and field enthusiast and was Georgia State Champion as a prep in the javelin in 1961. He attended the University of Tennessee and threw the javelin as a collegian. After moving to California, he began distance running in his spare time while being employed as a computer programmer at TRW, Inc. He has competed in many long distance races including the marathon. After getting an M.S. degree in computer science from U.C.L.A., he began his doctoral program at Stanford under a company-sponsored fellowship from TRW, Inc.

Chapter 1
Introducing the Computerized System

GENERAL DESCRIPTION

This book tells the track coach and the runner what they want to know about the interval method of training. It tells how fast, how far, how many times to repeat and how long to rest between each run. In addition, it presents speeds and distances for repeated runs beyond what is usually considered interval training. This was all made possible with the aid of the computer. For this reason the title "Computerized Running Training Programs" has been chosen. The book contains daily workout programs for runners in any event and of any ability, from sprinters to long distance runners and from world class to novice runners. Whether the runner is a world record holder or a junior high school athlete, this book contains a great variety of workout schedules designed specifically for him.

These workouts are presented in the form of a tabulation of times for each of many distances that might be used in a training program. Given with each time and distance are a suggested number of repetitions and the approximate rest interval required after each run in order to complete the workout. A single, complete table of speeds and distances is presented for *each* level of ability. These tables are hereafter referred to as the *pacing tables.*

Pacing tables are provided for many different levels of ability, ranging from performances equivalent to a 3:42.8 mile through those equivalent to an 8:43 mile. The level of performance is measured by an abbreviated scoring table which gives a point rating corresponding to the ability of the runner. Once the level of ability is established, the pacing table is selected which provides a source of "equivalent intensity" workout schedules.

The large number of tables, each containing 15 different times (speeds) for 20 different distances, is made possible through the use of the modern electronic computer. To achieve this, the computer was given a description for the relations between the variables in an interval workout: speed, distance, repetitions, and rest. This description (computer program) then generated the corresponding workouts for all ranges of abilities. The result is that training schedules for a champion can be determined in the same manner as for an average high school or college runner, each one obtaining the proper workout most suited to his needs. This book presents the first attempt to relate workout programs of runners of varied abilities in a systematic way.

The value of these tables is clearly evident: they become the coach's handbook and the runner's guide. They provide a vast source of workouts for modern runners which can be utilized to set up interesting, varied, and most of all, effective training schedules. In addition, the tables provide a measure of the potential of an athlete by relating his workouts to his expected performance on the track.

The most important features of the tables is that they provide the tools for the coach, or the runner himself, to "custom design" a training program that is geared for the athlete's own ability. Thus, he can avoid the unfortunate situation where the training schedule is designed for only the top performer in each event and the others must merely *hang on* as long as they can. In track it is important that each individual perform to the best of his ability. To do this, he must train in an optimum manner. Heretofore, it has been difficult enough for the coach to devise an "optimum" workout for his best performers. To also devise optimum workouts for his slower runners has been a formidable task. Now, with these tables he can do this

2

at the flip of a page. The result will be not only better performances from the best runners, but also better performances from the less capable runners.

With the wide selection of distances, speeds, and repetitions, the workout schedules can be designed to meet the objectives and needs of the individual runner. He can do speed work, pace work, endurance work, or any combination. All of these are available using the tables as a guide. Most of the conventional forms of interval running training are contained in the tables. In addition, some less conventional forms of training are listed. These may provide a source of workouts that can add variety to the daily routine.

The format, or arrangement, of the pacing tables has been carefully designed to simplify their use. Each page in the pacing tables contains a chart containing many workouts for *one level of ability*. A runner who has established his initial performance level need only to turn to that one chart to obtain a complete set of training schedules from which to choose his workout.

COMPONENTS OF THE SYSTEM

The computerized approach to running training is composed of five main elements: (1) performance rating tables, (2) pacing tables, (3) constant speed tables, (4) reduced speed tables, and (5) per mile average tables. Each of these elements is described below. By far, the most important element is the pacing tables, since all the interval workouts are obtained from them. However, the other elements are necessary for anyone to properly use the pacing tables. The discussion which follows simply introduces the various tables so the reader will have a feel for what they look like. Exactly how each is used can be found in the remainder of the book.

THE PERFORMANCE RATING TABLES

The performance rating tables are employed in the system to determine the level of ability of the individual athlete. The performance level is indicated by the assignment of a point score for a given performance in an event. A higher point score indicates a higher level of competition and greater ability. For ex-

3

ample, world class competition is usually at about 1000 points to 1050 points. National championship competition is at about 950 to 1000 points, whereas typical high school dual meet competition is at 600 to 800 points.

Figure 1.1 shows a sample performance rating table similar to those given as Table 1 in English Unit Tables and Metric Unit Tables, but covering a limited range. In the left hand column are the various point levels, ranging from 1070 to 1010 points. The other columns are headed by the classically run English distances. Under each distance is the time that it has to be run in to achieve that point level. For example, a 9.10 hundred yard dash receives 1042 points. Performances faster than this receive more points, while slower performances receive fewer points.

The times boxed in on Figure 1.1 represent the world records as of mid-1970. One can see that they are all reasonably close together in terms of point value. In addition one can see which world records are scored higher than others. One interpretation is that some world records are "ahead" of the others. All records progress with time, but they do not progress "in step." For example, the 880 yard and 800 meter records are poorer by comparison to most others, whereas the 200 meter and 400 meter records (19.8 and 43.8 respectively) are "ahead" of the others. The 880 record is due to be broken before the 400 meter record, providing the "right" athlete comes along.

The performance rating tables contained in the English and Metric Unit Tables of this book have point levels ranging from 1150 to 0 points, given at every 10 points. English Unit Tables contain the performance rating for English distances (yards and miles), while the Metric Unit Tables contain the performance rating for metric distances (meters and kilometers).

THE PACING TABLES

The pacing tables are the heart of the whole system, since each coach or athlete determines custom designed workouts from these tables. The purpose of the tables is to give a *guideline* for the level or intensity of each workout. To do this, the pacing tables are given for the various point levels which correspond to his all out effort for his particular event.

SCORING TABLES
CLASSICAL ENGLISH RACING DISTANCES
••

POINTS	100 YD	220 YD	440 YD	880 YD	1.00 MI	2.00 MI	3.00 MI	6.00 MI	10.00 MI	MARATHON
1070	8.99	-------	-------	1:41.8	3:46.3	8:07.7	12:33.9	26:17.9	45:22	2:07:02
1068	9.00	-------	44.4	1:41.9	3:46.6	8:08.2	12:34.7	26:19.6	45:25	2:07:10
1066	9.01	-------	-------	1:42.0	3:46.8	8:08.8	12:35.5	26:21.4	45:28	2:07:19
1064	-------	-------	-------	1:42.1	3:47.1	8:09.3	12:36.4	26:23.2	45:31	2:07:28
1062	9.02	-------	44.5	1:42.3	3:47.3	8:09.8	12:37.2	26:24.9	45:34	2:07:37
1060	9.03	20.0	-------	1:42.4	3:47.5	8:10.4	12:38.0	26:26.7	45:37	2:07:45
1058	9.04	-------	44.6	1:42.5	3:47.8	8:10.9	12:38.9	26:28.5	45:40	2:07:54
1056	-------	-------	-------	1:42.6	3:48.0	8:11.4	12:39.7	26:30.3	45:44	2:08:03
1054	9.05	-------	44.7	1:42.7	3:48.3	8:12.0	12:40.6	26:32.1	45:47	2:08:12
1052	9.06	-------	-------	1:42.8	3:48.5	8:12.5	12:41.4	26:33.8	45:50	2:08:21
1050	9.07	-------	-------	1:42.9	3:48.8	8:13.1	12:42.2	26:35.6	45:53	2:08:30
1048	-------	20.1	44.8	1:43.0	3:49.0	8:13.6	12:43.1	26:37.4	45:56	2:08:39
1046	9.08	-------	-------	1:43.1	3:49.3	8:14.1	12:43.9	26:39.2	45:59	2:08:48
1044	9.09	-------	44.9	1:43.2	3:49.5	8:14.7	12:44.8	26:41.0	46:02	2:08:56
1042	9.10	-------	-------	1:43.3	3:49.7	8:15.2	12:45.6	26:42.8	46:05	2:09:05
1040	-------	-------	45.0	1:43.4	3:50.0	8:15.8	12:46.5	26:44.7	46:09	2:09:14
1038	9.11	-------	-------	1:43.5	3:50.2	8:16.3	12:47.4	26:46.5	46:12	2:09:23
1036	9.12	20.2	-------	1:43.6	3:50.5	8:16.9	12:48.2	26:48.3	46:15	2:09:33
1034	9.13	-------	45.1	1:43.7	3:50.7	8:17.4	12:49.1	26:50.1	46:18	2:09:42
1032	9.14	-------	-------	1:43.8	3:51.0	8:18.0	12:49.9	26:52.0	46:21	2:09:51
1030	-------	-------	45.2	1:44.0	3:51.2	8:18.5	12:50.8	26:53.8	46:25	2:10:00
1028	9.15	-------	-------	1:44.1	3:51.5	8:19.1	12:51.7	26:55.6	46:28	2:10:09
1026	9.16	20.3	45.3	1:44.2	3:51.7	8:19.6	12:52.5	26:57.5	46:31	2:10:18
1024	9.17	-------	-------	1:44.4	3:52.0	8:20.2	12:53.4	26:59.3	46:34	2:10:27
1022	-------	-------	45.4	1:44.4	3:52.2	8:20.8	12:54.3	27:01.2	46:37	2:10:36
1020	9.18	-------	-------	1:44.5	3:52.5	8:21.3	12:55.2	27:03.0	46:41	2:10:46
1018	9.19	-------	-------	1:44.6	3:52.8	8:21.9	12:56.0	27:04.9	46:44	2:10:55
1016	9.20	-------	45.5	1:44.7	3:53.0	8:22.4	12:56.9	27:06.7	46:47	2:11:04
1014	9.21	20.4	-------	1:44.8	3:53.3	8:23.0	12:57.8	27:08.6	46:50	2:11:13
1012	-------	-------	45.6	1:44.9	3:53.5	8:23.6	12:58.7	27:10.5	46:54	2:11:23
1010	9.22	-------	-------	1:45.0	3:53.8	8:24.1	12:59.6	27:12.4	46:57	2:11:32

Figure 1.1   Sample Scoring Table Showing Classical English Racing Distances for the 1070 to 1010 Point Levels

A sample page from the complete set of pacing tables is presented in Figure 1.2. The first column on the left side, headed by "SPEED", lists the relative speed, in percentage of the maximum that a runner at this performance level could sustain over the particular distance. Broadly speaking, the sprint distances are for sprinters, the medium distances (220 to 880) are for middle distances runners and the longer distances are for distance runners.

The second column, headed by "REPS" (repetitions), indicates the number of times that the distance can be run at that speed with the given rest interval between each. The number listed under "REPS" is a typical number that can be done in a good, hard workout.

The third column, headed by "REST", lists the usual rest interval taken between each of the runs, given in minutes (M) or in seconds (S). As with the REPS, a range of values for the rest is given to allow some flexibility to the runner in terms of both his own response, his recovery characteristics and the form of "rest" that he takes (e.g., walking or slow jogging).

The number of repetitions and the rest intervals listed are not mathematically determined but are based on the response and heart rate recovery characteristics of *most* athletes. Some athletes may slightly exceed the number of reps at one distance, say 220 yards, but may fall just short of the listed number of another workout at a different distance, say 440 yards. The values listed have been found to apply to *most* runners who are somewhat accustomed to the interval form of training. The basis for the rest interval is discussed more thoroughly in Chapter 8.

The remainder of the columns of times are each headed by a distance, ranging from 110 yards in the upper section to 2 miles in the lower section. The numbers listed in each column are the times, in minutes and seconds, in which the distance is to be run. Since the computer calculates these exactly, they are given to a tenth of a second. It would *not* be expected, of course, that the runner cover the distance in this exact time in every attempt, but his *average* time over the workout should agree with the listed time within a few tenths of a second in the shorter distance and within a second or so in the longer distances. Also, for the table to hold a valid relationship to the workout actually performed, each run in the workout should be

760 POINT LEVEL PACING TABLE

SPEED	REPS	REST	110 YD	150 YD	165 YD	220 YD	275 YD	330 YD	352 YD	385 YD	440 YD	495 YD
95.0%	0- 1	---	11.1	15.3	17.0	23.0	29.8	37.4	40.5	45.4	53.7	1:02.3
92.5%	1- 2	4- 5 M	11.4	15.7	17.4	23.7	30.7	38.4	41.6	46.6	55.1	1:04.0
90.0%	2- 3	4- 5 M	11.7	16.2	17.9	24.3	31.5	39.5	42.8	47.9	56.7	1:05.8
87.5%	3- 4	3- 4 M	12.0	16.6	18.4	25.0	32.4	40.6	44.0	49.3	58.3	1:07.7
85.0%	4- 5	3- 4 M	12.4	17.1	18.9	25.8	33.4	41.8	45.3	50.7	1:00.0	1:09.7
82.5%	6- 7	2- 3 M	12.8	17.6	19.5	26.5	34.4	43.0	46.7	52.3	1:01.8	1:11.8
80.0%	8- 9	2- 3 M	13.2	18.2	20.1	27.4	35.4	44.4	48.1	53.9	1:03.7	1:14.0
77.5%	10-12	1- 2 M	13.6	18.8	20.8	28.2	36.6	45.8	49.7	55.6	1:05.8	1:16.4
75.0%	13-15	1- 2 M	14.0	19.4	21.5	29.2	37.8	47.3	51.3	57.5	1:08.0	1:19.0
72.5%	16-18	60-90 S	14.5	20.1	22.2	30.2	39.1	49.0	53.1	59.5	1:10.3	1:21.7
70.0%	19-21	60-90 S	15.0	20.8	23.0	31.3	40.5	50.7	55.0	1:01.6	1:12.9	1:24.6
67.5%	22-24	45-75 S	15.6	21.6	23.9	32.4	42.0	52.6	57.0	1:03.9	1:15.6	1:27.7
65.0%	25-29	45-75 S	16.2	22.4	24.8	33.7	43.6	54.6	59.2	1:06.3	1:18.5	1:31.1
62.5%	30-35	30-60 S	16.8	23.3	25.8	35.0	45.4	56.8	1:01.6	1:09.0	1:21.0	1:34.8
60.0%	36-40	30-60 S	17.6	24.3	26.8	36.5	47.3	59.2	1:04.2	1:11.8	1:25.0	-----

SPEED	REPS	REST	550 YD	660 YD	880 YD	1100 YD	1320 YD	1.00 MI	1.25 MI	1.50 MI	1.75 MI	2.00 MI
95.0%	0- 1	---	1:11.3	1:29.5	2:06.3	2:44.9	3:24.0	4:44.2	6:05.9	7:29.0	8:52.6	10:16.6
92.5%	1- 2	4- 5 M	1:13.2	1:31.9	2:09.8	2:49.3	3:29.5	4:51.9	6:15.8	7:41.1	9:07.0	10:33.3
90.0%	2- 3	4- 5 M	1:15.3	1:34.5	2:13.4	2:54.0	3:35.3	5:00.0	6:26.3	7:53.9	9:22.2	10:50.9
87.5%	3- 4	3- 4 M	1:17.4	1:37.2	2:17.2	2:59.0	3:41.4	5:08.6	6:37.3	8:07.5	9:38.3	11:09.5
85.0%	4- 5	3- 4 M	1:19.7	1:40.1	2:21.2	3:04.3	3:48.0	5:17.7	6:49.0	8:21.8	9:55.3	11:29.2
82.5%	6- 7	2- 3 M	1:22.1	1:43.1	2:25.5	3:09.9	3:54.9	5:27.3	7:01.4	-----	-----	-----
80.0%	8- 9	2- 3 M	1:24.7	1:46.3	2:30.0	3:15.8	4:02.2	5:37.5	-----	-----	-----	-----
77.5%	10-12	1- 2 M	1:27.4	1:49.7	2:34.9	3:22.1	4:10.0	-----	-----	-----	-----	-----
75.0%	13-15	1- 2 M	1:30.3	1:53.4	2:40.0	3:28.8	4:18.4	-----	-----	-----	-----	-----
72.5%	16-18	60-90 S	1:33.4	1:57.3	2:45.6	-----	-----	-----	-----	-----	-----	-----
70.0%	19-21	60-90 S	1:36.8	2:01.5	2:51.5	-----	-----	-----	-----	-----	-----	-----
67.5%	22-24	45-75 S	1:40.4	2:06.0	-----	-----	-----	-----	-----	-----	-----	-----
65.0%	25-29	45-75 S	1:44.2	-----	-----	-----	-----	-----	-----	-----	-----	-----
62.5%	30-35	30-60 S	-----	-----	-----	-----	-----	-----	-----	-----	-----	-----
60.0%	36-40	30-60 S	-----	-----	-----	-----	-----	-----	-----	-----	-----	-----

Figure 1.2 Sample Pacing Table for the 760 Point Level

7

evenly paced and the time of each run should be within about 2% of the time listed (roughly within 1 second for each minute).

CONSTANT SPEED TABLES

The constant speed tables simply give the times for intermediate distances at a constant speed (pace). One often wants to know what time he should run an intermediate distance, say 275 or 550 yards, at a known pace, usually expressed in seconds per 440. A couple of examples are: a runner performing a 220 in 30 seconds, or a 385 in 52.5 seconds, for a 60 second 440 pace.

In interval running, one often desires to run some fraction of the racing distance but at the planned race pace. For a 2:00 performance in the 880, the athlete might desire to run a certain number of repetitions of 275 yard intervals at the race pace of 2:00 for the 880, more typically expressed as a 60 second quarter pace (37.5 seconds).

Figure 1.3 shows an example of this table. In the left column are given times for the 440 yard distance. The remaining columns are headed by the intermediate distances and the times given are the elapsed times at that distance for the corresponding 440 yard time.

As an example, if an athlete desired to run 275 yard intervals at a 66 second 440 pace, he reads under the 275 yard column a time of 41.3 for the 66 second, 440 row (as circled in the figure).

The complete table is given as Table 2 in the English and Metric Unit Tables. Chapter 3 explains how to use this table in conjunction with the pacing tables.

REDUCED SPEED TABLES

The fourth kind of table is the reduced speed table which gives reduced speed level times based on a known mile average. An example of this table is given in Figure 1.4. The left column has the mile pace for a 100% effort run, and the remaining columns contain the mile pace for the reduced speed levels shown. This table is beneficial for the runner who is performing a long, continuous run. If an athlete can perform

INTERMEDIATE TIMES FOR CONSTANT SPEED RUNS
· ·

440 Y	110 Y	150 Y	165 Y	220 Y	275 Y	330 Y	352 Y	385 Y	495 Y	550 Y
43.0	10.8	14.7	16.1	21.5	26.9	32.3	34.4	37.6	48.4	53.8
44.0	11.0	15.0	16.5	22.0	27.5	33.0	35.2	38.5	49.5	55.0
45.0	11.3	15.3	16.9	22.5	28.1	33.8	36.0	39.4	50.6	56.3
46.0	11.5	15.7	17.3	23.0	28.8	34.5	36.8	40.3	51.8	57.5
47.0	11.8	16.0	17.6	23.5	29.4	35.3	37.6	41.1	52.9	58.8
48.0	12.0	16.4	18.0	24.0	30.0	36.0	38.4	42.0	54.0	1:00.0
49.0	12.3	16.7	18.4	24.5	30.6	36.8	39.2	42.9	55.1	1:01.3
50.0	12.5	17.0	18.8	25.0	31.3	37.5	40.0	43.8	56.3	1:02.5
51.0	12.8	17.4	19.1	25.5	31.9	38.3	40.8	44.6	57.4	1:03.8
52.0	13.0	17.7	19.5	26.0	32.5	39.0	41.6	45.5	58.5	1:05.0
53.0	13.3	18.1	19.9	26.5	33.1	39.8	42.4	46.4	59.6	1:06.3
54.0	13.5	18.4	20.3	27.0	33.8	40.5	43.2	47.3	1:00.8	1:07.5
55.0	13.8	18.8	20.6	27.5	34.4	41.3	44.0	48.1	1:01.9	1:08.8
56.0	14.0	19.1	21.0	28.0	35.0	42.0	44.8	49.0	1:03.0	1:10.0
57.0	14.3	19.4	21.4	28.5	35.6	42.8	45.6	49.9	1:04.1	1:11.3
58.0	14.5	19.8	21.8	29.0	36.3	43.5	46.4	50.8	1:05.3	1:12.5
59.0	14.8	20.1	22.1	29.5	36.9	44.3	47.2	51.6	1:06.4	1:13.8
1:00.0	15.0	20.5	22.5	30.0	37.5	45.0	48.0	52.5	1:07.5	1:15.0
1:01.0	15.3	20.8	22.9	30.5	38.1	45.8	48.8	53.4	1:08.6	1:16.3
1:02.0	15.5	21.1	23.3	31.0	38.8	46.5	49.6	54.3	1:09.8	1:17.5
1:03.0	15.8	21.5	23.6	31.5	39.4	47.3	50.4	55.1	1:10.9	1:18.8
1:04.0	16.0	21.8	24.0	32.0	40.0	48.0	51.2	56.0	1:12.0	1:20.0
1:05.0	16.3	22.2	24.4	32.5	40.6	48.8	52.0	56.9	1:13.1	1:21.3
1:06.0	16.5	22.5	24.8	33.0	41.3	49.5	52.8	57.8	1:14.3	1:22.5
1:07.0	16.8	22.8	25.1	33.5	41.9	50.3	53.6	58.6	1:15.4	1:23.8
1:08.0	17.0	23.2	25.5	34.0	42.5	51.0	54.4	59.5	1:16.5	1:25.0
1:09.0	17.3	23.5	25.9	34.5	43.1	51.8	55.2	1:00.4	1:17.6	1:26.3

Figure 1.3   Sample Constant Speed Table for the 43 to 1:09 Quarter Mile Averages

9

TABLE OF REDUCED SPEEDS FOR CONTINUOUS RUNNING TRAINING
•••

PER MILE AVERAGE

100.0 %	97.5 %	95.0 %	92.5 %	90.0 %	87.5 %	85.0 %	82.5 %	80.0 %
4:00.0	4:06.2	4:12.6	4:19.5	4:26.7	4:34.3	4:42.4	4:50.9	5:00.0
4:05.0	4:11.3	4:17.9	4:24.9	4:32.2	4:40.0	4:48.2	4:57.0	5:06.3
4:10.0	4:16.4	4:23.2	4:30.3	4:37.8	4:45.7	4:54.1	5:03.0	5:12.5
4:15.0	4:21.5	4:28.4	4:35.7	4:43.3	4:51.4	5:00.0	5:09.1	5:18.8
4:20.0	4:26.7	4:33.7	4:41.1	4:48.9	4:57.1	5:05.9	5:15.2	5:25.0
4:25.0	4:31.8	4:38.9	4:46.5	4:54.4	5:02.9	5:11.8	5:21.2	5:31.3
4:30.0	4:36.9	4:44.2	4:51.9	5:00.0	5:08.6	5:17.6	5:27.3	5:37.5
4:35.0	4:42.1	4:49.5	4:57.3	5:05.6	5:14.3	5:23.5	5:33.3	5:43.8
4:40.0	4:47.2	4:54.7	5:02.7	5:11.1	5:20.0	5:29.4	5:39.4	5:50.0
4:45.0	4:52.3	5:00.0	5:08.1	5:16.7	5:25.7	5:35.3	5:45.5	5:56.3
4:50.0	4:57.4	5:05.3	5:13.5	5:22.2	5:31.4	5:41.2	5:51.5	6:02.5
4:55.0	5:02.6	5:10.5	5:18.9	5:27.8	5:37.1	5:47.1	5:57.6	6:08.8
5:00.0	5:07.7	5:15.8	5:24.3	5:33.3	5:42.9	5:52.9	6:03.6	6:15.0
5:05.0	5:12.8	5:21.1	5:29.7	5:38.9	5:48.6	5:58.8	6:09.7	6:21.3
5:10.0	5:17.9	5:26.3	5:35.1	5:44.4	5:54.3	6:04.7	6:15.8	6:27.5
5:15.0	5:23.1	5:31.6	5:40.5	5:50.0	6:00.0	6:10.6	6:21.8	6:33.8
5:20.0	5:28.2	5:36.8	5:45.9	5:55.6	6:05.7	6:16.5	6:27.9	6:40.0
5:25.0	5:33.3	5:42.1	5:51.4	6:01.1	6:11.4	6:22.4	6:33.9	6:46.3
5:30.0	5:38.5	5:47.4	5:56.8	6:06.7	6:17.1	6:28.2	6:40.0	6:52.5
5:35.0	5:43.6	5:52.6	6:02.2	6:12.2	6:22.9	6:34.1	6:46.1	6:58.8
5:40.0	5:48.7	5:57.9	6:07.6	6:17.8	6:28.6	6:40.0	6:52.1	7:05.0
5:45.0	5:53.8	6:03.2	6:13.0	6:23.3	6:34.3	6:45.9	6:58.2	7:11.3
5:50.0	5:59.0	6:08.4	6:18.4	6:28.9	6:40.0	6:51.8	7:04.2	7:17.5
5:55.0	6:04.1	6:13.7	6:23.8	6:34.4	6:45.7	6:57.6	7:10.3	7:23.8
6:00.0	6:09.2	6:18.9	6:29.2	6:40.0	6:51.4	7:03.5	7:16.4	7:30.0

Figure 1.4   Sample Reduced Speed Table for the 4:00 to 6:00 Mile Averages

10

a given distance at say 6:00 per mile, with 100% effort as in competition, then in training he will typically run that same distance at some fraction (percentage speed) of his all out effort. From this table, the runner can obtain the proper pace for doing his training run.

As an example, most distance runners perform at 85% to 90% of their all out speed in a training run which is longer than their racing distance. If a particular runner's best average is 6:00 per mile for a long run, then he might run at 6:40 per mile (90% speed) in the training run. The table can also be referred to after a run to determine the speed level at which the run was just performed. Remember, speed should not be confused with "effort". Speed is expressed as a fraction of velocity (distance per unit time), while effort is expressed subjectively, i.e. how the runner feels, which may or may not correspond with the speed level.

The complete table is given in Table 3 in the English and Metric Unit Tables. Table 3 in the English Unit Tables contains per mile percentage speeds while Table 3 in the Metric Unit Tables contains per kilometer percentage speeds.

PER MILE AVERAGE TABLES

The fifth kind of table is the per mile average table which gives the per mile average time for a number of distances at the various point levels. An example of this table can be seen in Figure 1.5. This table is basically the same as the scoring table, except that the entries for the distances and point levels are per mile averages instead of total time.

This table is helpful to the distance runner who desires to do over-distance work. He can find the possible all out mile pace for a distance longer than his racing distance (even though he hasn't raced at it yet) by looking in this table at the column headed by this longer distance and *his* point level. This will give him a value for his potential performance in an all out effort. When he runs the distance in a training session, he will be able to determine his percentage speed by referring to the reduced speed tables for the percentage of the 100% speed. (See page 103 and 104 for a more detailed example).

The per mile average tables are contained in Table 5 of the English Unit Tables and give mile averages for distances ranging from 5 to 32 miles. There are no metric tables which show per kilometer averages.

POINTS	5.00 MI	6.00 MI	7.00 MI	8.00 MI	9.00 MI	10.00 MI	11.00 MI	12.00 MI	13.00 MI	14.00 MI
1050	4:22.7	4:25.9	4:28	4:31	4:33	4:35	4:37	4:38	4:40	4:41
1040	4:24.2	4:27.4	4:30	4:32	4:34	4:36	4:38	4:40	4:41	4:43
1030	4:25.7	4:29.0	4:31	4:34	4:36	4:38	4:40	4:41	4:43	4:44
1020	4:27.2	4:30.5	4:33	4:35	4:38	4:40	4:41	4:43	4:44	4:46
1010	4:28.7	4:32.1	4:35	4:37	4:39	4:41	4:43	4:45	4:46	4:48
1000	4:30.3	4:33.6	4:36	4:39	4:41	4:43	4:45	4:46	4:48	4:49
990	4:31.8	4:35.2	4:38	4:40	4:42	4:45	4:46	4:48	4:50	4:51
980	4:33.4	4:36.8	4:39	4:42	4:44	4:46	4:48	4:50	4:51	4:53
970	4:35.0	4:38.5	4:41	4:44	4:46	4:48	4:50	4:51	4:53	4:54
960	4:36.6	4:40.1	4:43	4:45	4:48	4:50	4:52	4:53	4:55	4:56
950	4:38.3	4:41.8	4:44	4:47	4:49	4:51	4:53	4:55	4:57	4:58
940	4:39.9	4:43.5	4:46	4:49	4:51	4:53	4:55	4:57	4:58	5:00
930	4:41.6	4:45.2	4:48	4:51	4:53	4:55	4:57	4:59	5:00	5:02
920	4:43.3	4:46.9	4:50	4:52	4:55	4:57	4:59	5:00	5:02	5:04
910	4:45.0	4:48.7	4:51	4:54	4:56	4:59	5:01	5:02	5:04	5:05
900	4:46.8	4:50.4	4:53	4:56	4:58	5:01	5:02	5:04	5:06	5:07
890	4:48.6	4:52.2	4:55	4:58	5:00	5:02	5:04	5:06	5:08	5:09
880	4:50.3	4:54.1	4:57	5:00	5:02	5:04	5:06	5:08	5:10	5:11
870	4:52.2	4:55.9	4:59	5:01	5:04	5:06	5:08	5:10	5:12	5:13
860	4:54.0	4:57.8	5:01	5:03	5:06	5:08	5:10	5:12	5:14	5:15
850	4:55.8	4:59.6	5:02	5:05	5:08	5:10	5:12	5:14	5:16	5:17
840	4:57.7	5:01.6	5:04	5:07	5:10	5:12	5:14	5:16	5:18	5:19
830	4:59.6	5:03.5	5:06	5:09	5:12	5:14	5:16	5:18	5:20	5:21
820	5:01.6	5:05.5	5:08	5:11	5:14	5:16	5:18	5:20	5:22	5:24
810	5:03.5	5:07.4	5:10	5:13	5:16	5:18	5:20	5:22	5:24	5:26
800	5:05.5	5:09.4	5:12	5:15	5:18	5:20	5:23	5:24	5:26	5:28
790	5:07.5	5:11.5	5:14	5:18	5:20	5:23	5:25	5:27	5:28	5:30
780	5:09.5	5:13.6	5:17	5:20	5:22	5:25	5:27	5:29	5:31	5:32
770	5:11.6	5:15.6	5:19	5:22	5:24	5:27	5:29	5:31	5:33	5:35
760	5:13.7	5:17.8	5:21	5:24	5:27	5:29	5:31	5:33	5:35	5:37
750	5:15.8	5:19.9	5:23	5:26	5:29	5:31	5:34	5:36	5:37	5:39
740	5:17.9	5:22.1	5:25	5:28	5:31	5:34	5:36	5:38	5:40	5:42

Figure 1.5   Sample Per Mile Averages Table for the 1000 to 690 Point Levels

12

Chapter 2
How to Use the System

DETERMINING THE PERFORMANCE LEVEL

Each competitive runner, whether or not he is at the peak of condition, is able to perform his chosen distance in a certain time. His performance time is an indication of his current state of condition and his ability, which may be described as his *level of performance.* Knowledge of his level of performance is important as it is directly related to his ability to perform a workout. One method for comparing his performance level with that of another runner who competes in a different event is to use an equalized scoring table. The scoring table gives a point score based on the performance time in the event. The complete performance rating scoring table is given as Table 1 in the English Unit Tables and as Table 1 in the Metric Unit Tables.

To use the performance rating table, one simply finds the performance time in the table for the distance run and looks to the left column to read the point score. This point level measures the relative ability of the athlete compared with all other point levels. Notice that relative ability is expressed irrespective of the athlete's event distance. For example, a 760 point level performer is a 440 yard runner who runs 52.0, or an 880 yard runner who runs 2:01, or a miler who runs 4:31, etc. These equivalent performances are boxed off in Figure 2.1. When the term "equivalent performances" is used, one must remember that these are considered equal competitive levels for all distances. A runner has to perform only one of the 760 point level performances to be considered a 760 point level runner. However, *nearly,* equal distances can be equated for a *single* athlete within his event category, e.g., a 4:30.8 miler may potentially be able to run about a 9:46 two mile if adequately trained. The athlete should always use the point level corresponding to the distance he is training for, i.e., a miler should use the point level for his best mile, regardless of what his point level is for other distances.

The point score also indicates the runner's capacity to perform a training workout. It is this application of the scoring table that is of greatest importance in using the pacing tables. Since there are factors other than physical condition and ability that influence the performance, it is not so important that the performance times listed in the rating table agree *exactly* with the time trial performance. All that is needed is an indication of the athlete's ability at the present time. For this reason the scoring table is printed in steps of 10 points in the English and Metric Unit Tables.

The pacing tables are given for every 20 points beginning with 1100 points and continuing to 0 points in the English Unit Tables. Therefore, the performance rating for training purposes need only be within ten points of the exact point score for the particular performance. *The important thing here is that there is a direct relationship between the athlete's performance level and his ability to perform an interval workout.* The performance rating table provides a measure of this ability. The pacing table given at each point level is designed for the ability of the runner whose performance matches the point score of the pacing table. This is the fundamental principle of the computerized system.

DETERMINING THE WORKOUT LEVEL

The most important instruction for using the pacing tables is to choose the table which *most nearly* matches the ability of the individual runner. A runner determines his point level from the performance rating table. He now wishes to obtain guidelines for his workouts. He simply finds the pacing table nearest his

SCORING TABLES
CLASSICAL ENGLISH RACING DISTANCES
••

POINTS	100 YD	220 YD	440 YD	880 YD	1.00 MI	2.00 MI	3.00 MI	6.00 MI	10.00 MI	MARATHON
850	9.90	22.0	49.5	1:54.7	4:16.2	9:14.0	14:17.4	29:57.9	51:46	2:25:16
840	9.95	22.1	49.8	1:55.3	4:17.8	9:17.4	14:22.8	30:09.3	52:06	2:26:13
830	9.99	22.2	50.0	1:56.0	4:19.3	9:20.9	14:28.3	30:20.9	52:26	2:27:11
820	10.04	22.3	50.3	1:56.7	4:20.9	9:24.4	14:33.8	30:32.7	52:46	2:28:10
810	10.08	22.4	50.6	1:57.4	4:22.5	9:28.0	14:39.4	30:44.6	53:07	2:29:10
800	10.13	22.6	50.9	1:58.1	4:24.1	9:31.6	14:45.0	30:56.7	53:28	2:30:10
790	10.18	22.7	51.1	1:58.8	4:25.8	9:35.3	14:50.8	31:08.9	53:50	2:31:11
780	10.23	22.8	51.4	1:59.5	4:27.4	9:39.0	14:56.6	31:21.3	54:11	2:32:14
770	10.28	22.9	51.7	2:00.2	4:29.1	9:42.8	15:02.5	31:33.9	54:33	2:33:16
760	**10.33**	**23.0**	**52.0**	**2:00.9**	**4:30.8**	**9:46.6**	**15:08.5**	**31:46.6**	**54:55**	**2:34:20**
750	10.38	23.1	52.3	2:01.7	4:32.6	9:50.4	15:14.5	31:59.5	55:18	2:35:25
740	10.43	23.2	52.6	2:02.4	4:34.3	9:54.3	15:20.6	32:12.6	55:41	2:36:30
730	10.48	23.4	52.9	2:03.2	4:36.1	9:58.3	15:26.9	32:25.8	56:04	2:37:37
720	10.53	23.5	53.2	2:03.9	4:37.9	10:02.3	15:33.1	32:39.3	56:28	2:38:44
710	10.58	23.6	53.5	2:04.7	4:39.7	10:06.4	15:39.5	32:52.9	56:51	2:39:53
700	10.63	23.7	53.8	2:05.5	4:41.6	10:10.5	15:46.0	33:06.7	57:16	2:41:02
690	10.68	23.8	54.1	2:06.3	4:43.4	10:14.7	15:52.6	33:20.7	57:40	2:42:13
680	10.74	24.0	54.4	2:07.1	4:45.3	10:19.0	15:59.2	33:34.9	58:05	2:43:24
670	10.79	24.1	54.7	2:07.9	4:47.2	10:23.3	16:06.0	33:49.3	58:30	2:44:37
660	10.85	24.2	55.1	2:08.7	4:49.2	10:27.6	16:12.8	34:04.0	58:56	2:45:50
650	10.90	24.4	55.4	2:09.5	4:51.2	10:32.0	16:19.7	34:18.8	59:22	2:47:05
640	10.96	24.5	55.7	2:10.4	4:53.2	10:36.5	16:26.8	34:33.8	59:48	2:48:21
630	11.01	24.6	56.0	2:11.2	4:55.2	10:41.1	16:33.9	34:49.1	1:00:15	2:49:38
620	11.07	24.7	56.4	2:12.1	4:57.2	10:45.7	16:41.2	35:04.6	1:00:42	2:50:56
610	11.12	24.9	56.7	2:13.0	4:59.3	10:50.4	16:48.5	35:20.3	1:01:10	2:52:15
600	11.18	25.0	57.1	2:13.9	5:01.4	10:55.1	16:56.0	35:36.3	1:01:38	2:53:36
590	11.24	25.2	57.4	2:14.8	5:03.6	10:59.9	17:03.6	35:52.5	1:02:06	2:54:58
580	11.30	25.3	57.8	2:15.7	5:05.8	11:04.8	17:11.2	36:09.0	1:02:35	2:56:21
570	11.36	25.4	58.1	2:16.6	5:08.0	11:09.8	17:19.0	36:25.7	1:03:04	2:57:46
560	11.42	25.6	58.5	2:17.5	5:10.2	11:14.8	17:27.0	36:42.7	1:03:34	2:59:11
550	11.48	25.7	58.9	2:18.5	5:12.5	11:20.0	17:35.0	36:59.9	1:04:04	3:00:39
540	11.54	25.9	59.2	2:19.5	5:14.8	11:25.2	17:43.2	37:17.4	1:04:35	3:02:07

Figure 2.1 Equivalent Performances at the 760 Point Level

15

point level from the complete set, listed as Table 4 in the English Unit Tables (and as Table 4 in the Metric Unit Tables). This procedure is perhaps clarified by looking at Figure 2.2.

It is important to note that *all times given in all the pacing tables are for a full running start.* This is more important for the shorter distance intervals than for 440 yards and up. Also, all runs are assumed to begin in the middle of a 440 track, i.e., half of a 110 yard interval is assumed to be on the curve. The positions of the typical workout distances on a track is shown in Figure 2.3.

In the *scoring tables,* the times given are for a standing start (or from a set of blocks) and all distances less than or equal to 110 meters (or about 120 yards) are assumed to be run on the straight, rather than partially on the curve.

For his training program the runner selects his workout schedule from the pacing table for *his* point level, but the specific choice of the daily workout at that level depends upon a number of factors which are discussed in the chapters which follow.

It must be emphasized that the workouts given by the charts are considered to be good, *hard,* workouts. They do *not* include the usual warmup activity nor the warmdown activity. The number of REPS and the REST intervals are based on the maximum number of runs that the typical athlete can maintain the speed (time) listed. Normally, if the runner attempts additional runs (with the same rest interval) he can no longer maintain the speed of each run, even with 100% effort (this does *not* hold true for distances less than 200 yards). The coach should consider this fact in his supervision of the workout. He may not believe that his runner should work out this hard, or he may believe that they should attempt to go beyond this. The tables reflect what *most* runners are able to do with the given rest intervals at the given speeds. The experience of many runners indicates that to exceed the workout given in the tables does not allow complete recovery for the following day's workout.

It is essential that the choice of the pacing tables be based on a trial that has actually been performed, rather than some goal or performance objective. The timetables are based on what the runner can do as a workout at the present time, using the time trial as a measure of his ability. His performance potential

```
                              SCORING TABLES
                   CLASSICAL ENGLISH RACING DISTANCES
                   ●●●●●●●●●●●●●●●●●●●●●●●●●●●●●●●●●●●●●●●●●
```

POINTS	100 YD	220 YD	440 YD	880 YD	1.00 MI	2.00 MI	3.00 MI	6.00 MI	10.00 MI	MARATHON
850	9.90	22.0	49.5	1:54.7	4:16.2	9:14.0	14:17.4	29:57.9	51:46	2:25:16
840	9.95	22.1	49.8	1:55.3	4:17.8	9:17.4	14:22.8	30:09.3	52:06	2:26:13
830	9.99	22.2	50.0	1:56.0	4:19.3	9:20.9	14:28.3	30:20.9	52:26	2:27:11
820	10.04	22.3	50.3	1:56.7	4:20.9	9:24.4	14:33.8	30:32.7	52:46	2:28:10
810	10.08	22.4	50.6	1:57.4	4:22.5	9:28.0	14:39.4	30:44.6	53:07	2:29:10
800	10.13	22.6	50.9	1:58.1	4:24.1	9:31.6	14:45.0	30:56.7	53:28	2:30:10
790	10.18	22.7	51.1	1:58.8	4:25.8	9:35.3	14:50.8	31:08.9	53:50	2:31:11
780	10.23	22.8	51.4	1:59.5	4:27.4	9:39.0	14:56.6	31:21.3	54:11	2:32:14
770	10.28	22.9	51.7	2:00.2	4:29.1	9:42.8	15:02.5	31:33.9	54:33	2:33:16
760	10.33	23.0	52.0	2:00.9	4:30.8	9:46.6	15:08.5	31:46.6	54:55	2:34:20
750	10.38	23.1	52.3	2:01.7	4:32.6	9:50.4	15:14.5	31:59.5	55:18	2:35:25
740	10.43	23.2	52.6	2:02.4	4:34.3	9:54.3	15:20.6	32:12.6	55:41	2:36:30
730	10.48	23.4	52.9	2:03.2	4:36.1	9:58.3	15:26.9	32:25.8	56:04	2:37:37
720	10.53	23.5	53.2	2:03.9	4:37.9	10:02.3	15:33.1	32:39.3	56:28	2:38:44
710	10.58	23.6	53.5	2:04.7	4:39.7	10:06.4	15:39.5	32:52.9	56:51	2:39:53
700	10.63	23.7	53.8	2:05.5	4:41.6	10:10.5	15:46.0	33:06.7	57:16	2:41:02
690										
680										

```
  760  POINT LEVEL PACING TABLE
  ●●●●●●●●●●●●●●●●●●●●●●●●●●●●●
```

SPEED	REPS	REST	110 YD	150 YD	165 YD	220 YD	275 YD	330 YD	352 YD	385 YD	440 YD	495 YD
95.0%	0- 1	---	11.1	15.3	17.0	23.0	29.8	37.4	40.5	45.4	53.7	1:02.3
92.5%	1- 2	4- 5 M	11.4	15.7	17.4	23.7	30.7	38.4	41.6	46.6	55.1	1:04.0
90.0%	2- 3	4- 5 M	11.7	16.2	17.9	24.3	31.5	39.5	42.8	47.9	56.7	1:05.8
87.5%	3- 4	3- 4 M	12.0	16.6	18.4	25.0	32.4	40.6	44.0	49.3	58.3	1:07.7
85.0%	4- 5	3- 4 M	12.4	17.1	18.9	25.8	33.4	41.8	45.3	50.7	1:00.0	1:09.7
82.5%	6- 7	2- 3 M	12.8	17.6	19.5	26.5	34.4	43.0	46.7	52.3	1:01.8	1:11.8
80.0%	8- 9	2- 3 M	13.2	18.2	20.1	27.4	35.4	44.4	48.1	53.9	1:03.7	1:14.0
77.5%	10-12	1- 2 M	13.6	18.8	20.8	28.2	36.6	45.8	49.7	55.6	1:05.8	1:16.4
75.0%	13-15	1- 2 M	14.0	19.4	21.5	29.2	37.8	47.3	51.3	57.5	1:08.0	1:19.0
72.5%	16-18	60-90 M	14.5	20.1	22.2	30.2	39.1	49.0	53.1	59.6	1:10.3	1:21.7
70.0%	19-21	60-90 S	15.0	20.8	23.0	31.3	40.5	50.7	55.0	1:01.6	1:12.9	1:24.6
67.5%	22-24	45-75 S	15.6	21.6	23.9	32.4	42.0	52.6	57.0	1:03.9	1:15.6	1:27.7
65.0%	25-29	45-75 S	16.2	22.4	24.8	33.7	43.6	54.6	59.2	1:06.3	1:18.5	1:31.1
62.5%	30-35	30-60 S	16.8	23.3	25.8	35.0	45.4	56.8	1:01.6	1:09.0	1:21.6	1:34.8
60.0%	36-40	30-60 S	17.6	24.3	26.8	36.5	47.3	59.2	1:04.2	1:11.8	1:25.0	-----

SPEED	REPS	REST	550 YD	660 YD	880 YD	1100 YD	1320 YD	1.00 MI	1.25 MI	1.50 MI	1.75 MI	2.00 MI
95.0%	0- 1	---	1:11.3	1:29.5	2:06.3	2:44.9	3:24.0	4:44.2	6:05.9	7:29.0	8:52.6	10:16.6

Figure 2.2 Procedure for Finding the Proper Pacing Table for a 4:30.8 Miler

17

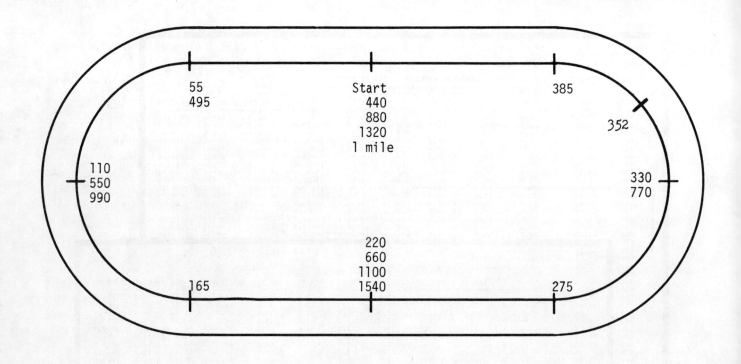

Figure 2.3 Position of Interval Distances on a Standard 440 Yard Track

18

will be brought out in the course of the conditioning program. As he improves in ability he can move up to higher level charts as indicated by his performance in the workouts and in trials or competition.

Two important points must be made concerning the rest intervals and the number of repetitions that are listed in the pacing tables. First, if a longer rest interval is taken then conditioned athletes will typically be able to exceed the number of repetitions that are listed in the tables. Some coaches have their distance runners perform a large number of repetitions of 220 yards for interval training; as many as 40, 60 and even 80 repetitions of 220 yards at about 60 to 65% speed. The rest interval taken during such workouts is longer than what is listed in the tables, usually a minimum of 90 seconds of walking and probably 90 seconds to 2 minutes. It should be emphasized that if more repetitions at a given speed are desired, a longer rest interval than given in the tables will allow such a workout to be performed.

It would be desirable to show the relationship between the numbers of repetitions and longer rest intervals. However, this relationship has not as yet been established. It is anticipated that this relationship will be defined as more analysis is made of the interval workout.

The second point is that the number of repetitions given indicates the typical response of a runner of corresponding ability, but individuals will vary in their workout performance. Furthermore, some runners perform much better in competition than indicated by their workouts, whereas other runners seem to do great workouts but do not meet expectations in competition. Although the values given in the tables have been found to be a valuable guideline for workout activity, they are not to be interpreted as absolute or inflexible. An important observation is that correlation among the various workouts within a single chart is stronger than the correlation between the workouts performed and a competitive performance. What this means is that first preference should be made for workouts that are at the same point level as workouts currently being performed and second preference should be made for workouts at the point level of a competitive performance.

Each pacing table contains the information needed to describe almost any type of interval workout that might be performed (see examples in Chapter 3). They can be used by any athlete from beginner to world champion. With these tables available, the athlete will be able to individualize his training and can progress according to his own rate. An added benefit of the pacing tables is that the various types of training can be more exactly defined and categorized. The overall training program can then be planned and structured in greater detail.

Now that one has determined which pacing table to reference from all those given, he will desire to know how to select different type workouts from his chart. The next chapter gives many of the possible workouts which one can obtain from the pacing tables. How these examples fit into the whole program, or how one decides which particular workout to do is discussed in subsequent chapters.

VALIDITY TESTS

A natural question to ask about this new computerized system is, "How do you know it is so good?" This system—and particularly the pacing tables—has been used and tested by many runners with excellent correlation and results.

Bill Fitzgerald, winner of five events in the 1969 U.S. Masters Championships (over 40), has a lifetime best of 4:28 in the mile and has been using the pacing tables to obtain his workouts for the past year. In December, 1969, Bill included workouts of 5x660 in 1:41, 5x220 in 26.5, 4x880 in 2:22.9, and 10x220 in 28.5. These workouts correspond quite well with the 740 point level pacing table, and on January 3, 1970, Bill set a Senior's Mile record of 4:35.2 in the All-American Games in San Francisco. His record time also was worth 740 points.

Some other examples of the validity of the system are the workouts of Stanford's Greg Brock, who was at the 920 point level in December, 1969, as a result of a 6:28 mile and a half and a 13:35 three mile. Greg had workouts of 12x440 of 64, 5x1320 in 3:21, and 20x440 in 67. These workouts correspond very closely to the 920 point level pacing table.

An interesting comparison can be made with the published workouts of Jim Ryun and the pacing tables. On May 13, 1966, Jim ran 8:25.2 for two miles which is worth approximately 1010 points. This was followed by a 3:53.7 mile on June 4 and a 1:44.9 880 on June 10, also good for about 1010 points.

On May 5, 1966, the afternoon workout of Jim was as follows (percentages are the speed levels taken from the 1020 point level pacing tables for the distance and time run):

Description of Worked Segment	Part of Total Workout*
2 x 220 in 25.5 (75%), 220 jog	1/6
440 jog	
2 x 330 in 40.5 (77.5%), 110 walk	1/6
440 jog	
2 x 440 in 56.8 (77.5%), 3 min. recovery	1/6
440 jog	
1 x 660 in 1:32 (80%)	1/8
440 jog	
2 x 440 in 57.0 (77.5%), 3 min. rest	1/6
440 jog	
2 x 220 in 24.5 (80%), 220 jog	1/6
4 x 150 shake downs	23/24 workout

*For example, the third segment of Jim's workout is 2 x 440 at 77.5% speed. From the pacing table, one finds 77.5% speed corresponds to 12 reps. This third segment is 2 reps, or 2/12 = 1/6 of a full workout.

Another workout performed on May 16 in the afternoon was as follows:

Description of Workout Segment	Part of Total Workout
1 x 1320 in 3:04 (90%)	1/3
440 jog	
1 x 440 in 53 (82.5%)	1/6
880 jog	
4 x 330 in 42.5 (75%), 110 walk	1/3
440 jog	
4 x 220 in 26 (75%), 220 jog	1/3
4 x 150 shake downs	1 1/6 workout

It can be seen that the workouts performed were the equivalent or nearly the equivalent of the full workout from the pacing tables at 1020 points. The second workout adds up to a little more than one complete workout, but there is an extra 440 jog between the segments which the pacing tables do not require; this allows a little more to be done.

As a final example at the lower end of the point scale, one of the authors was at the 500 point level in early 1970 (11:46 two mile) and among many workouts performed from the pacing tables did 3 x 1320 in 4:22, which also agrees favorably with the 500 point level pacing table.

Coach Marshall Clark, Stanford's Cross Country and Assistant Track Coach, finds the tables useful as a guideline for obtaining times for interval running at uncommon distances. An example is to have the distance runners perform interval runs of 550 yards; here the tables help in determining the proper interval time and number of reps.

22

Chapter 3
Example Workouts from the Pacing Tables

Figure 3.1 shows a sample pacing table for the 760 point level. Throughout this chapter the many example workouts from the pacing tables will be taken from this 760 point level ability. A runner at a different level will refer to his own point level pacing table given in Table 4. The type of workout can be the same, while only the time for the interval will be different.

STANDARD INTERVAL WORKOUTS

The standard interval workout can be read directly from the pacing table. For example, suppose a 760 point level *880 yard runner* desires to perform five 440 intervals with about a three to four minute rest (440 yard jog). From the 760 point table in Figure 3.1, he can extract a time of 60.0 seconds for each quarter. The athlete usually is able to perform four to five repetitions running at 85% speed. Expressed more concisely:

4 to 5 440's in 60 sec. with a 440 jog between each

760 POINT LEVEL PACING TABLE

SPEED	REPS	REST	110 YD	150 YD	165 YD	220 YD	275 YD	330 YD	352 YD	385 YD	440 YD	495 YD
95.0%	0- 1	---	11.1	15.3	17.0	23.0	29.8	37.4	40.5	45.4	53.7	1:02.3
92.5%	1- 2	4- 5 M	11.4	15.7	17.4	23.7	30.7	38.4	41.6	46.6	55.1	1:04.0
90.0%	2- 3	4- 5 M	11.7	16.2	17.9	24.3	31.5	39.5	42.8	47.9	56.7	1:05.8
87.5%	3- 4	3- 4 M	12.0	16.6	18.4	25.0	32.4	40.6	44.0	49.3	58.3	1:07.7
85.0%	4- 5	3- 4 M	12.4	17.1	18.9	25.8	33.4	41.8	45.3	50.7	1:00.0	1:09.7
82.5%	6- 7	2- 3 M	12.8	17.6	19.5	26.5	34.4	43.0	46.7	52.3	1:01.8	1:11.7
80.0%	8- 9	2- 3 M	13.2	18.2	20.1	27.4	35.4	44.4	48.1	53.9	1:03.7	1:14.0
77.5%	10-12	1- 2 M	13.6	18.8	20.8	28.2	36.6	45.8	49.7	55.6	1:05.8	1:16.4
75.0%	13-15	1- 2 M	14.0	19.4	21.5	29.2	37.8	47.3	51.3	57.5	1:08.0	1:19.0
72.5%	16-18	60-90 S	14.5	20.1	22.2	30.2	39.1	49.0	53.1	59.5	1:10.3	1:21.7
70.0%	19-21	60-90 S	15.0	20.8	23.0	31.3	40.5	50.7	55.0	1:01.6	1:12.9	1:24.6
67.5%	22-24	45-75 S	15.6	21.6	23.9	32.4	42.0	52.6	57.0	1:03.9	1:15.6	1:27.7
65.0%	25-29	45-75 S	16.2	22.4	24.8	33.7	43.6	54.6	59.2	1:06.3	1:18.5	1:31.1
62.5%	30-35	30-60 S	16.8	23.3	25.8	35.0	45.4	56.8	1:01.6	1:09.0	1:21.6	1:34.8
60.0%	36-40	30-60 S	17.6	24.3	26.8	36.5	47.3	59.2	1:04.2	1:11.8	1:25.0	-----

SPEED	REPS	REST	550 YD	660 YD	880 YD	1100 YD	1320 YD	1.00 MI	1.25 MI	1.50 MI	1.75 MI	2.00 MI
95.0%	0- 1	---	1:11.3	1:29.5	2:06.3	2:44.9	3:24.0	4:44.2	6:05.9	7:29.0	8:52.6	10:16.6
92.5%	1- 2	4- 5 M	1:13.2	1:31.9	2:09.8	2:49.3	3:29.5	4:51.9	6:15.8	7:41.1	9:07.0	10:33.3
90.0%	2- 3	4- 5 M	1:15.3	1:34.5	2:13.4	2:54.0	3:35.3	5:00.0	6:26.3	7:53.9	9:22.2	10:50.9
87.5%	3- 4	3- 4 M	1:17.4	1:37.2	2:17.2	2:59.0	3:41.4	5:08.6	6:37.3	8:07.5	9:38.3	11:09.5
85.0%	4- 5	3- 4 M	1:19.7	1:40.1	2:21.2	3:04.3	3:48.0	5:17.7	6:49.0	8:21.8	9:55.3	11:29.2
82.5%	6- 7	2- 3 M	1:22.1	1:43.1	2:25.5	3:09.9	3:54.9	5:27.3	7:01.4	-----	-----	-----
80.0%	8- 9	2- 3 M	1:24.7	1:46.3	2:30.0	3:15.8	4:02.2	5:37.5	-----	-----	-----	-----
77.5%	10-12	1- 2 M	1:27.4	1:49.7	2:34.9	3:22.1	4:10.0	-----	-----	-----	-----	-----
75.0%	13-15	1- 2 M	1:30.3	1:53.4	2:40.0	3:28.8	4:18.4	-----	-----	-----	-----	-----
72.5%	16-18	60-90 S	1:33.4	1:57.3	2:45.6	-----	-----	-----	-----	-----	-----	-----
70.0%	19-21	60-90 S	1:36.8	2:01.5	2:51.5	-----	-----	-----	-----	-----	-----	-----
67.5%	22-24	45-75 S	1:40.4	2:06.0	-----	-----	-----	-----	-----	-----	-----	-----
65.0%	25-29	45-75 S	1:44.2	-----	-----	-----	-----	-----	-----	-----	-----	-----
62.5%	30-35	30-60 S	-----	-----	-----	-----	-----	-----	-----	-----	-----	-----
60.0%	36-40	30-60 S	-----	-----	-----	-----	-----	-----	-----	-----	-----	-----

Figure 3.1   The 760 Point Level Pacing Table which is referred to for the Example Workouts described in Chapter 3

24

A 760 point level *sprinter* might desire to do two to three 165 yard dashes (90% speed). From the tables, he finds a time of 17.9 for each 165, with four to five minutes of rest (walking). Runs of 220 yards or less do not require as long a rest interval as runs longer than 220, thus a three to four minute rest here may be adequate. Again, expressing this workout in the short form:

2 to 3 165's in 17.9 with 3 to 4 minute rest between each

This workout may be contrasted with a 760 point level *distance runner* who might run four to five repeat miles (85.0%) in 5:17.7 with a three to four minute rest (440 jog with walking or about a 660 jog). This is expressed in short form as:

4 to 5 one-mile runs in 5:17.7 with a 440 jog in between

Another typical *distance runner's* workout is a high number of reps of a shorter distance, like 16 to 18 440's in 70.3 with a 90 second rest (about 220 jog) between each repetition, or more concisely:

16 to 18 440's in 70.3 with a 220 jog between each

To review the standard interval workout, you simply obtain the time for the desired distance, number of reps, and length of rest period from the pacing table which corresponds to the athlete's level of ability (points). On each page of the pacing tables, about 250 standard interval workouts are available.

WORK-DOWN (PROGRESSIVE) WORKOUTS

In order to bring variety into an interval training workout, an athlete might desire to change the distance he runs for each interval. One approach is to begin at an arbitrary distance and run each successive interval at a shorter distance but at a faster pace. The correct times for each distance may be obtained from the pacing tables.

Referring again to Figure 3.1 and assuming a runner is at the 760 point level, one can select times for a work-down or progressive workout. For the distance runner, a series of 2 mi., 1-½ mi., 1 mi., 880 and 440 would be a total of five intervals. From the pacing table, one can see that five reps corresponds to 85% speed. The times for each rep are read *along the row* of the 85% speed level. The athlete would perform (at the 85% level) interval times of 2 miles in 11:29, 1-½ miles in about 8:22, 1 mile in 5:18, 880 in 2:21, and a 440 in 60 seconds. These would all be done with about a 440 jog in between. This may be summarized as:

Warmup   1 x 2 miles in 11:29, 440 jog
               1 x 1-½ miles in 8:22, 440 jog
               1 x 1 mile in 5:18, 440 jog
               1 x 880 in 2:21, 440 jog
               1 x 440 in 1:00   Warmdown

One observation about this type of workout: a runner usually has to be cautious not to run the longer distances too fast. Going too fast in the early, longer runs will result in greater fatigue which will not allow the runner to complete the workout at the desired speed. Remember, these guidelines are for full intensity workouts, and more often than not, a pacing error in the early part of the workout results in the runner being unable to finish the workout on the desired pace.

As another example, a *middle distance runner* may desire to do two or three sets of step-down workouts. For example, one could do a set made up of a 440, 330, 220, and 110, or 4 intervals in each set. Now, to repeat this set three times gives a total of 12 reps in the workout. From the pacing tables, one can see that for 12 reps, the run should be at 75% speed. This means the 440 should be run in about

68, the 330 in 47.3, the 220 in 29.2, and the 110 in 14.0. The suggested rest period would be one to two minutes or a 150 to 220 yard jog. This would be done a total of three times, i.e., 440, 330, 220, 110 440, 330, 220, 110, 440, 330, 220, and 110. This may be more concisely written as: (after a warmup)

$$3 \times \left\{ \begin{array}{l} \text{440 in 68, 220 jog} \\ \text{330 in 47.3, 220 jog} \\ \text{220 in 29.2, 220 jog} \\ \text{110 in 14.0, 220 jog} \end{array} \right.$$

Another way of performing this same workout is to run all of the 440's, followed by all of the 330's, etc. This may be expressed as:

	3 x 440 in 68, 220 jog between each,
then	3 x 330 in 47:3, 220 jog between each,
then	3 x 220 in 29.2, 220 jog between each,
and then	3 x 110 in 14.0, 220 jog between each.

Some caution must be exercised in specifying sprints at the end of a workout since the likelihood of injury is greater under fatigue. This simply means that to do a step-down workout from, say, two miles to a 220 or 110 *could* be risky since a great deal of fatigue has already built up in the muscles by this time and to strain in a sprint might lead to an injury. Of course, a total, sprinting type of workout should not be harmful (under normal circumstances) as long as an adequate warmup has been performed.

To summarize this kind of workout, one first decides the total number of repetitions he is going to run. Then, one refers to that row (speed level) in the pacing tables which corresponds to the total reps. The times for the decreasing distances are read along that row, reading from right to left.

STEP-UP WORKOUTS

One sometimes desires to do the step-down approach in reverse by running each successive interval at a longer distance. The same procedure would be employed as described above in the step-down approach only the intervals would be run in reverse order. Most runners prefer, however, the step-down approach since it seems easier to do. This is perhaps more psychological than anything else, since each run is shorter than the previous one (except when multiple sets are run) and therefore seems easier.

As an example of a step-up workout, one may decide to do 3 sets of 220, 440, and 660 for a total of 9 repetitions. Nine repetitions in the tables indicates he will run each one at 80% speed with a two to three minute rest, or about a 220 to 330 jog between each one. From the example pacing tables, times of 27.4 for the 220, 63.7 for the 440, and 1:46.3 for the 660 are obtained for the 760 point level. This workout would be performed by running the 220, followed by the 440, and finally by the 660. This would be repeated three times. Summarizing, this workout can be done as follows:

$$
3 \times \left\{
\begin{array}{l}
220 \text{ in } 27.4, 220 \text{ to } 330 \text{ jog} \\
440 \text{ in } 1:03.7, 220 \text{ to } 330 \text{ jog} \\
660 \text{ in } 1:46.3, 220 \text{ to } 330 \text{ jog}
\end{array}
\right.
$$

STEP-UP, STEP-DOWN (PYRAMID) WORKOUTS

A very popular type of workout is the step-up, step-down approach. As the name implies, it is a combination of the step-up and the step-down kind of workouts. Here, a runner will begin with a particular distance, run successive intervals at longer distances through one-half of the total workout. Then he will reverse the process and run each interval at a shorter distance until he repeats the same interval he started with.

To obtain the times from the pacing tables for this kind of workout, one begins, as before, by deciding the total number of intervals he is going to run. This will correspond to a particular percentage speed,

28

from which all the times may be obtained.

For example, a typical distance runner's workout is to run a 440, 880, 1320, 1320, 880, and finally another 440. This is a total of six runs and therefore corresponds to an 82.5% speed. Going to the example table, times for the distances are: 61.8 seconds for the 440, 2:25.5 for the 880 and 3:54.9 (or 3:55) for the 1320. This workout would be run with about a quarter jog in between. This workout may be expressed in short form as:

Warmup
1 x 440 in 1:01.8, 440 jog
1 x 880 in 2:25.5, 440 jog
2 x 1320 in 3:55, 440 jog between each
1 x 880 in 2:25.5, 440 jog
1 x 440 in 1:01.8
Warmdown

This same approach may be taken for the 440 or 880 yard runners who might do a series of 110, 220, 330, 330, 220, and a 110. The time for each one would be obtained as above. The coach or runner can devise many combinations of this sort. Variety is brought into the daily workout with the assurance that the intensity is adequate.

SPEED PICK-UP, CONSTANT DISTANCE

Often to put variety in the workout session, runs each at a different relative speed may be combined, such as a run at 80% speed, followed by 82.5% speed, and so forth. To make up such combinations, we utilize a unique feature of the pacing tables. If the tables call for 8 reps of a run, then each run is 1/8 of the whole workout. A run at a speed for 20 reps (70% speed) is 1/20 of the whole workout and so forth. The runs at different speeds (and distances) can be combined providing *the total of these fractional work-*

outs does not exceed a whole workout! For example, a run at 82.5% speed is 1/6 of a whole workout, since it calls for 6 reps. A run at 87.5% speed is 1/3 of a workout, since it calls for 3 to 4 reps. Two runs at 87.5% combined with two runs at 82.5% would form a complete workout since 1/3+1/3+1/6+1/6 = 1. In a similar manner, the runner can perform several runs each at a different speed, providing the rule given above is followed. The arithmetic involved in figuring out this type of workout can become a little messy, so some examples are given here that can apply to all point levels and most any distance.

Speed Pick-Up Example No. 1

1 run at 75.0%, 1/14 workout
1 run at 77.5%, 1/11 workout
1 run at 80.0%, 1/8 workout
1 run at 82.5%, 1/6 workout
1 run at 85.0%, 1/4 workout
1 run at 87.5%, 1/3 workout
Total =   1 3/100 workout

A 760 point level middle distance runner could then run repeat 440's, each progressively faster, as follows:

440 in 68.0 (75.0%)
440 in 65.8 (77.5%)
440 in 63.7 (80.0%)
440 in 61.8 (82.5%)
440 in 60.0 (85.0%)
440 in 58.3 (87.5%)

30

An average rest interval of about 3 minutes would be appropriate.

Speed Pick-Up Example No. 2

4 runs at 72.5%, 1/4 workout
3 runs at 77.5%, 1/4 workout
2 runs at 80.0%, 1/4 workout
1 run at 85.0%, 1/4 workout
Total: 1 workout

Again the 760 point level *miler* might do:

4 x 440 in 70.3 (72.5%)
3 x 440 in 65.8 (77.5%)
2 x 440 in 63.7 (80.0%)
1 x 440 in 60.0 (85.0%)

An average rest interval of about 3 minutes would be used.

Speed Pick-Up Example No. 3

3 runs at 80.0%, about 1/3 workout
2 runs at 82.5%, about 1/3 workout
1 run at 87.5%, about 1/3 workout
Total: 1 workout

31

The distances can be different for each or some of the runs. The 760 point *half-miler* might do:

110 yards in   13.2 (80.0%)
220 yards in   27.4 (80.0%)
330 yards in   44.4 (80.0%)
440 yards in   61.8 (82.5%)
550 yards in 1:22.1 (82.5%)
660 yards in 1:37.2 (87.5%)

About 2 to 3 minutes of rest or a 330 yard jog between each would be appropriate. These runs could be in any order, either increasing distance, decreasing distance, or some other order.

These examples should demonstrate how speed pick-up workouts can be devised. Each run is like a building block, consisting of a part of a whole workout. These "blocks" can be put together as long as the total parts do not exceed a whole unit or workout.

ALTERNATE SPEED (COMBINATION) WORKOUTS

The speed pick-up workout is the first one to demonstrate a change in the level of speed during the workout. An expansion to this method is the generalized alternate speed workout. These types of workouts are usually a little more complicated to generate, but they do offer about the widest variety of intervals for a given training session.

The main principle behind the alternate speed workout is to take part of the workout at one speed and another part at a different speed. The simplest way to compose such a workout is to write down the *complete* workouts for two or more different speeds. Then take part of one and part of another to comprise the complete workout.

Let us consider the same 760 point level athlete again as an example. Suppose we construct two constant speed workouts as follows:

1. 4 x 440 in 60 sec., 3-4 min. rest (85%)
2. 10 x 440 in 65.8, 1-2 min. rest (77.5%)

Now, suppose we take ½ of the 85% speed workout and ½ of the 77.5% speed workout. We would then have the following alternate speed workout:

2 x 440 in 60 sec., 3-4 min. rest
5 x 440 in 65.8 sec., 1-2 min. rest

The way in which these intervals are actually performed could vary. For instance, one could run both of the 60 sec. quarters followed by the five 65.8 quarters, or one could do it in reverse by starting with the 65.8 440's, or one could do one 60 sec. 440 followed by two 65.8 sec. 440's, etc. This demonstrates some of the versatility of the pacing tables.

Let's examine another example. Suppose we write down the following constant speed workouts:

1. 12 x 220 at 77.5% speed (28.2 for 760 level)
2. 12 x 330 at 77.5% speed (45.8 for 760 level)
3. 9 x 440 at 80.0% speed (63.7 for 760 level)

Note that each rep number is on the high side of the table values. This can be balanced by increasing the rest interval to 3 minutes and the times slightly to 28.5, 46.0 and 64.0 seconds respectively. Now if we take 1/3 of each of these workouts, and combine them, we have a complete workout which can be a step-up step-down workout as follows (for a 760 point level):

$$3 \times \begin{cases} 220 \text{ in } 28.5 \ (77.5\%) \ 3 \text{ minute rest} \\ 330 \text{ in } 46.0 \ (77.5\%) \ 3 \text{ minute rest} \\ 440 \text{ in } 64.0 \ (80.0\%) \ 3 \text{ minute rest} \\ 330 \text{ in } 46.0 \ (77.5\%) \ 3 \text{ minute rest} \\ 220 \text{ in } 28.5 \ (77.5\%) \ 3 \text{ minute rest} \end{cases}$$

This workout would be done by a *miler* or a *half-miler* who is well advanced into his training program.

PACE WORKOUTS

One of the more common type of interval workout is the pre-defined pace workout. Usually, one desires to run repetitions of some sub-racing distance at the race pace. As an example, a miler may desire to do 440's or 660's in a workout at his race pace. A pace workout, however, does not necessarily have to be performed at a race pace; it may simply be any particular pace the athlete or coach desires. The problem then is to determine the distance, the number of repetitions that are to be run, and the actual interval time which corresponds to the desired pace.

The procedure for obtaining a pace interval workout is diagrammed visually in Figure 3.2 and is explained as follows. The pace is expressed in terms of a 440 yard time or split, i.e., a 4:00 miler runs at a 60 second 440 pace, and a 1:56 880 yard runner performs at a 58 second 440 yard pace. Therefore, we assume that the desired pace to be run is expressed as a number of seconds (or minutes and seconds) per 440 yards.

With this known pace, one then chooses the distance he desires to run in the training session. With these two variables determined, one may refer to the Intermediate Times For Constant Speed Runs (Table 2 in the English and Metric Unit Tables) to obtain the actual interval time to be run. One finds the pace

INTERMEDIATE TIMES FOR CONSTANT SPEED RUNS

440 Y	110 Y	150 Y	165 Y	220 Y	275 Y	330 Y	352 Y	385 Y	495 Y	550 Y
1:10.0	17.5	23.9	26.3	35.0	43.8	52.5	56.0	1:01.3	1:13.8	1:27.5
1:11.0	17.8	24.2	26.6	35.5	44.4	53.3	56.8	1:02.1	1:19.9	1:28.8
1:12.0	18.0	24.5	27.0	36.0	45.0	54.0	57.6	1:03.0	1:21.0	1:30.0
1:13.0	18.3	24.9	27.4	36.5	45.6	54.8	58.4	1:03.9	1:22.1	1:31.3
1:14.0	18.5	25.2	27.8	37.0	46.3	55.5	59.2	1:04.8	1:23.3	1:32.5
1:15.0	18.8	25.6	28.1	37.5	46.9	56.3	1:00.0	1:05.6	1:24.4	1:33.8
1:16.0	19.0	25.9	28.5	38.0	47.5	57.0	1:00.8	1:06.5	1:24.5	1:35.0
1:17.0	19.3	26.3	28.9	38.5	48.1	57.8	1:01.6	1:07.4	1:26.6	1:36.3
1:18.0	19.5	26.6	29.3	39.0	48.8	58.5	1:02.4	1:08.3	1:27.8	1:37.5
1:19.0	19.8	26.9	29.6	39.5	49.4	59.3	1:03.2	1:09.1	1:28.9	1:38.8
1:20.0	20.0	27.3	30.0	40.0	50.0	1:00.0	1:04.0	1:10.0	1:30.0	1:40.0
1:21.0	20.3	27.6	30.4	40.5	50.6	1:00.8	1:04.8	1:10.9	1:31.1	1:41.3

760 POINT LEVEL PACING TABLE

SPEED	REPS	REST	110 YD	150 YD	165 YD	220 YD	275 YD	330 YD	352 YD	385 YD	440 YD	495 YD
95.0%	0- 1	---	11.1	15.3	17.0	23.0	29.8	37.4	40.5	45.4	53.7	1:02.3
92.5%	1- 2	4- 5 M	11.4	15.7	17.4	23.7	30.7	38.4	41.6	46.6	55.1	1:04.0
90.0%	2- 3	4- 5 M	11.7	16.2	17.9	24.3	31.5	39.5	42.8	47.9	56.7	1:05.8
87.5%	3- 4	3- 4 M	12.0	16.6	18.4	25.0	32.4	40.6	44.0	49.3	58.3	1:07.7
85.0%	4- 5	3- 4 M	12.4	17.1	18.9	25.8	33.4	41.8	45.3	50.7	1:00.0	1:09.7
82.5%	6- 7	2- 3 M	12.8	17.6	19.5	26.5	34.4	43.0	46.7	52.3	1:01.8	1:11.8
80.0%	8- 9	2- 3 M	13.2	18.2	20.1	27.4	35.4	44.4	48.1	53.9	1:03.7	1:14.0
77.5%	10-12	1- 2 M	13.6	18.8	20.8	28.2	36.6	45.8	49.7	55.6	1:05.8	1:16.4
75.0%	13-15	1- 2 M	14.0	19.4	21.5	29.2	37.8	47.3	51.3	57.5	1:08.0	1:19.0
72.5%	16-18	60-90 S	14.5	20.1	22.2	30.2	39.1	49.0	53.1	59.5	1:10.3	1:21.7
70.0%	19-21	60-90 S	15.0	20.8	23.0	31.3	40.5	50.7	55.0	1:01.6	1:12.9	1:24.6
67.5%	22-24	45-75 S	15.6	21.6	23.9	32.4	42.0	52.6	57.0	1:03.9	1:15.6	1:27.7
65.0%	25-29	45-75 S	16.2	22.4	24.8	33.7	43.6	54.6	59.2	1:06.3	1:18.5	1:31.1
62.5%	30-35	30-60 S	16.8	23.3	25.8	35.0	45.4	56.8	1:01.6	1:09.0	1:21.6	1:34.8
60.0%	36-40	30-60 S	17.6	24.3	26.8	36.5	47.3	59.2	1:04.2	1:11.8	1:25.0	-----

SPEED	REPS	REST	550 YD	660 YD	880 YD	1100 YD	1320 YD	1.00 MI	1.25 MI	1.50 MI	1.75 MI	2.00 MI
95.0%	0- 1	---	1:11.3	1:29.5	2:06.3	2:44.9	3:24.0	4:44.2	6:05.9	7:29.0	8:52.6	10:16.6
92.5%	1- 2	4- 5 M	1:13.2	1:31.9	2:09.8	2:49.3	3:29.5	4:51.0	6:15.8	7:41.1	9:07.0	10:33.2

Figure 3.2 Procedure for Determining a Pace Workout from the Pacing Tables

35

time in the left-hand column and then moves across the row to the column headed by the desired interval distance. The time for the interval distance is then obtained; this time corresponds to the desired 440 pace originally specified.

Now, with the known distance and time for the interval, one refers to the runner's point level pacing table. Under the distance chosen for the interval, the closest time listed to the desired time is chosen. For this time, one may read the number of repetitions and the rest period from the left-hand columns of the pacing table. If the listed time is significantly different from the desired time, the number of reps can be adjusted to the intermediate number from those above or below the desired time.

Figure 3.2 shows an example. The coach or athlete has chosen a 75 second 440 pace and a distance of 495 yards for the workout. From the constant speed table, one easily finds a time of 1:24.4. One now has the interval distance (495 yards) and the time to run it (1:24.4) that will be at the desired pace (75 sec. quarter).

All that remains is to find the number of repetitions and rest period; this is found from the pacing table at the point level of the athlete, here 760 points. Looking at the 495 yard interval distance column, one can find 1:24.6 as the nearest time to 1:24.4.

Considering a jog from the 495 yard point on a track (see Figure 2.3) to the 660 yard point is 165 yards, it would be reasonable to make the rest interval a slow 165 yard jog, even though it might take a little over a minute. This workout can be summarized as:

19 - 21 x 495 yds. in 1:24.6 with 165 yd. jog between each.

Reviewing the determination of a pace workout, one chooses his pace and distance, finds the interval time for that pace in the constant speed table, and locates the number of reps and rest period from the pacing table.

TIME EQUIVALENT INTERVALS

One approach to training is to repeatedly run a distance in a time that is nearly equal to the competitive time for the racing distance. Such runs, in order to be repeated, would be at a pace slower than race pace but also at a distance less than the racing distance. Such interval running would be called "time equivalent" intervals. One way to obtain these times is to run 7/8 of the racing distances at 85% relative speed which is in the competitive time. For a 760 point level 440 runner, this would be 385 yards in about 51 to 52 seconds. At 85% speed he can run 4 to 5 repetitions with about a 3 minute rest between each.

Although the corresponding distances do not appear in the tables, in preference to more common distances, the same type of workout can be done for the 880 and the mile. For the 880 runner, he can run 770 yards (7/8 of 880 yards) at 85% speed and the time turns out to be the same as his 100% effort 880 yard time. For the 760 level example, he would run:

4 to 5 x 770 yds. in 2:01 with a 3-4 min. rest

For the 760 point level miler, he would run 1540 yards (3-½ laps) in 4:31 each or:

4 to 5 x 1540 yds. in 4:31 with a 3-4 min. rest between each

For a 2 miler, the time for 1.75 miles (7/8 of 2 miles) at 85% speed is nearly the same as his competitive 2 mile, so the same principle can be applied here as well.

EXAMPLES OF DIFFERENT POINT LEVELS

For all of the example workouts presented in this chapter so far, the single point level of 760 points was used. This was done to provide a consistent reference from which all the workout types could be explained. The problem with this is that most athletes are at some other point level than 760. It is the purpose of this section to demonstrate how the above described workouts for 760 points may be applied to other point levels.

Figure 3.3 shows a sample from the performance rating table given as Table 1 in the English and Metric Unit Tables. A distribution from 960 points to 560 points is given. An athlete who can run a mile in 4:00.4 would be considered a 960 point level performer. Our 760 point level runner can do a 4:30.8 mile, while a 560 point level miler can do 5:10.2. Each of these runners would refer to his respective point level pacing tables to obtain his workouts. Figure 3.4 and 3.5 show the pacing tables for the 960 and 560 point levels respectively. The 760 point level table was given as Figure 3.1.

Suppose each of these runners desired to do 4 to 6 repetitions of 440 yards with a 440 jog in between at 85% speed. From the 960 point level pacing table (Figure 3.4), a time of about 54 seconds is read; from the 760 point level table (Figure 3.1), a time of about 60 seconds can be found; and finally, from the 560 point level (Figure 3.5), table a time of 67.5 seconds can be read. Thus, all three athletes had decided to do the same workout, but the time in which each interval was to be run was different and was read from the respective point levels.

This same method of obtaining the interval time would be used by all other point levels and by all other types of runners, from sprinters to long distance runners.

Often on a team, the coach will desire groups of runners to work out together. If he wants them to all run the same time for the interval distance, then the proper number of repetitions for each runner could be determined by referencing the suggested number of repetitions for the desired interval distance time.

For example, suppose an 800, 760, and 720 point level athletes desired to work out together (possible since their point levels are fairly close together). Suppose they desired to run 60 second 440's. From the 800 point level pacing table, the athlete should be able to do 6 to 7 reps with about a 2 to 3 minute jog. The 760 point level runner should be able to do about 4 to 5 with a 3 to 4 minute rest, or about a 440 jog. The 720 point level runner should be able to do 3 to 4 reps with 3 to 4 minute rest. They could all run together and all take a rest interval of around three minutes, with each runner stopping after he has complet-

SCORING TABLES
CLASSICAL ENGLISH RACING DISTANCES
●●●

POINTS	100 YD	220 YD	440 YD	880 YD	1.00 MI	2.00 MI	3.00 MI	6.00 MI	10.00 MI	MARATHON
960	9.42	20.9	46.8	1:47.9	4:00.4	8:38.7	13:22.3	28:00.7	48:21	2:15:32
950	9.47	21.0	47.0	1:48.5	4:01.7	8:41.7	13:27.0	28:10.7	48:39	2:16:22
940	9.51	21.1	47.3	1:49.1	4:03.1	8:44.8	13:31.8	28:20.9	48:56	2:17:13
930	9.55	21.2	47.5	1:49.7	4:04.5	8:47.9	13:36.6	28:31.1	49:14	2:18:04
920	9.59	21.3	47.7	1:50.3	4:05.9	8:51.0	13:41.5	28:41.5	49:32	2:18:55
910	9.63	21.4	48.0	1:50.9	4:07.3	8:54.2	13:46.5	28:52.0	49:51	2:19:48
900	9.68	21.5	48.2	1:51.5	4:08.8	8:57.4	13:51.5	29:02.7	50:09	2:20:41
890	9.72	21.6	48.5	1:52.1	4:10.2	9:00.6	13:56.5	29:13.4	50:28	2:21:34
880	9.77	21.7	48.7	1:52.7	4:11.7	9:03.9	14:01.7	29:24.3	50:47	2:22:29
870	9.81	21.8	49.0	1:53.4	4:13.2	9:07.2	14:06.8	29:35.4	51:06	2:23:24
860	9.85	21.9	49.3	1:54.0	4:14.7	9:10.6	14:12.1	29:46.5	51:26	2:24:20
850	9.90	22.0	49.5	1:54.7	4:16.2	9:14.0	14:17.4	29:57.9	51:46	2:25:16
840	9.95	22.1	49.8	1:55.3	4:17.8	9:17.4	14:22.8	30:09.3	52:06	2:26:13
830	9.99	22.2	50.0	1:56.0	4:19.3	9:20.9	14:28.3	30:20.9	52:26	2:27:11
820	10.04	22.3	50.3	1:56.7	4:20.9	9:24.4	14:33.8	30:32.7	52:46	2:28:10
810	10.08	22.4	50.6	1:57.4	4:22.5	9:28.0	14:39.4	30:44.6	53:07	2:29:10
800	10.13	22.6	50.9	1:58.1	4:24.1	9:31.6	14:45.0	30:56.7	53:28	2:30:10
790	10.18	22.7	51.1	1:58.8	4:25.8	9:35.3	14:50.8	31:08.9	53:50	2:31:11
780	10.23	22.8	51.4	1:59.5	4:27.4	9:39.0	14:56.6	31:21.3	54:11	2:32:14
770	10.28	22.9	51.7	2:00.2	4:29.1	9:42.8	15:02.5	31:33.9	54:33	2:33:16
760	10.33	23.0	52.0	2:00.9	4:30.8	9:46.6	15:08.5	31:46.6	54:55	2:34:20
750	10.38	23.1	52.3	2:01.7	4:32.6	9:50.4	15:14.5	31:59.5	55:18	2:35:25
740	10.43	23.2	52.6	2:02.4	4:34.3	9:54.3	15:20.6	32:12.6	55:41	2:36:30
730	10.48	23.4	52.9	2:03.2	4:36.1	9:58.3	15:26.9	32:25.8	56:04	2:37:37
720	10.53	23.5	53.2	2:03.9	4:37.9	10:02.3	15:33.1	32:39.3	56:28	2:38:44
710	10.58	23.6	53.5	2:04.7	4:39.7	10:06.4	15:39.5	32:52.9	56:51	2:39:53
700	10.63	23.7	53.8	2:05.5	4:41.6	10:10.5	15:46.0	33:06.7	57:16	2:41:02
690	10.68	23.8	54.1	2:06.3	4:43.4	10:14.7	15:52.6	33:20.7	57:40	2:42:13
680	10.74	24.0	54.4	2:07.1	4:45.3	10:19.0	15:59.2	33:34.9	58:05	2:43:24
670	10.79	24.1	54.7	2:07.9	4:47.2	10:23.3	16:06.0	33:49.3	58:30	2:44:37
660	10.85	24.2	55.1	2:08.7	4:49.2	10:27.6	16:12.8	34:04.0	58:56	2:45:50
650	10.90	24.4	55.4	2:09.5	4:51.2	10:32.0	16:19.7	34:18.8	59:22	2:47:05
640	10.96	24.5	55.7	2:10.4	4:53.2	10:36.5	16:26.8	34:33.8	59:48	2:48:21
630	11.01	24.6	56.0	2:11.2	4:55.2	10:41.1	16:33.9	34:49.1	1:00:15	2:49:38
620	11.07	24.7	56.4	2:12.1	4:57.2	10:45.7	16:41.2	35:04.6	1:00:42	2:50:56
610	11.12	24.9	56.7	2:13.0	4:59.3	10:50.4	16:48.5	35:20.3	1:01:10	2:52:15
600	11.18	25.0	57.1	2:13.9	5:01.4	10:55.1	16:56.0	35:36.3	1:01:38	2:53:36
590	11.24	25.2	57.4	2:14.8	5:03.6	10:59.9	17:03.6	35:52.5	1:02:06	2:54:58
580	11.30	25.3	57.8	2:15.7	5:05.8	11:04.8	17:11.2	36:09.0	1:02:35	2:56:21
570	11.36	25.4	58.1	2:16.6	5:08.0	11:09.8	17:19.0	36:25.7	1:03:04	2:57:46
560	11.42	25.6	58.5	2:17.5	5:10.2	11:14.8	17:27.0	36:42.7	1:03:34	2:59:11

Figure 3.3   Sample Performance Rating Table for the 960 to 560 Point Levels

SPEED	REPS	REST	110 YD	150 YD	165 YD	220 YD	275 YD	330 YD	352 YD	385 YD	440 YD	495 YD
95.0%	0- 1	---	10.1	14.0	15.4	20.9	27.0	33.8	36.6	40.9	48.3	56.0
92.5%	1- 2	4- 5 M	10.4	14.3	15.9	21.5	27.8	34.7	37.6	42.0	49.6	57.5
90.0%	2- 3	4- 5 M	10.7	14.7	16.3	22.1	28.6	35.7	38.6	43.2	51.0	59.1
87.5%	3- 4	3- 4 M	11.0	15.2	16.8	22.7	29.4	36.7	39.7	44.4	52.4	1:00.8
85.0%	4- 5	3- 4 M	11.3	15.6	17.3	23.4	30.2	37.8	40.9	45.7	54.0	1:02.6
82.5%	6- 7	2- 3 M	11.6	16.1	17.8	24.1	31.1	38.9	42.1	47.1	55.6	1:04.5
80.0%	8- 9	2- 3 M	12.0	16.6	18.3	24.9	32.1	40.1	43.5	48.6	57.4	1:06.5
77.5%	10-12	1- 2 M	12.4	17.1	18.9	25.7	33.2	41.4	44.9	50.2	59.2	1:08.6
75.0%	13-15	1- 2 M	12.8	17.7	19.6	26.5	34.3	42.8	46.4	51.8	1:01.2	1:10.9
72.5%	16-18	60-90 S	13.3	18.3	20.2	27.4	35.4	44.3	48.0	53.6	1:03.3	1:13.4
70.0%	19-21	60-90 S	13.7	19.0	21.0	28.4	36.7	45.9	49.7	55.5	1:05.6	1:16.0
67.5%	22-24	45-75 S	14.2	19.7	21.7	29.5	38.1	47.6	51.5	57.6	1:08.0	1:18.8
65.0%	25-29	45-75 S	14.8	20.4	22.6	30.6	39.5	49.4	53.5	59.8	1:10.6	1:21.8
62.5%	30-35	30-60 S	15.4	21.2	23.5	31.8	41.1	51.4	55.6	1:02.2	1:13.4	1:25.1
60.0%	36-40	30-60 S	16.0	22.1	24.4	33.2	42.8	53.5	57.9	1:04.8	-----	-----

SPEED	REPS	REST	550 YD	660 YD	880 YD	1100 YD	1320 YD	1.00 MI	1.25 MI	1.50 MI	1.75 MI	2.00 MI
95.0%	0- 1	---	1:03.9	1:20.1	1:52.7	2:26.8	3:01.3	4:12.2	5:24.3	6:37.6	7:51.3	9:05.3
92.5%	1- 2	4- 5 M	1:05.7	1:22.3	1:55.8	2:30.8	3:06.2	4:19.0	5:33.1	6:48.3	8:04.0	9:20.0
90.0%	2- 3	4- 5 M	1:07.5	1:24.5	1:59.0	2:34.9	3:11.4	4:26.2	5:42.3	6:59.6	8:17.4	9:35.6
87.5%	3- 4	3- 4 M	1:09.4	1:27.0	2:02.4	2:39.4	3:16.9	4:33.8	5:52.1	7:11.6	8:31.7	9:52.0
85.0%	4- 5	3- 4 M	1:11.5	1:29.5	2:06.0	2:44.1	3:22.7	4:41.9	6:02.5	7:24.3	8:46.7	10:09.4
82.5%	6- 7	2- 3 M	1:13.6	1:32.2	2:09.8	2:49.0	3:28.8	4:50.4	6:13.4	-----	-----	-----
80.0%	8- 9	2- 3 M	1:15.9	1:35.1	2:13.9	2:54.3	3:35.3	4:59.5	-----	-----	-----	-----
77.5%	10-12	1- 2 M	1:18.4	1:38.2	2:18.2	2:59.9	3:42.3	-----	-----	-----	-----	-----
75.0%	13-15	1- 2 M	1:21.0	1:41.5	2:22.8	3:05.9	-----	-----	-----	-----	-----	-----
72.5%	16-18	60-90 S	1:23.8	1:45.0	2:27.7	-----	-----	-----	-----	-----	-----	-----
70.0%	19-21	60-90 S	1:26.8	1:48.7	-----	-----	-----	-----	-----	-----	-----	-----
67.5%	22-24	45-75 S	1:30.0	1:52.7	-----	-----	-----	-----	-----	-----	-----	-----
65.0%	25-29	45-75 S	1:33.5	-----	-----	-----	-----	-----	-----	-----	-----	-----
62.5%	30-35	30-60 S	-----	-----	-----	-----	-----	-----	-----	-----	-----	-----
60.0%	36-40	30-60 S	-----	-----	-----	-----	-----	-----	-----	-----	-----	-----

Figure 3.4 Sample 960 Point Level Pacing Table

SPEED	REPS	REST	110 YD	150 YD	165 YD	220 YD	275 YD	330 YD	352 YD	385 YD	440 YD	495 YD
95.0%	0- 1	---	12.3	17.0	18.8	25.6	33.3	41.8	45.4	50.9	1:00.4	1:10.3
92.5%	1- 2	4- 5 M	12.6	17.4	19.3	26.3	34.2	43.0	46.6	52.3	1:02.0	1:12.2
90.0%	2- 3	4- 5 M	12.9	17.9	19.8	27.0	35.1	44.2	47.9	53.8	1:03.8	1:14.2
87.5%	3- 4	3- 4 M	13.3	18.4	20.4	27.8	36.1	45.4	49.3	55.3	1:05.6	1:16.3
85.0%	4- 5	3- 4 M	13.7	19.0	21.0	28.6	37.2	46.7	50.7	56.9	1:07.5	1:18.6
82.5%	6- 7	2- 3 M	14.1	19.6	21.6	29.5	38.3	48.2	52.3	58.6	1:09.6	1:21.0
80.0%	8- 9	2- 3 M	14.6	20.2	22.3	30.4	39.5	49.7	53.9	1:00.5	1:11.7	1:23.5
77.5%	10-12	1- 2 M	15.0	20.8	23.0	31.4	40.8	51.3	55.7	1:02.4	1:14.0	1:26.2
75.0%	13-15	1- 2 M	15.5	21.5	23.8	32.5	42.2	53.0	57.5	1:04.5	1:16.5	1:29.0
72.5%	16-18	60-90 S	16.1	22.2	24.6	33.6	43.6	54.8	59.5	1:06.7	1:19.2	1:32.1
70.0%	19-21	60-90 S	16.6	23.0	25.5	34.8	45.2	56.8	1:01.6	1:09.1	1:22.0	1:35.4
67.5%	22-24	45-75 S	17.3	23.9	26.4	36.1	46.8	58.9	1:03.9	1:11.7	1:25.0	1:38.9
65.0%	25-29	45-75 S	17.9	24.8	27.5	37.4	48.6	1:01.1	1:06.4	1:14.4	1:28.3	1:42.7
62.5%	30-35	30-60 S	18.6	25.8	28.6	38.9	50.6	1:03.6	1:09.0	1:17.4	1:31.8	1:46.9
60.0%	36-40	30-60 S	19.4	26.9	29.8	40.6	52.7	1:06.2	1:11.9	1:20.6	1:35.6	1:51.3

SPEED	REPS	REST	550 YD	660 YD	880 YD	1100 YD	1320 YD	1.00 MI	1.25 MI	1.50 MI	1.75 MI	2.00 MI
95.0%	0- 1	---	1:20.6	1:41.5	2:23.7	3:08.0	3:53.0	5:25.5	6:59.9	8:35.8	10:12.4	11:49.4
92.5%	1- 2	4- 5 M	1:22.7	1:44.2	2:27.6	3:13.1	3:59.3	5:34.3	7:11.2	8:49.7	10:28.9	12:08.6
90.0%	2- 3	4- 5 M	1:25.0	1:47.1	2:31.7	3:18.5	4:06.0	5:43.6	7:23.2	9:04.4	10:46.4	12:28.8
87.5%	3- 4	3- 4 M	1:27.5	1:50.2	2:36.0	3:24.2	4:13.0	5:53.4	7:35.8	9:20.0	11:04.8	12:50.2
85.0%	4- 5	3- 4 M	1:30.0	1:53.4	2:40.6	3:30.2	4:20.5	6:03.8	7:49.3	9:36.4	11:24.4	13:12.9
82.5%	6- 7	2- 3 M	1:32.8	1:56.8	2:45.5	3:36.5	4:28.3	6:14.8	8:03.5	9:53.9	-----	-----
80.0%	8- 9	2- 3 M	1:35.7	2:00.5	2:50.7	3:43.3	4:36.7	6:26.6	-----	-----	-----	-----
77.5%	10-12	1- 2 M	1:38.8	2:04.4	2:56.2	3:50.5	4:45.7	-----	-----	-----	-----	-----
75.0%	13-15	1- 2 M	1:42.1	2:08.5	3:02.0	3:58.2	4:55.2	-----	-----	-----	-----	-----
72.5%	16-18	60-90 S	1:45.6	2:13.0	3:08.3	4:06.4	-----	-----	-----	-----	-----	-----
70.0%	19-21	60-90 S	1:49.3	2:17.7	3:15.0	-----	-----	-----	-----	-----	-----	-----
67.5%	22-24	45-75 S	1:53.4	2:22.8	-----	-----	-----	-----	-----	-----	-----	-----
65.0%	25-29	45-75 S	1:57.8	2:28.3	-----	-----	-----	-----	-----	-----	-----	-----
62.5%	30-35	30-60 S	2:02.5	-----	-----	-----	-----	-----	-----	-----	-----	-----
60.0%	36-40	30-60 S	-----	-----	-----	-----	-----	-----	-----	-----	-----	-----

Figure 3.5 Sample 560 Point Level Pacing Table

41

ed his appropriate number of repetitions. After 3 or 4 reps the 720 point level runner would stop; after 4 to 5 reps the 760 point level runner would stop; and the 800-pt. runner would go on to complete 6 or 7.

The particular example demonstrates that runners who are not at as high a point level as others, but are doing the distance in the same time, may easily refer to how many reps they should do. Overextending himself to "keep in there" during a workout may do more harm than good since he is tearing down rather than building up and cannot adequately recover for the following day's workout. The coach and the runner can determine when he should stop, and at that point he should do so.

This presentation should clear up any problems that might have occurred with only referencing 760 points earlier in this chapter.

HOW TO CHANGE POINT LEVELS

An important point that has not been described is how do you know when to move up to a higher training level or point level? First, the Pacing Tables have a built-in increase in training. This means that a runner who has established a performance level usually will not, initially, be able to perform the complete workout given for his level. He will have to work his way up to it by attempting the workouts given. For example, a miler who runs a 4:30.8 mile in a trial or competition would not likely be able to complete all his workouts at the 760 point level in the first week. By the time the runner is able to consistently perform the 760 point level workouts, especially at the higher suggested number of reps, he will usually beat his previous performance, and will then move to the next higher level. A single exceptional workout does not, however, demonstrate that he can consistently outperform the training level. Once he consistently exceeds the listed workouts for his level, he is ready to jump to the next level. Of course, a much improved competition time should indicate that a new workout level should be started.

This chapter should give the reader an indication of how versatile the system is. The coach or athlete will probably find that the tables lead to new ways in which he can develop many interesting kinds of workouts. Also he can use the tables to implement his own training philosophy.

42

With the example types of workouts outlined here and the tables at the end of this book, each coach and athlete will have no trouble organizing individualized workouts for every runner. The coach can concentrate on devising the workout type he wants his sprinters, middle distance, or distance runners to perform. Each runner simply looks up the particular times he should run for that type of workout specified by the coach.

OTHER CONSIDERATIONS

When a runner first begins to do interval running, he may find it a little difficult to complete the workout as specified by the pacing tables just because it is a new type of exercise. A distance runner who has been doing only continuous running training in pre-season will have to adjust to the interval running; therefore, the switch should be gradual. Also, by doing mostly interval running, the athlete will become "trained for interval running" and may be able to do *more* than the tables specify.

This chapter had presented a number of different types of workouts. Other chapters later in the book outline how these types of workouts may best be employed for the particular event category. Generally speaking, the reader should realize that the pacing table for a single point level is intended to be referenced by *all* event categories, from the sprinter through the distance runner. It should be noted that the workouts from the tables should be appropriate for the runner.

As an example, a 10.3 second 100 yard sprinter is just as much a 760 point level performer as a 4:30 miler, but it would be unreasonable to expect the sprinter to be able to perform repeat miles at 760 point level. Similarly, the miler would not be expected to perform low rep, high speed sprinting intervals from the table. A wide variety of workouts exist in each pacing table, but common sense should prevail as to their applicability for the individual athlete.

Another similar comparison can be made for two runners (say both are milers) who are at the same point level for their prime event but have different natural abilities with respect to speed. One of the milers may have more speed than the other, while the second miler may have more endurance. When these runners perform the shorter distance intervals, the miler with more speed may outperform the second miler. However, when these runners perform an overdistance, continuous run, the runner with more endurance may outperform the other. Again, common sense with respect to the variation between individuals and the usage of the pacing tables should be applied.

The reader may have already observed upon close examination of the pacing table that there is a range of values in the repetitions and rest columns, while the speed and distance columns are given as exact values. The computerized system generates precise values for speed, distance, and time. The repetitions and rest intervals are much more difficult to specify exactly since there are variances from one runner to the next and from environmental conditions on one day to another. (This is discussed in more detail in Chapter 8).

With this in mind, a runner may use the variable parts of the pacing tables to his advantage. At a given point level he may start by doing all the workouts with the longest suggested rest and minimum number of repetitions. He can then try to reduce the rest interval and increase the number of reps until he can do the maximum suggested reps with the minimum rest. At this time the runner will probably be able to attempt the easier workouts (minimum reps and maximum rest) at the next higher point level. Also he will have to adjust the reps if his actual performed speed is off. If he sets out to do 66 second 440's and does a 63, a 64, etc., he cannot expect to do the number of reps for 66 second quarters, but rather will be able to do the number of reps which correspond to his actual times performed in the workout.

The environment also affects the number of repetitions that can be performed. A hot and humid day may reduce the total number of reps by 1/5 of 1/3. See Chapter 6 for more discussion about environmental effects.

THE WARMUP AND WARMDOWN ACTIVITIES

The workouts given in the pacing tables for interval running do not include the warmup activity which is normally done before the actual workout, nor do they include a warmdown activity which should follow the interval workout. The warmup and warmdown activities should be done routinely by the runners each day before and after the formal workout and before competition. The warmup should consist of 20 to 30 minutes of pre-workout activity with jogging, calisthenics, stretching exercises and some faster running. The warmup before speed work or before competition should be more thorough than before an endurance workout such as a continuous run. It is a good idea to have two or three routine warmups that are appropriate for the type of event and type of workout that is to be done.

The warmdown or post-workout activity is important as it aides recovery from the effort. It can be a mile or two of light jogging or alternate jogging and walking until an athlete feels recovered. If the weather is cool, he should not linger too long while inactive to avoid getting chilled. Other books such as Fred Wilt's *Run Run Run* have specific warmup suggestions and may be referred to for additional comments.

Chapter 4
Suggestions for the "Jogger"

GETTING STARTED

In the last couple of years, there have been an increased interest and awareness by the general public as to the benefits of a consistent and active exercise program that maintains the whole body. Jogging becomes a leading way in which people have been able to satisfy their exercise needs.

The main principle behind jogging is to actively stress the total body-muscles, heart, lungs, and circulatory system—to condition them to a higher stress-tolerance level. This makes the unstressed body work less and results in one's feeling better in each day.

One begins a jogging program in a gradual manner so as to not over-exert the body before it has adjusted to the new, imposed stress. For those over thirty and all those of any age who have not been getting any exercise at all, a check with a doctor should be made first.

The general guidelines for jogging are quite straightforward. A warmup should be done first which is composed of general calisthenics to stretch the muscles of the legs and torso. Jogging for the first one to three months should simply be free jogging: easy running for 10 to 15 minutes, stopping to walk when tired or the heart is beating over 150 beats per minute.

After a few months, most joggers will be able to jog for the full 10 to 15 minutes without stopping. The pace may pick up to a good stride from the original slow jog. This is typically the steady-state condition which is prescribed to maintain one's condition.

PROVIDING VARIETY THROUGH STRESS JOGGING

In order to maintain interest in the exercise program consistent change must take place. Continuous running or jogging for most people will become boring and will result in not doing it just to provide a needed change.

An extension of the straight jogging or aerobics programs is Stress Jogging, a term coined by Payton Jordan, the 1968 Olympic Track Coach. In this system the jogger is instructed to do alternating speed jogging, varying from walking to a comfortable stride. The stride is usually faster than what would be done if the whole run were done at the same speed. The jogger should simply slow down and walk when he feels tired. This method has the added benefit over continuous jogging in that the muscles, including the heart, get added stress which results in better muscle tone.

A stress jogging program will provide the jogger with added physical benefits as well as the psychological benefits of an ever-changing schedule, which should help maintain the interest of the jogger. He can mix continuous runs with stress jogging to provide even more variety.

USING THE COMPUTERIZED SYSTEM

There are a large number of people who are doing more than casual jogging but are really not competing in races. These people desire to keep a record of their general progress and occasionally will run a mile for time to see how fit they are.

For these people—who desire to do systematic running but do not wish to do intensive training—the computerized tables described in this book may be used. One only needs to be able to run the equivalent of an 8:43 mile (the zero point level) or better. The pacing charts extend down to the zero point level, and the runner simply uses his pacing table in the same manner as the higher point level performers.

The jogger will need the facilities of a nearby high school or college track, or he can use measured distances in the neighborhood. Using the computerized system has added benefits over regular jogging of a systematic method for training and a reference (point level) which always lets the runner know where he is in terms of fitness.

Since the jogger is not normally interested in competing, and because he should make his training session a reasonably pleasant experience so that he will approach each workout with enthusiasm, the number of repetitions given in the tables should, therefore, be reduced by about 25%. This will result in a training session that does not have the severity that is associated with competition training. Also the preferred speeds and distances would be from 75% to 85% speed at 110 to 880 yards.

For a more specific discussion of jogging and aerobics, the books by Dr. Cooper, *Aerobics,* and Coach Bowerman, *Jogging,* should be consulted.

Chapter 5
Basic Concepts of Training

The pacing tables for interval running presented in this book provide over 250 different workouts for each capability level. There should be no problem in interpreting the workouts listed in the tables. A far more significant problem is how to select a workout from the tables and on what basis the selection is made.

To establish a rational basis for selecting the daily workout and for planning the overall training program, this chapter presents a general review of some basic concepts and principles of training. The next chapter discusses the various factors in choosing the workout and the following chapter discusses the training program. This information is presented in terms of the pacing tables for interval running when appropriate and is intended to establish a basis for the intelligent use of these tables.

THE RUNNING EVENTS

The competitive running events in track range from the 50 yard dash through the 1 hour run and longer. Road races range from about 3 miles to more than 50 miles. These may be divided into five categories which are defined all-inclusively as follows:

The Sprints—races at distances up to 275 yards or 250 meters.
The Long Sprints—races at distances over 275 yards or 250 meters up to 660 yards or 600 meters.
The Middle Distance Runs—races at distances over 660 yards or 600 meters up to 1-1/4 miles or 2000 meters.
The Distance Runs—races at distances over 1-1/4 miles or 2000 meters up to 10 miles or 16 kilometers.
The Long Distances—races at distances over 10 miles or 16 kilometers and longer.

These event categories are defined as such because each event has its unique requirements in terms of the type of training required and the type of physical and mental talent required. A very important point, also, is that a runner can usually compete at about an equal performance level throughout his event category and sometimes beyond. For example, a sprinter can usually perform about equally well at all sprint distances, but not necessarily in the long sprints, e.g., 440 yards. A 440 runner can usually run equally well at 300, 500 and possibly 600 yards. Some 440 men can run well at even 880 yards (such as Tom Courtney, 1956 Olympic Team). However, it should *never* be assumed that a runner can perform as well, on the point scale, at distances beyond his event category. At distances other than within his event category, the runner will simply perform at a lower point level. In other words, if his talent and his training properly match his event, he will score highest on the point scale at that event. Thus, the scoring table can be used to select a runner's best event, providing his training is properly taken into account.

SPEED AND DISTANCE

To clarify some of the discussion about using the pacing tables it is important that the difference between absolute speed and relative speed be made clear. In this discussion, four kinds of speed will be described. The terms employed to identify each, with definitions, are as follows:

1. *Absolute Maximum Speed*—the fastest running speed that can be performed by a runner over a short distance of 30 to 50 yards with a full running start. This speed is the "upper limit" of the runner, not influenced by the effects of muscular fatigue. Its value varies with the ability of the individual runner, of course.

2. *Maximum Event Speed*—or maximum effort speed, is the speed that the runner can sustain over a chosen distance with 100% effort. For example, a 440 yard run in 55 seconds is a speed of 8 yards each second and would be the maximum 440 yard event speed for a 660 point level performer.

3. *Submaximum Speed*—a running speed that is less than the maximum the runner could sustain over that distance and results in a submaximum effort. In this text it is expressed as the percentage of the maximum event speed for whatever distance is chosen.

4. *True Running Speed*—the running speed during any particular run, racing or training, without reference to the effort or ability of the runner, usually expressed as time per mile, such as 4:30 per mile, or as time per 440, such as 68 seconds per 440.

The speed that is listed in the left-hand column of the pacing tables is the submaximum speed expressed as a percentage of the maximum event speed for the performance level of the particular pacing table, such as 85%, 80%, etc.

It is obvious that to run farther, the runner must run slower because of man's limited capacity to supply oxygen to the muscles, as well as to carry away fatigue products from the muscles. Knowledge of the relationship between distance and the speed of the run is important, especially in training. For most runners, the speed for 100% effort decreases with increasing distance in a manner described by the Normal Performance Curve as shown in Figure 5.1. This curve represents the relative speed over all distances at one performance level rather than for one runner. A logarithmic scale is used to allow a greater range of distance to be presented.

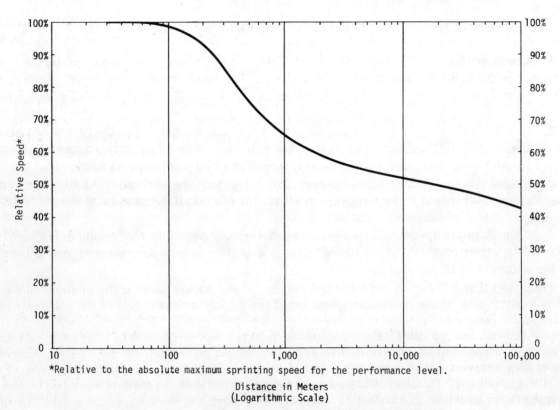

*Relative to the absolute maximum sprinting speed for the performance level.

Distance in Meters
(Logarithmic Scale)

Figure 5.1   NORMAL PERFORMANCE CURVE

52

The importance of this curve is that it can predict a runner's performance at a distance other than his event distance. Of course it does *not* say that a 52 second 440 yard runner should run a two mile in 9:46; first, because he is *not* trained for distance running and second, he may not have the capacity to perform distance runs on an equal par, even with training. The curve *does* predict his performance within his event category accurately enough for training purposes. Now, knowing the speed at different distances for 100% effort, we can mathematically determine speeds for submaximum effort by taking a fractional value, like 85% (.85), of the normal performance curve. Since these speeds require submaximum effort, runs at submaximum speed can be repeated, with rest intervals, numerous times. The principle of the pacing tables is *that the number of repetitions that the runner can perform depends only on the relative speed that he runs,* providing: (1) the run is longer than 220 yards and shorter than 2 miles, and (2) he is adequately conditioned to do the amount of running required in the workout. This principle is discussed more thoroughly in Chapter 8, and is consistent with current training schedules of most runners using interval running.

Provision (2) above simply means that a sprinter would not (and *could* not) do repeat 2 mile runs or the like, just as a six-miler would not do repeat 110 yard dashes at 90% of the speed for his performance level.

INTERVAL RUNNING

In general terms, interval running is a session which consists of repeated periods of running each followed by a limited rest period. The level of effort, or speed, of the run is always greater than could be sustained continuously for the full session. The rest periods may be either active rest, such as walking or slow jogging, or complete rest.

It has often been stated that there are an infinite number of combinations of these variables that can be chosen for a workout. This is misleading because the workout should conform to these two requirements:

1. It should be hard enough or tiring enough to yield a maximum training effect on the runner.

2. It should *not* be so exhausting that the runner cannot recover adequately for the next day's workout.

A workout meeting these two requirements will be called a *full intensity* workout. The workouts given in the tables are such workouts excepting those at less than 220 yards.

Since each runner has a limited capacity to perform a workout, the four variables of the interval running workout *cannot be arbitrarily chosen!* The ability and fitness of the runner determines the intensity of the workout that he can perform. The pacing tables provide an accurate means of determining the proper workout intensity for runners of various abilities. The coach or runner must still make the choice from the proper level table.

A common error is for an aspiring runner to attempt to do the same workouts as the champion runner. Such an approach is ridiculous, for the novice runner simply does not have the capacity to perform such workouts. He must build his capacity by working at his own level and gradually increasing as each month and year goes by. In terms of the tables, he must work his way up the point scale month by month and year by year.

The distances that are used in interval running range from about 50 yards to 2 miles or more, the choice of which depends on the event and the purpose of the training. The chart given as Figure 5.2 presents the general relationship between the event distances and the distances used in interval running. These are broad relationships and the reader should refer to the chapters which follow for a more specific discussion.

THE NATURE OF INTERVAL RUNNING

Interval running enables the runner to get more running at a faster speed than with continual running. It offers a number of other advantages in terms of the training effects, particularly for the sprinters and middle distance runners.

54

TYPE OF RUNNER	RACING DISTANCE	DISTANCE USED IN INTERVAL RUNNING
SPRINTERS	55 yards to 275 yards (50 meters to 250 meters)	30 yards to 330 yards (30 meters to 300 meters)
LONG SPRINTERS	275 yards to 660 yards (250 meters to 600 meters)	55 yards to 660 yards (50 meters to 600 meters)
MIDDLE DISTANCES	600 yards to 1-1/4 miles (600 meters to 2000 meters)	110 yards to 1-1/4 miles (100 meters to 2000 meters)
DISTANCES	1-1/4 miles to 10 miles (2000 meters to 16 kilometers)	220 yards to 2 miles (200 meters to 3200 meters)
LONG DISTANCES	10 miles and up (16 kilometers and up)	440 yards to 2 miles (400 meters to 3200 meters)

Figure 5.2   The Relationship between the Racing Distance and Distance Normally Used in Interval Running

Each run of an interval workout must be slower than for an "all out" effort over the same distance. With each run, some muscle fatigue builds up and with each successive run the fatigue accumulates to a point where to repeat the same run in the same time requires 100% effort. At this point, if not before, the interval workout should be stopped and a warmdown activity should be begun. To go beyond this point, the runner overextends himself and likely will not adequately recover for the next day's workout.

The heart rate or pulse of the runner is an indicator of his level of effort. In fact, it is an excellent indicator of effort to the point where the pulse reaches its maximum value (about 200 beats/minute), then the runner can further increase his speed (effort) but the pulse rate will not increase further. The speed at which this maximum pulse rate is reached is about 80% to 85% speed for the mile run [Ref. Karlsson, 1965]. This pace can be expressed as less than 60% speed for the 220, 60-62.5% for the 330, 60-65% for the 440, 70-75% speed for the 660, etc.

During a run at nominal speed over 220 yards or more, the heart rate reaches the near-maximum level during the run. However, when the individual stops running, his pulse rate immediately decreases rapidly. The rate of decrease is very nearly the same regardless of what distance was run. If the relative speed was low (60 to 80%) the pulse falls to a fairly constant rate within about 90 seconds. If the level of effort is higher, or if the run is in the latter phase of the interval workout, the time required for the pulse to level off becomes longer, approaching about 3 minutes for a 100% effort. Still, there appears to be no correlation between this transient (short term) recovery of the pulse rate and the distance of the run.

Following the short term recovery of the heart rate, a long term recovery of heart rate takes place which requires from 3 to 5 hours for it to return to the pre-exercise rest level. Thus, there is a short term recovery—phase 1, and a long term recovery—phase 2. The heart rate during phase 2 may be an indication of the total level of effort. For example, following a single run of 440 yards at about 65% speed the pulse rate falls to near rest value within 90 seconds; however, near the end of a workout of 28 or 30 of such runs, the heart rate falls to a value that is nearly double the rest rate. This high pulse rate during phase 2 recovery may indicate that the runner has had enough. Much of this is unconfirmed scientifically but indicated by observation of pulse rate recovery.

The length of the rest interval has been traditionally based on the heart rate; specifically, when the rate comes to less than 120 beats per minute, the next repetition should begin. At higher levels of effort, the length of the phase 1 recovery and the time for the pulse to drop to 120 are nearly the same. However, for lower levels of effort, the pulse rate falls to less than 120 very quickly, in 20 to 30 seconds, and continues to fall until the phase 2 recovery begins at 90 seconds from the time he stopped running. Depending on what criteria is chosen for the rest interval, it appears that it should be shorter, like 30 to 90 seconds for low levels of effort and longer, like 3 to 5 minutes for the higher levels of effort. This is also consistent with most runners' response, both physical and psychological, on the training track. See Chapter 8 for additional discussion of the recovery phase.

The rest intervals listed in the pacing tables are based on these observed characteristics. A range of values for the interval, such as 1-2 minutes, is given rather than a fixed value because there is some variation among individuals and their condition as well as differences in the environment; the temperature in particular causes variations.

It was pointed out earlier that the number of reps performed is dependent on the relative speed of the run. It is apparent from the discussion above that the rest interval is also dependent on the relative speed of the run. Thus, by selecting the relative speed of the run (relative to the maximum for the particular distance) we also, in effect, select the number of reps and the rest interval. The number of variables in the interval workout have, therefore, been reduced from four to two! So by stating the percentage speed and the distance, the interval workout is completely described by the tables.

TYPES OF INTERVAL RUNNING

In the discussion above, interval running has been used to describe the general form of interrupted running. Within this general form of training are several specific forms of interval running, each of which has specific benefits in terms of the training effects. The pacing tables offer an opportunity to define these various types of interval running in more precise terms. By dividing the workouts in the tables into several categories of training, the choice of the workouts can be made more easily.

To this point we have attempted to avoid the use of the term "interval training" in preference to interval running. *Interval training* is a specific form of interval running and its development is generally credited to Dr. Woldemar Gerschler, a noted German exercise physiologist. This specific form of interval running is properly described in terms of heart rate response rather than running speed. Interval training consists of repeated runs of sufficient speed to bring the heart rate up to 180 per minute or more, each followed by a rest interval sufficiently long to allow the heart rate to fall to 120 beats per minute. Using these criteria, the length of the run is usually 110 yards to 440 yards and the rest interval is typically 30 to 90 seconds, depending on the effort or speed of the runs. The speed necessary to get the heart rate up to 180 or more is not well defined; however, monitoring of heart rate by radio-telemetry has shown that even in a 2 mile run, the heart rate reaches 180 or more by the end of the first 440 yards [Ref. McArdle, 1967]. In interval running, the heart rate comes up to 180 more readily after the first few repetitions are completed at even a slower speed.

For those who check their pulse rates while training, it should be pointed out that the heart rate begins to drop immediately when running stops and drops very rapidly. So it is virtually impossible to check the peak heart rate while running except by radio telemetry or treadmill tests. Depending on the level of effort, the heart rate will decrease by 15% to 30% or more from its peak value within 15 seconds from when running is stopped. Thus, if the athlete takes his own pulse at 180 after a run, as measured over a 10 second interval (30 beats in 10 seconds), it probably was 200 to 205 during the run. If the pulse is measured in this manner, then a value of 160 to 170 within the first 15 seconds of the rest interval is sufficient to indicate a value of 180 or more during the run. (See Chapter 8 for additional comments on the heart rate recovery).

With these preliminary comments, we are now in a good position to define the various types of interval running, including interval training, in terms of the contents in the pacing tables. It is unfortunate, perhaps, that use of the term interval training has come to include virtually all forms of interval running; however, its use here will be limited to its original meaning as described above. Seven different types of interval running will be defined in terms of the tables, with some comment on the value and use of such type. These seven types are as follows:

1. *Sprint Interval Running*
2. *Fast Interval or Tempo Running*
3. *Stress Interval Running*
4. *Repetition Running*
5. *Interval Training*
6. *Slow Interval Running*
7. *Pace Interval Running*

In terms of the contents of the pacing tables they are defined as follows:

1. *Sprint Interval Running* is defined as running above 85% of maximum speed at the sprint distances, namely up to 275 yards. This form of training is used almost exclusively by the sprinters and long sprinters (440 men). The runners in other running events have little need for this fast training.

2. *Fast Interval or Tempo Running* is interval running at 77.5% to 85% speed at distances up to 680 yards. It is generally faster than the racing speed of middle distance and distance runs. It is often used by middle distance and distance runners for speed work to develop strength.

3. *Stress Interval Running* is interval running faster than 85% speed at the long-sprint distances, namely 275 to 660 yards. This form of training is used by the long sprinters (440 men) and middle distance runners, particularly 880 men, to improve their "staying power."

4. *Repetition Running* is interval running faster than 85% speed at the middle distances (660 yards and up) and longer. This form of training is often associated with Franz Stampfl, the famous English coach

of Roger Bannister and others. It is used by middle distance and distance runners often as preparation for the racing experience.

5. *Interval Training,* as described earlier, is running 60% to 75% speed at 110 to 440 yards. This form of interval running will generally meet the requirements for interval training as discussed earlier. Interval training is used specifically to increase the stroke volume of the heart and is most important to the middle distance runners.

6. *Slow Interval Running* includes the remainder of the interval running that is slower than the runner's racing speed. It is used mainly by distance runners to build general endurance and as a variation to continuous running.

7. *Pace Interval Running* is simply interval running at the planned racing speed, or pace, usually at 1/4 to 3/8 of the racing distance.

As an aid to referring to these various forms of interval running in the pacing tables, the region of each form of training is shown in Figure 5.3. Here again, the 760 point level table is used as an example. The pace used in this example is for a 4:30 mile. Some of the types of training refer to the pace of the runner's event so these areas within the tables would shift accordingly.

The chart presented as Figure 5.4 summarizes the use of interval running in terms of the various forms of interval running and the event categories. This chart presents some general guidelines for selecting an appropriate workout from the tables for the various events. The next two chapters will give more specific guidelines for setting up a workout program.

OTHER FORMS OF TRAINING

Interval running is a very controlled form of training where the stopwatch is used to measure the speed of every run. There are two other forms of training for running that are very important in most training programs. They are *fartlek training* and *continuous running training.*

1. *Fartlek* is the Swedish word meaning "play of speed" and more commonly *speed play.* Speed

760 POINT LEVEL PACING TABLE

SPEED	REPS	REST	110 YD	150 YD	165 YD	220 YD	275 YD	330 YD	352 YD	385 YD	440 YD	495 YD
95.0%	0- 1	---	11.1	15.3	17.0	23.0	29.8	37.4	40.5	45.4	51.7	1:02.3
92.5%	1- 2	4- 5 M	11.4	15.7	17.4	23.7	30.7	38.4	41.6	46.6	53.1	1:04.0
90.0%	2- 3	4- 5 M	11.7	16.2	17.9	24.3	31.5	39.5	42.8	47.9	54.7	1:05.8
87.5%	3- 4	3- 4 M	12.0	16.6	18.4	25.0	32.4	40.6	44.0	49.3	56.3	1:07.7
85.0%	4- 5	3- 4 M	12.4	17.1	18.9	25.8	33.4	41.8	45.3	50.7	1:00.0	1:09.7
82.5%	6- 7	2- 3 M	12.8	17.6	19.5	26.5	34.4	43.0	46.7	52.3	1:01.8	1:11.8
80.0%	8- 9	2- 3 M	13.2	18.2	20.1	27.4	35.6	44.4	48.1	53.9	1:03.7	1:14.0
77.5%	10-12	1- 2 M	13.6	18.8	20.8	28.2	36.6	45.8	49.7	55.6	1:05.8	1:16.4
75.0%	13-15	1- 2 M	14.0	19.4	21.5	29.2	37.8	47.3	51.3	57.5	1:08.0	1:19.0
72.5%	16-18	60-90 S	14.5	20.1	22.2	30.2	39.1	49.0	53.1	59.5	1:10.5	1:21.7
70.0%	19-21	60-90 S	15.0	20.8	23.0	31.3	40.5	50.7	55.0	1:01.8	1:12.9	1:24.6
67.5%	22-24	45-75 S	15.6	21.6	23.9	32.4	42.0	52.6	57.0	1:04.3	1:15.6	1:27.7
65.0%	25-29	45-75 S	16.2	22.4	24.8	33.6	43.6	54.6	59.2	1:06.3	1:18.5	1:31.1
62.5%	30-35	30-60 S	16.8	23.3	25.7	35.0	45.4	56.8	1:01.6	1:09.0	1:21.6	1:34.8
60.0%	36-40	30-60 S	17.6	24.3	26.8	36.5	47.3	59.1	1:04.2	1:11.8	1:25.0	-----

SPEED	REPS	REST	550 YD	660 YD	880 YD	1100 YD	1320 YD	1.00 MI	1.25 MI	1.50 MI	1.75 MI	2.00 MI
95.0%	0- 1	---	1:11.3	1:29.3	2:09.0	2:49.0	3:34.0	4:44.0	6:05.0	7:29.0	8:52.0	10:16.0
92.5%	1- 2	4- 5 M	1:13.3	1:31.3	2:09.8	2:58.9	3:55.3	4:54.0	6:26.9	7:53.9	9:07.0	10:31.8
90.0%	2- 3	4- 5 M	1:15.5	1:34.5	2:17.3	3:01.0	3:55.5	5:08.9	6:37.3	8:07.5	9:38.3	11:09.5
87.5%	3- 4	3- 4 M	1:17.4									
85.0%	4- 5	3- 4 M	1:19.7	1:40.1	2:21.2	3:04.3	3:48.0	5:17.0	6:49.0	8:21.8	9:55.3	11:29.2
82.5%	6- 7	2- 3 M	1:22.1	1:43.5	2:25.5	3:09.9	3:54.9	5:27.0	7:01.4	-----	-----	-----
80.0%	8- 9	2- 3 M	1:24.7	1:46.3	2:30.0	3:15.8	4:02.2	5:37.5	-----	-----	-----	-----
77.5%	10-12	1- 2 M	1:27.4	1:49.7	2:34.9	3:22.1	4:10.0	-----	-----	-----	-----	-----
75.0%	13-15	1- 2 M	1:30.3	1:53.4	2:40.0	3:28.8	4:18.4	-----	-----	-----	-----	-----
72.5%	16-18	60-90 S	1:33.4	1:57.3	2:45.5	-----	-----	-----	-----	-----	-----	-----
70.0%	19-21	60-90 S	1:36.8	2:01.5	2:51.5	-----	-----	-----	-----	-----	-----	-----
67.5%	22-24	45-75 S	1:40.4	2:06.0	-----	-----	-----	-----	-----	-----	-----	-----
65.0%	25-29	45-75 S	1:44.2	-----	-----	-----	-----	-----	-----	-----	-----	-----
62.5%	30-35	30-60 S	-----	-----	-----	-----	-----	-----	-----	-----	-----	-----
60.0%	36-40	30-60 S	-----	-----	-----	-----	-----	-----	-----	-----	-----	-----

Pace Interval Running
4:30 Mile Pace Line

Sprint Interval Running

Stress Interval Running

Fast Interval Running

Interval Training

Slow Interval Running

Repetition Running

Figure 5.3   Pictorial Representation of the Different Forms of Interval Running

61

TRACK EVENT CATEGORY / TYPE OF INTERVAL RUNNING	SPRINTS	LONG SPRINTS	MIDDLE DISTANCES	DISTANCES	LONG DISTANCES
	Race: Up to 275 yards Train: Interval Running 30 to 330 yards Continuous Running up to 5 miles	Race: 275 to 660 yards Train: Interval Running 55 to 660 yards Continuous Running up to 8 miles	Race: 660 to 1¼ miles Train: Interval Running 110 to 1¼ miles Continuous Running 3 to 15 miles	Race: 1¼ to 10 miles Train: Interval Running 220 yds. to 2 miles Continuous Running 5 to 20 miles	Race: 10 miles and longer Train: Interval Running 440 yards to 2 miles Continuous Running 10 to 30 miles
Sprint Interval Running Up to 275 yards at 87.5 to 95% speed	For speed and strength development, usually done at 30 to 165 yards.	For speed and strength development, usually done at 55 to 275 yards.	Sprint Interval Running not suggested for middle distance runners.	Sprint Interval Running not suggested for distance runners.	Sprint Interval Running not suggested for long distance runners.
Fast Interval Running Up to 660 yards at 77.5 to 85% speed	For stamina development and coordination, usually done at 110 to 275 yards.	For stamina development and coordination, usually done at 110 to 385 yards.	For speed and strength development, usually done at 165 to 550 yards.	For speed and strength development, usually done at 440 to 660 yds. in early season training.	Fast Interval Running not suggested for long distance runners except as a supplementary workout.
Stress Interval Running 275 to 660 yards at 87.5 to 95% speed	For anaerobic endurance development, usually done at 275 to 330 yards.	For anaerobic endurance development, usually done at 275 to 495 yards.	For anaerobic endurance development, usually done at 440 to 660 yards late season.	Stress Interval Running not suggested for distance runners.	Stress Interval Running not suggested for long distance runners.
Repetition Running 660 yards to 2 miles at 87.5 to 95% speed	Repetition Running is not used by sprinters.	Repetition Running is not used in a long sprinter's training program.	For stamina development, usually done at 660 yards to 1320 yards in early season training.	For stamina development, usually done at 1320 yards to 2 miles in early season training.	For stamina development usually at 1 mile to 2 miles in late season training.
Interval Training 110 to 440 yards at 60 to 75% speed	For general endurance development, usually done at 110 to 220 yards.	For general endurance development, usually done at 110 to 330 yards.	For general endurance development, usually done at 220 to 440 yards.	For general endurance development, usually done at 220 to 440 yds.	For general endurance development. usually at 330 to 440 yards with high number of repetitions.
Slow Interval Running 495 yards and longer at slower than race pace	Slow interval running not suggested for sprinters training program.	For aerobic endurance development, usually done at 550 to 880 yds. pre-season.	For aerobic endurance development, usually done at 550 to 2200 yds. pre-season.	For aerobic endurance development, usually at 660 yards to 2 miles.	For aerobic endurance, usually at 880 yards to 2 miles.
Pace Interval Running ¼ to ½ of event distance at racing speed	Pace Interval Running not applicable to sprint training.	For development of pace judgement, usually done at 150 to 352 yards, in early season training.	For development of pace judgement, usually done at 330 to 880 yards.	For development of pace judgement, usually at 880 yards to 1 mile.	Pace Interval Running seldom used by long distance runners.

Figure 5.4 Use of the Various Types of Interval Running According to Event Category

62

play is the most descriptive term for this form of training for it consists of running with wide variation of speed in an informal but intense manner. In essence, it is varied interval running without the aid of a stopwatch or measured course. It could best be described by an example: Jog 15 to 20 minutes until warm, then go into a series of 200 to 300 yard fast-slow runs with the fast runs at a 60 to 66 second 440 pace. These would be followed (without stopping) by a sustained drive for ½ to ¾ mile at a pace approaching racing speed for the 2 mile. Jog until you catch your breath, then sprint 300 yards or so, preferably uphill (if available), then do a sustained run of ½ to ¾ mile or so. This type of activity is continued until the runner has covered a distance of 3 to 10 miles, depending on his state of training and his condition. It is important to note that the fast-slow runs during fartlek training need not follow any particular order in terms of distances, hills, and speeds, but should be adapted to the terrain and environment of the individual runner. Fartlek training is probably most effectively done by runners who are experienced, in good condition and who have good self-discipline since the runner is completely on his own without the motivation of the stopwatch and track. Probably its greatest benefit is the freedom from the track and stopwatch and can be a refreshing variation from track training and over-distance training.

2. *Continuous Running Training* is simply running at a somewhat constant speed over a relatively long distance. The distance of the run varies greatly. For the beginning jogger or schoolboy, a mile or two is enough initially. For the long distance runner (marathoner), the runs may range from 15 to 30 miles or more. Continuous running training includes jogging, distance runs (3 to 10 miles) and long distance runs (10 to 30 miles and more). The latter is referred to as marathon training, often associated with the Arthur Lydiard (New Zealand coach) training schedules. Marathon training is a major part of the Lydiard method of training and his success has brought about a re-examination of the value of such training.

Continuous running training is the oldest form of training, being practiced by the road racers of the late 1920's and 1930's. Its practice was advised by the great Arthur Newton, who was the greatest long distance runner of that era when road races of 50 miles or more were popular. The track world ignored his ideas, perhaps because he never raced at a distance less than 10 miles (and that only once!) and rarely at less than 26 miles. His choice of racing distances and corresponding performances were probably due to his age and to his style of running, which was described as a "shuffle", rather than a limitation of his training.

Continuous running is coming to be recognized as the most effective training for developing general endurance. A great deal of testimonial evidence indicates that continuous running training is very beneficial not only to long distance runners, but to distance and middle distance runners as well.

The effect of continuous running training is apparently to develop the capillaries in the muscle tissue (refer to "Continuous Running Training," by Toni Nett in *Run Run Run* by Fred Wilt, p. 174). This enables the circulatory system to better deliver oxygen to the muscle cells. Continuous running training should be a basic part of every training program, and especially for middle distances and longer.

The *speed* of the continuous run is important, but again must be relative to the ability of the individual. The range of abilities in long distance running are far greater than in the shorter distances, with the fastest runners nearly *twice* as fast as the slowest. Likewise the training speeds must be adjusted accordingly just as in interval running. Here again it is most convenient to select the speed in training with continuous runs in terms of the percentage of the speed for 100% effort as in competition. To provide an aid in this regard, the computer was put to work to print percentage speed tables called "Reduced Speeds For Continuous Running Training" which appear as Table 3 in both the English and Metric Unit Tables.

These are used in conjunction with the Per-Mile Average Tables for long distance runs (Table 5, English Unit Tables). From this table, the runner can find his predicted per-mile average for this performance level (100% effort). He then refers to the table of Reduced Speeds and can select what speed he should run a long distance that may be unfamiliar to him. The percentage speeds may be related to qualitative terms as follows:

FAST   —92.5% to 95% speed
MEDIUM   —87.5% to 90% speed
EASY   —82.5% to 85% speed
SLOW   —80% speed or less

Most runners using this form of training use *medium* speed, or about 90% as fast as they would race the distance. Others prefer the *easy* to *slow* speed. *Medium* speed continuous runs allow adequate recovery from day-to-day, whereas *fast* runs usually must be followed by an *easy* run the next day to recover. Another important consideration is the distance of the run in comparison to the average daily mileage. Some guidance in this regard may be summarized as follows:

Distance	Speed	Percentage
Equal to average daily mileage	Medium—Fast	87.5%—95%
1-1/2 times average daily mileage	Easy—Medium	82.5%—90.0%
2 times average daily mileage	Slow—Easy	80.0%—85.0%
More than 2 times average daily mileage	Slow	80.0% or less

For example, a runner averaging seven miles a day would go at about 85% of his performance rated speed on a 14-mile run. A runner averaging 10 miles day would go at 80% speed for a 25-mile run, etc.

THE ELEMENTS OF RUNNING PERFORMANCE

To this point in the discussion, the various types of training and the different kinds of workouts have been reviewed and defined in terms of the contents of the pacing tables for interval running. To provide a basis for the intelligent use of these tables in the training program, these need to be tied together with the running events and the needs of the individual. Much of the remainder of this book will be concerned with the rationale for proper selection of the workout and planning of the overall program.

The initial step in establishing a rational basis for workout selection is to examine the running performance and separate it into its basic elements. These elements can be weighed as to their importance in the various events, and correlated with specific forms of training and workouts. A step-by-step approach can then be made to the total training program.

The ability to perform well in running events may be considered as a combination of four basic abilities:

1. SPRINTING SPEED
2. ANAEROBIC ENDURANCE
3. AEROBIC ENDURANCE
4. RUNNING EFFICIENCY

The relative importance of each of these elements of a performance establishes the training emphasis.

1. *Sprinting speed* is a result of muscular strength, fast neuromuscular reactions, low muscle viscosity (friction), and coordinated movement. Of these, only two can be improved significantly by training; strength and coordination. Increased strength is an aid to sprinting ability providing there is no significant increase in muscle size. More important, perhaps, is that there be *balanced* strength among the muscle groups involved in sprinting. Muscle viscosity, or muscle friction, may be reduced slightly through training, but its significance is difficult to measure. Fast reactions are an inborn trait and cannot be improved by training. Coordinated movement can be greatly improved by training and may be the most trainable aspect of sprinting.

2. *Anaerobic Endurance* is the athlete's capacity to perform anaerobic work. The muscle performs work by means of anaerobic (without oxygen) and aerobic (with oxygen) metabolic processes. Anaerobic work is that portion of the total work output that is due to the anaerobic process. The rate at which the circulatory system can supply oxygen to the muscle cells is limited; therefore, high effort, short duration (up to a few minutes) work is mostly due to the anaerobic process. The events from the sprints through the middle distances demand mostly anaerobic work. Anaerobic endurance is increased by anaerobic train-

ing, which includes sprint interval, stress interval, repetition running and fast interval running.

3. *Aerobic Endurance* is the athlete's capacity to perform aerobic work. Aerobic work is that portion of the total work output that is due to aerobic processes. It is the steady state work capacity as opposed to the short term work capacity. The role of aerobic endurance increases as the duration of the event increases; thus it is of major importance in the distance and long distance runs. The relative energy yield from each process based on an individual with high capacitance of each is portrayed in Figure 5.5. This is indicative of the relative importance of anaerobic and aerobic processes; however, individual variations must be considered. Aerobic endurance is increased by aerobic training which includes slow continuous running, interval training, and slow interval running.

4. *Running Efficiency* is the result of coordinated movement. Coordinated movement is that in which there is a minimum waste of physiological energy. Body movement in which the waste of energy is not minimized is called incoordinated movement. Running efficiency comes about through the practice of running and its effect is to decrease the amount of oxygen required for a fixed running speed. This is congruous to increasing the running speed for a fixed oxygen requirement. Running efficiency is not usually emphasized in training discussions since it is not a physiological result of training, because the physiological results are to increase the oxygen-carrying capacity, not decrease the requirements. Running efficiency is most important in the distance runs because any wasted energy results in premature fatigue.

In sprinting, coordinated movement allows maximum speed to be achieved whereas uncoordinated movement delays the leg action and slows the speed of the runner. Running efficiency is achieved by consistent, daily workouts and is optimized at the racing speed by pace interval running. Many coaches feel that no conscious effort needs to be made toward improving coordination, although emphasis on *relaxation* is the most common form of improving one's running efficiency.

THE APPROACH TO TRAINING

Having identified the basic elements of a performance above, the approach to training for better

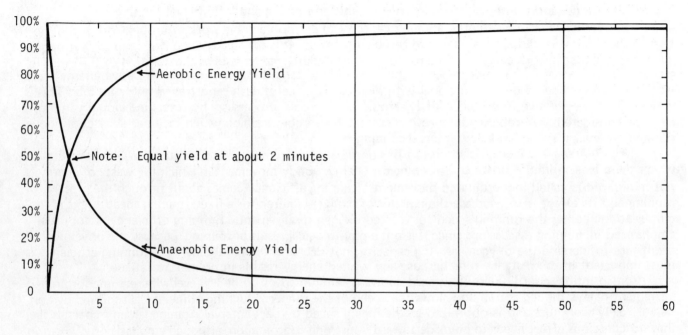

Figure 5.5* Relative Energy Yield from Aerobic and Anaerobic Processes

*From Jour. AMA, Vol. 205, No. 11, Sept. 9, 1968, p. 70

performance in running is to train each of these elements: speed, anaerobic endurance, aerobic endurance and running efficiency, according to its relative importance to the event. The next step is to evaluate the relative importance of each of these elements to the particular events and to identify the type of training that will most effectively develop each element. This is presented in the next chapter and provides a basis for selection of the workout as well as planning the whole training program. Before presenting the specifics of the events and the training for them, a few of the general principles of physical training are worthy of review. In this brief review, some viewpoints may not be in full accord with traditional ideas, but they are worthy of consideration.

Training for running is a process of adaptation. Adaptation takes place in three forms: increased skill or efficiency, increased strength and increased capacity for work (endurance), both anaerobic and aerobic. The greater efficiency results in a reduced energy requirement whereas greater strength and endurance increases the energy output capacity. All three are a factor in improved performance. In terms of strength and endurance, the nature of the human body is to always have a reserve beyond normal demands made upon it. The normal demand, then, is the daily workout. The reserve capacity is used in a competitive performance, though not completely. The degree to which the reserve capacity is used is determined by motivation.

To utilize the human body's capacity for adaptation in training we apply the *principle of progressive loading*. If a load, in the form of a workout, is imposed regularly, and if the load is nearly equal to the body's normal capacity to sustain the load, the body will adapt by increasing its capacity for the load in order to maintain its reserve. This is the elementary principle of all strength and endurance training. The load (workout or performance) can then be increased to match the increased capacity, which results in greater capacity, and so forth. This is continued until the individual achieves his ultimate capability, or he becomes psychologically distracted and discontinues his training. His ultimate capability is limited by his inborn talent and his limited capacity to adapt.

The principle of progressive loading is often incorrectly called the overload principle. To overload is to exceed capacity and if applied to athletes, will result in physical breakdown in the form of chronic injuries, staleness and an associated decline in performance. In training, it is important *not* to overload the athlete but to properly load him with a workout he can perform and come back the next day with sufficient reserve to do the same amount of work.

Chapter 6
Factors in Choosing the Workout

The pacing tables contain such a wide selection of workouts for an individual that the first reaction to them is to ask, "Which one is the best to use?" The answer is that it depends upon a number of factors, each of which must be considered to make a proper choice of the daily workout. In any systematic training program the coach and/or runner has something in mind when he decides on the workout program even though he may not consciously think about some of the more obvious factors. Most of these considerations are given and discussed in this chapter to provide a sound basis for choosing the daily workout. One consideration that is not discussed here is the psychological makeup of the runner, his likes and dislikes, attitude, etc. These must be handled by the coach on an individual basis.

THE RUNNER AND HIS EVENT

The most important consideration in the runner's workout program is his event or the category of events in which he plans to compete. This is a most obvious consideration; however, it is worthwhile to discuss what it means in terms of the workouts and training program.

71

Once the runner has chosen his event category, hopefully on the basis of demonstrated talent in this event compared to other events, his training will be directed toward meeting the physical demands of the event. The relative importance of each of the elements, defined in Chapter 5, in the various event categories provides a basis for the type of training that must be undertaken. In Figure 6.1, the importance of each element is ranked as essential, important, helpful or less important.

Event Category	Sprinting Speed	Anaerobic Endurance	Aerobic Endurance	Running Efficiency
Sprints	Essential	Helpful	Unimportant	Helpful
Long Sprints	Essential	Essential	Helpful	Helpful
Middle Distance	Important ✓	Important ✓	Important ✓	Important ✓
Distance	Helpful	Helpful	Essential	Essential
Long Distance	Helpful	Helpful	Essential	Essential

Figure 6.1—Importance of Training Elements to Event Category

In Chapter 5, one will recall the seven types of interval training that were defined (sprint interval, pace work, etc.). These seven types can be associated with the above named training elements. The most effective type of training to develop each of the training elements can be summarized as follows:

1. *Speed.* . . .Sprint Interval, Fast Interval Training

2. *Anaerobic Capacity*. . . .Stress, Fast Interval, Repetition Running
3. *Aerobic Capacity*. . . .Continuous Running, Interval Training, Slow Interval Running
4. *Running Efficiency*. . . .Pace Work, Volume Running, Daily Workout

(Volume in this text means the quantity of running done in a workout or the amount of "running practice" that the athlete performs).

Now from Figure 6.1 and the above classifications one can determine the types of training that each event category demands, i.e.

EVENT CATEGORY	with Figure 6.1 gives	Importance of Training Elements for Each Category	with Above gives	Type of Training for Each Training Element	with Below gives	Type of Training for each Event Category

The above diagram can be expanded to show, in detail, the types of training which should be employed in each of the five event categories (the following can be considered support information for Figure 5:4):

1. *The Sprints* demand mostly   sprint interval running from 30 to 165 yards and some fast interval running from 100 to 220 yards.

2. *The Long Sprints* demand more stress training and fast interval running with less emphasis on sprint interval training. The stress training is usually done at 275 to 550 yards and the fast interval training at 110 to 440 yards.

3. *The Middle Distances* demand all forms of training with speed being the least important of the four given above. Anaerobic and aerobic capacity are equally important; however, aerobic capacity takes longer to develop so the majority of preseason training is spent in aerobic training. Middle distance

training, then, consists of continuous running training (early), slow interval running, interval training, fast interval running, stress training and some repetition running. Pace work, of course, is included. The degree of emphasis on each type of training depends upon whether the athlete performs at the shorter (e.g. 880 yards) or longer of the middle distance category (e.g. 1 mile).

   4. *The Distance Runs* demand predominately aerobic training consisting of continuous running and interval running with some slow interval running and repetition running. The slow interval training is done at 440 yards and repetition running at 1 to 2 miles.

   5. *The Long Distance Runs* demand only aerobic training with only enough interval training to add a little variety to the training routine. Continuous runs make up the bulk of the program with some slow interval work with high repetitions at less than 70% speed.

   This summarizes the event factors in the training program, although additional comments will be forthcoming.

THE PERFORMANCE GOAL

   The competitive runner who is serious about his training has some performance goal he wants to achieve. This goal, in turn, provides the incentive that drives him to train so intensely. The performance goal has a great deal of influence on the choice of the workouts within the overall training program as well as influencing the total structure of the training program. Performance goals certainly are one of the greatest motivating forces in track and must be an integral part of the workout program.

   The greatest difficulty in setting performance goals is to set them just within reach but not beyond. If the performance goal for the season is set unreasonably high, the athlete can become very discouraged with his progress and this in turn can affect his training. The performance rating tables included in this book are of great help in establishing realistic performance goals for the individual athlete. The scoring tables may be helpful to provide some guidelines for setting performance goals in the following ways:

   1. In an athlete's first year of training, he can reasonably expect to improve about 100 points or

more on the performance rating scale. If he is not yet fully matured, he may improve even more, up to 200 points or so.

2. In his second year of training he may improve some 50 to 100 points in his best performance of the season compared to the previous year's best performance.

3. In the third and subsequent years of training, the athlete should not expect to improve more than 50 points from one season to the next under normal circumstances.

As an example, a high school freshman may run a 5:01 mile (600 points). As a sophomore he might expect to improve to 4:40 or better (710 points). As a junior he might achieve a 4:31 (760 points) and as a senior could expect to improve to about 4:24 (800 points). This rate of improvement would be typical; however, it would certainly vary with the individual. *An athlete who improves much more rapidly than this certainly has unusual talent and should be encouraged to develop into a top class competitor.* A rate of improvement greatly less than this may indicate he is near his limit in ability. The quality and extent of the training program must also be taken into consideration in the evaluation of the athlete's rate of progress.

With the performance goal set for the season, the runner will want to emphasize developing his maximum skill while running at that speed or pace. Table 2 in the English and Metric Unit Tables should be used to determine the times that various interval distances are to be run if performed at a desired pace. If an athlete's goal is a 4:36 mile, his pace is 69 seconds for each 440 yards. By referring to the Table of Intermediate Times for Constant Speed Runs in the English Unit Table, he can choose to run 220 yards in 34.5, 275 yards in 43.1, 330 yards in 51.8, 550 yards in 86.3, etc. Then by referring to the pacing table for *his performance level* (**not** that for his goal performance), the time for the chosen distance is found that is nearest his pace time and the REPS and REST columns state how many and with what rest interval. This procedure was diagrammed in Figure 3.2 when explanation for pace workouts was given.

If a miler is shooting for a 4:24 mile (66 second 440) but is presently at the 760 point level (4:30.8 mile), the pace work for his 4:24 mile goal may be any one of the following (taken from the 760 point level table):

1. 27 x 220y in 33.7
2. 23 x 275y in 42.0
3. 17 x 330y in 49.0
4. 15 x 352y in 52.0
5. 13 x 385y in 57.5
6. 11 x 440y in 1:05.8
7. 7 x 550y in 1:22.1
8. 4 x 660y in 1:37.2
9. 2 x 880y in 2:13.4
10 1 x 1100y in 2:45

Note that at least ten different workouts can be done for pace work on his performance goal. The last three workouts listed are repetition running as defined earlier and would be used late in the season in final preparation for competition.

The importance of the performance goal in the workout program is that it establishes a set of workouts which are pace work in pursuit of that goal. The amount of work done at the *desired speed* is established by his *present level* of ability. As the athlete's condition improves he will be able to do more and more of the interval work at the same pace. As this occurs he is also moving up on his performance ability as a competitor.

Although pace work as such is an important part of the workout, it need not take up the bulk of the workout program. In fact, too much training done at the same speed can lead to boredom and staleness on the part of the runner.

THE COMPETITIVE SEASON

A third factor that must be considered in choosing the daily workout is the season of the year as related to the competitive season. The peak of the season typically occurs in late spring and the runner will want to achieve his peak during this season. The type of training done during the year is directed, in greater or lesser degree, toward building to this peak season.

This building process assumes the runner is training the year around. Year around training is typical among middle distance and distance runners and essential for long distance runners. Including the peak season, the five periods or "seasons" are: (1) Summer, (2) Fall, (3) Winter, (4) early Spring, and (5) late Spring. The kind of training emphasized in each season is outlined below. The transition from one season to the next comes about as a gradual shift in emphasis rather than abrupt change in the workout patterns.

1. *Summer* is the post-competitive period when training is loosely structured and informal. It is a good period to do foundation work for the next year by developing strength through weight training and basic endurance through easy distance running. The more severe interval training should be used sparingly unless there is summer competition. Sprinters can benefit most by weight training in the off season which would include summer and fall for them. The endurance work in the form of long easy runs is of great benefit to the middle distance and distance runners. Interval running done in the summer is usually slow intervals, at low relative speed and high numbers of repetitions. Interval training, in itself, is a more severe form of training. Basic strength and endurance work in the form of weight training and continuous running in the summer and fall seasons make the interval training which follows much more effective in preparing the runner for competition.

2. *Fall* is the season for cross country competition for the middle distance and distance runners. Even as such it is the building period for the track season. The sprinters and especially long sprinters (440 men) can benefit greatly from cross country running. During this season the training may be balanced among continuous running training, fartlek and slow interval running with some moderately fast interval running to develop strength and quickness. The interval running can also be done on a cross country course with accurately measured distances.

3. *Winter* or pre-competitive season follows the cross country season and precedes the competitive

indoor track or early outdoor track competition. During this period the emphasis is on more interval running and less on the continuous runs. The interval running in the preseason shifts from mostly slow intervals as the competitive season approaches. Occasionally stress training and sprint workouts are appropriate the last few weeks before the first track competition. Stress training should not be overdone, however, as it is severe and psychologically tiring on the runner.

4. *Early Spring* or early season brings competition on a regular basis, but the athlete is still pointing to the championship meets in the late season. His workouts shift to more fast interval, stress and repetition running and pace work. Some slow interval work or continuous runs are done on easy days or the day before competition. During this season the workouts are designed to sharpen the runner's skill and increase his anaerobic work capacity. If the runner is competing every week, stress running type workouts, in addition to the competitive runs, should be limited to once a week.

5. *Late Spring* is the peak of the season, and the runner needs to direct all his energies to high level competition. Thus, the workout schedule is less exhausting and designed to further sharpen his running skill. The bulk of the workouts are fast interval with fewer stress workouts than in the early season. The emphasis is more on speed than on endurance. The workouts must be of sufficient volume consistent with the runner's event, but the workout will generally be less than full intensity, i.e. the number of REPS is reduced by 15 to 25%.

It will be found that the performance levels achieved in late season competition may exceed the runner's ability to perform the workouts which correspond to that level. This is attributed to the workouts being initially scaled to non-competition time trials in fall or pre-season. Practice time trials do not have the high performance incentive that championship competitions have and therefore the athlete's performance will probably exceed his workout level when actual competition really gets underway. At this point, the runner should use the table that matches his workouts rather than his performance times and move up according to his training.

THE PREVIOUS AND SUBSEQUENT WORKOUTS

Because of the nature of the various types of workouts and the body's response to them, the workouts should follow a preferred sequence. For example, a hard sprint workout would not be performed on consecutive days because the effects of fatigue from the first day's workout may cause an injury to occur in the following day of hard sprinting.

The workouts from day to day should also be arranged to avoid boredom and staleness. It is not advisable, for example, to do pace work every day or even as much as three times a week for such would be very boring to the runner and its effect is no more valuable than other types of workouts. The first guideline that can be given is to categorize the workout types:

1. Sprint workouts or fast interval workouts. . . . .Speed
2. Slow interval workouts or continuous runs. . . . .Endurance
3. Pace interval, repetition runs or stress workouts. . . . .Pace

The workouts then follow the sequence: speed, endurance, pace, or speed, pace, endurance. It is typical that a Saturday workout be not on the track, and therefore, an endurance type workout would be most easily implemented. On Monday the runner would be well rested and could perform a speed workout on this day. The weekly sequence for the pre-competitive season (fall, winter) would then be:

Mon.	—	Speed
Tue.	—	Endurance
Wed.	—	Pace
Thu.	—	Speed
Fri.	—	Pace
Sat.	—	Endurance
Sun.	—	Rest or Endurance

The intensity of the speed workout or the choice of the pace workout depends upon the season and other factors as discussed earlier, but this basic sequence is satisfactory throughout most of the season. During the competitive seasons, when competing on Saturday, Friday's workout should be an easy endurance type which has a therapeutic effect. The weekly sequence during a competitive season (early spring, late spring) might be:

Mon. — Speed
Tue. — Endurance
Wed. — Pace
Thu. — Speed
Fri. — Easy Endurance
Sat. — Competition
Sun. — Rest or Endurance

THE ENVIRONMENT

Certainly one of the most important factors in choosing the day's workout is the conditions of the environment, specifically, the weather (temperature, wind, rain, snow), the condition of the track or cross country course, and other considerations such as academic schedule, traveling and the like. Each of these must be taken into account and it is generally up to the coach or the runner's judgment to choose alternate workouts when the environment changes.

The weather during outdoor season is the strongest influence on the workout schedule. During rainy weather the runners may "take to the road" if the track condition is bad. If windy, sprint work with the wind and recovery jogging against the wind is good. If it is cold, sprinting is ill-advised and a slow interval workout may be substituted.

Of particular concern in the warmer climates is the kind of workout in hot weather. Because high temperatures limit the rate at which the body can rid itself of its heat, workouts during hot weather (above 90° F. or so) should be of shorter duration or at a much slower speed than normal. Thus sprint workouts or stress workouts are more appropriate since they consist of only a few repetitions at high relative speed. During continued hot weather other adjustments can be made such as lengthening the rest interval in the normal workout or slowing the continuous runs to 80-85%. Full workouts may be performed in the cooler morning, but doing only morning workouts may result in not being able to cope with a hot afternoon race.

Chapter 7
The Training Program

THE ROLE OF REPETITION RUNNING IN THE OVERALL PROGRAM

It is foolhardy to suggest that interval running should be used totally in a training program. The important thing is that interval running be used intelligently in the training program and be properly balanced with continuous running training, and fartlek training. The more successful runners of today are for the most part using a combination of the various training methods. A review of the training schedules of world record holder Jim Ryun, for example, reveals that a combination of long continuous runs, interval running and repetition runs make up his overall training program.

The most serious mistake a coach or runner can make is to adopt a single, inflexible training philosophy that is not adaptable to the individual runner. The training program must be designed to meet the needs of the competitive event and the needs of the individual athlete. The great advantage that is provided by the pacing tables is that they provide the equipment for the coach or runner to design workouts for the needs of the individual competitor. It is, again, not suggested that repetition running be the total makeup of the training program.

82

A logical approach to training is to build the aerobic endurance during the early phase of the program, then build the anaerobic endurance and strength during the latter phase of the program. One argument for this approach is that improved aerobic endurance enables the runner to perform more intense training sessions in the later part of the program than can be done through interval running alone. Also, it appears that the incidence of leg injuries is less when a base of endurance training is accomplished. This approach to the training program is similar to the Arthur Lydiard method and to that discussed by Rosandich [1969]. The review article by Rosandich is highly recommended and appears in the February 1969 issue of *The Athletic Journal*.

This approach is to begin with continuous running training, then fartlek running and slow interval running, followed by interval training and fast interval running, then a final phase of stress interval and repetition running. Per Rosandich, this approach is termed the American Technique of Distance Training and is essentially the approach used in this book.

THE BUILDING BLOCK APPROACH

Putting together the various elements of training into a complete training program leads to a sequence in which the basic endurance is developed first. The other types of training are sequenced as shown by the diagram in Figure 7.1.

This sequence shown is based on the principle that fast training can be more effectively done with a base of endurance training.

The continuous running (e.g. jogging) and slow interval training can be performed by one who is initially completely unfit. Therefore, it is reasonable that this be the first phase of the training program.

As the runner develops strength, muscle tone and endurance from the jogging or marathon type of training, he is then more able to effectively perform the more intense fast interval running with high repetitions. The slow intervals can be moved up in relative speed (percentage) as the runner's general endurance improves. Also, Swedish fartlek training can be used more effectively when the runner is already in good

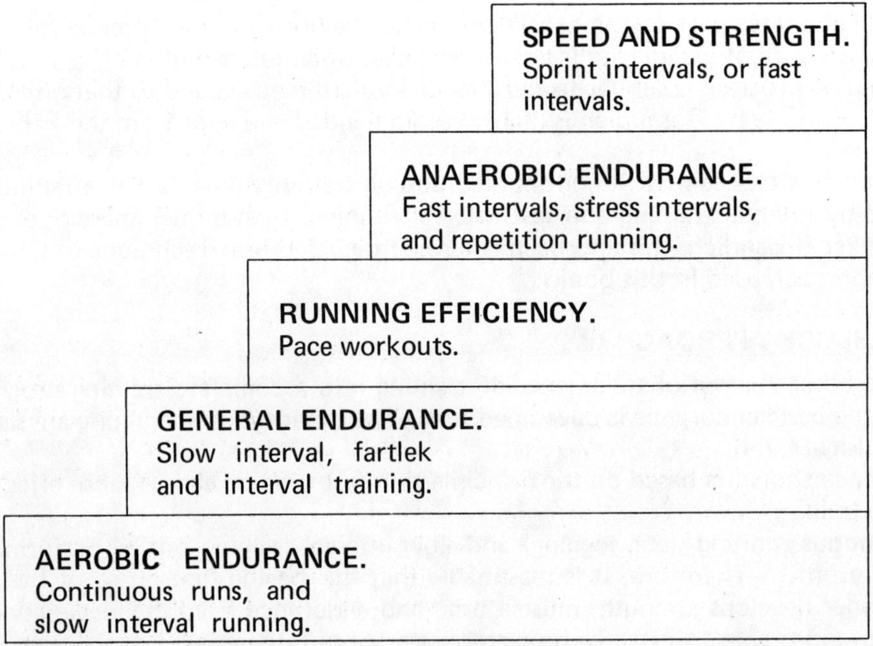

SPEED AND STRENGTH.
Sprint intervals, or fast intervals.

ANAEROBIC ENDURANCE.
Fast intervals, stress intervals, and repetition running.

RUNNING EFFICIENCY.
Pace workouts.

GENERAL ENDURANCE.
Slow interval, fartlek and interval training.

AEROBIC ENDURANCE.
Continuous runs, and slow interval running.

Figure 7.1 The Building Block Approach

general condition. This basic and general endurance program gives the runner, whether he is a sprinter or distance runner, a base of good sound conditioning upon which he can build the specific type of running skill needed for his event.

For novice runners, the endurance program of long continuous running and general conditioning strengthens the tendons, joints and muscles so that fewer injuries occur during the more severe sprint and fast interval training that is needed for top competition. The important factor in using endurance training is that it takes time to realize the effects but the results are long lasting. Ideally, the endurance program should be from 3 to 6 months duration as a minimum. Endurance training can bring about continuing improvement even after 2 and 3 years of only this type of workout. In view of this it may be advisable to engage this type of training with the pre-high school age runners for a year or two to build their basic endurance before subjecting them to the more severe forms of interval training.

THE TRAINING EMPHASIS

It must be made clear that in changing from one type of training to another as the season progresses, the change is not made in an abrupt manner but more as gradual shift in emphasis from one type to another. It is not advisable for a runner to only do slow interval training, for example, then switch abruptly to fast or sprint interval training every day of the week. The training programs for many runners consist of a blend of the various types of training with one particular type receiving more emphasis than the others, depending on the season, the event, the individual's needs, etc.

Just as these factors determine the single workout, the same factors determine the type of training that is emphasized in the various phases of the program. Assuming a six day-a-week workout program, a *beginning* runner might plan his training program along the following 9 month schedule (39 weeks). One can assume that time trials could be incorporated after the first two months. Actual competitive races would probably be done during the last two months.

SAMPLE BEGINNER'S PROGRAM

8 weeks: Continuous runs daily.

2 weeks: Continuous runs, 5 days; slow intervals, 1 day.

4 weeks: Continuous runs, 4 days; slow intervals, 2 days.

4 weeks: Continuous runs, 3 days; slow intervals, 2 days; fast intervals, 1 day.

6 weeks: Slow intervals, 3 days; continuous runs, 2 days; fast intervals, 1 day.

3 weeks: Fast intervals, 2 days; slow intervals, 2 days; pace, 1 day; continuous runs, 1 day.

3 weeks: Fast intervals, 1 day; pace, 1 day; repetition, 1 day; slow, 1 day; continuous, 1 day; interval training, 1 day.

4 weeks: Fast intervals, 1 day; pace, 1 day; stress, 1 day; slow, 1 day; interval training, 1 day; interval training, 1 day; repetition, 1 day.

3 weeks: Fast interval, 2 days; pace, 2 days; stress, 1 day; repetition, 1 day.

2 weeks: Fast interval, 2 days; stress, 1 day; slow, 2 days; pace, 1 day.

—————

39 weeks total

TRAINING FOR THE PEAK

When the peak of the competitive season arrives, the runner can do little to increase his basic endurance in the few weeks that remain. The process of developing basic endurance is slow and gradual and takes months to achieve significant results. The emphasis must now be on running efficiency, knowledge of pace and anaerobic endurance. However, the workouts must be of sufficient intensity to sustain his work capacity, yet conserve his strength for the weekly competition. This does not mean a letdown by any means, but by this time the runner should know very well just what and how much he can do. He must simply avoid overextending himself. His workouts at this point must be designed to do the following:

1. Improve and maintain his anaerobic endurance.
2. Maintain his aerobic endurance by consistent training on a par with his ability.
3. Prevent possible injury by avoiding unusual and unnecessary strain in the workouts.
4. Most of all, sharpen his running efficiency and increase his knowledge of pace.

The workouts, then, emphasize pace and sustained effort without excess strain. The workouts are not as exhausting as in the pre-season since he is normally competing every week. The bulk of the workouts are fast interval, on or just faster than race pace. Sprint or fast interval workouts occur no more than twice a week, stress or repetition runs once a week and an easy continuous run the day after competition.

For most events, the workout the day before competition may consist of the usual warmup activity, a few acceleration runs and a warmdown (typically light jogging for 10 minutes or so). The intensity of the workout is not as great in later season so that the runner can direct his efforts, both physical and mental, toward the important competition each week.

THE OVERALL PROGRAM STRUCTURE

It is neither feasible nor practical to present day-by-day workout schedules for each of the event categories, for each runner trains under a different set of circumstances. For him to follow a pre-set, rigorous schedule that makes no allowance for variations of his physical state of well-being or of his environment would stifle him more than condition him. What is presented, then, is merely a brief outline of the types of workouts he *may* do, what is to be emphasized, and the purpose of the short term and the long term program. These outlines are given in terms of the event categories, the pacing tables, and the five seasons as defined previously.

These program outlines are intended to be used as a guide in setting up a training program particularly if the coach or the runner doing the planning is relatively inexperienced. The more experienced coaches and runners will certainly have their own ideas about training programs for each event but can still utilize the pacing tables and associated charts to good advantage.

The program outlines are presented for each event category since each has its unique training requirements. Within the event category, the program is structured around five seasons: Summer (post-competitive), Fall (cross-country), Winter (pre-competitive), Early Spring (early competitive), and Late Spring (late competitive). Within each season is given a sample outline of a weekly workout schedule in terms of the type of training and what is emphasized.

The detailed workout schedule for each day is left for the coach or the runner to devise. In fact, the information in this book enables the runner to select his own workouts which he may more willingly accept than if his coach dictates his workouts.

The training program outlines that are presented represent a particular philosophy of training which may be accepted, modified, or rejected by the user, but *they provide a starting point* for training programs based on the computerized system. As these tables come into more widespread use, many types of training programs will evolve and many improvements will be made.

The following discussion is presented as a summary of most of the material given in Chapters 5, and 6. The training program outlines are divided into the five event categories which were defined in Chapter 5 (sprints, long sprints, middle distance, distance, and long distance).

For each of these five event categories a short general discussion is presented to describe the overall training emphasis and year around considerations. Reference to the role of the training elements (speed, anaerobic capacity, aerobic capacity, and efficiency) from Chapter 5 are also given. An example weekly schedule is given *only* to demonstrate how the structure may be implemented.

The coach or runner should, in practice, generate the specific daily workouts from the emphasis given in the structure of each season; variation should be provided by the many kinds of workouts described in Chapter 3.

The most important information presented in this chapter is the structure for each season; from it, all the individual workouts can be generated.

A PROGRAM FOR SPRINTERS

The program for sprinters is built around the particular requirements of the sprint events. In addition to the natural talent required for sprinting, the sprinter must train for precise timing and coordination, muscular strength and conditioning. His need for endurance is to enable him to do longer and harder workouts. To prevent injury he must be in top physical condition and must have good strength, not only in his legs but particularly in his back and abdominal muscles. The training program must include, in addition to the running training, development work for the upper body and practice from the starting blocks.

The general pattern for the sprinter's training program includes the summer and fall as a period of general conditioning, endurance work, and development work in the form of weight training and calisthenics. During the winter, or pre-season, the emphasis is on sharpening his timing and coordination and building up anaerobic endurance. The pre-season is the period of the hardest work for the sprinter. In the early season, there is a greater emphasis on refinement of his timing and coordination which continues through the late season. The greatest danger for the sprinter is injury due to muscle pulls. Although the exact cause of pulls is not completely understood, workouts can be designed to prevent unnecessary strains and allow adequate recovery from hard workouts and competition.

Some of the special workout activities for sprinters are:

1. "Form runs" — full stride (about 80% to 90% speed) runs of from 100 yards to 275 yards with concentration on relaxation, coordinated movement, and timing.

2. "Pickups" — acceleration runs of from 55 to 100 yards concentrating on rhythm and coordination, starting at full stride and finishing at near top speed.

3. "Bursts" — sprints of from 25 to 55 yards with a full running start, "pushing the limit" in speed, with absolute concentration on speed and coordination (never do these when fatigued or with tight muscles); for speed and power development.

4. "Starts" — starting from the blocks and accelerating to full stride, concentrating on form, drive, stride length, body lean, etc.

The warmup is routinely done every day prior to the formal workout. An adequate warmup would be: ¾ to 1 mile jog, calisthenics (stretching and loosening exercises) and a few (4 to 6) easy pickups of about 55 to 75 yards.

The following discussion is made with reference to Table 7.1 which outlines the sprinter's training program.

SUMMER

Since summer usually follows the peak of the competitive season, the workout should be informal, i.e., not rigorous, and should emphasize maintaining good physical condition but without the intense speed work. Some fast running three times a week and easy continuous running the remainder is the general pattern. Participation in other sports such as basketball, football, soccer or baseball is typical and should be encouraged. The running games such as soccer and basketball are particularly good.

FALL

In the fall, the workout schedule intensifies somewhat and is a little more rigorous. The emphasis is

	SUMMER Post-Competitive	FALL Early Pre-Season	WINTER Late Pre-Season	EARLY SPRING Early Season	LATE SPRING Late Season
BASIC PROGRAM STRUCTURE	1 day Sprint Intervals 3 days Fast Intervals 2 days Interval Training 1 day Continuous Running	2 days Sprint Intervals 2 days Fast Intervals 1 day Interval Training 1 day Stress Training 1 day Continuous Running	2 days Sprint Intervals 2 days Fast Intervals 2 days Stress Training 1 day Continuous Running	3 days Sprint Intervals 1 day Stress Training 1 day Fast Intervals 1 day Continuous Running 1 day Competition	3 days Sprint Intervals 1 day Stress Training 2 days Fast Intervals 1 day Competition
MON	Sprint Intervals 55's to 275's at 87.5 to 95% speed	Sprint Intervals 55's to 275's at 87.5 to 95% speed	Sprint Intervals 55's to 275's at 87.5 to 95% speed	Sprint Intervals 55's to 275's at 87.5 to 95% speed	Sprint Intervals 55's to 275's at 87.5 to 95% speed
TUE	Fast Intervals 110's to 330's at 77.5 to 85% speed	Fast Intervals 110's to 330's at 77.5 to 85% speed	Stress Training 275's to 440's at 87.5% to 95% speed	Stress Training 275's to 440's at 87.5 to 95% speed	Stress Training 275's to 440's at 87.5 to 95% speed
WED	Interval Training 110's to 330's at 70 to 75% speed	Interval Training 110's to 330's at 70 to 75% speed	Fast Intervals 110's to 330's at 77.5 to 85% speed	Sprint Intervals 55's to 275's at 87.5 to 95% speed	Sprint Intervals 55's to 275's at 87.5 to 95% speed
THU	Fast Intervals 110's to 330's at 77.5 to 85% speed	Sprint Intervals 55's to 275's at 87.5 to 95% speed	Sprint Intervals 55's to 275's at 87.5 to 95% speed	Fast Intervals 110's to 330's at 77.5 to 85% speed	Fast Intervals 110's to 330's at 77.5 to 85% speed
FRI	Interval Training 110's to 330's at 70 to 75% speed	Fast Intervals 110's to 330's at 77.5 to 85% speed	Stress Training 275's to 440's at 87.5 to 95% speed	Sprint Intervals 55's to 110's at 87.5 to 95% speed	Sprint Intervals 55's to 110's at 87.5 to 95% speed
SAT	Fast Intervals 110's to 330's at 77.5 to 85% speed	Stress Training 275's to 440's at 87.5 to 95% speed	Fast Intervals 110's to 330 at 77.5 to 85% speed	Competition	Competition
SUN	Continuous Run 3 to 5 miles Slow	Continuous Run 4 to 6 miles Slow	Continuous Run 3 to 5 miles Easy	Continuous Run 2 to 4 miles Easy	Fast Intervals 110's to 330's at 77.5 to 85% speed

TABLE 7.1   A TRAINING PROGRAM OUTLINE FOR SPRINTERS

on moderate stamina development. Some of the sprinters may be involved with other team sports such as football or soccer. Some weight training and specialized calisthenics for leg, abdominal and back strength is advisable. This should be done three times a week on the days that the fast running is done and following the workout. On the alternate days, easy continuous running or slow intervals for endurance and stretching exercises are suggested.

WINTER

In the pre-season, the emphasis shifts from general conditioning to the development of the special skills for sprinting: the starts, acceleration and speed bursts. He should make a special effort to concentrate mentally on good muscular coordination and explosive power. After the fall program, he should be in good physical condition and have good stamina. In the latter phase of the pre-season, some stress runs are in order—about once a week for sprinters, in the form of 275's, 330's or 385's at 90% speed, with the shorter of these in the first part of the pre-season and the longer stress runs in the latter part of the pre-season.

EARLY SPRING

This season assumes that the runner is competing every week but not at championship meets. The emphasis is on sharpening the skill of the sprinter: timing in the starts, relay baton passing practice (if appropriate), short bursts of "super speed" sprinting and pickups for improving his sprinting skill. Sprint intervals as form runs and stress runs round out the program.

LATE SPRING

In late spring the runner is making final preparations for the big championship meets. The emphasis is on further sharpening his timing and coordination. He should cautiously avoid any unusual activity which could cause muscle strain. The weekly program emphasizes the speed *bursts,* fast *pickups,* and *form runs* at a higher speed level than in the earlier part of the season.

It is evident that the pacing tables are not utilized as extensively with the sprinter's workouts as they are with the longer distances. This is principally because much of the sprinting practice is done at near top speed making it necessary to restrict the distance to a fraction of the racing distance. At these distances (25 to 55 yards), stopwatch times are difficult to obtain accurately and their significance is questionable. The *form runs* and *stress runs* can be based on the pacing table times.

A PROGRAM FOR LONG SPRINTERS

The long sprints include the 440 yard and 400 meter dashes. The training program for the long sprinter is built around the particular needs of this event category. The long sprinter needs the speed of the sprinter and the "staying power" of the middle distance runner. He needs endurance to recover quickly from his event and to effectively perform the necessary workouts. He needs to achieve the greatest running speed with the least expenditure of energy so his skill in the running motion is very important. To develop his staying power, or anaerobic endurance, he needs to do more stress training than the sprinter. As with sprinters, his upper body strength is important, so his workouts should include calisthenics and weight training in the off season. Practice from starting blocks is not particularly important for the long sprints, however, speed training in the form of *bursts, pickups* and *form runs,* as described on page 90, is beneficial.

The pattern for the year's training program includes basic development and endurance work in the summer and fall. Quarter-milers can benefit from cross country running as it builds endurance. In the pre-season, the long sprinter emphasizes speed work and stress training to a greater degree. In the early season, he continues to sharpen his running skill with speed work and increases his anaerobic endurance with stress training. However, because of weekly competition, the training schedule is not quite as intense as during the pre-season. In the late season, the training schedule emphasizes mostly speed work and stress training, but the latter only once a week with the high level competition coming each weekend. The following breakdown into each season is made with reference to Table 7.2 which summarizes the long sprinter's program.

		SUMMER Post Competitive	FALL Early Pre-Season	WINTER Late Pre-Season	EARLY SPRING Early Season	LATE SPRING Late Season
BASIC PROGRAM STRUCTURE		1 day Fast Intervals 2 days Interval Training 1 day Stress Training 3 days Continuous Runs	2 days Fast Intervals 1 day Stress Training 2 days Interval Training 2 days Continuous Runs	1 day Sprint Intervals 2 days Stress Training 1 day Fast Intervals 2 days Pace Intervals 1 day Interval Training	2 days Sprint Intervals 2 days Pace Intervals 1 day Stress Training 1 day Fast Intervals 1 day Competition	2 days Sprint Intervals 2 days Fast Intervals 1 day Stress Training 1 day Pace Intervals 1 day Competition
TYPICAL **WEEKLY** **SCHEDULE**	M O N	Fast Intervals 110's to 275's at 77.5 to 85% speed	Fast Intervals 110's to 275's at 77.5 to 85% speed	Sprint Intervals 110's to 275's at 87.5 to 95% speed	Sprint Intervals 110's to 275's at 87.5 to 95% speed	Sprint Intervals 110's to 275's at 87.5 to 95% speed
	T U E	Continuous Run 4 to 6 miles Easy	Interval Training 110's to 440's at 65 to 75% speed	Pace Intervals 110's to 275's at 82.5 to 87.5% speed	Stress Training 275's to 660's at 87.5 to 95% speed	Stress Training 275's to 660's at 87.5 to 95% speed
	W E D	Interval Training 110's to 440's at 65 to 75% speed	Continuous Runs Fartlek, 4 to 6 miles	Stress Training 275's to 660's at 87.5 to 95% speed	Pace Intervals 110's to 275's at 82.5 to 87.5% speed	Pace Intervals 110's to 275's at 82.5 to 87.5% speed
	T H U	Continuous Runs 4 to 6 miles Easy	Fast Intervals 110's to 275's at 77.5 to 85% speed	Pace Intervals 110's to 275's at 82.5 to 87.5% speed	Sprint Intervals 110's to 275's at 87.5 to 95% speed	Sprint Intervals 110's to 275's at 87.5 to 95% speed
	F R I	Stress Training 275's to 660's at 87.5 to 95% speed	Stress Training 275's to 660's at 87.5 to 95% speed	Interval Training 110's to 440's at 65 to 75% speed	Pace Intervals 110's to 275's at 82.5 to 87.5% speed	Fast Intervals 110's to 275's at 77.5 to 85% speed
	S A T	Interval Training 110's to 440's at 65 to 75% speed	Interval Training 110's to 440's at 65 to 75% speed	Stress Intervals 275's to 660's at 87.5 to 95% speed	Competition	Competition
	S U N	Continuous Run 5 to 7 miles Slow	Continuous Run 5 to 7 miles Easy	Fast Intervals 110's to 275's at 77.5 to 85% speed	Fast Intervals 110's to 275's at 77.5 to 85% speed	Fast Intervals 110's to 275's at 77.5 to 85% speed

TABLE 7.2   A TRAINING PROGRAM OUTLINE FOR LONG SPRINTERS

SUMMER

The summer program is informal and the runner is usually on his own, without coaching supervision. The summer program consists mostly of continuous runs with fast intervals and sprint intervals done to maintain leg strength and quickness. Preparation for cross country running should be made. If a seventh day of training is performed, it should be a continuous run.

FALL

The long sprinters may participate in competitive cross country or at least work out with the cross country team whenever possible. The workouts are more intense and formal than in the summer. The emphasis is on stamina development with continuous runs, interval runs and speed play workouts. There should be enough speed work to maintain leg strength and quickness.

WINTER

As with the sprinters, the pre-season training emphasizes the special requirements of the long sprints speed, anaerobic endurance and running efficiency. Pace work distances are 165, 220 and 275 yard runs. Stress training runs are at 275, 330, 385, 440 or 495 yards. Sprint interval runs are from 100 to 165 yards. Speed training is similar to that of the sprinter with bursts of 25 to 55 yards and pickup runs of 55 to 110 yards.

EARLY SPRING

In the early competitive season it is assumed that the runner is competing every week. The competition run is a "stress workout" so only one other stress workout is done in the week's workout. The emphasis is now on speed, anaerobic endurance and running efficiency.

LATE SPRING

In the late spring the emphasis is on sharpening his coordination and increasing the "staying power" of the runner. The late competition assumes greater importance, the intensity of the training program is reduced a little and the runner eases up the day before competition. Only a light workout the day after the competition should be done.

THE PROGRAM FOR MIDDLE DISTANCE RUNNERS

Middle distance running is unique in that it requires a balance of anaerobic endurance, aerobic endurance, running efficiency and speed with the latter being the least important. As aerobic endurance requires much longer to develop, the year's training program is mostly aerobic endurance training in the summer and fall seasons. With a foundation of endurance, the runner can more effectively do the fast interval training necessary for his event. The building block approach described previously is most applicable to the middle distance runner because of the plurality of his event requirements. The weekly schedules are given as examples and the specific distances given can be varied from week to week or combination workouts can be substituted if desired. Many of these were described in Chapter 3. The training program is discussed below according to each season. Table 7.3 summarizes the program.

SUMMER

For the middle distance runner the summer season can consist almost totally of endurance training in the form of continuous runs and slow interval runs. It is assumed that the runner does not have supervision and thus can most easily perform long continuous runs but may wish to do interval training once or twice a week. His weekly mileage total should be upwards from 50 miles per week or 8 miles a day. His program must be adapted, of course, to his own situation such as job, facilities, schedule, etc. The most important thing is that he *run daily*.

		SUMMER Post Competitive	FALL Early Pre-Season	WINTER Late Pre-Season	EARLY SPRING Early Season	LATE SPRING Late Season
BASIC PROGRAM STRUCTURE		4 days Continuous Runs 2 days Slow Intervals 1 day Interval Training	3 days Continuous Runs 2 days Slow Intervals 1 day Interval Training 1 day Fast Intervals	2 days Continuous Runs 2 days Interval Training 1 day Fast Intervals 1 day Pace Intervals 1 day Repetition Running	1 day Fast Intervals 1 day Stress Training 1 day Pace Intervals 1 day Interval Training 1 day Repetition Running 1 day Continuous Run 1 day Competition	1 day Fast Intervals 1 day Stress Training 1 day Pace Intervals 1 day Interval Training 2 days Continuous Runs 1 day Competition
TYPICAL WEEKLY SCHEDULE	MON	Slow Intervals 550's to 1 mile at 65 to 85% speed	Interval Training 110's to 440's at 60 to 75% speed	Fast Intervals 330's to 660's at 77.5 to 85% speed	Fast Intervals 330's to 660's at 77.5 to 85% speed	Fast Intervals 330's to 660's at 77.5 to 85% speed
	TUE	Continuous Run 7 to 10 miles Fast	Slow Intervals 550's to 1 mile at 65 to 85% speed	Repetition Running 660's to 1 mile at 87.5 to 95% speed	Stress Training 330's to 660's at 87.5 to 95% speed	Stress Training 330's to 660's at 87.5 to 95% speed
	WED	Slow Intervals 550's to 1 mile at 65 to 85% speed	Continuous Run 8 to 12 miles of Fartlek Running	Interval Training 110's to 440's at 60 to 75% speed	Interval Training 110's to 440's at 60 to 75% speed	Interval Training 110's to 440's at 60 to 75% speed
	THU	Continuous Run 8 to 12 miles Medium	Fast Intervals 330's to 660's at 77.5 to 85% speed	Pace Intervals 330's to 880's at 77.5 to 87.5% speed	Repetition Running 660's to 1 mile at 87.5 to 95% speed	Pace Intervals 330's to 880's at 77.5 to 87.5% speed
	FRI	Interval Training 110's to 440's at 60 to 75% speed	Continuous Run 7 to 10 miles of Fartlek Running	Interval Training 110's to 440's at 60 to 75% speed	Pace Intervals 330's to 880's at 77.5 to 87.5% speed	Continuous Run 3 to 5 miles Easy
	SAT	Continuous Run 10 to 15 miles Easy	Slow Intervals 550's to 1 mile at 65 to 85% speed	Continuous Run 10 to 15 miles Easy	Competition	Competition
	SUN	Continuous Run 5 to 7 miles Medium	Continuous Run 6 to 8 miles Medium	Continuous Run 6 to 8 miles Medium	Continuous Run 5 to 7 miles Medium	Continuous Run 5 to 7 miles Medium

TABLE 7.3   A TRAINING PROGRAM OUTLINE FOR MIDDLE DISTANCE RUNNERS

FALL

The fall season brings cross country running for most middle distance runners and more fast interval running and speed play workouts. The weekly mileage should be upwards from 70 miles or 10 to 12 miles per day. Twice a day workouts may be performed with a continuous run in the morning and an interval workout in the afternoon. If this is done the number of repetitions from the table should be reduced by about 1/5. Alternatively, an easy run of 5 miles or so can follow the interval workout to increase the daily mileage.

WINTER

In the pre-competitive season, the emphasis is more on quality workouts and less on quantity. A 7 to 10 miles per day program is adequate with a longer run on weekends. A stress or repetition running workout is done once or twice a week in the latter phase of the pre-season. The runners specializing in the 880 yard and 800 meter events will need more speed work and stress training than the milers and 1500 meter specialists. However, their training is basically the same.

EARLY SPRING

In the early competitive season the usual weekly competition dictates a modified training program compared to the pre-season. The workout the day before competition should be at a reduced intensity unless the competition is of little significance. The number of "good workouts" is effectively reduced to only four or five a week instead of six or seven that can be done in the pre-season. The emphasis in the training shifts to more speed work in the form of fast interval training, pace work and stress training. The endurance work can be done the day after competition in the manner of a long, easy continuous run.

LATE SPRING

The late season competition is usually the most important and the runner wants to "peak out" at

98

the championship meets. At this point in time most of the improvement in his performance is due to greater running efficiency and to a higher motivation. The emphasis in his training is then on the pace work and speed work, the latter to further develop strength and sharpen his coordination. The weekly schedule should taper off the two days before competition, leaving only three days of rigorous workouts.

A PROGRAM FOR DISTANCE RUNNERS

Two fundamental requirements dictate the structure of the training program of the distance runner: they are aerobic work capacity and running efficiency. The bulk of the training program is endurance training in the form of long continuous runs and slow, high repetition interval running. The effect of endurance training is in some proportion to the time spent in training and to expose oneself to extended periods of running requires that the running be at a slow average speed. To run for 2 or 3 hours a day demands that the run be at a slow pace, otherwise physical breakdown will occur. It also requires a long, gradual buildup of many months in order to endure the high volume workouts. Endurance training does not exclude interval training; however, to complete the desired distance or duration of running restricts the type of interval training to very high repetitions or the longer interval distances such as repeated 880's, miles, two miles, etc. The distance running training program follows the same pattern as for the middle distances with the endurance program in summer, fall and winter and more speed (relatively speaking) in the early and late spring. The distance runner should maintain a higher daily mileage than is necessary for middle distance runners. Twelve miles a day or more is typical. Distance running still requires strength and quickness in the running stride so a certain amount of speed work is appropriate and beneficial, particularly just prior to and during the competitive season. Pace work to maximize the running efficiency at the planned race pace fills out the distance runner's program. The description of the training program below is divided into the five seasons and is summarized in Table 7.4.

		SUMMER Post Competitive	FALL Early Pre-Season	WINTER Late Pre-Season	EARLY SPRING Early Season	LATE SPRING Late Season
BASIC **PROGRAM** **STRUCTURE**		4 days Continuous Runs 1 day Fartlek Running 2 days Slow Intervals	2 days Continuous Runs 2 days Fartlek Running 2 days Interval Training 1 day Slow Intervals	2 days Continuous Runs 2 days Interval Training 1 day Fast Intervals 1 day Repetition Running 1 day Pace Intervals	2 days Continuous Run 1 day Interval Training 2 days Fast Intervals 1 day Interval Training 1 day Competition	1 day Continuous Run 1 day Interval Training 2 days Pace Intervals 1 day Fast Intervals 1 day Repetition Runs 1 day Competition
TYPICAL **WEEKLY** **SCHEDULE**	**MON**	Continuous Run 12 to 15 miles Medium	Interval Training 220's to 440's at 60 to 75% speed	Interval Training 220's to 440's at 60 to 75% speed	Interval Training 220's to 440's at 60 to 75% speed	Fast Intervals 330's to 1 mile at 60 to 85% speed
	TUE	Slow Intervals 660's to 2 miles at 60 to 85% speed	Fartlek Running 10 to 12 miles	Pace Intervals 660's to 1 mile at 72.5 to 85% speed	Repetition Running 880's to 2 miles at 87.5 to 95% speed	Repetition Running 880's to 2 miles at 87.5 to 95% speed
	WED	Continuous Run 8 to 10 miles Fast	Slow Intervals 660's to 2 miles at 70 to 85% speed	Continuous Run 10 to 12 miles Medium	Fast Intervals 330's to 1 mile at 65 to 85% speed	Pace Intervals 660's to 1 mile at 72.5 to 85% speed
	THU	Fartlek Running 10 to 12 miles	Fartlek Running 8 to 10 miles	Fast Intervals 330's to 1 mile at 65 to 85% speed	Pace Intervals 660's to 1 mile at 72.5 to 85% speed	Interval Training 220's to 440's at 60 to 75% speed
	FRI	Slow Intervals 660's to 2 miles at 70 to 85% speed	Interval Training 220's to 440's at 60 to 75% speed	Interval Training 220's to 440's at 60 to 75% speed	Continuous Run 10 to 12 miles Easy	Pace Intervals 660's to 1 mile at 72.5 to 85% speed
	SAT	Continuous Run 15 to 18 miles Easy	Continuous Run 6 to 10 miles Fast or cross country race	Repetition Running 880's to 2 miles at 87.5 to 95% speed	Competition	Competition
	SUN	Continuous Run 7 to 10 miles Medium	Continuous Run 14 to 18 miles Slow	Continuous Run 12 to 15 miles Easy	Continuous Run 8 to 10 miles Medium	Continuous Run 8 to 10 miles Easy

TABLE 7.4   A TRAINING PROGRAM OUTLINE FOR DISTANCE RUNNERS

SUMMER

The post-competitive period is the best time to lay the groundwork for the following year. The prescription for the distance runner is run, run, run, as far as you can. Fifteen miles a day, twenty miles a day, or more; as much as the situation (job, school, etc.) will allow. The training need not be intense, in terms of all-out effort, but usually at an 80% to 90% speed for the long distance runs. Interval running sessions with repeated slow 880's, 1320's, miles or two-miles are effective and add variety to the workout schedule.

FALL

If the distance runner is in school, he will normally compete in cross country runs, and his training is essentially the same as prescribed for the middle distance runners who also are cross country runners. The daily mileage quota should be maintained at about 12 to 15 if time permits. Variable speed (fartlek) over cross country courses is the most appropriate form of interval training in the fall season. Occasionally track workouts are good to evaluate training progress. The fall workouts are still basically endurance workouts throughout.

WINTER

In the pre-competitive season, the distance runner shifts his training emphasis from all endurance to some speed work and some pace work, yet endurance type workouts still dominate. Moderate speed work once a week and pace work once a week are adequate with the balance being continuous runs or slow interval workouts. Two-a-day workouts may still be done.

EARLY SPRING

With weekly competition a slight let-up on the pre-competition day is usual. The amount of speed work increases to twice each week and pace work can remain at once a week but over a longer distance interval. The balance of the week can remain slow interval running or continuous runs as the individual chooses, but the weekly mileage should be sustained to about 80% of that in the pre-season.

LATE SPRING

The higher level competition requires a moderate let-up on the day before the meet. The distance runner should not require a complete lay-off but should have a relatively light workout or "rest day." The workouts now emphasize more "on pace" running to sharpen the coordination; enough speed work to maintain strength and quickness and endurance work to maintain his aerobic work capacity. Because of the weekly competition and "rest day," the weekly mileage total is usually only about 70% to 75% of the preseason levels.

A PROGRAM FOR LONG DISTANCE RUNNERS

The long distance runner typically is aiming at a top performance in two, three or four most important races scattered throughout the year. Particularly with marathon racing, it is not possible to race at top effort every week or even every month because the event is so physically demanding that complete recovery may take from 3 to 6 weeks. Thus the "seasonal" program presented for the shorter events is not appropriate for the long distance runner. Rather, a six to nine month program pointing toward a particular race is a more sensible approach.

For long distance races which, as defined in Chapter 5, typically last about 1 hour and longer, the basic requirement is *aerobic endurance.* The long distance runner has little need for speed work as such and can better utilize his time in training doing endurance running.

It is interesting to observe that a distance runner can be in top condition for six to 10 mile races, yet not be able to perform a comparable level 26 mile race. The physiological reason for this is not entirely clear. It can merely be said that his biochemical system is not adequately prepared to sustain him for a 2-½ to 3 hours of *continuous* effort. To properly train for a two to three hour (or more) race, the runner must be exposed to continuous running of at least that duration. The frequent dilemma is that most individuals are limited in the amount of time available for training—by their job, school, family obligations, etc. Therefore a compromise is often necessary and one must often find the type of training program that brings the most results with the least amount of time spent in training.

The choice of relative speed in the long runs depends on the distance being run compared to the average daily mileage (in his current training routine). For example, if the longest run made in practice is 20 miles, then runs of 20 miles or longer should *not* be run at faster than 90% of his performance level speed for the distance being run. If his training run is about equal to his daily average then his practice speed can be from 90% to 95% of his racing speed for the distance. It is noted for example that the present world's best marathoner (Derek Clayton at 2:08:33 for 4:54 per mile) runs 26 miles in a workout in about 2:30:00, or 5:45 per mile, which is only 86% of his top racing speed! The great Ron Clarke does his practice 10 to 15 mile runs at about 90% to 95% of his racing speed for these distances. In fact, in observing a larger number of long distance runners of varying ability, it is found that they typically run in training at about 90% to 95% speed for continuous runs. Specific guidelines were given in Chapter 5 for the choice of speed on continuous runs. For example, if the runner can do 10 miles in 60 minutes in competition, his training runs at ten miles would usually be in 60 ÷ .90 or about 66½ minutes. Training runs at 85% to 90% speed allows adequate recovery for the next day's workout, whereas faster speed will often result in incomplete recovery.

To provide a helpful aid to the long distance runner in determining the proper speed for him to set out on his long runs, an additional set of tables was printed by the computer. These tables are presented as Table 5 in the English Unit Tables. These tables are to be used in conjunction with the Table of Reduced Speeds for continuous runs, which is Table 3 in the English and Metric Unit Tables. Table 5 lists the per mile average time for 100% effort for a number of long distance runs at the various performance levels. To cite an example (see Figure 7.2), a runner who has run 13 miles in 1:16:21 is a 690 point level performer. If he trains for the long distances, he should be able to perform near the 690 point level. Table 1c says that at the 690 point level, a 25 mile run would be run in 2:33:58 which is at 6:09 per mile (from Table 5, Per

Mile Average Tables). With this value, he turns to the Reduced Speed Table (Table 3) and might choose 90.0% speed for the 25 mile run which is 6:51 per mile. With this special table, the long distance runner can avoid setting out at too fast a pace on a long run, particularly a run that is much longer than usual.

For the road runners, it is suggested that a number of mileage check points be noted along the course so that the runner can check his speed with his watch, particularly in the early part of the run. Street maps can be a helpful aid by noting mentally where the 1 mile, 2 mile, 5 mile, etc., points are to check his initial running speed.

Some interval running is of value for the long distance runner, particularly to improve leg speed and leg strength. Repeated runs of 880 yards, such as 20 x 880 at 75% speed, to repeated 2 miles, such as 5 x 2 miles at 85% speed are the type of interval training used. However, the interval training is used only 2 or 3 days a week at the most.

Long distance runners who are fortunate enough to have frequent opportunities to compete usually enter races which range from 6 miles to 26 miles. To do this requires excellent all around fitness for both the shorter distance races as well as the long marathon events. Knowledge of pace in the various races is essential. This knowledge is acquired by practice runs at a variety of distances at the 85 to 95% speed. For this reason it is preferable to run varying distances on succeeding days rather than the same distance every day. For example, a weekly schedule with a total of 100 miles might be structured as follows:

Sunday	—24 mile run at 85% speed
Monday	—12 mile run at 90% speed
Tuesday	—5 x 2 miles at 85% speed (10 miles total)
Wednesday	—18 mile run at 90% speed
Thursday	—12 mile run at 95% speed
Friday	—20 x 880 at 70% speed (12 miles total)
Saturday	—10 mile run at 95% speed

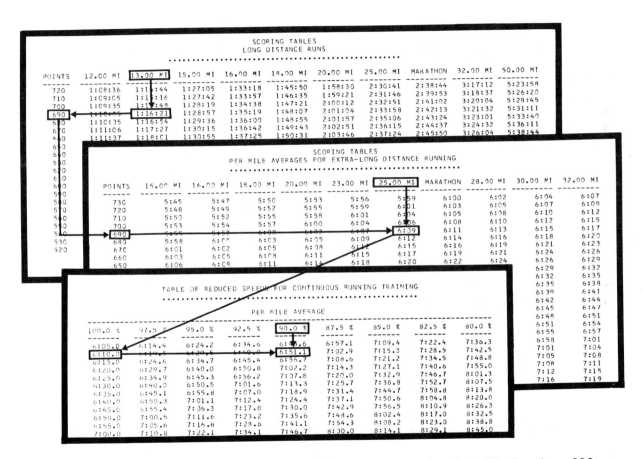

Figure 7.2 Procedure to Determine the Mile Pace for a 90% Speed 25-Mile Run by a 690 Point Level, 1:16:21 13 Miler

104a

This type of schedule has all the elements of a good sound training program for a long distance runner. It has sufficient "speed work" with the 880 and 2 mile intervals, a very long run and a moderately long run each week and a 10 to 12 mile run in the remaining days. This type of schedule requires between 1 and 2 hours of running each day except the long run on the weekend. This program is about minimum for long distance runners to compete effectively at distances up to 26 miles. Those having ample time available for training would want to spend 2 to 3 hours a day running with 2 or even 3 workouts each day.

A frequent situation is that of a middle distance or distance runner or even a jogger wanting to compete in (or complete) a 26 mile marathon race for the first time. In contrast to the usual training program for distance runners, marathon running requires a degree of special preparation. A brief outline of that type of training program that is necessary to prepare the "first timer" for the marathon race is given here.

The length of the program depends upon the amount of training the runner is currently doing. Two measures of his current training are important: (1) his average daily mileage and (2) his longest weekly continuous run. A jogger who is running about 3 miles a day and a "long" run each week of 6 miles will need 9 to 12 months to adequately prepare himself for a marathon run. A distance runner who is averaging 10 miles a day and a weekly long run of 15 miles should plan on about 3 to 6 months of preparation for a 26 mile event.

The two measures given above are a valid criteria of the long distance training program. A novice marathoner should, as a minimum, set a training goal of 12 miles a day average with a weekly long run of 18 to 25 miles. By comparison, experienced marathoners will run 15 to 25 miles a day with a weekly long run of 20 to 30 miles.

Rather than present a detailed weekly schedule, it can be simplified to suggest that a 10% to 15% increase in the training mileage each week is a reasonable program with the weekly pattern being similar to that presented on the previous page. The amount of training done will usually be limited by the amount of time available and the dedication of the individual runner. But, the minimum goal should be 12 miles a day and a 25 mile run each week. With marathon training, the more running, the better. Speed work is not so important as mileage.

The most important thing the novice runner must learn is his exact capability. In long distance running, more than any other type of event, knowledge of *pace* is critical, for to misjudge his pace in the long event results in disastrous and agonizing consequences. More novice marathoners (and some experienced) do poorly because of poor judgment of pace than because of inadequate training. It is for this reason the aspiring marathoner must do a number of practice runs of 23 to 28 miles. In doing so, he can fairly accurately determine what his performance limit is. In his first race he must be conservative in his judgment of his ability and start out a little slower than he believes he is capable.

Experienced marathoners are very individualistic about their training programs but it is generally observed that they peak their training programs, in terms of mileage and exertion, about 2 to 3 weeks before the "big race." During the last 2 weeks or so, there is a gradual tapering off in training intensity. The competitor then enters the race fresh and ready for a top performance.

In summary, some basic guidelines for doing distance training have been given which should enable the inexperienced long distance runner to plan his own program around his own schedule and goals. The time available to train is the usual limiting factor on long distance runners and each one must set his own standards. The key elements of his overall program are: adequate mileage, both daily and weekly, knowledge of pace and knowledge of ability. Inexperienced runners would be advised to discuss their training and race plans with an experienced marathoner rather than someone who has never experienced this type of training and discipline.

Chapter 8
The Basis for the Tables

FEATURES OF THE TABLES

Of the five different types of tables presented in this book, the most useful and the most revolutionary, are the Pacing Tables for interval running. The Scoring Tables are important in this context as they provide a means to relate the performance ability of a runner to the appropriate Pacing Table. The mathematical basis of the scoring tables has been documented for publication in a journal (Ref. Gardner, 1970). The other tables are obtained by simple arithmetic so there is little need to explain them further. The Pacing Tables for interval running, as the most significant part of this work, are deserving of some explanation of their basis. This explanation is given for the benefit of those who are interested in more than just the use of these tables.

The most significant features of the pacing tables are: (1) that they are provided for, and are useful to, runners over a wide range of ability, (2) that runs made at the same relative (percentage) speed over different distances allow the same number of repetitions to be performed, (3) that the rest interval taken after the longer runs is the same as that taken after the shorter runs. Many who have not actually tried the different workouts in the tables have questioned the validity of these latter two features but those who have done the various workouts can attest to the fact that the pacing tables do work. The pacing tables are derived from three basic principles:

1. The principle of the normal performance curve.
2. The principle of normalized running speed.
3. The principle of transient recovery.

Each of these principles is discussed in sequence in the following pages.

THE NORMAL PERFORMANCE CURVE

The first principle is that the relationship between the true running speed for 100% effort and the distance of the run follows a mathematical curve and is similar for all runners throughout each event category. This relationship is portrayed by the normal performance curve (Figure 5.1). This principle enables one to predict a performance at one distance based on a performance at another distance but within the same event category. Of course, it does not predict an exact competitive performance, since there are many tactical, psychological, and environmental factors which affect each performance. To obtain a reference time for training purposes, however, the accuracy of the normal performance curve is sufficient. It should be noted that a performance in an event that is not the runner's specialty will typically be at a lower performance level than his performances in his own event. Yet, the normal performance curve still applies, but at a lower performance level, and provides a valid reference for computing training speeds. In essence, the scoring table gives a normal performance curve for each level of ability; the times given at each point level indicate the speed at the various distances along each curve. The validity of this curve is indicated by one athlete scoring nearly the same number of points at different distances. Some notable examples of this are the performances of Jim Ryun in 1966:

2 miles	8:25.2	1010 points*
880 yards	1:44.9	1010 points*
1 mile	3:53.7	1010 points*
1 mile	3:51.2	1030 points*

and the performances of Ron Clarke:

2 miles	8:19.6	1030 points*
3 miles	12:50.4	1030 points*
6 miles	26:46.	1040 points*

Similar comparisons can be made with the performance of other athletes at their levels of ability. It should be noted that the athlete must be trained for the event in which he is competing for him to score at a near equal level to his other events. There are individuals who are exceptions to the normal performance curve such as Lee Evans' 400 meter record (43.8) which vastly exceeds his best performance at 220 yards (20.7). In using the normal performance curve to compute training speeds, its validity is established in spite of these exceptions. The application of the normal performance curve in deriving the pacing tables is that it predicts the maximum speed of a runner at distances other than his event distance. These speeds are those used on a basis for computing training speeds at the various levels of ability.

NORMALIZED RUNNING SPEED

To normalize means to divide by the maximum value, yielding a value that is less than (or equal to) one. This value can be expressed as a percentage of the maximum. In a training run, the speed of the run

(*Rounded to the nearest 10 points, i.e. times read from Table 1, English Unit Tables).

is not as fast as would be done in competition or in a time trial. This is true for either interval running or continuous running. The principle of normalized running speed is that if the normalized running speed is the same, its effect in terms of exertion level (relative), recovery, degree of exhaustion, etc. is the same, even though the actual speed of different runners, because of their individual ability, is different. As an example, suppose one runner can run 440 yards in 48 seconds with 100% effort. Another runner can run 440 yards in 56 seconds with 100% effort. If each runs the 440 at 80% of their maximum speed then the first runner would run it in 60 seconds and the second runner would have a time of 70 seconds. Since speed is inversely related to distance, the 100% time is divided by the decimal percentage: $48 \div 0.80 = 60$ seconds. Now, if the first runner can also run 880 yards in 1:56, he may for a workout run 880's at 80% of this speed which is 116 seconds $\div$ .80 = 145 seconds or 2:25.

The extension of this principle is that the number of repetitions that can be performed is dependent on the normalized speed and not on the absolute speed. This enables us to give a fixed relationship between the percentage speed and the repetitions. The range of distances for which this applies is limited to those normally used in interval running, namely 220 yards to 1 mile or so. However, distance and long distance runners can use up to 2 miles or more in interval running and the principle still applies. The shorter distances, less than 220 yards, also can be used in the same manner by sprinters, since their total workout load is usually lower than those in the longer events. Now only the rest interval needs to be determined and this is discussed below.

TRANSIENT RECOVERY

The third principle is that the transient recovery (i.e. short term recovery) of the heart rate depends primarily on the total effort of the run and not on the distance of the run within the limits stated above. The heart rate has been the usual criteria for determining the length of the rest interval. Informal monitoring of heart rate indicates that the heart rate recovery is related to the effort or relative speed of the run. These relationships are indicated in Figure 8.1, although these are not scientifically established and indicate trends only.

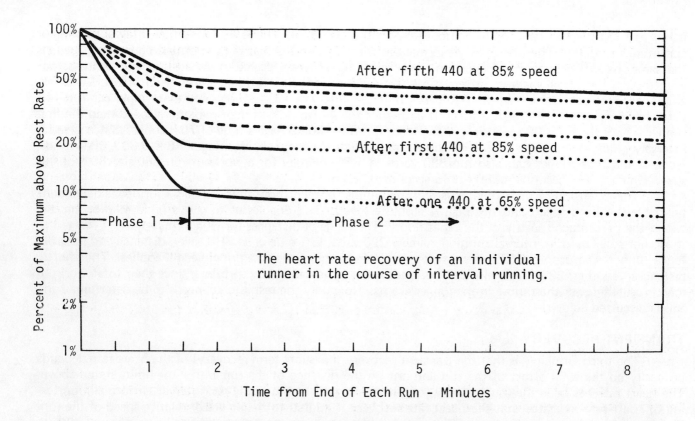

Figure 8.1   Normalized Heart Rate Versus Time Of Rest Interval

111

The profiles of the heart rate recovery given in the figure were obtained from an individual running repeated 440 yards with 3 minutes rest. The dashed lines indicate anticipated recovery based on observations of other runners. Other observations have shown that these same recovery profiles occur at both longer and shorter distances. The dotted lines indicate the normal recovery rate that would occur if no additional runs were made. Phase 2 recovery rate is such that it takes about 4 to 5 hours for the pulse to return to the pre-exercise rest level.

The rest interval has usually been based on the heart rate falling to 120 beats per minute, or about halfway between the pre-exercise rest pulse and the maximum, which is about 200 beats per minute for young, trained athletes. As indicated in Figure 8.1, the recovery of the heart rate to normal rest value has two distinct phases: phase 1, which has a characteristic time constant of about 90 seconds, and phase 2 which has a characteristic time constant of about 60 minutes.* The phase 1 period may be interpreted as the time required to ventilate the CO_2 from the bloodstream. If so, then the "proper" rest interval should be the length of the phase 1 recovery. This is interpreted as the time when the pulse rate is no longer decreasing rapidly. This ranges from about 90 seconds after low effort runs to about 5 minutes after a maximum effort run. If the criterion for the rest interval is the 120 beats per minute value, then the interval

---

*A "time constant" is the term used to describe a mathematical function of the form $f(t) = ke^{-t/T}$, where T is the time constant of the function and is the time for the function to fall to 37% of its initial value. The heart rate recovery after a maximum effort can be described by a mathematical function which has the form

$$\frac{\Delta HR}{\Delta HR_{max}} = Ae^{-t/T_1} + Be^{-t/T_2}$$

where T_1 is about 90 seconds, T_2 is about 60 minutes, ΔHR is the heart rate above rest value, ΔHR_{max} is the maximum above rest value, and t is the elapsed time from the end of the exercise.

should be somewhat shorter for the initial low effort runs because the pulse falls below 120 within 20 to 40 seconds after a low speed (like 60-65%) run. An important observation, however, is that the heart rate at the end of phase 1 recovery increases with each repetition and eventually follows the same pattern as it does after a single run with 100% effort. At this point (if not before), the workout should be ended with a warmdown activity. There is not, as yet, sufficient data to exactly define the number of repetitions required at the various speeds in terms of the heart rate recovery patterns, but it is hoped that future studies will provide us with this information. The rest intervals given in the pacing tables are based on the information presented above.

The number of repetitions given in the tables are based on the experience of typical runners but are usually maximum values. In practice, the criterion for ending the interval running workout is when the runner can no longer hold to the desired pace even with maximum effort. This happens because of the cumulative fatigue that occurs in interval running. With each successive run, there is an increase in the muscular fatigue which is not recovered in the rest interval. This builds up in the course of the workout until the runner "ties up" and cannot run at the desired speed. To go this far in a workout is probably beyond what is necessary for optimum training effect but again there is not sufficient scientific knowledge on the effects of interval training to exactly define the optimum number of repetitions. The number of repetitions given in the tables are about the *maximum* that can be done by typical runners of corresponding ability. Of course, if a longer rest interval is taken then the runner can do more repetitions than are listed. Some coaches may want their runners to do more than the listed number of repetitions. If so, they can increase the rest interval and achieve more repetitions. We have not, as yet, determined the *exact* relationship between increased and decreased rest and the number of repetitions. This will be established in the future.

SUMMARY AND EVALUATION

In this book we have presented a totally new approach to the organization and presentation of training schedules. To achieve this, the computer was used to perform the extensive calculations and printing that was required to obtain the various tables. The bulk of the text portion of the book was included to provide some guidance for the use of these tables. How they are actually used by the coach or individual athlete must be left to his own judgment. In terms of the type of training done by the runner, the tables do not suggest any new secret training method nor a radical departure from established methods. Rather, as stated early in the book, they are intended as a guideline for workout activity.

As a guideline, the workouts given and the workouts performed by individual runners continue to agree far better than the authors had anticipated. The workouts in the tables do represent hard workouts, yet they are reasonable. It is not suggested that the runners do hard interval training on a daily basis and most runners of today do not do hard interval running daily. Therefore, the runner and coach who uses these schedules should not expect that they be used every day for every workout.

Additional work is being done every day on this approach to training schedules and particularly to relate the variation of reps with the rest interval. When such work is complete it will be published for the use of everyone. The authors believe that this material is only the first step in completely defining the response of an athlete on the training track.

Bibliography

Amado, Fernando. *Systeme Rationnel pour Classer les Performances Athletiques*, 2 vols. Lisbon, Portugal: Federacao Portuguesa de Athletismo p. da Alegria, 1962.

Astrand, Per-Olof. "Physical Performance as a Function of Age," *Journal of the American Medical Association*, Vol. 205, No. 11, (September, 1968).

Bowerman, William J. and W. E. Harris. *Jogging*. New York: Grosset and Dunlap, 1967.

Congress of the International Amateur Athletic Federation. *Scoring Table for Men's Track and Field Events*. London: Council of the I.A.A.F., 1962.

Cooper, Kenneth H. *Aerobics*. New York: M. Evans and Company, Inc., 1968. (Edition also available from Bantam Books, Inc.).

Costill, David L. *What Research Tells the Coach About Distance Running.* Washington, D.C.: American Association for Health, Physical Education and Recreation, 1968.

Craig, Albert B. "Limitations of the Human Organism: Analysis of World Records and Olympic Performance," *Journal of the American Medical Association*, Vol. 205, No. 11, (September, 1968).

Dill, David B. "Physiological Adjustments to Altitude Changes," *Journal of the American Medical Association*, Vol. 205, No. 11, (September, 1968).

Doherty, J. Kenneth. *Modern Training for Running.* Englewood Cliffs: Prentice-Hall, 1968.

Faulkner, John A. "New Perspectives in Training for Maximum Performance," *Journal of the American Medical Association*, Vol. 205, No. 11, (September, 1968).

Fox, Edward L., Sid Robinson, and David L. Wiegman. "Metabolic Energy Sources During Continuous and Interval Running," *Journal of Applied Physiology*, Vol. 27, No. 2, (August, 1969).

Gardner, James B. and J. Gerry Purdy. "Computerized Track Scoring Tables," submitted to *Medicine and Science In Sports*, December, 1969 (to be published Fall, 1970).

Hyman, Martin and Bruce Tulloh. *Long Distance Running.* London: Amateur Athletic Association, 1966.

Jarver, L. (Jess). *The How and Why of Physical Conditioning for Sport.* Adelaide, Australia: Rigby Limited, 1964.

Jordan, Payton and Bud Spencer. *Champions in the Making.* Englewood Cliffs: Prentice-Hall, Inc., 1968.

116

Karlsson, Jan, Per-Olof Astrand, and Bjorn Ekblom. "Training of the Oxygen Transport System in Man," *Journal of Applied Physiology*, Vol. 22, No. 6, (December, 1965).

Lydiard, Arthur. *Running Training Schedules.* Los Altos, California: Track and Field News, 1965.

McArdle, William D., Guido F. Foglia, and Anthony V. Patti. "Telemetered Cardiac Response to Selected Running Events," *Journal of Applied Physiology*, Vol. 23, No. 4, (October, 1967).

McIlroy, Malcolm B. "Respiratory Response to Exercise in Sick and Healthy People," *Physical Therapy*, Vol. 48, No. 5, (May, 1968).

Novak, Ladislav P., Robert E. Hyatt, and John F. Alexander. "Body Composition and Physiologic Function of Athletes," *Journal of the American Medical Association*, Vol. 205, No. 11, (September, 1968).

Ogilvie, Bruce C. "Psychological Consistencies Within the Personality of High-Level Competitors," *Journal of the American Medical Association*, Vol. 205, No. 11, (September, 1968).

Pickering, R.J. *Strength Training for Athletics.* Eastborne, England: Amateur Athletic Association, 1968.

Purdy, J. Gerry and James B. Gardner. "Computerized Individual Workouts," *Scholastic Coach*, Vol. 39, No. 8, (April, 1970).

Rosandich, Thomas P. "The American Technique of Distance Training," *The Athletic Journal*, (February, 1969).

Rose, Kenneth D. and F. Lowell Dunn. "Telemeter Electrocardiography: A Study of Heart Function in Athletics," *Nebraska State Medical Journal*, (September, 1964).

Saltin, Bengt and Per-Olof Astrand. "Maximal Oxygen Uptake in Athletes," *Journal of Applied Physiology*, Vol. 23, No. 3, (September, 1967).

Schneider, E. G., S. Robinson, and J. L. Newton. "Oxygen Debt in Aerobic Work," *Journal of Applied Physiology*, Vol. 25, No. 1, (July, 1968).

Shepard, Roy J. "The Heart and Circulation Under Stress of Olympic Conditions," *Journal of the American Medical Association*, Vol. 205, No. 11, (September, 1968).

Slocum, Donald B. and Stanley L. James. "Biomechanics of Running," *Journal of the American Medical Association*, Vol. 205, No. 11, (September, 1968).

Smodkla, Vojin N. "Sports Medicine in the World Today," *Journal of the American Medical Association*, Vol. 205, No. 11, (September, 1968).

Stampfl, Franz. *Franz Stampfl on Running.* New York: MacMillan Company, 1955.

Wilt, Fred. *How They Train.* Los Altos, California: Track and Field News, 1959.

Wilt, Fred. *Run Run Run.* Los Altos, California: Track and Field News, 1964.

English Unit Tables

This part of the book contains all of the tables generated in English units, i.e., yards and miles. The first table is actually three. Table 1a gives the performance rating (point score) for the classical English racing distances. Table 1b gives the performance rating for non-classical English racing distances. Table 1c gives the performance rating for long English racing distances. The second table, Table 2, lists the intermediate times for constant speed runs. Table 3 contains the reduced speed tables. Table 4 contains the pacing tables given in 20 point steps, and Table 5 contains the per mile average tables.

Table 1: Performance Rating Tables

On the following 12 pages are three sets of performance rating (or scoring) tables. Both sets are employed to determine a point level (between 0 and 1150) for a given performance in the stated event. The first set of performance rating tables (Table 1a) contains the classical racing distances, the second table (Table 1b) contains the non-classical racing distances, and the third set (Table 1c) contains the per mile average tables.

The classical racing distance scoring table is used to look up a point level for the events which are most commonly run. The non-classical racing distance scoring table is employed to find the point level for events which are usually run as time trials. For example, the 660 is often run as a time trial for half milers.

In fact, the non-classical scoring table can be used to measure the performance of an odd run distance compared with the classical distance. As a result, a time trial performance point level found in the non-classical scoring table may be referenced in the classical scoring table to find the time that should be expected at the full racing distance.

As an example, suppose a 440 yard dashman runs a 39.5 second 330. From Table 1b, one can see that this is worth 620 points. Now, from Table 1a, 620 points is awarded for a 56.4 second 440. Thus, the coach and runner have a measure of how well the athlete performed in the time trial and they can expect him to perform fairly close to the time quoted for the 440 or race day.

The rating tables are given in 10 point steps. The point level is determined by the time value *nearest* the performance time.

SCORING TABLES
CLASSICAL ENGLISH RACING DISTANCES   TABLE 1A

••

POINTS	100 YD	220 YD	440 YD	880 YD	1.00 MI	2.00 MI	3.00 MI	6.00 MI	10.00 MI	MARATHON
1150	8.70	19.2	42.7	1:37.9	3:37.1	7:47.4	12:02.2	25:10.7	43:25	2:01:29
1140	8.74	19.3	42.9	1:38.3	3:38.2	7:49.8	12:06.0	25:18.8	43:39	2:02:09
1130	8.77	19.4	43.1	1:38.8	3:39.4	7:52.3	12:09.8	25:26.9	43:53	2:02:49
1120	8.81	19.5	43.3	1:39.3	3:40.5	7:54.8	12:13.7	25:35.2	44:08	2:03:30
1110	8.84	19.6	43.5	1:39.8	3:41.6	7:57.3	12:17.7	25:43.5	44:22	2:04:12
1100	8.88	-------	43.7	1:40.3	3:42.8	7:59.9	12:21.7	25:52.0	44:37	2:04:53
1090	8.92	19.7	43.9	1:40.8	3:44.0	8:02.4	12:25.7	26:00.5	44:52	2:05:36
1080	8.95	19.8	44.1	1:41.3	3:45.1	8:05.1	12:29.8	26:09.2	45:07	2:06:18
1070	8.99	19.9	44.3	1:41.8	3:46.3	8:07.7	12:33.9	26:17.9	45:22	2:07:02
1060	9.03	20.0	44.6	1:42.4	3:47.5	8:10.4	12:38.0	26:26.7	45:37	2:07:45
1050	9.07	20.1	44.8	1:42.9	3:48.8	8:13.1	12:42.2	26:35.6	45:53	2:08:30
1040	9.11	20.2	45.0	1:43.4	3:50.0	8:15.8	12:46.5	26:44.7	46:09	2:09:14
1030	9.14	20.3	45.2	1:44.0	3:51.2	8:18.5	12:50.8	26:53.8	46:25	2:10:00
1020	9.18	-------	45.4	1:44.5	3:52.5	8:21.3	12:55.2	27:03.0	46:41	2:10:46
1010	9.22	20.4	45.6	1:45.0	3:53.8	8:24.1	12:59.6	27:12.4	46:57	2:11:32
1000	9.26	20.5	45.9	1:45.6	3:55.1	8:27.0	13:04.0	27:21.8	47:13	2:12:19
990	9.30	20.6	46.1	1:46.2	3:56.4	8:29.9	13:08.5	27:31.4	47:30	2:13:06
980	9.34	20.7	46.3	1:46.7	3:57.7	8:32.8	13:13.1	27:41.0	47:47	2:13:54
970	9.38	20.8	46.6	1:47.3	3:59.0	8:35.7	13:17.7	27:50.8	48:04	2:14:43
960	9.42	20.9	46.8	1:47.9	4:00.4	8:38.7	13:22.3	28:00.7	48:21	2:15:32
950	9.47	21.0	47.0	1:48.5	4:01.7	8:41.7	13:27.0	28:10.7	48:39	2:16:22
940	9.51	21.1	47.3	1:49.1	4:03.1	8:44.8	13:31.8	28:20.9	48:56	2:17:13
930	9.55	21.2	47.5	1:49.7	4:04.5	8:47.9	13:36.6	28:31.1	49:14	2:18:04
920	9.59	21.3	47.7	1:50.3	4:05.9	8:51.0	13:41.5	28:41.5	49:32	2:18:55
910	9.63	21.4	48.0	1:50.9	4:07.3	8:54.2	13:46.5	28:52.0	49:51	2:19:48
900	9.68	21.5	48.2	1:51.5	4:08.8	8:57.4	13:51.5	29:02.7	50:09	2:20:41
890	9.72	21.6	48.5	1:52.1	4:10.2	9:00.6	13:56.5	29:13.4	50:28	2:21:34
880	9.77	21.7	48.7	1:52.7	4:11.7	9:03.9	14:01.7	29:24.3	50:47	2:22:29
870	9.81	21.8	49.0	1:53.4	4:13.2	9:07.2	14:06.8	29:35.4	51:06	2:23:24
860	9.85	21.9	49.3	1:54.0	4:14.7	9:10.6	14:12.1	29:46.5	51:26	2:24:20
850	9.90	22.0	49.5	1:54.7	4:16.2	9:14.0	14:17.4	29:57.9	51:46	2:25:16
840	9.95	22.1	49.8	1:55.3	4:17.8	9:17.4	14:22.8	30:09.3	52:06	2:26:13

122

SCORING TABLES
CLASSICAL ENGLISH RACING DISTANCES

TABLE 1A (CONT.)

POINTS	100 YD	220 YD	440 YD	880 YD	1.00 MI	2.00 MI	3.00 MI	6.00 MI	10.00 MI	MARATHON
830	9.99	22.2	50.0	1:56.0	4:19.3	9:20.9	14:28.3	30:20.9	52:26	2:27:11
820	10.04	22.3	50.3	1:56.7	4:20.9	9:24.4	14:33.8	30:32.7	52:46	2:28:10
810	10.08	22.4	50.6	1:57.4	4:22.5	9:28.0	14:39.4	30:44.6	53:07	2:29:10
800	10.13	22.6	50.9	1:58.1	4:24.1	9:31.6	14:45.0	30:56.7	53:28	2:30:10
790	10.18	22.7	51.1	1:58.8	4:25.8	9:35.3	14:50.8	31:08.9	53:50	2:31:11
780	10.23	22.8	51.4	1:59.5	4:27.4	9:39.0	14:56.5	31:21.3	54:11	2:32:14
770	10.28	22.9	51.7	2:00.2	4:29.1	9:42.8	15:02.5	31:33.9	54:33	2:33:16
760	10.33	23.0	52.0	2:00.9	4:30.8	9:46.6	15:08.5	31:46.6	54:55	2:34:20
750	10.38	23.1	52.3	2:01.7	4:32.6	9:50.4	15:14.5	31:59.5	55:18	2:35:25
740	10.43	23.2	52.6	2:02.4	4:34.3	9:54.3	15:20.6	32:12.6	55:41	2:36:30
730	10.48	23.4	52.9	2:03.2	4:36.1	9:58.3	15:26.9	32:25.8	56:04	2:37:37
720	10.53	23.5	53.2	2:03.9	4:37.9	10:02.3	15:33.1	32:39.3	56:28	2:38:44
710	10.58	23.6	53.5	2:04.7	4:39.7	10:06.4	15:39.5	32:52.9	56:51	2:39:53
700	10.63	23.7	53.8	2:05.5	4:41.6	10:10.5	15:46.0	33:06.7	57:16	2:41:02
690	10.68	23.8	54.1	2:06.3	4:43.4	10:14.7	15:52.6	33:20.7	57:40	2:42:13
680	10.74	24.0	54.4	2:07.1	4:45.3	10:19.0	15:59.2	33:34.9	58:05	2:43:24
670	10.79	24.1	54.7	2:07.9	4:47.2	10:23.3	16:06.0	33:49.3	58:30	2:44:37
660	10.85	24.2	55.1	2:08.7	4:49.2	10:27.6	16:12.8	34:04.0	58:56	2:45:50
650	10.90	24.4	55.4	2:09.5	4:51.2	10:32.0	16:19.7	34:18.8	59:22	2:47:05
640	10.96	24.5	55.7	2:10.4	4:53.2	10:36.5	16:26.8	34:33.8	59:48	2:48:21
630	11.01	24.6	56.0	2:11.2	4:55.2	10:41.1	16:33.9	34:49.1	1:00:15	2:49:38
620	11.07	24.7	56.4	2:12.1	4:57.2	10:45.7	16:41.2	35:04.6	1:00:42	2:50:56
610	11.12	24.9	56.7	2:13.0	4:59.3	10:50.4	16:48.5	35:20.3	1:01:10	2:52:15
600	11.18	25.0	57.1	2:13.9	5:01.4	10:55.1	16:56.0	35:36.3	1:01:38	2:53:36
590	11.24	25.2	57.4	2:14.8	5:03.6	10:59.9	17:03.6	35:52.5	1:02:06	2:54:58
580	11.30	25.3	57.8	2:15.7	5:05.8	11:04.8	17:11.2	36:09.0	1:02:35	2:56:21
570	11.36	25.4	58.1	2:16.6	5:08.0	11:09.8	17:19.0	36:25.7	1:03:04	2:57:46
560	11.42	25.6	58.5	2:17.5	5:10.2	11:14.8	17:27.0	36:42.7	1:03:34	2:59:11
550	11.48	25.7	58.9	2:18.5	5:12.5	11:20.0	17:35.0	36:59.9	1:04:04	3:00:39
540	11.54	25.9	59.2	2:19.5	5:14.8	11:25.2	17:43.2	37:17.4	1:04:35	3:02:07
530	11.60	26.0	59.6	2:20.4	5:17.1	11:30.4	17:51.5	37:35.2	1:05:06	3:03:38
520	11.67	26.2	1:00.0	2:21.4	5:19.5	11:35.8	17:59.9	37:53.2	1:05:38	3:05:09

123

POINTS	100 YD	220 YD	440 YD	880 YD	1.00 MI	2.00 MI	3.00 MI	6.00 MI	10.00 MI	MARATHON
510	11.73	26.3	1:00.4	2:22.4	5:21.9	11:41.2	18:08.4	38:11.6	1:06:10	3:06:42
500	11.79	26.5	1:00.8	2:23.5	5:24.3	11:46.8	18:17.1	38:30.3	1:06:43	3:08:17
490	11.86	26.6	1:01.2	2:24.5	5:26.8	11:52.4	18:26.0	38:49.2	1:07:16	3:09:54
480	11.92	26.8	1:01.6	2:25.5	5:29.3	11:58.1	18:35.0	39:08.5	1:07:50	3:11:32
470	11.99	26.9	1:02.0	2:26.6	5:31.9	12:03.9	18:44.1	39:28.1	1:08:24	3:13:11
460	12.06	27.1	1:02.4	2:27.7	5:34.5	12:09.8	18:53.4	39:48.1	1:08:59	3:14:53
450	12.13	27.3	1:02.8	2:28.8	5:37.1	12:15.7	19:02.8	40:08.3	1:09:35	3:16:36
440	12.19	27.4	1:03.3	2:29.9	5:39.8	12:21.8	19:12.4	40:28.9	1:10:11	3:18:21
430	12.26	27.6	1:03.7	2:31.0	5:42.5	12:28.0	19:22.1	40:49.9	1:10:48	3:20:08
420	12.33	27.7	1:04.1	2:32.2	5:45.3	12:34.3	19:32.0	41:11.3	1:11:26	3:21:57
410	12.40	27.9	1:04.6	2:33.4	5:48.1	12:40.7	19:42.1	41:33.0	1:12:04	3:23:48
400	12.48	28.1	1:05.0	2:34.5	5:51.0	12:47.2	19:52.4	41:55.1	1:12:43	3:25:41
390	12.55	28.3	1:05.5	2:35.7	5:53.9	12:53.8	20:02.8	42:17.6	1:13:22	3:27:36
380	12.62	28.4	1:05.9	2:37.0	5:56.9	13:00.6	20:13.5	42:40.5	1:14:03	3:29:34
370	12.70	28.6	1:06.4	2:38.2	5:59.9	13:07.4	20:24.3	43:03.8	1:14:44	3:31:33
360	12.77	28.8	1:06.9	2:39.5	6:02.9	13:14.4	20:35.3	43:27.5	1:15:26	3:33:35
350	12.85	29.0	1:07.4	2:40.8	6:06.0	13:21.5	20:46.5	43:51.7	1:16:08	3:35:39
340	12.92	29.2	1:07.8	2:42.1	6:09.2	13:28.7	20:57.9	44:16.4	1:16:52	3:37:46
330	13.00	29.3	1:08.3	2:43.4	6:12.4	13:36.1	21:09.5	44:41.5	1:17:36	3:39:55
320	13.08	29.5	1:08.8	2:44.7	6:15.7	13:43.6	21:21.4	45:07.1	1:18:21	3:42:07
310	13.16	29.7	1:09.4	2:46.1	6:19.0	13:51.2	21:33.5	45:33.1	1:19:07	3:44:21
300	13.24	29.9	1:09.9	2:47.5	6:22.4	13:59.0	21:45.8	45:59.7	1:19:54	3:46:38
290	13.32	30.1	1:10.4	2:48.9	6:25.9	14:06.9	21:58.3	46:26.8	1:20:42	3:48:58
280	13.41	30.3	1:10.9	2:50.3	6:29.4	14:15.0	22:11.1	46:54.5	1:21:31	3:51:21
270	13.49	30.5	1:11.5	2:51.8	6:33.0	14:23.2	22:24.1	47:22.7	1:22:21	3:53:47
260	13.57	30.7	1:12.0	2:53.3	6:36.6	14:31.6	22:37.4	47:51.4	1:23:12	3:56:15
250	13.66	30.9	1:12.6	2:54.8	6:40.4	14:40.1	22:50.9	48:20.8	1:24:03	3:58:48
240	13.75	31.1	1:13.2	2:56.3	6:44.2	14:48.9	23:04.7	48:50.8	1:24:56	4:01:23
230	13.84	31.4	1:13.7	2:57.9	6:48.0	14:57.8	23:18.8	49:21.4	1:25:51	4:04:02
220	13.93	31.6	1:14.3	2:59.5	6:52.0	15:06.8	23:33.2	49:52.6	1:26:46	4:06:44
210	14.02	31.8	1:14.9	3:01.1	6:56.0	15:16.1	23:47.9	50:24.5	1:27:42	4:09:30
200	14.11	32.0	1:15.5	3:02.8	7:00.1	15:25.6	24:02.9	50:57.1	1:28:40	4:12:20

POINTS	100 YD	220 YD	440 YD	880 YD	1.00 MI	2.00 MI	3.00 MI	6.00 MI	10.00 MI	MARATHON
190	14.20	32.2	1:16.1	3:04.5	7:04.2	15:35.2	24:18.3	51:30.4	1:29:39	4:15:13
180	14.29	32.5	1:16.8	3:06.2	7:08.5	15:45.1	24:33.9	52:04.4	1:30:39	4:18:11
170	14.39	32.7	1:17.4	3:07.9	7:12.8	15:55.1	24:49.9	52:39.2	1:31:41	4:21:13
160	14.49	32.9	1:18.0	3:09.7	7:17.3	16:05.4	25:06.2	53:14.8	1:32:44	4:24:19
150	14.58	33.2	1:18.7	3:11.5	7:21.8	16:15.9	25:22.9	53:51.2	1:33:49	4:27:30
140	14.68	33.4	1:19.4	3:13.4	7:26.4	16:26.7	25:40.0	54:28.4	1:34:55	4:30:45
130	14.78	33.7	1:20.1	3:15.3	7:31.1	16:37.6	25:57.5	55:06.5	1:36:03	4:34:05
120	14.89	33.9	1:20.7	3:17.2	7:35.9	16:48.9	26:15.3	55:45.5	1:37:12	4:37:30
110	14.99	34.2	1:21.4	3:19.2	7:40.9	17:00.3	26:33.6	56:25.4	1:38:23	4:41:00
100	15.09	34.4	1:22.2	3:21.2	7:45.9	17:12.1	26:52.3	57:06.3	1:39:36	4:44:36
90	15.20	34.7	1:22.9	3:23.2	7:51.0	17:24.1	27:11.5	57:48.2	1:40:50	4:48:17
80	15.31	34.9	1:23.6	3:25.3	7:56.3	17:36.4	27:31.1	58:31.1	1:42:07	4:52:04
70	15.42	35.2	1:24.4	3:27.4	8:01.7	17:49.0	27:51.2	59:15.1	1:43:25	4:55:57
60	15.53	35.5	1:25.2	3:29.6	8:07.2	18:01.9	28:11.8	1:00:00.2	1:44:45	4:59:56
50	15.64	35.8	1:25.9	3:31.8	8:12.8	18:15.1	28:32.9	1:00:46.5	1:46:08	5:04:02
40	15.76	36.0	1:26.7	3:34.1	8:18.5	18:28.6	28:54.5	1:01:34.0	1:47:33	5:08:15
30	15.87	36.3	1:27.6	3:36.4	8:24.4	18:42.5	29:16.7	1:02:22.7	1:49:00	5:12:34
20	15.99	36.6	1:28.4	3:38.8	8:30.4	18:56.7	29:39.4	1:03:12.7	1:50:29	5:17:02
10	16.11	36.9	1:29.2	3:41.2	8:36.6	19:11.3	30:02.8	1:04:04.1	1:52:01	5:21:36
0	16.23	37.2	1:30.1	3:43.6	8:43.0	19:26.3	30:26.8	1:04:56.9	1:53:35	5:26:19

POINTS	60 YD	165 YD	300 YD	330 YD	660 YD	1000 YD	1320 YD	1.50 MI	4.00 MI	5.00 MI
1150	5.58	14.5	27.1	30.3	1:09.9	1:53.8	2:36.5	5:41.2	16:20.9	20:43.7
1140	5.61	-------	27.2	30.4	1:10.3	1:54.3	2:37.3	5:43.0	16:26.1	20:50.3
1130	5.63	14.6	27.3	30.6	1:10.6	1:54.9	2:38.1	5:44.8	16:31.4	20:57.0
1120	5.65	-------	27.4	30.7	1:10.9	1:55.5	2:38.9	5:46.6	16:36.7	21:03.8
1110	5.68	14.7	27.6	30.8	1:11.3	1:56.1	2:39.7	5:48.4	16:42.1	21:10.7
1100	5.70	14.8	27.7	31.0	1:11.6	1:56.7	2:40.6	5:50.3	16:47.5	21:17.6
1090	5.72	-------	27.8	31.1	1:12.0	1:57.2	2:41.4	5:52.1	16:53.0	21:24.6
1080	5.75	14.9	27.9	31.2	1:12.4	1:57.8	2:42.2	5:54.0	16:58.6	21:31.7
1070	5.77	15.0	28.1	31.4	1:12.7	1:58.4	2:43.1	5:55.9	17:04.2	21:38.8
1060	5.79	-------	28.2	31.5	1:13.1	1:59.1	2:43.9	5:57.9	17:09.9	21:46.1
1050	5.82	15.1	28.3	31.7	1:13.4	1:59.7	2:44.8	5:59.8	17:15.7	21:53.4
1040	5.84	15.2	28.4	31.8	1:13.8	2:00.3	2:45.7	6:01.8	17:21.5	22:00.8
1030	5.87	-------	28.6	32.0	1:14.2	2:00.9	2:46.6	6:03.8	17:27.4	22:08.3
1020	5.89	15.3	28.7	32.1	1:14.6	2:01.6	2:47.5	6:05.8	17:33.3	22:15.9
1010	5.92	15.4	28.8	32.3	1:14.9	2:02.2	2:48.4	6:07.8	17:39.3	22:23.5
1000	5.94	-------	29.0	32.4	1:15.3	2:02.9	2:49.3	6:09.9	17:45.4	22:31.3
990	5.97	15.5	29.1	32.6	1:15.7	2:03.5	2:50.2	6:12.0	17:51.5	22:39.1
980	5.99	15.6	29.2	32.7	1:16.1	2:04.2	2:51.1	6:14.1	17:57.8	22:47.0
970	6.02	-------	29.4	32.9	1:16.5	2:04.9	2:52.1	6:16.2	18:04.1	22:55.1
960	6.05	15.7	29.5	33.0	1:16.9	2:05.5	2:53.0	6:18.4	18:10.4	23:03.2
950	6.07	15.8	29.7	33.2	1:17.3	2:06.2	2:54.0	6:20.6	18:16.9	23:11.4
940	6.10	-------	29.8	33.4	1:17.7	2:06.9	2:55.0	6:22.8	18:23.4	23:19.7
930	6.13	15.9	30.0	33.5	1:18.2	2:07.6	2:56.0	6:25.0	18:30.0	23:28.1
920	6.15	16.0	30.1	33.7	1:18.6	2:08.3	2:57.0	6:27.3	18:36.7	23:36.6
910	6.18	16.1	30.2	33.9	1:19.0	2:09.1	2:58.0	6:29.5	18:43.4	23:45.2
900	6.21	-------	30.4	34.0	1:19.4	2:09.8	2:59.0	6:31.8	18:50.3	23:54.0
890	6.23	16.2	30.5	34.2	1:19.9	2:10.5	3:00.0	6:34.2	18:57.2	24:02.8
880	6.26	16.3	30.7	34.4	1:20.3	2:11.3	3:01.1	6:36.6	19:04.2	24:11.7
870	6.29	16.4	30.8	34.5	1:20.7	2:12.0	3:02.1	6:39.0	19:11.3	24:20.8
860	6.32	-------	31.0	34.7	1:21.2	2:12.8	3:03.2	6:41.4	19:18.5	24:29.9
850	6.35	16.5	31.2	34.9	1:21.6	2:13.6	3:04.3	6:43.8	19:25.8	24:39.2
840	6.38	16.6	31.3	35.1	1:22.1	2:14.3	3:05.4	6:46.3	19:33.2	24:48.6

126

● ●

POINTS	60 YD	165 YD	300 YD	330 YD	660 YD	1000 YD	1320 YD	1.50 MI	4.00 MI	5.00 MI
830	6.41	16.7	31.5	35.3	1:22.6	2:15.1	3:06.5	6:48.8	19:40.6	24:58.1
820	6.44	-------	31.6	35.4	1:23.0	2:15.9	3:07.6	6:51.4	19:48.2	25:07.8
810	6.47	16.8	31.8	35.6	1:23.5	2:16.7	3:08.7	6:54.0	19:55.8	25:17.5
800	6.50	16.9	31.9	35.8	1:24.0	2:17.5	3:09.9	6:56.6	20:03.6	25:27.4
790	6.53	17.0	32.1	36.0	1:24.5	2:18.4	3:11.0	6:59.2	20:11.4	25:37.4
780	6.56	17.1	32.3	36.2	1:25.0	2:19.2	3:12.2	7:01.9	20:19.4	25:47.6
770	6.59	17.2	32.4	36.4	1:25.5	2:20.0	3:13.4	7:04.6	20:27.5	25:57.9
760	6.62	-------	32.6	36.6	1:26.0	2:20.9	3:14.6	7:07.3	20:35.6	26:08.3
750	6.65	17.3	32.8	36.8	1:26.5	2:21.8	3:15.8	7:10.1	20:43.9	26:18.9
740	6.68	17.4	33.0	37.0	1:27.0	2:22.6	3:17.1	7:13.0	20:52.3	26:29.6
730	6.72	17.5	33.1	37.2	1:27.5	2:23.5	3:18.3	7:15.8	21:00.8	26:40.5
720	6.75	17.6	33.3	37.4	1:28.0	2:24.4	3:19.6	7:18.7	21:09.5	26:51.5
710	6.78	17.7	33.5	37.6	1:28.6	2:25.3	3:20.9	7:21.6	21:18.2	27:02.6
700	6.81	17.8	33.7	37.8	1:29.1	2:26.3	3:22.2	7:24.6	21:27.1	27:13.9
690	6.85	17.9	33.9	38.0	1:29.7	2:27.2	3:23.5	7:27.6	21:36.1	27:25.4
680	6.88	-------	34.0	38.2	1:30.2	2:28.1	3:24.8	7:30.7	21:45.2	27:37.0
670	6.92	18.0	34.2	38.4	1:30.8	2:29.1	3:26.2	7:33.8	21:54.4	27:48.8
660	6.95	18.1	34.4	38.6	1:31.3	2:30.1	3:27.6	7:36.9	22:03.8	28:00.8
650	6.99	18.2	34.6	38.8	1:31.9	2:31.1	3:29.0	7:40.1	22:13.3	28:13.0
640	7.02	18.3	34.8	39.1	1:32.5	2:32.1	3:30.4	7:43.3	22:22.9	28:25.3
630	7.06	18.4	35.0	39.3	1:33.1	2:33.1	3:31.8	7:46.6	22:32.7	28:37.8
620	7.09	18.5	35.2	39.5	1:33.7	2:34.1	3:33.2	7:49.9	22:42.7	28:50.5
610	7.13	18.6	35.4	39.7	1:34.3	2:35.1	3:34.7	7:53.3	22:52.7	29:03.3
600	7.16	18.7	35.6	40.0	1:34.9	2:36.2	3:36.2	7:56.7	23:03.0	29:16.4
590	7.20	18.8	35.8	40.2	1:35.5	2:37.2	3:37.7	8:00.2	23:13.4	29:29.7
580	7.24	18.9	36.0	40.4	1:36.2	2:38.3	3:39.2	8:03.7	23:23.9	29:43.1
570	7.28	19.0	36.2	40.7	1:36.8	2:39.4	3:40.8	8:07.3	23:34.6	29:56.8
560	7.32	19.1	36.4	40.9	1:37.4	2:40.5	3:42.4	8:10.9	23:45.5	30:10.7
550	7.35	19.2	36.6	41.2	1:38.1	2:41.7	3:43.9	8:14.6	23:56.5	30:24.8
540	7.39	19.3	36.9	41.4	1:38.8	2:42.8	3:45.6	8:18.3	24:07.7	30:39.1
530	7.43	19.4	37.1	41.7	1:39.4	2:44.0	3:47.2	8:22.1	24:19.1	30:53.7
520	7.47	19.5	37.3	41.9	1:40.1	2:45.1	3:48.9	8:25.9	24:30.7	31:08.4

SCORING TABLES
NON-CLASSICAL ENGLISH RACING DISTANCES

TABLE 1B (CONT.)

POINTS	60 YD	165 YD	300 YD	330 YD	660 YD	1000 YD	1320 YD	1.50 MI	4.00 MI	5.00 MI
510	7.51	19.7	37.5	42.2	1:40.8	2:46.3	3:50.6	8:29.8	24:42.4	31:23.4
500	7.55	19.8	37.8	42.4	1:41.5	2:47.5	3:52.3	8:33.8	24:54.3	31:38.7
490	7.59	19.9	38.0	42.7	1:42.2	2:48.8	3:54.0	8:37.8	25:06.5	31:54.2
480	7.64	20.0	38.2	43.0	1:42.9	2:50.0	3:55.8	8:41.9	25:18.8	32:10.0
470	7.68	20.1	38.5	43.2	1:43.7	2:51.3	3:57.6	8:46.1	25:31.3	32:26.0
460	7.72	20.2	38.7	43.5	1:44.4	2:52.6	3:59.4	8:50.3	25:44.1	32:42.3
450	7.76	20.3	38.9	43.8	1:45.2	2:53.9	4:01.3	8:54.6	25:57.0	32:58.9
440	7.81	20.5	39.2	44.1	1:45.9	2:55.2	4:03.1	8:59.0	26:10.2	33:15.7
430	7.85	20.6	39.4	44.3	1:46.7	2:56.5	4:05.1	9:03.4	26:23.6	33:32.9
420	7.90	20.7	39.7	44.6	1:47.5	2:57.9	4:07.0	9:07.9	26:37.2	33:50.3
410	7.94	20.8	39.9	44.9	1:48.3	2:59.3	4:09.0	9:12.5	26:51.1	34:08.1
400	7.99	20.9	40.2	45.2	1:49.1	3:00.7	4:11.0	9:17.1	27:05.2	34:26.1
390	8.03	21.1	40.5	45.5	1:49.9	3:02.1	4:13.0	9:21.9	27:19.6	34:44.5
380	8.08	21.2	40.7	45.8	1:50.7	3:03.5	4:15.1	9:26.7	27:34.2	35:03.2
370	8.13	21.3	41.0	46.1	1:51.6	3:05.0	4:17.2	9:31.6	27:49.1	35:22.2
360	8.17	21.5	41.3	46.4	1:52.4	3:06.5	4:19.3	9:36.6	28:04.2	35:41.6
350	8.22	21.6	41.5	46.8	1:53.3	3:08.0	4:21.5	9:41.7	28:19.6	36:01.4
340	8.27	21.7	41.8	47.1	1:54.2	3:09.6	4:23.7	9:46.8	28:35.3	36:21.5
330	8.32	21.9	42.1	47.4	1:55.1	3:11.2	4:25.9	9:52.1	28:51.3	36:42.0
320	8.37	22.0	42.4	47.7	1:56.0	3:12.8	4:28.2	9:57.5	29:07.7	37:02.9
310	8.42	22.1	42.7	48.1	1:56.9	3:14.4	4:30.6	10:02.9	29:24.3	37:24.2
300	8.47	22.3	43.0	48.4	1:57.9	3:16.0	4:32.9	10:08.5	29:41.2	37:45.9
290	8.52	22.4	43.3	48.7	1:58.8	3:17.7	4:35.3	10:14.1	29:58.5	38:08.0
280	8.58	22.5	43.6	49.1	1:59.8	3:19.4	4:37.8	10:19.9	30:16.1	38:30.6
270	8.63	22.7	43.9	49.4	2:00.8	3:21.2	4:40.3	10:25.8	30:34.0	38:53.6
260	8.68	22.8	44.2	49.8	2:01.8	3:22.9	4:42.8	10:31.8	30:52.3	39:17.1
250	8.74	23.0	44.5	50.2	2:02.8	3:24.7	4:45.4	10:37.9	31:11.0	39:41.0
240	8.79	23.1	44.8	50.5	2:03.9	3:26.6	4:48.0	10:44.1	31:30.0	40:05.5
230	8.85	23.3	45.2	50.9	2:04.9	3:28.4	4:50.7	10:50.4	31:49.5	40:30.4
220	8.90	23.5	45.5	51.3	2:06.0	3:30.4	4:53.5	10:56.9	32:09.3	40:55.9
210	8.96	23.6	45.8	51.7	2:07.1	3:32.3	4:56.2	11:03.5	32:29.6	41:21.9
200	9.02	23.8	46.2	52.1	2:08.2	3:34.3	4:59.1	11:10.2	32:50.3	41:48.4

128

SCORING TABLES
NON-CLASSICAL ENGLISH RACING DISTANCES

TABLE 1B (CONT.)

POINTS	60 YD	165 YD	300 YD	330 YD	660 YD	1000 YD	1320 YD	1.50 MI	4.00 MI	5.00 MI
190	9.08	23.9	46.5	52.5	2:09.4	3:36.3	5:02.0	11:17.1	33:11.5	42:15.6
180	9.14	24.1	46.8	52.9	2:10.5	3:38.3	5:04.9	11:24.1	33:33.1	42:43.3
170	9.20	24.3	47.2	53.3	2:11.7	3:40.4	5:07.9	11:31.3	33:55.1	43:11.7
160	9.26	24.4	47.6	53.7	2:12.9	3:42.5	5:11.0	11:38.6	34:17.7	43:40.7
150	9.32	24.6	47.9	54.1	2:14.1	3:44.7	5:14.1	11:46.1	34:40.8	44:10.3
140	9.38	24.8	48.3	54.5	2:15.4	3:46.9	5:17.3	11:53.7	35:04.4	44:40.6
130	9.45	24.9	48.7	55.0	2:16.6	3:49.2	5:20.6	12:01.5	35:28.5	45:11.6
120	9.51	25.1	49.1	55.4	2:17.9	3:51.5	5:23.9	12:09.5	35:53.2	45:43.4
110	9.58	25.3	49.5	55.9	2:19.2	3:53.8	5:27.3	12:17.6	36:18.5	46:15.9
100	9.64	25.5	49.8	56.3	2:20.6	3:56.2	5:30.8	12:25.9	36:44.4	46:49.2
90	9.71	25.7	50.3	56.8	2:21.9	3:58.7	5:34.3	12:34.5	37:10.9	47:23.2
80	9.78	25.9	50.7	57.3	2:23.3	4:01.2	5:38.0	12:43.2	37:38.0	47:58.2
70	9.85	26.1	51.1	57.7	2:24.7	4:03.7	5:41.7	12:52.1	38:05.8	48:33.9
60	9.92	26.2	51.5	58.2	2:26.2	4:06.3	5:45.4	13:01.2	38:34.3	49:10.6
50	9.99	26.4	51.9	58.7	2:27.7	4:09.0	5:49.3	13:10.6	39:03.5	49:48.3
40	10.06	26.6	52.4	59.2	2:29.2	4:11.7	5:53.3	13:20.2	39:33.5	50:26.9
30	10.14	26.8	52.8	59.7	2:30.7	4:14.5	5:57.3	13:30.0	40:04.3	51:06.5
20	10.21	27.1	53.3	1:00.3	2:32.3	4:17.3	6:01.5	13:40.0	40:35.8	51:47.1
10	10.29	27.3	53.7	1:00.8	2:33.9	4:20.2	6:05.7	13:50.4	41:08.2	52:28.9
0	10.36	27.5	54.2	1:01.3	2:35.5	4:23.2	6:10.0	14:00.9	41:41.5	53:11.8

• •

POINTS	12.00 MI	13.00 MI	15.00 MI	16.00 MI	18.00 MI	20.00 MI	25.00 MI	MARATHON	32.00 MI	50.00 MI
1150	52:42	57:24	1:C6:50	1:11:35	1:21:09	1:30:49	1:55:20	2:01:29	2:30:44	4:06:49
1140	53:00	57:42	1:07:11	1:11:58	1:21:35	1:31:19	1:55:58	2:02:09	2:31:34	4:08:12
1130	53:17	58:01	1:C7:34	1:12:22	1:22:02	1:31:49	1:56:37	2:02:49	2:32:24	4:09:35
1120	53:34	58:20	1:07:56	1:12:46	1:22:29	1:32:19	1:57:15	2:03:30	2:33:15	4:11:00
1110	53:52	58:40	1:08:18	1:13:10	1:22:57	1:32:50	1:57:55	2:04:12	2:34:06	4:12:25
1100	54:10	58:59	1:08:41	1:13:34	1:23:25	1:33:21	1:58:34	2:04:53	2:34:58	4:13:51
1C90	54:28	59:19	1:C9:04	1:13:59	1:23:53	1:33:52	1:59:14	2:05:36	2:35:51	4:15:18
1080	54:46	59:39	1:09:27	1:14:24	1:24:21	1:34:24	1:59:55	2:06:18	2:36:44	4:16:47
1070	55:05	59:59	1:09:51	1:14:49	1:24:50	1:34:56	2:00:36	2:07:02	2:37:38	4:18:16
1C60	55:24	1:00:19	1:10:15	1:15:15	1:25:19	1:35:29	2:01:18	2:07:45	2:38:33	4:19:46
1050	55:43	1:00:40	1:10:39	1:15:40	1:25:48	1:36:02	2:02:00	2:08:30	2:39:28	4:21:18
1040	56:02	1:01:01	1:11:03	1:16:07	1:26:18	1:36:35	2:02:42	2:09:14	2:40:24	4:22:50
1030	56:21	1:01:22	1:11:28	1:16:33	1:26:48	1:37:09	2:03:25	2:10:00	2:41:20	4:24:24
1020	56:41	1:01:43	1:11:53	1:17:00	1:27:18	1:37:43	2:04:08	2:10:46	2:42:17	4:25:58
1010	57:00	1:02:05	1:12:18	1:17:27	1:27:49	1:38:17	2:04:52	2:11:32	2:43:15	4:27:34
1000	57:21	1:02:27	1:12:44	1:17:54	1:28:20	1:38:52	2:05:37	2:12:19	2:44:14	4:29:11
990	57:41	1:02:49	1:13:10	1:18:22	1:28:52	1:39:28	2:06:22	2:13:06	2:45:13	4:30:49
980	58:01	1:03:11	1:13:36	1:18:50	1:29:23	1:40:03	2:07:08	2:13:54	2:46:13	4:32:28
970	58:22	1:03:34	1:14:02	1:19:18	1:29:56	1:40:39	2:07:54	2:14:43	2:47:13	4:34:09
960	58:43	1:03:57	1:14:29	1:19:47	1:30:28	1:41:16	2:08:40	2:15:32	2:48:15	4:35:51
950	59:04	1:04:20	1:14:56	1:20:16	1:31:01	1:41:53	2:09:28	2:16:22	2:49:17	4:37:34
940	59:26	1:04:44	1:15:23	1:20:45	1:31:35	1:42:31	2:10:16	2:17:13	2:50:20	4:39:18
930	59:48	1:05:07	1:15:51	1:21:15	1:32:09	1:43:09	2:11:04	2:18:04	2:51:23	4:41:04
920	1:00:10	1:05:32	1:16:19	1:21:45	1:32:43	1:43:47	2:11:53	2:18:55	2:52:28	4:42:51
910	1:00:32	1:05:56	1:16:48	1:22:16	1:33:18	1:44:25	2:12:43	2:19:48	2:53:33	4:44:39
900	1:00:55	1:06:21	1:17:17	1:22:47	1:33:53	1:45:05	2:13:33	2:20:41	2:54:39	4:46:29
890	1:01:18	1:06:46	1:17:46	1:23:18	1:34:28	1:45:45	2:14:24	2:21:34	2:55:46	4:48:20
880	1:01:41	1:07:11	1:18:15	1:23:50	1:35:04	1:46:26	2:15:15	2:22:29	2:56:54	4:50:13
870	1:02:04	1:07:37	1:18:45	1:24:22	1:35:41	1:47:06	2:16:08	2:23:24	2:58:03	4:52:07
860	1:02:28	1:08:02	1:19:16	1:24:54	1:36:18	1:47:48	2:17:01	2:24:20	2:59:12	4:54:03
850	1:02:52	1:08:29	1:19:46	1:25:27	1:36:55	1:48:30	2:17:54	2:25:16	3:00:23	4:56:00
840	1:03:17	1:08:55	1:20:17	1:26:01	1:37:33	1:49:12	2:18:49	2:26:13	3:01:34	4:57:59

130

POINTS	12.00 MI	13.00 MI	15.00 MI	16.00 MI	18.00 MI	20.00 MI	25.00 MI	MARATHON	32.00 MI	50.00 MI
830	1:03:41	1:09:22	1:20:49	1:26:34	1:38:11	1:49:56	2:19:44	2:27:11	3:02:47	4:59:59
820	1:04:06	1:09:50	1:21:21	1:27:09	1:38:50	1:50:39	2:20:39	2:28:10	3:04:00	5:02:01
810	1:04:32	1:10:17	1:21:53	1:27:43	1:39:30	1:51:23	2:21:36	2:29:10	3:05:15	5:04:04
800	1:04:58	1:10:45	1:22:26	1:28:19	1:40:10	1:52:08	2:22:33	2:30:10	3:06:30	5:06:10
790	1:05:24	1:11:14	1:22:59	1:28:54	1:40:50	1:52:54	2:23:31	2:31:11	3:07:46	5:08:17
780	1:05:50	1:11:43	1:23:33	1:29:30	1:41:31	1:53:40	2:24:30	2:32:14	3:09:04	5:10:26
770	1:06:17	1:12:12	1:24:07	1:30:07	1:42:13	1:54:26	2:25:30	2:33:16	3:10:22	5:12:36
760	1:06:44	1:12:41	1:24:41	1:30:44	1:42:55	1:55:14	2:26:30	2:34:20	3:11:42	5:14:49
750	1:07:11	1:13:11	1:25:16	1:31:22	1:43:38	1:56:02	2:27:31	2:35:25	3:13:03	5:17:03
740	1:07:39	1:13:42	1:25:52	1:32:00	1:44:21	1:56:50	2:28:34	2:36:30	3:14:24	5:19:19
730	1:08:08	1:14:13	1:26:28	1:32:38	1:45:05	1:57:40	2:29:37	2:37:37	3:15:47	5:21:38
720	1:08:36	1:14:44	1:27:05	1:33:18	1:45:50	1:58:30	2:30:41	2:38:44	3:17:12	5:23:58
710	1:09:05	1:15:16	1:27:42	1:33:57	1:46:35	1:59:21	2:31:46	2:39:53	3:18:37	5:26:20
700	1:09:35	1:15:48	1:28:19	1:34:38	1:47:21	2:00:12	2:32:51	2:41:02	3:20:04	5:28:45
690	1:10:05	1:16:21	1:28:57	1:35:19	1:48:07	2:01:04	2:33:58	2:42:13	3:21:32	5:31:11
680	1:10:35	1:16:54	1:29:36	1:36:00	1:48:55	2:01:57	2:35:06	2:43:24	3:23:01	5:33:40
670	1:11:06	1:17:27	1:30:15	1:36:42	1:49:43	2:02:51	2:36:15	2:44:37	3:24:32	5:36:11
660	1:11:37	1:18:01	1:30:55	1:37:25	1:50:31	2:03:46	2:37:24	2:45:50	3:26:04	5:38:44
650	1:12:09	1:18:36	1:31:36	1:38:09	1:51:21	2:04:41	2:38:35	2:47:05	3:27:37	5:41:20
640	1:12:41	1:19:11	1:32:17	1:38:53	1:52:11	2:05:37	2:39:47	2:48:21	3:29:12	5:43:58
630	1:13:14	1:19:47	1:32:58	1:39:37	1:53:02	2:06:34	2:41:00	2:49:38	3:30:48	5:46:38
620	1:13:47	1:20:23	1:33:41	1:40:23	1:53:53	2:07:32	2:42:14	2:50:56	3:32:25	5:49:21
610	1:14:20	1:21:00	1:34:24	1:41:09	1:54:46	2:08:31	2:43:29	2:52:15	3:34:05	5:52:07
600	1:14:55	1:21:37	1:35:07	1:41:56	1:55:39	2:09:31	2:44:46	2:53:36	3:35:45	5:54:55
590	1:15:29	1:22:15	1:35:52	1:42:43	1:56:33	2:10:32	2:46:04	2:54:58	3:37:28	5:57:46
580	1:16:04	1:22:53	1:36:36	1:43:31	1:57:28	2:11:33	2:47:22	2:56:21	3:39:12	6:00:40
570	1:16:40	1:23:32	1:37:22	1:44:20	1:58:23	2:12:36	2:48:42	2:57:46	3:40:57	6:03:36
560	1:17:17	1:24:12	1:38:09	1:45:10	1:59:20	2:13:40	2:50:04	2:59:11	3:42:45	6:06:36
550	1:17:53	1:24:52	1:38:56	1:46:01	2:00:18	2:14:44	2:51:27	3:00:39	3:44:34	6:09:38
540	1:18:31	1:25:33	1:39:44	1:46:52	2:01:16	2:15:50	2:52:51	3:02:07	3:46:25	6:12:44
530	1:19:09	1:26:15	1:40:32	1:47:44	2:02:16	2:16:57	2:54:16	3:03:38	3:48:18	6:15:52
520	1:19:48	1:26:57	1:41:22	1:48:37	2:03:16	2:18:04	2:55:43	3:05:09	3:50:12	6:19:04

POINTS	12.00 MI	13.00 MI	15.00 MI	16.00 MI	18.00 MI	20.00 MI	25.00 MI	MARATHON	32.00 MI	50.00 MI
510	1:20:27	1:27:40	1:42:12	1:49:31	2:04:18	2:19:13	2:57:11	3:06:42	3:52:09	6:22:19
500	1:21:07	1:28:24	1:43:03	1:50:26	2:05:20	2:20:24	2:58:41	3:08:17	3:54:07	6:25:38
490	1:21:48	1:29:08	1:43:55	1:51:22	2:06:24	2:21:35	3:00:13	3:09:54	3:56:08	6:28:59
480	1:22:29	1:29:53	1:44:48	1:52:19	2:07:28	2:22:48	3:01:45	3:11:32	3:58:11	6:32:25
470	1:23:11	1:30:39	1:45:42	1:53:17	2:08:34	2:24:01	3:03:20	3:13:11	4:00:15	6:35:54
460	1:23:54	1:31:26	1:46:37	1:54:15	2:09:41	2:25:16	3:04:56	3:14:53	4:02:22	6:39:27
450	1:24:38	1:32:14	1:47:32	1:55:15	2:10:49	2:26:33	3:06:34	3:16:36	4:04:32	6:43:04
440	1:25:22	1:33:02	1:48:29	1:56:16	2:11:58	2:27:51	3:08:14	3:18:21	4:06:43	6:46:44
430	1:26:07	1:33:51	1:49:27	1:57:18	2:13:08	2:29:10	3:09:55	3:20:08	4:08:57	6:50:29
420	1:26:53	1:34:41	1:50:25	1:58:21	2:14:20	2:30:30	3:11:38	3:21:57	4:11:14	6:54:18
410	1:27:40	1:35:33	1:51:25	1:59:25	2:15:33	2:31:52	3:13:24	3:23:48	4:13:33	6:58:11
400	1:28:27	1:36:24	1:52:26	2:00:30	2:16:48	2:33:16	3:15:11	3:25:41	4:15:54	7:02:09
390	1:29:16	1:37:17	1:53:28	2:01:37	2:18:03	2:34:41	3:17:00	3:27:36	4:18:18	7:06:11
380	1:30:05	1:38:11	1:54:31	2:02:44	2:19:20	2:36:08	3:18:51	3:29:34	4:20:45	7:10:18
370	1:30:55	1:39:06	1:55:35	2:03:53	2:20:39	2:37:36	3:20:44	3:31:33	4:23:15	7:14:30
360	1:31:47	1:40:02	1:56:40	2:05:04	2:21:59	2:39:06	3:22:40	3:33:35	4:25:48	7:18:46
350	1:32:39	1:40:59	1:57:47	2:06:15	2:23:21	2:40:38	3:24:37	3:35:39	4:28:23	7:23:08
340	1:33:32	1:41:57	1:58:55	2:07:28	2:24:44	2:42:11	3:26:37	3:37:46	4:31:02	7:27:35
330	1:34:26	1:42:56	2:00:05	2:08:43	2:26:09	2:43:47	3:28:39	3:39:55	4:33:44	7:32:07
320	1:35:21	1:43:57	2:01:15	2:09:59	2:27:35	2:45:24	3:30:44	3:42:07	4:36:29	7:36:45
310	1:36:18	1:44:58	2:02:27	2:11:16	2:29:03	2:47:03	3:32:51	3:44:21	4:39:17	7:41:29
300	1:37:15	1:46:01	2:03:41	2:12:35	2:30:33	2:48:44	3:35:01	3:46:38	4:42:09	7:46:19
290	1:38:14	1:47:05	2:04:56	2:13:56	2:32:05	2:50:28	3:37:14	3:48:58	4:45:05	7:51:14
280	1:39:13	1:48:10	2:06:12	2:15:18	2:33:39	2:52:13	3:39:29	3:51:21	4:48:04	7:56:17
270	1:40:14	1:49:17	2:07:31	2:16:42	2:35:15	2:54:00	3:41:47	3:53:47	4:51:07	8:01:25
260	1:41:17	1:50:25	2:08:50	2:18:08	2:36:52	2:55:50	3:44:08	3:56:15	4:54:14	8:06:41
250	1:42:20	1:51:35	2:10:12	2:19:35	2:38:32	2:57:42	3:46:32	3:58:48	4:57:24	8:12:03
240	1:43:25	1:52:46	2:11:35	2:21:05	2:40:14	2:59:37	3:49:00	4:01:23	5:00:39	8:17:32
230	1:44:32	1:53:58	2:13:00	2:22:36	2:41:58	3:01:34	3:51:30	4:04:02	5:03:59	8:23:09
220	1:45:39	1:55:12	2:14:27	2:24:09	2:43:44	3:03:34	3:54:04	4:06:44	5:07:23	8:28:54
210	1:46:49	1:56:28	2:15:55	2:25:44	2:45:33	3:05:36	3:56:41	4:09:30	5:10:51	8:34:47
200	1:47:59	1:57:45	2:17:26	2:27:22	2:47:24	3:07:41	3:59:22	4:12:20	5:14:24	8:40:48

POINTS	12.00 MI	13.00 MI	15.00 MI	16.00 MI	18.00 MI	20.00 MI	25.00 MI	MARATHON	32.00 MI	50.00 MI
190	1:49:12	1:59:04	2:18:59	2:29:02	2:49:18	3:09:49	4:02:06	4:15:13	5:18:02	8:46:57
180	1:50:26	2:00:25	2:20:34	2:30:43	2:51:14	3:12:00	4:04:54	4:18:11	5:21:46	8:53:15
170	1:51:41	2:01:48	2:22:11	2:32:28	2:53:13	3:14:14	4:07:46	4:21:13	5:25:34	8:59:43
160	1:52:59	2:03:12	2:23:50	2:34:14	2:55:15	3:16:31	4:10:43	4:24:19	5:29:28	9:06:20
150	1:54:18	2:04:39	2:25:32	2:36:04	2:57:19	3:18:51	4:13:43	4:27:30	5:33:28	9:13:06
140	1:55:39	2:06:08	2:27:16	2:37:56	2:59:27	3:21:14	4:16:48	4:30:45	5:37:33	9:20:03
130	1:57:02	2:07:38	2:29:02	2:39:50	3:01:38	3:23:42	4:19:57	4:34:05	5:41:45	9:27:11
120	1:58:27	2:09:11	2:30:51	2:41:47	3:03:52	3:26:12	4:23:11	4:37:30	5:46:03	9:34:29
110	1:59:54	2:10:47	2:32:43	2:43:48	3:06:09	3:28:47	4:26:30	4:41:00	5:50:27	9:42:00
100	2:01:23	2:12:24	2:34:38	2:45:51	3:08:29	3:31:25	4:29:54	4:44:36	5:54:59	9:49:42
90	2:02:55	2:14:05	2:36:35	2:47:57	3:10:54	3:34:08	4:33:24	4:48:17	5:59:37	9:57:36
80	2:04:29	2:15:47	2:38:36	2:50:07	3:13:22	3:36:54	4:36:59	4:52:04	6:04:23	10:05:43
70	2:06:05	2:17:33	2:40:40	2:52:20	3:15:54	3:39:46	4:40:39	4:55:57	6:09:16	10:14:04
60	2:07:44	2:19:21	2:42:47	2:54:37	3:18:30	3:42:41	4:44:26	4:59:56	6:14:18	10:22:38
50	2:09:25	2:21:12	2:44:57	2:56:57	3:21:10	3:45:42	4:48:18	5:04:02	6:19:28	10:31:28
40	2:11:09	2:23:06	2:47:11	2:59:21	3:23:54	3:48:47	4:52:17	5:08:15	6:24:46	10:40:32
30	2:12:56	2:25:03	2:49:29	3:01:49	3:26:43	3:51:57	4:56:23	5:12:34	6:30:14	10:49:52
20	2:14:46	2:27:03	2:51:50	3:04:21	3:29:37	3:55:13	5:00:36	5:17:02	6:35:51	10:59:29
10	2:16:39	2:29:07	2:54:15	3:06:57	3:32:36	3:58:35	5:04:56	5:21:36	6:41:38	11:09:24
0	2:18:35	2:31:14	2:56:45	3:09:38	3:35:39	4:02:02	5:09:24	5:26:19	6:47:35	11:19:36

Table 2: Intermediate Times for Constant Speed Runs

On the next four pages are tables to compute odd distance pace times such as a 275 yard time for a given 440 pace. This table is employed to aid in the construction of pace workouts which were described in detail in Chapter 3. The known 440 pace is given in the left-hand column, while the intermediate times and distances are given in the succeeding columns to the right.

INTERMEDIATE TIMES FOR CONSTANT SPEED RUNS

440 Y	110 Y	150 Y	165 Y	220 Y	275 Y	330 Y	352 Y	385 Y	495 Y	550 Y
43.0	10.8	14.7	16.1	21.5	26.9	32.3	34.4	37.6	48.4	53.8
44.0	11.0	15.0	16.5	22.0	27.5	33.0	35.2	38.5	49.5	55.0
45.0	11.3	15.3	16.9	22.5	28.1	33.8	36.0	39.4	50.6	56.3
46.0	11.5	15.7	17.3	23.0	28.8	34.5	36.8	40.3	51.8	57.5
47.0	11.8	16.0	17.6	23.5	29.4	35.3	37.6	41.1	52.9	58.8
48.0	12.0	16.4	18.0	24.0	30.0	36.0	38.4	42.0	54.0	1:00.0
49.0	12.3	16.7	18.4	24.5	30.6	36.8	39.2	42.9	55.1	1:01.3
50.0	12.5	17.0	18.8	25.0	31.3	37.5	40.0	43.8	56.3	1:02.5
51.0	12.8	17.4	19.1	25.5	31.9	38.3	40.8	44.6	57.4	1:03.8
52.0	13.0	17.7	19.5	26.0	32.5	39.0	41.6	45.5	58.5	1:05.0
53.0	13.3	18.1	19.9	26.5	33.1	39.8	42.4	46.4	59.6	1:06.3
54.0	13.5	18.4	20.3	27.0	33.8	40.5	43.2	47.3	1:00.8	1:07.5
55.0	13.8	18.8	20.6	27.5	34.4	41.3	44.0	48.1	1:01.9	1:08.8
56.0	14.0	19.1	21.0	28.0	35.0	42.0	44.8	49.0	1:03.0	1:10.0
57.0	14.3	19.4	21.4	28.5	35.6	42.8	45.6	49.9	1:04.1	1:11.3
58.0	14.5	19.8	21.8	29.0	36.3	43.5	46.4	50.8	1:05.3	1:12.5
59.0	14.8	20.1	22.1	29.5	36.9	44.3	47.2	51.6	1:06.4	1:13.8
1:00.0	15.0	20.5	22.5	30.0	37.5	45.0	48.0	52.5	1:07.5	1:15.0
1:01.0	15.3	20.8	22.9	30.5	38.1	45.8	48.8	53.4	1:08.6	1:16.3
1:02.0	15.5	21.1	23.3	31.0	38.8	46.5	49.6	54.3	1:09.8	1:17.5
1:03.0	15.8	21.5	23.6	31.5	39.4	47.3	50.4	55.1	1:10.9	1:18.8
1:04.0	16.0	21.8	24.0	32.0	40.0	48.0	51.2	56.0	1:12.0	1:20.0
1:05.0	16.3	22.2	24.4	32.5	40.6	48.8	52.0	56.9	1:13.1	1:21.3
1:06.0	16.5	22.5	24.8	33.0	41.3	49.5	52.8	57.8	1:14.3	1:22.5
1:07.0	16.8	22.8	25.1	33.5	41.9	50.3	53.6	58.6	1:15.4	1:23.8
1:08.0	17.0	23.2	25.5	34.0	42.5	51.0	54.4	59.5	1:16.5	1:25.0
1:09.0	17.3	23.5	25.9	34.5	43.1	51.8	55.2	1:00.4	1:17.6	1:26.3

INTERMEDIATE TIMES FOR CONSTANT SPEED RUNS

440 Y	110 Y	150 Y	165 Y	220 Y	275 Y	330 Y	352 Y	385 Y	495 Y	550 Y
1:10.0	17.5	23.9	26.3	35.0	43.8	52.5	56.C	1:01.3	1:18.8	1:27.5
1:11.0	17.8	24.2	26.6	35.5	44.4	53.3	56.8	1:02.1	1:19.9	1:28.8
1:12.0	18.0	24.5	27.C	36.0	45.0	54.0	57.6	1:03.0	1:21.0	1:30.0
1:13.0	18.3	24.9	27.4	36.5	45.6	54.8	58.4	1:03.9	1:22.1	1:31.3
1:14.C	18.5	25.2	27.8	37.0	46.3	55.5	59.2	1:04.8	1:23.3	1:32.5
1:15.0	18.8	25.6	28.1	37.5	46.9	56.3	1:00.C	1:05.6	1:24.4	1:33.8
1:16.0	19.0	25.9	28.5	38.0	47.5	57.0	1:00.8	1:06.5	1:25.5	1:35.0
1:17.0	19.3	26.3	28.9	38.5	48.1	57.8	1:01.6	1:07.4	1:26.6	1:36.3
1:18.0	19.5	26.6	29.3	39.0	48.8	58.5	1:02.4	1:08.3	1:27.8	1:37.5
1:19.0	19.8	26.9	29.6	39.5	49.4	59.3	1:03.2	1:09.1	1:28.9	1:38.8
1:20.0	20.0	27.3	3C.0	40.0	50.0	1:00.0	1:04.0	1:10.0	1:30.0	1:40.0
1:21.0	20.3	27.6	30.4	40.5	50.6	1:00.8	1:04.8	1:10.9	1:31.1	1:41.3
1:22.0	20.5	28.0	30.8	41.0	51.3	1:01.5	1:05.6	1:11.8	1:32.3	1:42.5
1:23.0	20.8	28.3	31.1	41.5	51.9	1:02.3	1:06.4	1:12.6	1:33.4	1:43.8
1:24.0	21.0	28.6	31.5	42.0	52.5	1:03.0	1:07.2	1:13.5	1:34.5	1:45.0
1:25.C	21.3	29.0	31.9	42.5	53.1	1:03.8	1:08.0	1:14.4	1:35.6	1:46.3
1:26.0	21.5	29.3	32.3	43.0	53.8	1:04.5	1:C8.8	1:15.3	1:36.8	1:47.5
1:27.0	21.8	29.7	32.6	43.5	54.4	1:05.3	1:09.6	1:16.1	1:37.9	1:48.8
1:28.0	22.0	30.0	33.0	44.0	55.0	1:06.0	1:10.4	1:17.0	1:39.0	1:50.0
1:29.0	22.3	30.3	33.4	44.5	55.6	1:06.8	1:11.2	1:17.9	1:40.1	1:51.3
1:30.0	22.5	30.7	33.8	45.0	56.3	1:07.5	1:12.0	1:18.8	1:41.3	1:52.5
1:31.0	22.8	31.0	34.1	45.5	56.9	1:08.3	1:12.8	1:19.6	1:42.4	1:53.8
1:32.0	23.0	31.4	34.5	46.0	57.5	1:09.0	1:13.6	1:20.5	1:43.5	1:55.0
1:33.0	23.3	31.7	34.9	46.5	58.1	1:09.8	1:14.4	1:21.4	1:44.6	1:56.3
1:34.0	23.5	32.0	35.3	47.0	58.8	1:10.5	1:15.2	1:22.3	1:45.8	1:57.5
1:35.0	23.8	32.4	35.6	47.5	59.4	1:11.3	1:16.C	1:23.1	1:46.9	1:58.8
1:36.0	24.0	32.7	36.0	48.0	1:00.0	1:12.0	1:16.8	1:24.0	1:48.0	2:00.0

136

INTERMEDIATE TIMES FOR CONSTANT SPEED RUNS

440 Y	660 Y	770 Y	880 Y	1100 Y	1320 Y	1.0 M	1.25 M	1.50 M	1.75 M	2.00 M
43.0	1:04.5	1:15.3	1:26.0	1:47.5	2:09.0	2:52.0	3:35.0	4:18.0	5:01.0	5:44.0
44.0	1:06.0	1:17.0	1:28.0	1:50.0	2:12.0	2:56.0	3:40.0	4:24.0	5:08.0	5:52.0
45.0	1:07.5	1:18.8	1:30.0	1:52.5	2:15.0	3:00.0	3:45.0	4:30.0	5:15.0	6:00.0
46.0	1:09.0	1:20.5	1:32.0	1:55.0	2:18.0	3:04.0	3:50.0	4:36.0	5:22.0	6:08.0
47.0	1:10.5	1:22.3	1:34.0	1:57.5	2:21.0	3:08.0	3:55.0	4:42.0	5:29.0	6:16.0
48.0	1:12.0	1:24.0	1:36.0	2:00.0	2:24.0	3:12.0	4:00.0	4:48.0	5:36.0	6:24.0
49.0	1:13.5	1:25.8	1:38.0	2:02.5	2:27.0	3:16.0	4:05.0	4:54.0	5:43.0	6:32.0
50.0	1:15.0	1:27.5	1:40.0	2:05.0	2:30.0	3:20.0	4:10.0	5:00.0	5:50.0	6:40.0
51.0	1:16.5	1:29.3	1:42.0	2:07.5	2:33.0	3:24.0	4:15.0	5:06.0	5:57.0	6:48.0
52.0	1:18.0	1:31.0	1:44.0	2:10.0	2:36.0	3:28.0	4:20.0	5:12.0	6:04.0	6:56.0
53.0	1:19.5	1:32.8	1:46.0	2:12.5	2:39.0	3:32.0	4:25.0	5:18.0	6:11.0	7:04.0
54.0	1:21.0	1:34.5	1:48.0	2:15.0	2:42.0	3:36.0	4:30.0	5:24.0	6:18.0	7:12.0
55.0	1:22.5	1:36.3	1:50.0	2:17.5	2:45.0	3:40.0	4:35.0	5:30.0	6:25.0	7:20.0
56.0	1:24.0	1:38.0	1:52.0	2:20.0	2:48.0	3:44.0	4:40.0	5:36.0	6:32.0	7:28.0
57.0	1:25.5	1:39.8	1:54.0	2:22.5	2:51.0	3:48.0	4:45.0	5:42.0	6:39.0	7:36.0
58.0	1:27.0	1:41.5	1:56.0	2:25.0	2:54.0	3:52.0	4:50.0	5:48.0	6:46.0	7:44.0
59.0	1:28.5	1:43.3	1:58.0	2:27.5	2:57.0	3:56.0	4:55.0	5:54.0	6:53.0	7:52.0
1:00.0	1:30.0	1:45.0	2:00.0	2:30.0	3:00.0	4:00.0	5:00.0	6:00.0	7:00.0	8:00.0
1:01.0	1:31.5	1:46.8	2:02.0	2:32.5	3:03.0	4:04.0	5:05.0	6:06.0	7:07.0	8:08.0
1:02.0	1:33.0	1:48.5	2:04.0	2:35.0	3:06.0	4:08.0	5:10.0	6:12.0	7:14.0	8:16.0
1:03.0	1:34.5	1:50.3	2:06.0	2:37.5	3:09.0	4:12.0	5:15.0	6:18.0	7:21.0	8:24.0
1:04.0	1:36.0	1:52.0	2:08.0	2:40.0	3:12.0	4:16.0	5:20.0	6:24.0	7:28.0	8:32.0
1:05.0	1:37.5	1:53.8	2:10.0	2:42.5	3:15.0	4:20.0	5:25.0	6:30.0	7:35.0	8:40.0
1:06.0	1:39.0	1:55.5	2:12.0	2:45.0	3:18.0	4:24.0	5:30.0	6:36.0	7:42.0	8:48.0
1:07.0	1:40.5	1:57.3	2:14.0	2:47.5	3:21.0	4:28.0	5:35.0	6:42.0	7:49.0	8:56.0
1:08.0	1:42.0	1:59.0	2:16.0	2:50.0	3:24.0	4:32.0	5:40.0	6:48.0	7:56.0	9:04.0
1:09.0	1:43.5	2:00.8	2:18.0	2:52.5	3:27.0	4:36.0	5:45.0	6:54.0	8:03.0	9:12.0

INTERMEDIATE TIMES FOR CONSTANT SPEED RUNS
• •

440 Y	660 Y	770 Y	880 Y	1100 Y	1320 Y	1.0 M	1.25 M	1.50 M	1.75 M	2.00 M
1:10.0	1:45.0	2:02.5	2:20.0	2:55.0	3:30.0	4:40.0	5:50.0	7:00.0	8:10.0	9:20.0
1:11.0	1:46.5	2:04.3	2:22.0	2:57.5	3:33.0	4:44.0	5:55.0	7:06.0	8:17.0	9:28.0
1:12.0	1:48.0	2:06.0	2:24.0	3:00.0	3:36.0	4:48.0	6:00.0	7:12.0	8:24.0	9:36.0
1:13.0	1:49.5	2:07.8	2:26.0	3:02.5	3:39.0	4:52.0	6:05.0	7:18.0	8:31.0	9:44.0
1:14.0	1:51.0	2:09.5	2:28.0	3:05.0	3:42.0	4:56.0	6:10.0	7:24.0	8:38.0	9:52.0
1:15.0	1:52.5	2:11.3	2:30.0	3:07.5	3:45.0	5:00.0	6:15.0	7:30.0	8:45.0	0:00.0
1:16.0	1:54.0	2:13.0	2:32.0	3:10.0	3:48.0	5:04.0	6:20.0	7:36.0	8:52.0	0:08.0
1:17.0	1:55.5	2:14.8	2:34.0	3:12.5	3:51.0	5:08.0	6:25.0	7:42.0	8:59.0	0:16.0
1:18.0	1:57.0	2:16.5	2:36.0	3:15.0	3:54.0	5:12.0	6:30.0	7:48.0	9:06.0	0:24.0
1:19.0	1:58.5	2:18.3	2:38.0	3:17.5	3:57.0	5:16.0	6:35.0	7:54.0	9:13.0	0:32.0
1:20.0	2:00.0	2:20.0	2:40.0	3:20.0	4:00.0	5:20.0	6:40.0	8:00.0	9:20.0	0:40.0
1:21.0	2:01.5	2:21.8	2:42.0	3:22.5	4:03.0	5:24.0	6:45.0	8:06.0	9:27.0	0:48.0
1:22.0	2:03.0	2:23.5	2:44.0	3:25.0	4:06.0	5:28.0	6:50.0	8:12.0	9:34.0	0:56.0
1:23.0	2:04.5	2:25.3	2:46.0	3:27.5	4:09.0	5:32.0	6:55.0	8:18.0	9:41.0	1:04.0
1:24.0	2:06.0	2:27.0	2:48.0	3:30.0	4:12.0	5:36.0	7:00.0	8:24.0	9:48.0	1:12.0
1:25.0	2:07.5	2:28.8	2:50.0	3:32.5	4:15.0	5:40.0	7:05.0	8:30.0	9:55.0	1:20.0
1:26.0	2:09.0	2:30.5	2:52.0	3:35.0	4:18.0	5:44.0	7:10.0	8:36.0	0:02.0	1:28.0
1:27.0	2:10.5	2:32.3	2:54.0	3:37.5	4:21.0	5:48.0	7:15.0	8:42.0	0:09.0	1:36.0
1:28.0	2:12.0	2:34.0	2:56.0	3:40.0	4:24.0	5:52.0	7:20.0	8:48.0	0:16.0	1:44.0
1:29.0	2:13.5	2:35.8	2:58.0	3:42.5	4:27.0	5:56.0	7:25.0	8:54.0	0:23.0	1:52.0
1:30.0	2:15.0	2:37.5	3:00.0	3:45.0	4:30.0	6:00.0	7:30.0	9:00.0	0:30.0	2:00.0
1:31.0	2:16.5	2:39.3	3:02.0	3:47.5	4:33.0	6:04.0	7:35.0	9:06.0	0:37.0	2:08.0
1:32.0	2:18.0	2:41.0	3:04.0	3:50.0	4:36.0	6:08.0	7:40.0	9:12.0	0:44.0	2:16.0
1:33.0	2:19.5	2:42.8	3:06.0	3:52.5	4:39.0	6:12.0	7:45.0	9:18.0	0:51.0	2:24.0
1:34.0	2:21.0	2:44.5	3:08.0	3:55.0	4:42.0	6:16.0	7:50.0	9:24.0	0:58.0	2:32.0
1:35.0	2:22.5	2:46.3	3:10.0	3:57.5	4:45.0	6:20.0	7:55.0	9:30.0	1:05.0	2:40.0
1:36.0	2:24.0	2:48.0	3:12.0	4:00.0	4:48.0	6:24.0	8:00.0	9:36.0	1:12.0	2:48.0

Table 3: Reduced Speeds for Continuous Running Training

On the following two pages is a table to determine the percentage of all out speed to be performed in a submaximum, continuous run workout. The 100% speed mile pace is given in the left column, and the reduced speeds for that mile pace are given in the subsequent columns. Thus, a 6:00 mile pace for a particular distance should be run at 7:03 per mile for 85% speed of that particular distance. All times listed are for a per mile average.

TABLE OF REDUCED SPEEDS FOR CONTINUOUS RUNNING TRAINING
• •

PER MILE AVERAGE

100.0 %	97.5 %	95.0 %	92.5 %	90.0 %	87.5 %	85.0 %	82.5 %	80.0 %
4:00.0	4:06.2	4:12.6	4:19.5	4:26.7	4:34.3	4:42.4	4:50.9	5:00.0
4:05.0	4:11.3	4:17.9	4:24.9	4:32.2	4:40.0	4:48.2	4:57.0	5:06.3
4:10.0	4:16.4	4:23.2	4:30.3	4:37.8	4:45.7	4:54.1	5:03.0	5:12.5
4:15.0	4:21.5	4:28.4	4:35.7	4:43.3	4:51.4	5:00.0	5:09.1	5:18.8
4:20.0	4:26.7	4:33.7	4:41.1	4:48.9	4:57.1	5:05.9	5:15.2	5:25.0
4:25.0	4:31.8	4:38.9	4:46.5	4:54.4	5:02.9	5:11.8	5:21.2	5:31.3
4:30.0	4:36.9	4:44.2	4:51.9	5:00.0	5:08.6	5:17.6	5:27.3	5:37.5
4:35.0	4:42.1	4:49.5	4:57.3	5:05.6	5:14.3	5:23.5	5:33.3	5:43.8
4:40.0	4:47.2	4:54.7	5:02.7	5:11.1	5:20.0	5:29.4	5:39.4	5:50.0
4:45.0	4:52.3	5:00.0	5:08.1	5:16.7	5:25.7	5:35.3	5:45.5	5:56.3
4:50.0	4:57.4	5:05.3	5:13.5	5:22.2	5:31.4	5:41.2	5:51.5	6:02.5
4:55.0	5:02.6	5:10.5	5:18.9	5:27.8	5:37.1	5:47.1	5:57.6	6:08.8
5:00.0	5:07.7	5:15.8	5:24.3	5:33.3	5:42.9	5:52.9	6:03.6	6:15.0
5:05.0	5:12.8	5:21.1	5:29.7	5:38.9	5:48.6	5:58.8	6:09.7	6:21.3
5:10.0	5:17.9	5:26.3	5:35.1	5:44.4	5:54.3	6:04.7	6:15.8	6:27.5
5:15.0	5:23.1	5:31.6	5:40.5	5:50.0	6:00.0	6:10.6	6:21.8	6:33.8
5:20.0	5:28.2	5:36.8	5:45.9	5:55.6	6:05.7	6:16.5	6:27.9	6:40.0
5:25.0	5:33.3	5:42.1	5:51.4	6:01.1	6:11.4	6:22.4	6:33.9	6:46.3
5:30.0	5:38.5	5:47.4	5:56.8	6:06.7	6:17.1	6:28.2	6:40.0	6:52.5
5:35.0	5:43.6	5:52.6	6:02.2	6:12.2	6:22.9	6:34.1	6:46.1	6:58.8
5:40.0	5:48.7	5:57.9	6:07.6	6:17.8	6:28.6	6:40.0	6:52.1	7:05.0
5:45.0	5:53.8	6:03.2	6:13.0	6:23.3	6:34.3	6:45.9	6:58.2	7:11.3
5:50.0	5:59.0	6:08.4	6:18.4	6:28.9	6:40.0	6:51.8	7:04.2	7:17.5
5:55.0	6:04.1	6:13.7	6:23.8	6:34.4	6:45.7	6:57.6	7:10.3	7:23.8
6:00.0	6:09.2	6:18.9	6:29.2	6:40.0	6:51.4	7:03.5	7:16.4	7:30.0

TABLE OF REDUCED SPEEDS FOR CONTINUOUS RUNNING TRAINING

PER MILE AVERAGE

100.0 %	97.5 %	95.0 %	92.5 %	90.0 %	87.5 %	85.0 %	82.5 %	80.0 %
6:05.0	6:14.4	6:24.2	6:34.6	6:45.6	6:57.1	7:09.4	7:22.4	7:36.3
6:10.0	6:19.5	6:29.5	6:40.0	6:51.1	7:02.9	7:15.3	7:28.5	7:42.5
6:15.0	6:24.6	6:34.7	6:45.4	6:56.7	7:08.6	7:21.2	7:34.5	7:48.8
6:20.0	6:29.7	6:40.0	6:50.8	7:02.2	7:14.3	7:27.1	7:40.6	7:55.0
6:25.0	6:34.9	6:45.3	6:56.2	7:07.8	7:20.0	7:32.9	7:46.7	8:01.3
6:30.0	6:40.0	6:50.5	7:01.6	7:13.3	7:25.7	7:38.8	7:52.7	8:07.5
6:35.0	6:45.1	6:55.8	7:07.0	7:18.9	7:31.4	7:44.7	7:58.8	8:13.8
6:40.0	6:50.3	7:01.1	7:12.4	7:24.4	7:37.1	7:50.6	8:04.8	8:20.0
6:45.0	6:55.4	7:06.3	7:17.8	7:30.0	7:42.9	7:56.5	8:10.9	8:26.3
6:50.0	7:00.5	7:11.6	7:23.2	7:35.6	7:48.6	8:02.4	8:17.0	8:32.5
6:55.0	7:05.6	7:16.8	7:28.6	7:41.1	7:54.3	8:08.2	8:23.0	8:38.8
7:00.0	7:10.8	7:22.1	7:34.1	7:46.7	8:00.0	8:14.1	8:29.1	8:45.0
7:05.0	7:15.9	7:27.4	7:39.5	7:52.2	8:05.7	8:20.0	8:35.2	8:51.3
7:10.0	7:21.0	7:32.6	7:44.9	7:57.8	8:11.4	8:25.9	8:41.2	8:57.5
7:15.0	7:26.2	7:37.9	7:50.3	8:03.3	8:17.1	8:31.8	8:47.3	9:03.8
7:20.0	7:31.3	7:43.2	7:55.7	8:08.9	8:22.9	8:37.6	8:53.3	9:10.0
7:25.0	7:36.4	7:48.4	8:01.1	8:14.4	8:28.6	8:43.5	8:59.4	9:16.3
7:30.0	7:41.5	7:53.7	8:06.5	8:20.0	8:34.3	8:49.4	9:05.5	9:22.5
7:35.0	7:46.7	7:58.9	8:11.9	8:25.6	8:40.0	8:55.3	9:11.5	9:28.8
7:40.0	7:51.8	8:04.2	8:17.3	8:31.1	8:45.7	9:01.2	9:17.6	9:35.0
7:45.0	7:56.9	8:09.5	8:22.7	8:36.7	8:51.4	9:07.1	9:23.6	9:41.3
7:50.0	8:02.1	8:14.7	8:28.1	8:42.2	8:57.1	9:12.9	9:29.7	9:47.5
7:55.0	8:07.2	8:20.0	8:33.5	8:47.8	9:02.9	9:18.8	9:35.8	9:53.8
8:00.0	8:12.3	8:25.3	8:38.9	8:53.3	9:08.6	9:24.7	9:41.8	10:00.0

Table 4: Pacing Tables for Repetition Running

The pacing tables given on the subsequent pages are to be utilized by the individual athlete who has determined his point level from the Performance Rating Tables given in Table 1a, Table 1b, and Table 1c. For a point level between two successive pacing tables, the athlete should reference the lower one until he can perform the workout at that level; then, he may use the next higher level.

The pacing tables are given in increments of 20 points. A 760 point level runner (a runner who can perform at least one event at the 760 point level) simply references the 760 point level pacing table, while the 450 point level runner would initially reference the 440 point level pacing table. Proper usage of the tables is contained in the text, with Chapters 2 and 3 the most important.

1100 POINT LEVEL PACING TABLE

SPEED	REPS	REST	110 YD	150 YD	165 YD	220 YD	275 YD	330 YD	352 YD	385 YD	440 YD	495 YD
95.0%	0- 1	---	9.5	13.1	14.5	19.7	25.4	31.7	34.3	38.3	45.1	52.3
92.5%	1- 2	4- 5 M	9.8	13.5	14.9	20.2	26.1	32.5	35.2	39.3	46.4	53.7
90.0%	2- 3	4- 5 M	10.1	13.9	15.3	20.8	26.8	33.4	36.2	40.4	47.7	55.2
87.5%	3- 4	3- 4 M	10.3	14.3	15.8	21.4	27.6	34.4	37.2	41.6	49.0	56.8
85.0%	4- 5	3- 4 M	10.7	14.7	16.2	22.0	28.4	35.4	38.3	42.8	50.5	58.4
82.5%	6- 7	2- 3 M	11.0	15.1	16.7	22.7	29.2	36.5	39.5	44.1	52.0	1:00.2
80.0%	8- 9	2- 3 M	11.3	15.6	17.3	23.4	30.1	37.6	40.7	45.5	53.6	1:02.1
77.5%	10-12	1- 2 M	11.7	16.1	17.8	24.1	31.1	38.8	42.0	46.9	55.3	1:04.1
75.0%	13-15	1- 2 M	12.1	16.7	18.4	24.9	32.2	40.1	43.4	48.5	57.2	1:06.2
72.5%	16-18	60-90 S	12.5	17.2	19.0	25.8	33.3	41.5	44.9	50.2	59.2	1:08.5
70.0%	19-21	60-90 S	12.9	17.8	19.7	26.7	34.4	43.0	46.5	52.0	1:01.3	1:10.9
67.5%	22-24	45-75 S	13.4	18.5	20.5	27.7	35.7	44.6	48.2	53.9	1:03.5	1:13.6
65.0%	25-29	45-75 S	13.9	19.2	21.2	28.8	37.1	46.3	50.1	56.0	1:06.0	1:16.4
62.5%	30-35	30-60 S	14.5	20.0	22.1	29.9	38.6	48.1	52.1	58.2	1:08.6	-----
60.0%	36-40	30-60 S	15.1	20.8	23.0	31.2	40.2	50.1	54.3	1:00.6	-----	-----

SPEED	REPS	REST	550 YD	660 YD	880 YD	1100 YD	1320 YD	1.00 MI	1.25 MI	1.50 MI	1.75 MI	2.00 MI
95.0%	0- 1	---	59.6	1:14.6	1:44.8	2:16.3	2:48.3	3:53.8	5:00.4	6:08.0	7:16.1	8:24.4
92.5%	1- 2	4- 5 M	1:01.3	1:16.6	1:47.6	2:20.0	2:52.8	4:00.1	5:08.5	6:18.0	7:27.9	8:38.1
90.0%	2- 3	4- 5 M	1:03.0	1:18.7	1:50.6	2:23.9	2:57.6	4:06.8	5:17.1	6:28.5	7:40.3	8:52.5
87.5%	3- 4	3- 4 M	1:04.8	1:21.0	1:53.8	2:28.0	3:02.7	4:13.8	5:26.1	6:39.6	7:53.5	9:07.7
85.0%	4- 5	3- 4 M	1:06.7	1:23.4	1:57.1	2:32.4	3:08.1	4:21.3	5:35.7	6:51.3	8:07.4	9:23.8
82.5%	6- 7	2- 3 M	1:08.7	1:25.9	2:00.7	2:37.0	3:13.8	4:29.2	5:45.9	-----	-----	-----
80.0%	8- 9	2- 3 M	1:10.8	1:28.6	2:04.5	2:41.9	3:19.8	4:37.6	-----	-----	-----	-----
77.5%	10-12	1- 2 M	1:13.1	1:31.4	2:08.5	2:47.1	3:26.3	-----	-----	-----	-----	-----
75.0%	13-15	1- 2 M	1:15.5	1:34.5	2:12.8	2:52.7	-----	-----	-----	-----	-----	-----
72.5%	16-18	60-90 S	1:18.1	1:37.8	2:17.3	-----	-----	-----	-----	-----	-----	-----
70.0%	19-21	60-90 S	1:20.9	1:41.2	-----	-----	-----	-----	-----	-----	-----	-----
67.5%	22-24	45-75 S	1:23.9	1:45.0	-----	-----	-----	-----	-----	-----	-----	-----
65.0%	25-29	45-75 S	1:27.2	-----	-----	-----	-----	-----	-----	-----	-----	-----
62.5%	30-35	30-60 S	-----	-----	-----	-----	-----	-----	-----	-----	-----	-----
60.0%	36-40	30-60 S	-----	-----	-----	-----	-----	-----	-----	-----	-----	-----

1080 POINT LEVEL PACING TABLE

SPEED	REPS	REST	110 YD	150 YD	165 YD	220 YD	275 YD	330 YD	352 YD	385 YD	440 YD	495 YD
95.0%	0- 1	---	9.6	13.3	14.7	19.9	25.6	31.9	34.6	38.6	45.6	52.8
92.5%	1- 2	4- 5 M	9.9	13.6	15.1	20.4	26.3	32.8	35.5	39.7	46.8	54.2
90.0%	2- 3	4- 5 M	10.1	14.0	15.5	21.0	27.0	33.7	36.5	40.8	48.1	55.7
87.5%	3- 4	3- 4 M	10.4	14.4	15.9	21.6	27.8	34.7	37.5	42.0	49.5	57.3
85.0%	4- 5	3- 4 M	10.7	14.8	16.4	22.2	28.6	35.7	38.7	43.2	50.9	59.0
82.5%	6- 7	2- 3 M	11.1	15.3	16.9	22.9	29.5	36.8	39.8	44.5	52.5	1:00.8
80.0%	8- 9	2- 3 M	11.4	15.7	17.4	23.6	30.4	37.9	41.1	45.9	54.1	1:02.7
77.5%	10-12	1- 2 M	11.8	16.3	18.0	24.3	31.4	39.2	42.4	47.4	55.9	1:04.7
75.0%	13-15	1- 2 M	12.2	16.8	18.6	25.1	32.4	40.5	43.8	48.9	57.7	1:06.8
72.5%	16-18	60-90 S	12.6	17.4	19.2	26.0	33.6	41.9	45.3	50.6	59.7	1:09.2
70.0%	19-21	60-90 S	13.0	18.0	19.9	26.9	34.8	43.4	46.9	52.4	1:01.8	1:11.6
67.5%	22-24	45-75 S	13.5	18.7	20.6	27.9	36.0	45.0	48.7	54.4	1:04.1	1:14.3
65.0%	25-29	45-75 S	14.0	19.4	21.4	29.0	37.4	46.7	50.5	56.5	1:06.6	1:17.1
62.5%	30-35	30-60 S	14.6	20.2	22.3	30.2	38.9	48.6	52.6	58.7	1:09.3	-----
60.0%	36-40	30-60 S	15.2	21.0	23.2	31.4	40.5	50.6	54.8	1:01.2	-----	-----

SPEED	REPS	REST	550 YD	660 YD	880 YD	1100 YD	1320 YD	1.00 MI	1.25 MI	1.50 MI	1.75 MI	2.00 MI
95.0%	0- 1	---	1:00.2	1:15.3	1:45.9	2:17.7	2:50.0	3:56.3	5:03.6	6:12.0	7:20.8	8:29.9
92.5%	1- 2	4- 5 M	1:01.8	1:17.4	1:48.7	2:21.5	2:54.6	4:02.7	5:11.8	6:22.0	7:32.7	8:43.7
90.0%	2- 3	4- 5 M	1:03.6	1:19.5	1:51.8	2:25.4	2:59.5	4:09.4	5:20.4	6:32.6	7:45.3	8:58.2
87.5%	3- 4	3- 4 M	1:05.4	1:21.8	1:54.9	2:29.5	3:04.6	4:16.5	5:29.6	6:43.9	7:58.6	9:13.6
85.0%	4- 5	3- 4 M	1:07.3	1:24.2	1:58.3	2:33.9	3:10.0	4:24.1	5:39.3	6:55.7	8:12.7	9:29.9
82.5%	6- 7	2- 3 M	1:09.3	1:26.8	2:01.9	2:38.6	3:15.8	4:32.1	5:49.6	-----	-----	-----
80.0%	8- 9	2- 3 M	1:11.5	1:29.5	2:05.7	2:43.6	3:21.9	4:40.6	-----	-----	-----	-----
77.5%	10-12	1- 2 M	1:13.8	1:32.3	2:09.8	2:48.8	3:28.4	-----	-----	-----	-----	-----
75.0%	13-15	1- 2 M	1:16.3	1:35.4	2:14.1	2:54.5	-----	-----	-----	-----	-----	-----
72.5%	16-18	60-90 S	1:18.9	1:38.7	2:18.7	-----	-----	-----	-----	-----	-----	-----
70.0%	19-21	60-90 S	1:21.7	1:42.2	-----	-----	-----	-----	-----	-----	-----	-----
67.5%	22-24	45-75 S	1:24.8	1:46.0	-----	-----	-----	-----	-----	-----	-----	-----
65.0%	25-29	45-75 S	1:28.0	-----	-----	-----	-----	-----	-----	-----	-----	-----
62.5%	30-35	30-60 S	-----	-----	-----	-----	-----	-----	-----	-----	-----	-----
60.0%	36-40	30-60 S	-----	-----	-----	-----	-----	-----	-----	-----	-----	-----

1060 POINT LEVEL PACING TABLE

SPEED	REPS	REST	110 YD	150 YD	165 YD	220 YD	275 YD	330 YD	352 YD	385 YD	440 YD	495 YD
95.0%	0- 1	---	9.7	13.4	14.8	20.0	25.8	32.2	34.9	39.0	46.0	53.3
92.5%	1- 2	4- 5 M	10.0	13.7	15.2	20.6	26.5	33.1	35.8	40.1	47.2	54.7
90.0%	2- 3	4- 5 M	10.2	14.1	15.6	21.1	27.3	34.0	36.8	41.2	48.6	56.2
87.5%	3- 4	3- 4 M	10.5	14.5	16.0	21.7	28.1	35.0	37.9	42.3	49.9	57.9
85.0%	4- 5	3- 4 M	10.8	14.9	16.5	22.4	28.9	36.0	39.0	43.6	51.4	59.6
82.5%	6- 7	2- 3 M	11.2	15.4	17.0	23.1	29.8	37.1	40.2	44.9	53.0	1:01.4
80.0%	8- 9	2- 3 M	11.5	15.9	17.6	23.8	30.7	38.3	41.4	46.3	54.6	1:03.3
77.5%	10-12	1- 2 M	11.9	16.4	18.1	24.5	31.7	39.5	42.8	47.8	56.4	1:05.3
75.0%	13-15	1- 2 M	12.3	16.9	18.7	25.4	32.7	40.8	44.2	49.4	58.3	1:07.5
72.5%	16-18	60-90 S	12.7	17.5	19.4	26.2	33.9	42.2	45.7	51.1	1:00.3	1:09.8
70.0%	19-21	60-90 S	13.2	18.1	20.1	27.2	35.1	43.8	47.4	52.9	1:02.4	1:12.3
67.5%	22-24	45-75 S	13.6	18.8	20.8	28.2	36.4	45.4	49.1	54.9	1:04.7	1:15.0
65.0%	25-29	45-75 S	14.2	19.5	21.6	29.3	37.8	47.1	51.0	57.0	1:07.2	1:17.9
62.5%	30-35	30-60 S	14.7	20.3	22.5	30.4	39.3	49.0	53.1	59.3	1:09.9	1:21.0
60.0%	36-40	30-60 S	15.3	21.2	23.4	31.7	40.9	51.0	55.3	1:01.8	-----	-----

SPEED	REPS	REST	550 YD	660 YD	880 YD	1100 YD	1320 YD	1.00 MI	1.25 MI	1.50 MI	1.75 MI	2.00 MI
95.0%	0- 1	---	1:00.8	1:16.1	1:47.0	2:19.2	2:51.8	3:58.8	5:06.8	6:16.0	7:25.6	8:35.5
92.5%	1- 2	4- 5 M	1:02.5	1:18.1	1:49.8	2:22.9	2:56.5	4:05.2	5:15.1	6:26.2	7:37.6	8:49.4
90.0%	2- 3	4- 5 M	1:04.2	1:20.3	1:52.9	2:26.9	3:01.4	4:12.1	5:23.9	6:36.9	7:50.4	9:04.1
87.5%	3- 4	3- 4 M	1:06.0	1:22.6	1:56.1	2:31.1	3:06.5	4:19.3	5:33.1	6:48.2	8:03.8	9:19.7
85.0%	4- 5	3- 4 M	1:08.0	1:25.0	1:59.5	2:35.5	3:12.0	4:26.9	5:42.9	7:00.2	8:18.0	9:36.1
82.5%	6- 7	2- 3 M	1:10.0	1:27.6	2:03.2	2:40.2	3:17.8	4:35.0	5:53.3	-----	-----	-----
80.0%	8- 9	2- 3 M	1:12.2	1:30.4	2:07.0	2:45.3	3:24.0	4:43.6	-----	-----	-----	-----
77.5%	10-12	1- 2 M	1:14.5	1:33.3	2:11.1	2:50.6	3:30.6	-----	-----	-----	-----	-----
75.0%	13-15	1- 2 M	1:17.0	1:36.4	2:15.5	2:56.3	-----	-----	-----	-----	-----	-----
72.5%	16-18	60-90 S	1:19.7	1:39.7	2:20.1	-----	-----	-----	-----	-----	-----	-----
70.0%	19-21	60-90 S	1:22.5	1:43.3	-----	-----	-----	-----	-----	-----	-----	-----
67.5%	22-24	45-75 S	1:25.6	1:47.1	-----	-----	-----	-----	-----	-----	-----	-----
65.0%	25-29	45-75 S	1:28.9	-----	-----	-----	-----	-----	-----	-----	-----	-----
62.5%	30-35	30-60 S	-----	-----	-----	-----	-----	-----	-----	-----	-----	-----
60.0%	36-40	30-60 S	-----	-----	-----	-----	-----	-----	-----	-----	-----	-----

1040 POINT LEVEL PACING TABLE
· ·

SPEED	REPS	REST	110 YD	150 YD	165 YD	220 YD	275 YD	330 YD	352 YD	385 YD	440 YD	495 YD
95.0%	0- 1	---	9.8	13.5	14.9	20.2	26.1	32.5	35.2	39.4	46.4	53.8
92.5%	1- 2	4- 5 M	10.0	13.9	15.3	20.7	26.8	33.4	36.2	40.4	47.7	55.3
90.0%	2- 3	4- 5 M	10.3	14.2	15.7	21.3	27.5	34.3	37.2	41.6	49.0	56.8
87.5%	3- 4	3- 4 M	10.6	14.6	16.2	21.9	28.3	35.3	38.3	42.7	50.4	58.4
85.0%	4- 5	3- 4 M	10.9	15.1	16.7	22.6	29.1	36.4	39.4	44.0	51.9	1:00.1
82.5%	6- 7	2- 3 M	11.3	15.5	17.2	23.3	30.0	37.5	40.6	45.3	53.5	1:02.0
80.0%	8- 9	2- 3 M	11.6	16.0	17.7	24.0	31.0	38.6	41.8	46.8	55.2	1:03.9
77.5%	10-12	1- 2 M	12.0	16.5	18.3	24.8	32.0	39.9	43.2	48.3	56.9	1:06.0
75.0%	13-15	1- 2 M	12.4	17.1	18.9	25.6	33.0	41.2	44.6	49.9	58.8	1:08.2
72.5%	16-18	60-90 S	12.8	17.7	19.5	26.5	34.2	42.6	46.2	51.6	1:00.9	1:10.5
70.0%	19-21	60-90 S	13.3	18.3	20.2	27.4	35.4	44.2	47.8	53.4	1:03.0	1:13.0
67.5%	22-24	45-75 S	13.8	19.0	21.0	28.4	36.7	45.8	49.6	55.4	1:05.4	1:15.7
65.0%	25-29	45-75 S	14.3	19.7	21.8	29.5	38.1	47.6	51.5	57.5	1:07.9	1:18.6
62.5%	30-35	30-60 S	14.9	20.5	22.7	30.7	39.6	49.5	53.6	59.8	1:10.6	1:21.8
60.0%	36-40	30-60 S	15.5	21.4	23.6	32.0	41.3	51.5	55.8	1:02.3	-----	-----

SPEED	REPS	REST	550 YD	660 YD	880 YD	1100 YD	1320 YD	1.00 MI	1.25 MI	1.50 MI	1.75 MI	2.00 MI
95.0%	0- 1	---	1:01.4	1:16.9	1:48.1	2:20.6	2:53.6	4:01.4	5:10.2	6:20.1	7:30.5	8:41.2
92.5%	1- 2	4- 5 M	1:03.1	1:18.9	1:51.0	2:24.4	2:58.3	4:07.9	5:18.6	6:30.4	7:42.7	8:55.3
90.0%	2- 3	4- 5 M	1:04.8	1:21.1	1:54.1	2:28.4	3:03.3	4:14.8	5:27.4	6:41.2	7:55.5	9:10.1
87.5%	3- 4	3- 4 M	1:06.7	1:23.4	1:57.3	2:32.7	3:08.5	4:22.0	5:36.8	6:52.7	8:09.1	9:25.8
85.0%	4- 5	3- 4 M	1:08.6	1:25.9	2:00.8	2:37.2	3:14.1	4:29.8	5:46.7	7:04.8	8:23.5	9:42.5
82.5%	6- 7	2- 3 M	1:10.7	1:28.5	2:04.4	2:41.9	3:19.9	4:37.9	5:57.2	-----	-----	-----
80.0%	8- 9	2- 3 M	1:12.9	1:31.3	2:08.3	2:47.0	3:26.2	4:46.6	-----	-----	-----	-----
77.5%	10-12	1- 2 M	1:15.3	1:34.2	2:12.5	2:52.4	3:32.8	-----	-----	-----	-----	-----
75.0%	13-15	1- 2 M	1:17.8	1:37.4	2:16.9	2:58.1	-----	-----	-----	-----	-----	-----
72.5%	16-18	60-90 S	1:20.5	1:40.7	2:21.6	-----	-----	-----	-----	-----	-----	-----
70.0%	19-21	60-90 S	1:23.3	1:44.3	-----	-----	-----	-----	-----	-----	-----	-----
67.5%	22-24	45-75 S	1:26.4	1:48.2	-----	-----	-----	-----	-----	-----	-----	-----
65.0%	25-29	45-75 S	1:29.8	-----	-----	-----	-----	-----	-----	-----	-----	-----
62.5%	30-35	30-60 S	-----	-----	-----	-----	-----	-----	-----	-----	-----	-----
60.0%	36-40	30-60 S	-----	-----	-----	-----	-----	-----	-----	-----	-----	-----

1020 POINT LEVEL PACING TABLE

SPEED	REPS	REST	110 YD	150 YD	165 YD	220 YD	275 YD	330 YD	352 YD	385 YD	440 YD	495 YD
95.0%	0- 1	---	9.9	13.6	15.0	20.4	26.3	32.8	35.6	39.7	46.9	54.3
92.5%	1- 2	4- 5 M	10.1	14.0	15.4	20.9	27.0	33.7	36.5	40.8	48.2	55.8
90.0%	2- 3	4- 5 M	10.4	14.4	15.9	21.5	27.8	34.7	37.5	42.0	49.5	57.4
87.5%	3- 4	3- 4 M	10.7	14.8	16.3	22.1	28.6	35.7	38.6	43.2	50.9	59.0
85.0%	4- 5	3- 4 M	11.0	15.2	16.8	22.8	29.4	36.7	39.7	44.4	52.4	1:00.7
82.5%	6- 7	2- 3 M	11.3	15.7	17.3	23.5	30.3	37.8	41.0	45.8	54.0	1:02.6
80.0%	8- 9	2- 3 M	11.7	16.2	17.9	24.2	31.2	39.0	42.2	47.2	55.7	1:04.5
77.5%	10-12	1- 2 M	12.1	16.7	18.4	25.0	32.2	40.3	43.6	48.7	57.5	1:06.6
75.0%	13-15	1- 2 M	12.5	17.2	19.0	25.8	33.3	41.6	45.0	50.3	59.4	1:08.8
72.5%	16-18	60-90 S	12.9	17.8	19.7	26.7	34.5	43.0	46.6	52.1	1:01.5	1:11.2
70.0%	19-21	60-90 S	13.4	18.5	20.4	27.7	35.7	44.6	48.3	53.9	1:03.6	1:13.7
67.5%	22-24	45-75 S	13.9	19.1	21.2	28.7	37.0	46.2	50.1	55.9	1:06.0	1:16.5
65.0%	25-29	45-75 S	14.4	19.9	22.0	29.8	38.5	48.0	52.0	58.1	1:08.5	1:19.4
62.5%	30-35	30-60 S	15.0	20.7	22.9	31.0	40.0	49.9	54.1	1:00.4	1:11.3	1:22.6
60.0%	36-40	30-60 S	15.6	21.5	23.8	32.3	41.7	52.0	56.3	1:02.9	-----	-----

SPEED	REPS	REST	550 YD	660 YD	880 YD	1100 YD	1320 YD	1.00 MI	1.25 MI	1.50 MI	1.75 MI	2.00 MI
95.0%	0- 1	---	1:02.0	1:17.6	1:49.2	2:22.1	2:55.5	4:04.0	5:13.6	6:24.3	7:35.5	8:47.0
92.5%	1- 2	4- 5 M	1:03.7	1:19.7	1:52.1	2:26.0	3:00.2	4:10.6	5:22.1	6:34.7	7:47.8	9:01.2
90.0%	2- 3	4- 5 M	1:05.5	1:22.0	1:55.3	2:30.0	3:05.3	4:17.5	5:31.0	6:45.7	8:00.8	9:16.3
87.5%	3- 4	3- 4 M	1:07.3	1:24.3	1:58.5	2:34.3	3:10.5	4:24.9	5:40.5	6:57.3	8:14.6	9:32.2
85.0%	4- 5	3- 4 M	1:09.3	1:26.8	2:02.0	2:38.8	3:16.1	4:32.7	5:50.5	7:09.6	8:29.1	9:49.0
82.5%	6- 7	2- 3 M	1:11.4	1:29.4	2:05.7	2:43.6	3:22.1	4:41.0	6:01.1	-----	-----	-----
80.0%	8- 9	2- 3 M	1:13.7	1:32.2	2:09.7	2:48.8	3:28.4	4:49.7	-----	-----	-----	-----
77.5%	10-12	1- 2 M	1:16.0	1:35.2	2:13.8	2:54.2	3:35.1	-----	-----	-----	-----	-----
75.0%	13-15	1- 2 M	1:18.6	1:38.3	2:18.3	3:00.0	-----	-----	-----	-----	-----	-----
72.5%	16-18	60-90 S	1:21.3	1:41.7	2:23.1	-----	-----	-----	-----	-----	-----	-----
70.0%	19-21	60-90 S	1:24.2	1:45.4	-----	-----	-----	-----	-----	-----	-----	-----
67.5%	22-24	45-75 S	1:27.3	1:49.3	-----	-----	-----	-----	-----	-----	-----	-----
65.0%	25-29	45-75 S	1:30.7	-----	-----	-----	-----	-----	-----	-----	-----	-----
62.5%	30-35	30-60 S	-----	-----	-----	-----	-----	-----	-----	-----	-----	-----
60.0%	36-40	30-60 S	-----	-----	-----	-----	-----	-----	-----	-----	-----	-----

1000 POINT LEVEL PACING TABLE
• •

SPEED	REPS	REST	110 YD	150 YD	165 YD	220 YD	275 YD	330 YD	352 YD	385 YD	440 YD	495 YD
95.0%	0- 1	---	9.9	13.7	15.2	20.6	26.6	33.2	35.9	40.1	47.4	54.9
92.5%	1- 2	4- 5 M	10.2	14.1	15.6	21.1	27.3	34.0	36.9	41.2	48.6	56.4
90.0%	2- 3	4- 5 M	10.5	14.5	16.0	21.7	28.0	35.0	37.9	42.4	50.0	57.9
87.5%	3- 4	3- 4 M	10.8	14.9	16.5	22.3	28.8	36.0	39.0	43.6	51.4	59.6
85.0%	4- 5	3- 4 M	11.1	15.3	17.0	23.0	29.7	37.1	40.1	44.9	52.9	1:01.3
82.5%	6- 7	2- 3 M	11.4	15.8	17.5	23.7	30.6	38.2	41.3	46.2	54.5	1:03.2
80.0%	8- 9	2- 3 M	11.8	16.3	18.0	24.4	31.5	39.4	42.6	47.7	56.2	1:05.2
77.5%	10-12	1- 2 M	12.2	16.8	18.6	25.2	32.5	40.6	44.0	49.2	58.1	1:07.3
75.0%	13-15	1- 2 M	12.6	17.4	19.2	26.0	33.6	42.0	45.5	50.8	1:00.0	1:09.5
72.5%	16-18	60-90 S	13.0	18.0	19.9	26.9	34.8	43.4	47.0	52.6	1:02.1	1:11.9
70.0%	19-21	60-90 S	13.5	18.6	20.6	27.9	36.0	45.0	48.7	54.5	1:04.3	1:14.5
67.5%	22-24	45-75 S	14.0	19.3	21.3	28.9	37.4	46.7	50.5	56.5	1:06.7	1:17.2
65.0%	25-29	45-75 S	14.5	20.1	22.2	30.1	38.8	48.5	52.5	58.7	1:09.2	1:20.2
62.5%	30-35	30-60 S	15.1	20.9	23.1	31.3	40.4	50.4	54.6	1:01.0	1:12.0	1:23.4
60.0%	36-40	30-60 S	15.7	21.7	24.0	32.6	42.0	52.5	56.8	1:03.5	-----	-----

SPEED	REPS	REST	550 YD	660 YD	880 YD	1100 YD	1320 YD	1.00 MI	1.25 MI	1.50 MI	1.75 MI	2.00 MI
95.0%	0- 1	---	1:02.7	1:18.4	1:50.3	2:23.6	2:57.4	4:06.7	5:17.1	6:28.6	7:40.7	8:53.0
92.5%	1- 2	4- 5 M	1:04.3	1:20.6	1:53.3	2:27.5	3:02.2	4:13.3	5:25.7	6:39.1	7:53.1	9:07.4
90.0%	2- 3	4- 5 M	1:06.1	1:22.8	1:56.5	2:31.6	3:07.3	4:20.4	5:34.7	6:50.2	8:06.2	9:22.6
87.5%	3- 4	3- 4 M	1:08.0	1:25.2	1:59.8	2:36.0	3:12.6	4:27.8	5:44.3	7:02.0	8:20.1	9:38.6
85.0%	4- 5	3- 4 M	1:10.0	1:27.7	2:03.3	2:40.5	3:18.3	4:35.7	5:54.4	7:14.4	8:34.8	9:55.7
82.5%	6- 7	2- 3 M	1:12.1	1:30.3	2:07.1	2:45.4	3:24.3	4:44.1	6:05.1	-----	-----	-----
80.0%	8- 9	2- 3 M	1:14.4	1:33.2	2:11.0	2:50.6	3:30.7	4:52.9	-----	-----	-----	-----
77.5%	10-12	1- 2 M	1:16.8	1:36.2	2:15.3	2:56.1	3:37.5	-----	-----	-----	-----	-----
75.0%	13-15	1- 2 M	1:19.4	1:39.4	2:19.8	3:01.9	-----	-----	-----	-----	-----	-----
72.5%	16-18	60-90 S	1:22.1	1:42.8	2:24.6	-----	-----	-----	-----	-----	-----	-----
70.0%	19-21	60-90 S	1:25.0	1:46.5	-----	-----	-----	-----	-----	-----	-----	-----
67.5%	22-24	45-75 S	1:28.2	1:50.4	-----	-----	-----	-----	-----	-----	-----	-----
65.0%	25-29	45-75 S	1:31.6	-----	-----	-----	-----	-----	-----	-----	-----	-----
62.5%	30-35	30-60 S	-----	-----	-----	-----	-----	-----	-----	-----	-----	-----
60.0%	36-40	30-60 S	-----	-----	-----	-----	-----	-----	-----	-----	-----	-----

980 POINT LEVEL PACING TABLE

SPEED	REPS	REST	110 YD	150 YD	165 YD	220 YD	275 YD	330 YD	352 YD	385 YD	440 YD	495 YD
95.0%	0- 1	---	10.0	13.8	15.3	20.8	26.8	33.5	36.2	40.5	47.8	55.4
92.5%	1- 2	4- 5 M	10.3	14.2	15.7	21.3	27.5	34.4	37.2	41.6	49.1	56.9
90.0%	2- 3	4- 5 M	10.6	14.6	16.2	21.9	28.3	35.3	38.3	42.8	50.5	58.5
87.5%	3- 4	3- 4 M	10.9	15.0	16.6	22.5	29.1	36.3	39.4	44.0	51.9	1:00.2
85.0%	4- 5	3- 4 M	11.2	15.5	17.1	23.2	29.9	37.4	40.5	45.3	53.5	1:02.0
82.5%	6- 7	2- 3 M	11.5	15.9	17.6	23.9	30.9	38.5	41.7	46.7	55.1	1:03.8
80.0%	8- 9	2- 3 M	11.9	16.4	18.2	24.6	31.8	39.7	43.0	48.1	56.8	1:05.8
77.5%	10-12	1- 2 M	12.3	17.0	18.8	25.4	32.8	41.0	44.4	49.7	58.6	1:07.9
75.0%	13-15	1- 2 M	12.7	17.5	19.4	26.3	33.9	42.4	45.9	51.3	1:00.6	1:10.2
72.5%	16-18	60-90 S	13.1	18.1	20.1	27.2	35.1	43.9	47.5	53.1	1:02.7	1:12.6
70.0%	19-21	60-90 S	13.6	18.8	20.8	28.2	36.4	45.4	49.2	55.0	1:04.9	1:15.2
67.5%	22-24	45-75 S	14.1	19.5	21.5	29.2	37.7	47.1	51.0	57.0	1:07.3	1:18.0
65.0%	25-29	45-75 S	14.7	20.2	22.4	30.3	39.2	48.9	53.0	59.2	1:09.9	1:21.0
62.5%	30-35	30-60 S	15.2	21.0	23.3	31.5	40.7	50.9	55.1	1:01.6	1:12.7	1:24.3
60.0%	36-40	30-60 S	15.9	21.9	24.2	32.9	42.4	53.0	57.4	1:04.2	-----	-----

SPEED	REPS	REST	550 YD	660 YD	880 YD	1100 YD	1320 YD	1.00 MI	1.25 MI	1.50 MI	1.75 MI	2.00 MI
95.0%	0- 1	---	1:03.3	1:19.3	1:51.5	2:25.2	2:59.4	4:09.4	5:20.7	6:33.0	7:45.9	8:59.1
92.5%	1- 2	4- 5 M	1:05.0	1:21.4	1:54.5	2:29.1	3:04.2	4:16.2	5:29.3	6:43.7	7:58.5	9:13.6
90.0%	2- 3	4- 5 M	1:06.8	1:23.7	1:57.7	2:33.3	3:09.3	4:23.3	5:38.5	6:54.9	8:11.8	9:29.0
87.5%	3- 4	3- 4 M	1:08.7	1:26.1	2:01.1	2:37.6	3:14.7	4:30.8	5:48.1	7:06.7	8:25.8	9:45.3
85.0%	4- 5	3- 4 M	1:10.7	1:28.6	2:04.6	2:42.3	3:20.5	4:38.8	5:58.4	7:19.3	8:40.7	10:02.5
82.5%	6- 7	2- 3 M	1:12.9	1:31.3	2:08.4	2:47.2	3:26.5	4:47.2	6:09.2	-----	-----	-----
80.0%	8- 9	2- 3 M	1:15.2	1:34.1	2:12.4	2:52.4	3:33.0	4:56.2	-----	-----	-----	-----
77.5%	10-12	1- 2 M	1:17.6	1:37.2	2:16.7	2:58.0	3:39.8	-----	-----	-----	-----	-----
75.0%	13-15	1- 2 M	1:20.2	1:40.4	2:21.3	3:03.9	-----	-----	-----	-----	-----	-----
72.5%	16-18	60-90 S	1:22.9	1:43.9	2:26.1	-----	-----	-----	-----	-----	-----	-----
70.0%	19-21	60-90 S	1:25.9	1:47.6	-----	-----	-----	-----	-----	-----	-----	-----
67.5%	22-24	45-75 S	1:29.1	1:51.6	-----	-----	-----	-----	-----	-----	-----	-----
65.0%	25-29	45-75 S	1:32.5	-----	-----	-----	-----	-----	-----	-----	-----	-----
62.5%	30-35	30-60 S	-----	-----	-----	-----	-----	-----	-----	-----	-----	-----
60.0%	36-40	30-60 S	-----	-----	-----	-----	-----	-----	-----	-----	-----	-----

960 POINT LEVEL PACING TABLE

SPEED	REPS	REST	110 YD	150 YD	165 YD	220 YD	275 YD	330 YD	352 YD	385 YD	440 YD	495 YD
95.0%	0- 1	----	10.1	14.0	15.4	20.9	27.0	33.8	36.6	40.9	48.3	56.0
92.5%	1- 2	4- 5 M	10.4	14.3	15.9	21.5	27.8	34.7	37.6	42.0	49.6	57.5
90.0%	2- 3	4- 5 M	10.7	14.7	16.3	22.1	28.6	35.7	38.6	43.2	51.0	59.1
87.5%	3- 4	3- 4 M	11.0	15.2	16.8	22.7	29.4	36.7	39.7	44.4	52.4	1:00.8
85.0%	4- 5	3- 4 M	11.3	15.6	17.3	23.4	30.2	37.8	40.9	45.7	54.0	1:02.6
82.5%	6- 7	2- 3 M	11.6	16.1	17.8	24.1	31.1	38.9	42.1	47.1	55.6	1:04.5
80.0%	8- 9	2- 3 M	12.0	16.6	18.3	24.9	32.1	40.1	43.5	48.6	57.4	1:06.5
77.5%	10-12	1- 2 M	12.4	17.1	18.9	25.7	33.2	41.4	44.9	50.2	59.2	1:08.6
75.0%	13-15	1- 2 M	12.8	17.7	19.6	26.5	34.3	42.8	46.4	51.8	1:01.2	1:10.9
72.5%	16-18	60-90 S	13.3	18.3	20.2	27.4	35.4	44.3	48.0	53.6	1:03.3	1:13.4
70.0%	19-21	60-90 S	13.7	19.0	21.0	28.4	36.7	45.9	49.7	55.5	1:05.6	1:16.0
67.5%	22-24	45-75 S	14.2	19.7	21.7	29.5	38.1	47.6	51.5	57.6	1:08.0	1:18.8
65.0%	25-29	45-75 S	14.8	20.4	22.6	30.6	39.5	49.4	53.5	59.8	1:10.6	1:21.8
62.5%	30-35	30-60 S	15.4	21.2	23.5	31.8	41.1	51.4	55.6	1:02.2	1:13.4	1:25.1
60.0%	36-40	30-60 S	16.0	22.1	24.4	33.2	42.8	53.5	57.9	1:04.8	-----	-----

SPEED	REPS	REST	550 YD	660 YD	880 YD	1100 YD	1320 YD	1.00 MI	1.25 MI	1.50 MI	1.75 MI	2.00 MI
95.0%	0- 1	----	1:03.9	1:20.1	1:52.7	2:26.8	3:01.3	4:12.2	5:24.3	6:37.6	7:51.3	9:05.3
92.5%	1- 2	4- 5 M	1:05.7	1:22.3	1:55.8	2:30.8	3:06.2	4:19.0	5:33.1	6:48.3	8:04.0	9:20.0
90.0%	2- 3	4- 5 M	1:07.5	1:24.5	1:59.0	2:34.9	3:11.4	4:26.2	5:42.3	6:59.6	8:17.4	9:35.6
87.5%	3- 4	3- 4 M	1:09.4	1:27.0	2:02.4	2:39.4	3:16.9	4:33.8	5:52.1	7:11.6	8:31.7	9:52.0
85.0%	4- 5	3- 4 M	1:11.5	1:29.5	2:06.0	2:44.1	3:22.7	4:41.9	6:02.5	7:24.3	8:46.7	10:09.4
82.5%	6- 7	2- 3 M	1:13.6	1:32.2	2:09.8	2:49.0	3:28.8	4:50.4	6:13.4	-----	-----	-----
80.0%	8- 9	2- 3 M	1:15.9	1:35.1	2:13.9	2:54.3	3:35.3	4:59.5	-----	-----	-----	-----
77.5%	10-12	1- 2 M	1:18.4	1:38.2	2:18.2	2:59.9	3:42.3	-----	-----	-----	-----	-----
75.0%	13-15	1- 2 M	1:21.0	1:41.5	2:22.8	3:05.9	-----	-----	-----	-----	-----	-----
72.5%	16-18	60-90 S	1:23.8	1:45.0	2:27.7	-----	-----	-----	-----	-----	-----	-----
70.0%	19-21	60-90 S	1:26.8	1:48.7	-----	-----	-----	-----	-----	-----	-----	-----
67.5%	22-24	45-75 S	1:30.0	1:52.7	-----	-----	-----	-----	-----	-----	-----	-----
65.0%	25-29	45-75 S	1:33.5	-----	-----	-----	-----	-----	-----	-----	-----	-----
62.5%	30-35	30-60 S	-----	-----	-----	-----	-----	-----	-----	-----	-----	-----
60.0%	36-40	30-60 S	-----	-----	-----	-----	-----	-----	-----	-----	-----	-----

940 POINT LEVEL PACING TABLE
• •

SPEED	REPS	REST	110 YD	150 YD	165 YD	220 YD	275 YD	330 YD	352 YD	385 YD	440 YD	495 YD
95.0%	0- 1	----	10.2	14.1	15.6	21.1	27.3	34.1	37.0	41.3	48.8	56.6
92.5%	1- 2	4- 5 M	10.5	14.5	16.0	21.7	28.0	35.0	38.0	42.4	50.1	58.1
90.0%	2- 3	4- 5 M	10.8	14.9	16.4	22.3	28.8	36.0	39.0	43.6	51.5	59.7
87.5%	3- 4	3- 4 M	11.1	15.3	16.9	22.9	29.6	37.0	40.1	44.9	53.0	1:01.4
85.0%	4- 5	3- 4 M	11.4	15.7	17.4	23.6	30.5	38.1	41.3	46.2	54.5	1:03.2
82.5%	6- 7	2- 3 M	11.7	16.2	17.9	24.3	31.4	39.3	42.6	47.6	56.2	1:05.1
80.0%	8- 9	2- 3 M	12.1	16.7	18.5	25.1	32.4	40.5	43.9	49.1	57.9	1:07.2
77.5%	10-12	1- 2 M	12.5	17.3	19.1	25.9	33.5	41.8	45.3	50.7	59.8	1:09.3
75.0%	13-15	1- 2 M	12.9	17.8	19.7	26.8	34.6	43.2	46.8	52.3	1:01.8	1:11.7
72.5%	16-18	60-90 S	13.4	18.5	20.4	27.7	35.8	44.7	48.4	54.1	1:03.9	1:14.1
70.0%	19-21	60-90 S	13.8	19.1	21.1	28.7	37.1	46.3	50.2	56.1	1:06.2	1:16.8
67.5%	22-24	45-75 S	14.4	19.8	21.9	29.7	38.4	48.0	52.0	58.2	1:08.7	1:19.6
65.0%	25-29	45-75 S	14.9	20.6	22.8	30.9	39.9	49.9	54.0	1:00.4	1:11.3	1:22.7
62.5%	30-35	30-60 S	15.5	21.4	23.7	32.1	41.5	51.9	56.2	1:02.8	1:14.2	1:26.0
60.0%	36-40	30-60 S	16.2	22.3	24.7	33.5	43.2	54.0	58.5	1:05.4	-----	-----

SPEED	REPS	REST	550 YD	660 YD	880 YD	1100 YD	1320 YD	1.00 MI	1.25 MI	1.50 MI	1.75 MI	2.00 MI
95.0%	0- 1	----	1:04.6	1:20.9	1:53.9	2:28.4	3:03.4	4:15.1	5:28.0	6:42.2	7:56.8	9:11.7
92.5%	1- 2	4- 5 M	1:06.4	1:23.1	1:57.0	2:32.4	3:08.3	4:22.0	5:36.9	6:53.0	8:09.6	9:26.6
90.0%	2- 3	4- 5 M	1:08.2	1:25.4	2:00.3	2:36.7	3:13.6	4:29.3	5:46.3	7:04.5	8:23.2	9:42.3
87.5%	3- 4	3- 4 M	1:10.2	1:27.9	2:03.7	2:41.1	3:19.1	4:37.0	5:56.2	7:16.6	8:37.6	9:59.0
85.0%	4- 5	3- 4 M	1:12.2	1:30.5	2:07.4	2:45.9	3:24.9	4:45.1	6:06.6	7:29.5	8:52.8	10:16.6
82.5%	6- 7	2- 3 M	1:14.4	1:33.2	2:11.2	2:50.9	3:31.2	4:53.8	6:17.7	-----	-----	-----
80.0%	8- 9	2- 3 M	1:16.7	1:36.1	2:15.3	2:56.2	3:37.8	5:02.9	-----	-----	-----	-----
77.5%	10-12	1- 2 M	1:19.2	1:39.2	2:19.7	3:01.9	3:44.8	-----	-----	-----	-----	-----
75.0%	13-15	1- 2 M	1:21.8	1:42.5	2:24.3	3:08.0	-----	-----	-----	-----	-----	-----
72.5%	16-18	60-90 S	1:24.7	1:46.1	2:29.3	-----	-----	-----	-----	-----	-----	-----
70.0%	19-21	60-90 S	1:27.7	1:49.9	-----	-----	-----	-----	-----	-----	-----	-----
67.5%	22-24	45-75 S	1:30.9	1:53.9	-----	-----	-----	-----	-----	-----	-----	-----
65.0%	25-29	45-75 S	1:34.4	-----	-----	-----	-----	-----	-----	-----	-----	-----
62.5%	30-35	30-60 S	-----	-----	-----	-----	-----	-----	-----	-----	-----	-----
60.0%	36-40	30-60 S	-----	-----	-----	-----	-----	-----	-----	-----	-----	-----

151

920 POINT LEVEL PACING TABLE
●●●●●●●●●●●●●●●●●●●●●●●●●●●

SPEED	REPS	REST	110 YD	150 YD	165 YD	220 YD	275 YD	330 YD	352 YD	385 YD	440 YD	495 YD
95.0%	0- 1	---	10.3	14.2	15.7	21.3	27.6	34.5	37.3	41.7	49.3	57.2
92.5%	1- 2	4- 5 M	10.6	14.6	16.1	21.9	28.3	35.4	38.3	42.9	50.6	58.7
90.0%	2- 3	4- 5 M	10.9	15.0	16.6	22.5	29.1	36.4	39.4	44.1	52.0	1:00.3
87.5%	3- 4	3- 4 M	11.2	15.4	17.1	23.2	29.9	37.4	40.5	45.3	53.5	1:02.1
85.0%	4- 5	3- 4 M	11.5	15.9	17.6	23.8	30.8	38.5	41.7	46.6	55.1	1:03.9
82.5%	6- 7	2- 3 M	11.9	16.4	18.1	24.6	31.7	39.7	43.0	48.1	56.8	1:05.8
80.0%	8- 9	2- 3 M	12.2	16.9	18.7	25.3	32.7	40.9	44.3	49.6	58.5	1:07.9
77.5%	10-12	1- 2 M	12.6	17.4	19.3	26.1	33.8	42.2	45.7	51.2	1:00.4	1:10.1
75.0%	13-15	1- 2 M	13.0	18.0	19.9	27.0	34.9	43.6	47.3	52.9	1:02.4	1:12.4
72.5%	16-18	60-90 S	13.5	18.6	20.6	28.0	36.1	45.1	48.9	54.7	1:04.6	1:14.9
70.0%	19-21	60-90 S	14.0	19.3	21.3	28.9	37.4	46.8	50.7	56.6	1:06.9	1:17.6
67.5%	22-24	45-75 S	14.5	20.0	22.1	30.0	38.8	48.5	52.5	58.7	1:09.4	1:20.4
65.0%	25-29	45-75 S	15.0	20.8	23.0	31.2	40.3	50.4	54.5	1:01.0	1:12.0	1:23.5
62.5%	30-35	30-60 S	15.6	21.6	23.9	32.4	41.9	52.4	56.7	1:03.4	1:14.9	1:26.9
60.0%	36-40	30-60 S	16.3	22.5	24.9	33.8	43.6	54.5	59.1	1:06.1	-----	-----

SPEED	REPS	REST	550 YD	660 YD	880 YD	1100 YD	1320 YD	1.00 MI	1.25 MI	1.50 MI	1.75 MI	2.00 MI
95.0%	0- 1	---	1:05.3	1:21.8	1:55.2	2:30.1	3:05.5	4:18.0	5:31.9	6:46.9	8:02.4	9:18.2
92.5%	1- 2	4- 5 M	1:07.1	1:24.0	1:58.3	2:34.1	3:10.5	4:25.0	5:40.8	6:57.9	8:15.4	9:33.3
90.0%	2- 3	4- 5 M	1:08.9	1:26.4	2:01.6	2:38.4	3:15.8	4:32.4	5:50.3	7:09.5	8:29.2	9:49.2
87.5%	3- 4	3- 4 M	1:10.9	1:28.8	2:05.1	2:42.9	3:21.4	4:40.2	6:00.3	7:21.8	8:43.7	10:06.1
85.0%	4- 5	3- 4 M	1:13.0	1:31.4	2:08.8	2:47.7	3:27.3	4:48.4	6:10.9	7:34.7	8:59.1	10:23.9
82.5%	6- 7	2- 3 M	1:15.2	1:34.2	2:12.7	2:52.8	3:33.6	4:57.1	6:22.1	-----	-----	-----
80.0%	8- 9	2- 3 M	1:17.5	1:37.2	2:16.8	2:58.2	3:40.2	5:06.4	-----	-----	-----	-----
77.5%	10-12	1- 2 M	1:20.0	1:40.3	2:21.2	3:04.0	3:47.3	-----	-----	-----	-----	-----
75.0%	13-15	1- 2 M	1:22.7	1:43.6	2:25.9	3:10.1	-----	-----	-----	-----	-----	-----
72.5%	16-18	60-90 S	1:25.6	1:47.2	2:31.0	-----	-----	-----	-----	-----	-----	-----
70.0%	19-21	60-90 S	1:28.6	1:51.0	-----	-----	-----	-----	-----	-----	-----	-----
67.5%	22-24	45-75 S	1:31.9	1:55.2	-----	-----	-----	-----	-----	-----	-----	-----
65.0%	25-29	45-75 S	1:35.4	-----	-----	-----	-----	-----	-----	-----	-----	-----
62.5%	30-35	30-60 S	-----	-----	-----	-----	-----	-----	-----	-----	-----	-----
60.0%	36-40	30-60 S	-----	-----	-----	-----	-----	-----	-----	-----	-----	-----

900 POINT LEVEL PACING TABLE
....

SPEED	REPS	REST	110 YD	150 YD	165 YD	220 YD	275 YD	330 YD	352 YD	385 YD	440 YD	495 YD
95.0%	0- 1	---	10.4	14.3	15.9	21.5	27.8	34.8	37.7	42.2	49.8	57.8
92.5%	1- 2	4- 5 M	10.7	14.7	16.3	22.1	28.6	35.7	38.7	43.3	51.2	59.3
90.0%	2- 3	4- 5 M	11.0	15.1	16.7	22.7	29.4	36.7	39.8	44.5	52.6	1:01.0
87.5%	3- 4	3- 4 M	11.3	15.6	17.2	23.4	30.2	37.8	40.9	45.8	54.1	1:02.7
85.0%	4- 5	3- 4 M	11.6	16.0	17.7	24.1	31.1	38.9	42.1	47.1	55.7	1:04.6
82.5%	6- 7	2- 3 M	12.0	16.5	18.3	24.8	32.0	40.1	43.4	48.5	57.4	1:06.5
80.0%	8- 9	2- 3 M	12.3	17.0	18.8	25.6	33.0	41.3	44.8	50.1	59.1	1:08.6
77.5%	10-12	1- 2 M	12.7	17.6	19.4	26.4	34.1	42.6	46.2	51.7	1:01.1	1:10.8
75.0%	13-15	1- 2 M	13.2	18.2	20.1	27.3	35.3	44.1	47.7	53.4	1:03.1	1:13.2
72.5%	16-18	60-90 S	13.6	18.8	20.8	28.2	36.5	45.6	49.4	55.2	1:05.3	1:15.7
70.0%	19-21	60-90 S	14.1	19.5	21.5	29.2	37.8	47.2	51.2	57.2	1:07.6	1:18.4
67.5%	22-24	45-75 S	14.6	20.2	22.3	30.3	39.2	49.0	53.1	59.3	1:10.1	1:21.3
65.0%	25-29	45-75 S	15.2	21.0	23.2	31.5	40.7	50.8	55.1	1:01.6	1:12.8	1:24.4
62.5%	30-35	30-60 S	15.8	21.8	24.1	32.7	42.3	52.9	57.3	1:04.1	1:15.7	1:27.8
60.0%	36-40	30-60 S	16.4	22.7	25.1	34.1	44.1	55.1	59.7	1:06.8	1:18.9	-----

SPEED	REPS	REST	550 YD	660 YD	880 YD	1100 YD	1320 YD	1.00 MI	1.25 MI	1.50 MI	1.75 MI	2.00 MI
95.0%	0- 1	---	1:06.0	1:22.7	1:56.5	2:31.8	3:07.6	4:21.0	5:35.8	6:51.7	8:08.1	9:24.9
92.5%	1- 2	4- 5 M	1:07.8	1:24.9	1:59.6	2:35.9	3:12.7	4:28.1	5:44.8	7:02.8	8:21.3	9:40.2
90.0%	2- 3	4- 5 M	1:09.7	1:27.3	2:03.0	2:40.2	3:18.0	4:35.5	5:54.4	7:14.6	8:35.3	9:56.3
87.5%	3- 4	3- 4 M	1:11.6	1:29.8	2:06.5	2:44.8	3:23.7	4:43.4	6:04.5	7:27.0	8:50.0	10:13.3
85.0%	4- 5	3- 4 M	1:13.8	1:32.4	2:10.2	2:49.6	3:29.7	4:51.8	6:15.3	7:40.1	9:05.6	10:31.4
82.5%	6- 7	2- 3 M	1:16.0	1:35.2	2:14.1	2:54.8	3:36.0	5:00.6	6:26.6	-----	-----	-----
80.0%	8- 9	2- 3 M	1:18.4	1:38.2	2:18.3	3:00.2	3:42.8	5:10.0	-----	-----	-----	-----
77.5%	10-12	1- 2 M	1:20.9	1:41.4	2:22.8	3:06.1	3:49.9	-----	-----	-----	-----	-----
75.0%	13-15	1- 2 M	1:23.6	1:44.8	2:27.6	3:12.3	-----	-----	-----	-----	-----	-----
72.5%	16-18	60-90 S	1:26.5	1:48.4	2:32.6	-----	-----	-----	-----	-----	-----	-----
70.0%	19-21	60-90 S	1:29.6	1:52.2	-----	-----	-----	-----	-----	-----	-----	-----
67.5%	22-24	45-75 S	1:32.9	1:56.4	-----	-----	-----	-----	-----	-----	-----	-----
65.0%	25-29	45-75 S	1:36.4	-----	-----	-----	-----	-----	-----	-----	-----	-----
62.5%	30-35	30-60 S	-----	-----	-----	-----	-----	-----	-----	-----	-----	-----
60.0%	36-40	30-60 S	-----	-----	-----	-----	-----	-----	-----	-----	-----	-----

880 POINT LEVEL PACING TABLE

SPEED	REPS	REST	110 YD	150 YD	165 YD	220 YD	275 YD	330 YD	352 YD	385 YD	440 YD	495 YD
95.0%	0- 1	---	10.5	14.5	16.0	21.7	28.1	35.1	38.1	42.6	50.3	58.4
92.5%	1- 2	4- 5 M	10.8	14.9	16.4	22.3	28.9	36.1	39.1	43.7	51.7	59.9
90.0%	2- 3	4- 5 M	11.1	15.3	16.9	22.9	29.7	37.1	40.2	45.0	53.1	1:01.6
87.5%	3- 4	3- 4 M	11.4	15.7	17.4	23.6	30.5	38.2	41.3	46.2	54.6	1:03.4
85.0%	4- 5	3- 4 M	11.7	16.2	17.9	24.3	31.4	39.3	42.6	47.6	56.2	1:05.2
82.5%	6- 7	2- 3 M	12.1	16.7	18.4	25.0	32.4	40.5	43.8	49.0	57.9	1:07.2
80.0%	8- 9	2- 3 M	12.4	17.2	19.0	25.8	33.4	41.7	45.2	50.6	59.8	1:09.3
77.5%	10-12	1- 2 M	12.8	17.8	19.6	26.6	34.4	43.1	46.7	52.2	1:01.7	1:11.6
75.0%	13-15	1- 2 M	13.3	18.3	20.3	27.5	35.6	44.5	48.2	53.9	1:03.7	1:13.9
72.5%	16-18	60-90 S	13.7	19.0	21.0	28.5	36.8	46.0	49.9	55.8	1:05.9	1:16.5
70.0%	19-21	60-90 S	14.2	19.7	21.7	29.5	38.1	47.7	51.7	57.8	1:08.3	1:19.2
67.5%	22-24	45-75 S	14.8	20.4	22.5	30.6	39.6	49.5	53.6	59.9	1:10.8	1:22.2
65.0%	25-29	45-75 S	15.3	21.2	23.4	31.8	41.1	51.4	55.6	1:02.2	1:13.6	1:25.3
62.5%	30-35	30-60 S	15.9	22.0	24.3	33.0	42.7	53.4	57.9	1:04.7	1:16.5	1:28.7
60.0%	36-40	30-60 S	16.6	22.9	25.4	34.4	44.5	55.6	1:00.3	1:07.4	1:19.7	-----

SPEED	REPS	REST	550 YD	660 YD	880 YD	1100 YD	1320 YD	1.00 MI	1.25 MI	1.50 MI	1.75 MI	2.00 MI
95.0%	0- 1	---	1:06.7	1:23.6	1:57.8	2:33.5	3:09.8	4:24.1	5:39.8	6:56.6	8:14.0	9:31.7
92.5%	1- 2	4- 5 M	1:08.5	1:25.9	2:01.0	2:37.7	3:14.9	4:31.3	5:49.0	7:07.9	8:27.4	9:47.2
90.0%	2- 3	4- 5 M	1:10.4	1:28.3	2:04.3	2:42.1	3:20.3	4:38.8	5:58.6	7:19.8	8:41.5	10:03.5
87.5%	3- 4	3- 4 M	1:12.4	1:30.8	2:07.9	2:46.7	3:26.0	4:46.8	6:08.9	7:32.4	8:56.4	10:20.8
85.0%	4- 5	3- 4 M	1:14.5	1:33.5	2:11.7	2:51.6	3:32.1	4:55.2	6:19.7	7:45.7	9:12.2	10:39.0
82.5%	6- 7	2- 3 M	1:16.8	1:36.3	2:15.6	2:56.8	3:38.5	5:04.1	6:31.3	-----	-----	-----
80.0%	8- 9	2- 3 M	1:19.2	1:39.3	2:19.9	3:02.3	3:45.3	5:13.6	-----	-----	-----	-----
77.5%	10-12	1- 2 M	1:21.8	1:42.5	2:24.4	3:08.2	3:52.6	-----	-----	-----	-----	-----
75.0%	13-15	1- 2 M	1:24.5	1:45.9	2:29.2	3:14.5	-----	-----	-----	-----	-----	-----
72.5%	16-18	60-90 S	1:27.4	1:49.6	2:34.4	-----	-----	-----	-----	-----	-----	-----
70.0%	19-21	60-90 S	1:30.5	1:53.5	-----	-----	-----	-----	-----	-----	-----	-----
67.5%	22-24	45-75 S	1:33.9	1:57.7	-----	-----	-----	-----	-----	-----	-----	-----
65.0%	25-29	45-75 S	1:37.5	-----	-----	-----	-----	-----	-----	-----	-----	-----
62.5%	30-35	30-60 S	-----	-----	-----	-----	-----	-----	-----	-----	-----	-----
60.0%	36-40	30-60 S	-----	-----	-----	-----	-----	-----	-----	-----	-----	-----

860 POINT LEVEL PACING TABLE
• •

SPEED	REPS	REST	110 YD	150 YD	165 YD	220 YD	275 YD	330 YD	352 YD	385 YD	440 YD	495 YD
95.0%	0- 1	---	10.6	14.6	16.2	21.9	28.4	35.5	38.5	43.0	50.9	59.0
92.5%	1- 2	4- 5 M	10.9	15.0	16.6	22.5	29.1	36.5	39.5	44.2	52.2	1:00.6
90.0%	2- 3	4- 5 M	11.2	15.4	17.1	23.2	30.0	37.5	40.6	45.4	53.7	1:02.3
87.5%	3- 4	3- 4 M	11.5	15.9	17.5	23.8	30.8	38.5	41.8	46.7	55.2	1:04.1
85.0%	4- 5	3- 4 M	11.8	16.3	18.1	24.5	31.7	39.7	43.0	48.1	56.8	1:05.9
82.5%	6- 7	2- 3 M	12.2	16.8	18.6	25.3	32.7	40.9	44.3	49.6	58.6	1:07.9
80.0%	8- 9	2- 3 M	12.6	17.4	19.2	26.1	33.7	42.1	45.7	51.1	1:00.4	1:10.1
77.5%	10-12	1- 2 M	13.0	17.9	19.8	26.9	34.8	43.5	47.1	52.7	1:02.3	1:12.3
75.0%	13-15	1- 2 M	13.4	18.5	20.5	27.8	35.9	45.0	48.7	54.5	1:04.4	1:14.7
72.5%	16-18	60-90 S	13.9	19.2	21.2	28.8	37.2	46.5	50.4	56.4	1:06.6	1:17.3
70.0%	19-21	60-90 S	14.4	19.8	21.9	29.8	38.5	48.2	52.2	58.4	1:09.0	1:20.1
67.5%	22-24	45-75 S	14.9	20.6	22.7	30.9	39.9	50.0	54.1	1:00.6	1:11.6	1:23.0
65.0%	25-29	45-75 S	15.5	21.4	23.6	32.1	41.5	51.9	56.2	1:02.9	1:14.3	1:26.2
62.5%	30-35	30-60 S	16.1	22.2	24.6	33.4	43.1	54.0	58.5	1:05.4	1:17.3	1:29.7
60.0%	36-40	30-60 S	16.7	23.1	25.6	34.7	44.9	56.2	1:00.9	1:08.1	1:20.5	-----

SPEED	REPS	REST	550 YD	660 YD	880 YD	1100 YD	1320 YD	1.00 MI	1.25 MI	1.50 MI	1.75 MI	2.00 MI
95.0%	0- 1	---	1:07.4	1:24.5	1:59.1	2:35.3	3:12.0	4:27.3	5:43.9	7:01.7	8:20.1	9:38.8
92.5%	1- 2	4- 5 M	1:09.2	1:26.8	2:02.4	2:39.5	3:17.2	4:34.5	5:53.2	7:13.1	8:33.6	9:54.4
90.0%	2- 3	4- 5 M	1:11.2	1:29.2	2:05.8	2:43.9	3:22.7	4:42.1	6:03.0	7:25.1	8:47.9	10:10.9
87.5%	3- 4	3- 4 M	1:13.2	1:31.8	2:09.4	2:48.6	3:28.4	4:50.2	6:13.3	7:37.9	9:02.9	10:28.4
85.0%	4- 5	3- 4 M	1:15.4	1:34.5	2:13.2	2:53.6	3:34.6	4:58.7	6:24.3	7:51.3	9:18.9	10:46.9
82.5%	6- 7	2- 3 M	1:17.6	1:37.4	2:17.2	2:58.8	3:41.1	5:07.8	6:36.0	-----	-----	-----
80.0%	8- 9	2- 3 M	1:20.1	1:40.4	2:21.5	3:04.4	3:48.0	5:17.4	-----	-----	-----	-----
77.5%	10-12	1- 2 M	1:22.6	1:43.6	2:26.0	3:10.4	3:55.3	-----	-----	-----	-----	-----
75.0%	13-15	1- 2 M	1:25.4	1:47.1	2:30.9	3:16.7	-----	-----	-----	-----	-----	-----
72.5%	16-18	60-90 S	1:28.3	1:50.8	2:36.1	-----	-----	-----	-----	-----	-----	-----
70.0%	19-21	60-90 S	1:31.5	1:54.7	2:41.7	-----	-----	-----	-----	-----	-----	-----
67.5%	22-24	45-75 S	1:34.9	1:59.0	-----	-----	-----	-----	-----	-----	-----	-----
65.0%	25-29	45-75 S	1:38.5	-----	-----	-----	-----	-----	-----	-----	-----	-----
62.5%	30-35	30-60 S	-----	-----	-----	-----	-----	-----	-----	-----	-----	-----
60.0%	36-40	30-60 S	-----	-----	-----	-----	-----	-----	-----	-----	-----	-----

840 POINT LEVEL PACING TABLE
•••••••••••••••••••••••••••••

SPEED	REPS	REST	110 YD	150 YD	165 YD	220 YD	275 YD	330 YD	352 YD	385 YD	440 YD	495 YD
95.0%	0- 1	---	10.7	14.8	16.3	22.2	28.7	35.9	38.9	43.5	51.4	59.6
92.5%	1- 2	4- 5 M	11.0	15.2	16.8	22.8	29.4	36.8	39.9	44.7	52.8	1:01.2
90.0%	2- 3	4- 5 M	11.3	15.6	17.2	23.4	30.3	37.8	41.0	45.9	54.3	1:02.9
87.5%	3- 4	3- 4 M	11.6	16.0	17.7	24.1	31.1	38.9	42.2	47.2	55.8	1:04.7
85.0%	4- 5	3- 4 M	11.9	16.5	18.2	24.8	32.0	40.1	43.4	48.6	57.4	1:06.7
82.5%	6- 7	2- 3 M	12.3	17.0	18.8	25.5	33.0	41.3	44.7	50.1	59.2	1:08.7
80.0%	8- 9	2- 3 M	12.7	17.5	19.4	26.3	34.0	42.6	46.1	51.6	1:01.0	1:10.8
77.5%	10-12	1- 2 M	13.1	18.1	20.0	27.2	35.1	44.0	47.6	53.3	1:03.0	1:13.1
75.0%	13-15	1- 2 M	13.5	18.7	20.7	28.1	36.3	45.4	49.2	55.1	1:05.1	1:15.5
72.5%	16-18	60-90 S	14.0	19.3	21.4	29.0	37.6	47.0	50.9	57.0	1:07.3	1:18.1
70.0%	19-21	60-90 S	14.5	20.0	22.1	30.1	38.9	48.7	52.7	59.0	1:09.8	1:20.9
67.5%	22-24	45-75 S	15.0	20.8	23.0	31.2	40.3	50.5	54.7	1:01.2	1:12.3	1:23.9
65.0%	25-29	45-75 S	15.6	21.6	23.8	32.4	41.9	52.4	56.8	1:03.5	1:15.1	1:27.2
62.5%	30-35	30-60 S	16.2	22.4	24.8	33.7	43.6	54.5	59.1	1:06.1	1:18.1	1:30.6
60.0%	36-40	30-60 S	16.9	23.4	25.8	35.1	45.4	56.8	1:01.5	1:08.8	1:21.4	-----

SPEED	REPS	REST	550 YD	660 YD	880 YD	1100 YD	1320 YD	1.00 MI	1.25 MI	1.50 MI	1.75 MI	2.00 MI
95.0%	0- 1	---	1:08.2	1:25.5	2:00.5	2:37.1	3:14.3	4:30.5	5:48.1	7:06.9	8:26.3	9:46.0
92.5%	1- 2	4- 5 M	1:10.0	1:27.8	2:03.8	2:41.4	3:19.5	4:37.8	5:57.5	7:18.4	8:39.9	10:01.8
90.0%	2- 3	4- 5 M	1:12.0	1:30.2	2:07.2	2:45.9	3:25.1	4:45.5	6:07.4	7:30.6	8:54.4	10:18.5
87.5%	3- 4	3- 4 M	1:14.0	1:32.8	2:10.8	2:50.6	3:30.9	4:53.7	6:17.9	7:43.5	9:09.7	10:36.2
85.0%	4- 5	3- 4 M	1:16.2	1:35.6	2:14.7	2:55.6	3:37.1	5:02.3	6:29.0	7:57.1	9:25.8	10:54.9
82.5%	6- 7	2- 3 M	1:18.5	1:38.5	2:18.8	3:00.9	3:43.7	5:11.5	6:40.8	-----	-----	-----
80.0%	8- 9	2- 3 M	1:20.9	1:41.5	2:23.1	3:06.6	3:50.7	5:21.2	-----	-----	-----	-----
77.5%	10-12	1- 2 M	1:23.6	1:44.8	2:27.7	3:12.6	3:58.1	-----	-----	-----	-----	-----
75.0%	13-15	1- 2 M	1:26.3	1:48.3	2:32.7	3:19.0	-----	-----	-----	-----	-----	-----
72.5%	16-18	60-90 S	1:29.3	1:52.0	2:37.9	-----	-----	-----	-----	-----	-----	-----
70.0%	19-21	60-90 S	1:32.5	1:56.0	2:43.6	-----	-----	-----	-----	-----	-----	-----
67.5%	22-24	45-75 S	1:35.9	2:00.3	-----	-----	-----	-----	-----	-----	-----	-----
65.0%	25-29	45-75 S	1:39.6	-----	-----	-----	-----	-----	-----	-----	-----	-----
62.5%	30-35	30-60 S	-----	-----	-----	-----	-----	-----	-----	-----	-----	-----
60.0%	36-40	30-60 S	-----	-----	-----	-----	-----	-----	-----	-----	-----	-----

820 POINT LEVEL PACING TABLE

SPEED	REPS	REST	110 YD	150 YD	165 YD	220 YD	275 YD	330 YD	352 YD	385 YD	440 YD	495 YD
95.0%	0- 1	---	10.8	14.9	16.5	22.4	28.9	36.2	39.3	43.9	51.9	1:00.3
92.5%	1- 2	4- 5 M	11.1	15.3	16.9	23.0	29.7	37.2	40.3	45.1	53.4	1:01.9
90.0%	2- 3	4- 5 M	11.4	15.7	17.4	23.6	30.6	38.2	41.4	46.4	54.8	1:03.6
87.5%	3- 4	3- 4 M	11.7	16.2	17.9	24.3	31.4	39.3	42.6	47.7	56.4	1:05.5
85.0%	4- 5	3- 4 M	12.0	16.6	18.4	25.0	32.4	40.5	43.9	49.1	58.1	1:07.4
82.5%	6- 7	2- 3 M	12.4	17.1	19.0	25.8	33.3	41.7	45.2	50.6	59.8	1:09.4
80.0%	8- 9	2- 3 M	12.8	17.7	19.6	26.6	34.4	43.0	46.6	52.2	1:01.7	1:11.6
77.5%	10-12	1- 2 M	13.2	18.3	20.2	27.4	35.5	44.4	48.1	53.9	1:03.7	1:13.9
75.0%	13-15	1- 2 M	13.6	18.9	20.9	28.3	36.7	45.9	49.7	55.7	1:05.8	1:16.4
72.5%	16-18	60-90 S	14.1	19.5	21.6	29.3	37.9	47.5	51.4	57.6	1:08.1	1:19.0
70.0%	19-21	60-90 S	14.6	20.2	22.4	30.4	39.3	49.2	53.3	59.6	1:10.5	1:21.8
67.5%	22-24	45-75 S	15.2	21.0	23.2	31.5	40.7	51.0	55.3	1:01.8	1:13.1	1:24.9
65.0%	25-29	45-75 S	15.7	21.8	24.1	32.7	42.3	52.9	57.4	1:04.2	1:15.9	1:28.1
62.5%	30-35	30-60 S	16.4	22.6	25.0	34.0	44.0	55.1	59.7	1:06.8	1:19.0	1:31.6
60.0%	36-40	30-60 S	17.1	23.6	26.1	35.4	45.8	57.4	1:02.2	1:09.6	1:22.3	-----

SPEED	REPS	REST	550 YD	660 YD	880 YD	1100 YD	1320 YD	1.00 MI	1.25 MI	1.50 MI	1.75 MI	2.00 MI
95.0%	0- 1	---	1:08.9	1:26.5	2:01.9	2:39.0	3:16.6	4:33.8	5:52.4	7:12.2	8:32.6	9:53.3
92.5%	1- 2	4- 5 M	1:10.8	1:28.8	2:05.2	2:43.3	3:21.9	4:41.2	6:01.9	7:23.9	8:46.5	10:09.4
90.0%	2- 3	4- 5 M	1:12.8	1:31.3	2:08.7	2:47.8	3:27.5	4:49.0	6:12.0	7:36.2	9:01.1	10:26.3
87.5%	3- 4	3- 4 M	1:14.8	1:33.9	2:12.4	2:52.6	3:33.5	4:57.3	6:22.6	7:49.3	9:16.5	10:44.2
85.0%	4- 5	3- 4 M	1:17.0	1:36.6	2:16.3	2:57.7	3:39.7	5:06.0	6:33.8	8:03.1	9:32.9	11:03.1
82.5%	6- 7	2- 3 M	1:19.4	1:39.6	2:20.4	3:03.1	3:46.4	5:15.3	6:45.8	-----	-----	-----
80.0%	8- 9	2- 3 M	1:21.8	1:42.7	2:24.8	3:08.8	3:53.5	5:25.1	-----	-----	-----	-----
77.5%	10-12	1- 2 M	1:24.5	1:46.0	2:29.5	3:14.9	4:01.0	-----	-----	-----	-----	-----
75.0%	13-15	1- 2 M	1:27.3	1:49.5	2:34.4	3:21.4	-----	-----	-----	-----	-----	-----
72.5%	16-18	60-90 S	1:30.3	1:53.3	2:39.8	-----	-----	-----	-----	-----	-----	-----
70.0%	19-21	60-90 S	1:33.5	1:57.4	2:45.5	-----	-----	-----	-----	-----	-----	-----
67.5%	22-24	45-75 S	1:37.0	2:01.7	-----	-----	-----	-----	-----	-----	-----	-----
65.0%	25-29	45-75 S	1:40.7	-----	-----	-----	-----	-----	-----	-----	-----	-----
62.5%	30-35	30-60 S	-----	-----	-----	-----	-----	-----	-----	-----	-----	-----
60.0%	36-40	30-60 S	-----	-----	-----	-----	-----	-----	-----	-----	-----	-----

800 POINT LEVEL PACING TABLE

SPEED	REPS	REST	110 YD	150 YD	165 YD	220 YD	275 YD	330 YD	352 YD	385 YD	440 YD	495 YD
95.0%	0- 1	----	10.9	15.0	16.6	22.6	29.2	36.6	39.7	44.4	52.5	1:01.0
92.5%	1- 2	4- 5 M	11.2	15.4	17.1	23.2	30.0	37.6	40.7	45.6	53.9	1:02.6
90.0%	2- 3	4- 5 M	11.5	15.9	17.6	23.8	30.9	38.6	41.9	46.9	55.4	1:04.3
87.5%	3- 4	3- 4 M	11.8	16.3	18.1	24.5	31.7	39.7	43.1	48.2	57.0	1:06.2
85.0%	4- 5	3- 4 M	12.2	16.8	18.6	25.2	32.7	40.9	44.3	49.6	58.7	1:08.1
82.5%	6- 7	2- 3 M	12.5	17.3	19.1	26.0	33.7	42.1	45.7	51.1	1:00.5	1:10.2
80.0%	8- 9	2- 3 M	12.9	17.9	19.7	26.8	34.7	43.5	47.1	52.7	1:02.4	1:12.4
77.5%	10-12	1- 2 M	13.3	18.4	20.4	27.7	35.8	44.9	48.6	54.4	1:04.4	1:14.7
75.0%	13-15	1- 2 M	13.8	19.0	21.1	28.6	37.0	46.4	50.3	56.3	1:06.5	1:17.2
72.5%	16-18	60-90 S	14.3	19.7	21.8	29.6	38.3	48.0	52.0	58.2	1:08.8	1:19.9
70.0%	19-21	60-90 S	14.8	20.4	22.6	30.7	39.7	49.7	53.8	1:00.3	1:11.3	1:22.7
67.5%	22-24	45-75 S	15.3	21.2	23.4	31.8	41.2	51.5	55.8	1:02.5	1:13.9	1:25.8
65.0%	25-29	45-75 S	15.9	22.0	24.3	33.0	42.7	53.5	58.0	1:04.9	1:16.8	1:29.1
62.5%	30-35	30-60 S	16.5	22.9	25.3	34.3	44.4	55.6	1:00.3	1:07.5	1:19.8	1:32.7
60.0%	36-40	30-60 S	17.2	23.8	26.3	35.8	46.3	58.0	1:02.8	1:10.3	1:23.1	-----

SPEED	REPS	REST	550 YD	660 YD	880 YD	1100 YD	1320 YD	1.00 MI	1.25 MI	1.50 MI	1.75 MI	2.00 MI
95.0%	0- 1	----	1:09.7	1:27.5	2:03.4	2:40.9	3:19.0	4:37.2	5:56.8	7:17.7	8:39.1	10:00.9
92.5%	1- 2	4- 5 M	1:11.6	1:29.8	2:06.7	2:45.3	3:24.4	4:44.7	6:06.4	7:29.5	8:53.1	10:17.1
90.0%	2- 3	4- 5 M	1:13.6	1:32.3	2:10.2	2:49.8	3:30.1	4:52.6	6:16.6	7:42.0	9:07.9	10:34.3
87.5%	3- 4	3- 4 M	1:15.7	1:35.0	2:13.9	2:54.7	3:36.1	5:01.0	6:27.4	7:55.2	9:23.6	10:52.4
85.0%	4- 5	3- 4 M	1:17.9	1:37.8	2:17.9	2:59.8	3:42.4	5:09.8	6:38.8	8:09.2	9:40.2	11:11.6
82.5%	6- 7	2- 3 M	1:20.3	1:40.7	2:22.1	3:05.3	3:49.1	5:19.2	6:50.8	-----	-----	-----
80.0%	8- 9	2- 3 M	1:22.8	1:43.9	2:26.5	3:11.1	3:56.3	5:29.2	-----	-----	-----	-----
77.5%	10-12	1- 2 M	1:25.4	1:47.2	2:31.2	3:17.2	4:03.9	-----	-----	-----	-----	-----
75.0%	13-15	1- 2 M	1:28.3	1:50.8	2:36.3	3:23.8	-----	-----	-----	-----	-----	-----
72.5%	16-18	60-90 S	1:31.3	1:54.6	2:41.6	-----	-----	-----	-----	-----	-----	-----
70.0%	19-21	60-90 S	1:34.6	1:58.7	2:47.4	-----	-----	-----	-----	-----	-----	-----
67.5%	22-24	45-75 S	1:38.1	2:03.1	-----	-----	-----	-----	-----	-----	-----	-----
65.0%	25-29	45-75 S	1:41.9	-----	-----	-----	-----	-----	-----	-----	-----	-----
62.5%	30-35	30-60 S	-----	-----	-----	-----	-----	-----	-----	-----	-----	-----
60.0%	36-40	30-60 S	-----	-----	-----	-----	-----	-----	-----	-----	-----	-----

780 POINT LEVEL PACING TABLE
•••••••••••••••••••••••••••••••

SPEED	REPS	REST	110 YD	150 YD	165 YD	220 YD	275 YD	330 YD	352 YD	385 YD	440 YD	495 YD
95.0%	0- 1	---	11.0	15.2	16.8	22.8	29.5	37.0	40.1	44.9	53.1	1:01.6
92.5%	1- 2	4- 5 M	11.3	15.6	17.2	23.4	30.3	38.0	41.2	46.1	54.5	1:03.3
90.0%	2- 3	4- 5 M	11.6	16.0	17.7	24.1	31.2	39.0	42.3	47.4	56.0	1:05.1
87.5%	3- 4	3- 4 M	11.9	16.5	18.2	24.8	32.1	40.2	43.5	48.7	57.6	1:06.9
85.0%	4- 5	3- 4 M	12.3	17.0	18.8	25.5	33.0	41.3	44.8	50.2	59.3	1:08.9
82.5%	6- 7	2- 3 M	12.6	17.5	19.3	26.3	34.0	42.6	46.2	51.7	1:01.1	1:11.0
80.0%	8- 9	2- 3 M	13.0	18.0	19.9	27.1	35.1	43.9	47.6	53.3	1:03.0	1:13.2
77.5%	10-12	1- 2 M	13.5	18.6	20.6	28.0	36.2	45.3	49.2	55.0	1:05.1	1:15.6
75.0%	13-15	1- 2 M	13.9	19.2	21.3	28.9	37.4	46.9	50.8	56.9	1:07.3	1:18.1
72.5%	16-18	60-90 S	14.4	19.9	22.0	29.9	38.7	48.5	52.5	58.8	1:09.6	1:20.8
70.0%	19-21	60-90 S	14.9	20.6	22.8	31.0	40.1	50.2	54.4	1:00.9	1:12.1	1:23.7
67.5%	22-24	45-75 S	15.5	21.4	23.6	32.1	41.6	52.1	56.4	1:03.2	1:14.7	1:26.8
65.0%	25-29	45-75 S	16.0	22.2	24.5	33.3	43.2	54.1	58.6	1:05.6	1:17.6	1:30.1
62.5%	30-35	30-60 S	16.7	23.1	25.5	34.7	44.9	56.2	1:00.9	1:08.2	1:20.7	1:33.7
60.0%	36-40	30-60 S	17.4	24.0	26.6	36.1	46.8	58.6	1:03.5	1:11.1	1:24.1	-----

SPEED	REPS	REST	550 YD	660 YD	880 YD	1100 YD	1320 YD	1.00 MI	1.25 MI	1.50 MI	1.75 MI	2.00 MI
95.0%	0- 1	---	1:10.5	1:28.5	2:04.8	2:42.9	3:21.5	4:40.7	6:01.3	7:23.3	8:45.8	10:08.7
92.5%	1- 2	4- 5 M	1:12.4	1:30.9	2:08.2	2:47.3	3:26.9	4:48.3	6:11.1	7:35.2	9:00.0	10:25.1
90.0%	2- 3	4- 5 M	1:14.4	1:33.4	2:11.8	2:51.9	3:32.6	4:56.3	6:21.4	7:47.9	9:15.0	10:42.5
87.5%	3- 4	3- 4 M	1:16.5	1:36.1	2:15.5	2:56.8	3:38.7	5:04.7	6:32.3	8:01.3	9:30.8	11:00.8
85.0%	4- 5	3- 4 M	1:18.8	1:38.9	2:19.5	3:02.0	3:45.2	5:13.7	6:43.8	8:15.4	9:47.6	11:20.3
82.5%	6- 7	2- 3 M	1:21.2	1:41.9	2:23.7	3:07.5	3:52.0	5:23.2	6:56.1	-----	-----	-----
80.0%	8- 9	2- 3 M	1:23.7	1:45.1	2:28.2	3:13.4	3:59.2	5:33.3	-----	-----	-----	-----
77.5%	10-12	1- 2 M	1:26.4	1:48.5	2:33.0	3:19.6	4:06.9	-----	-----	-----	-----	-----
75.0%	13-15	1- 2 M	1:29.3	1:52.1	2:38.1	3:26.3	-----	-----	-----	-----	-----	-----
72.5%	16-18	60-90 S	1:32.4	1:55.9	2:43.6	-----	-----	-----	-----	-----	-----	-----
70.0%	19-21	60-90 S	1:35.7	2:00.1	2:49.4	-----	-----	-----	-----	-----	-----	-----
67.5%	22-24	45-75 S	1:39.2	2:04.5	-----	-----	-----	-----	-----	-----	-----	-----
65.0%	25-29	45-75 S	1:43.0	-----	-----	-----	-----	-----	-----	-----	-----	-----
62.5%	30-35	30-60 S	-----	-----	-----	-----	-----	-----	-----	-----	-----	-----
60.0%	36-40	30-60 S	-----	-----	-----	-----	-----	-----	-----	-----	-----	-----

760 POINT LEVEL PACING TABLE
....

SPEED	REPS	REST	110 YD	150 YD	165 YD	220 YD	275 YD	330 YD	352 YD	385 YD	440 YD	495 YD
95.0%	0- 1	----	11.1	15.3	17.0	23.0	29.8	37.4	40.5	45.4	53.7	1:02.3
92.5%	1- 2	4- 5 M	11.4	15.7	17.4	23.7	30.7	38.4	41.6	46.6	55.1	1:04.0
90.0%	2- 3	4- 5 M	11.7	16.2	17.9	24.3	31.5	39.5	42.8	47.9	56.7	1:05.8
87.5%	3- 4	3- 4 M	12.0	16.6	18.4	25.0	32.4	40.6	44.0	49.3	58.3	1:07.7
85.0%	4- 5	3- 4 M	12.4	17.1	18.9	25.8	33.4	41.8	45.3	50.7	1:00.0	1:09.7
82.5%	6- 7	2- 3 M	12.8	17.6	19.5	26.5	34.4	43.0	46.7	52.3	1:01.8	1:11.8
80.0%	8- 9	2- 3 M	13.2	18.2	20.1	27.4	35.4	44.4	48.1	53.9	1:03.7	1:14.0
77.5%	10-12	1- 2 M	13.6	18.8	20.8	28.2	36.6	45.8	49.7	55.6	1:05.8	1:16.4
75.0%	13-15	1- 2 M	14.0	19.4	21.5	29.2	37.8	47.3	51.3	57.5	1:08.0	1:19.0
72.5%	16-18	60-90 S	14.5	20.1	22.2	30.2	39.1	49.0	53.1	59.5	1:10.3	1:21.7
70.0%	19-21	60-90 S	15.0	20.8	23.0	31.3	40.5	50.7	55.0	1:01.6	1:12.9	1:24.6
67.5%	22-24	45-75 S	15.6	21.6	23.9	32.4	42.0	52.6	57.0	1:03.9	1:15.6	1:27.7
65.0%	25-29	45-75 S	16.2	22.4	24.8	33.7	43.6	54.6	59.2	1:06.3	1:18.5	1:31.1
62.5%	30-35	30-60 S	16.8	23.3	25.8	35.0	45.4	56.8	1:01.6	1:09.0	1:21.6	1:34.8
60.0%	36-40	30-60 S	17.6	24.3	26.8	36.5	47.3	59.2	1:04.2	1:11.8	1:25.0	-----

SPEED	REPS	REST	550 YD	660 YD	880 YD	1100 YD	1320 YD	1.00 MI	1.25 MI	1.50 MI	1.75 MI	2.00 MI
95.0%	0- 1	----	1:11.3	1:29.5	2:06.3	2:44.9	3:24.0	4:44.2	6:05.9	7:29.0	8:52.6	10:16.6
92.5%	1- 2	4- 5 M	1:13.2	1:31.9	2:09.8	2:49.3	3:29.5	4:51.9	6:15.8	7:41.1	9:07.0	10:33.3
90.0%	2- 3	4- 5 M	1:15.3	1:34.5	2:13.4	2:54.0	3:35.3	5:00.0	6:26.3	7:53.9	9:22.2	10:50.9
87.5%	3- 4	3- 4 M	1:17.4	1:37.2	2:17.2	2:59.0	3:41.4	5:08.6	6:37.3	8:07.5	9:38.3	11:09.5
85.0%	4- 5	3- 4 M	1:19.7	1:40.1	2:21.2	3:04.3	3:48.0	5:17.7	6:49.0	8:21.8	9:55.3	11:29.2
82.5%	6- 7	2- 3 M	1:22.1	1:43.1	2:25.5	3:09.9	3:54.9	5:27.3	7:01.4	-----	-----	-----
80.0%	8- 9	2- 3 M	1:24.7	1:46.3	2:30.0	3:15.8	4:02.2	5:37.5	-----	-----	-----	-----
77.5%	10-12	1- 2 M	1:27.4	1:49.7	2:34.9	3:22.1	4:10.0	-----	-----	-----	-----	-----
75.0%	13-15	1- 2 M	1:30.3	1:53.4	2:40.0	3:28.8	4:18.4	-----	-----	-----	-----	-----
72.5%	16-18	60-90 S	1:33.4	1:57.3	2:45.6	-----	-----	-----	-----	-----	-----	-----
70.0%	19-21	60-90 S	1:36.8	2:01.5	2:51.5	-----	-----	-----	-----	-----	-----	-----
67.5%	22-24	45-75 S	1:40.4	2:06.0	-----	-----	-----	-----	-----	-----	-----	-----
65.0%	25-29	45-75 S	1:44.2	-----	-----	-----	-----	-----	-----	-----	-----	-----
62.5%	30-35	30-60 S	-----	-----	-----	-----	-----	-----	-----	-----	-----	-----
60.0%	36-40	30-60 S	-----	-----	-----	-----	-----	-----	-----	-----	-----	-----

740 POINT LEVEL PACING TABLE
•••••••••••••••••••••••••••••

SPEED	REPS	REST	110 YD	150 YD	165 YD	220 YD	275 YD	330 YD	352 YD	385 YD	440 YD	495 YD
95.0%	0- 1	---	11.2	15.5	17.1	23.3	30.2	37.8	41.0	45.9	54.3	1:03.1
92.5%	1- 2	4- 5 M	11.5	15.9	17.6	23.9	31.0	38.8	42.1	47.1	55.8	1:04.8
90.0%	2- 3	4- 5 M	11.8	16.3	18.1	24.6	31.8	39.9	43.2	48.4	57.3	1:06.6
87.5%	3- 4	3- 4 M	12.2	16.8	18.6	25.3	32.7	41.0	44.5	49.8	58.9	1:08.5
85.0%	4- 5	3- 4 M	12.5	17.3	19.1	26.0	33.7	42.2	45.8	51.3	1:00.7	1:10.5
82.5%	6- 7	2- 3 M	12.9	17.8	19.7	26.8	34.7	43.5	47.2	52.8	1:02.5	1:12.6
80.0%	8- 9	2- 3 M	13.3	18.4	20.3	27.6	35.8	44.9	48.6	54.5	1:04.5	1:14.9
77.5%	10-12	1- 2 M	13.7	19.0	21.0	28.5	37.0	46.3	50.2	56.2	1:06.5	1:17.3
75.0%	13-15	1- 2 M	14.2	19.6	21.7	29.5	38.2	47.9	51.9	58.1	1:08.8	1:19.9
72.5%	16-18	60-90 S	14.7	20.3	22.4	30.5	39.5	49.5	53.7	1:00.1	1:11.1	1:22.6
70.0%	19-21	60-90 S	15.2	21.0	23.2	31.6	40.9	51.3	55.6	1:02.3	1:13.7	1:25.6
67.5%	22-24	45-75 S	15.8	21.8	24.1	32.8	42.4	53.2	57.7	1:04.6	1:16.4	1:28.7
65.0%	25-29	45-75 S	16.4	22.6	25.0	34.0	44.1	55.2	59.9	1:07.0	1:19.3	1:32.2
62.5%	30-35	30-60 S	17.0	23.5	26.0	35.4	45.8	57.4	1:02.3	1:09.7	1:22.5	1:35.8
60.0%	36-40	30-60 S	17.7	24.5	27.1	36.9	47.7	59.8	1:04.9	1:12.6	1:26.0	-----

SPEED	REPS	REST	550 YD	660 YD	880 YD	1100 YD	1320 YD	1.00 MI	1.25 MI	1.50 MI	1.75 MI	2.00 MI
95.0%	0- 1	---	1:12.1	1:30.6	2:07.9	2:46.9	3:26.5	4:47.9	6:10.7	7:34.9	8:59.7	10:24.8
92.5%	1- 2	4- 5 M	1:14.1	1:33.0	2:11.3	2:51.4	3:32.1	4:55.7	6:20.7	7:47.2	9:14.2	10:41.7
90.0%	2- 3	4- 5 M	1:16.1	1:35.6	2:15.0	2:56.2	3:38.0	5:03.9	6:31.3	8:00.2	9:29.6	10:59.5
87.5%	3- 4	3- 4 M	1:18.3	1:38.4	2:18.9	3:01.2	3:44.2	5:12.6	6:42.5	8:13.9	9:45.9	11:18.3
85.0%	4- 5	3- 4 M	1:20.6	1:41.2	2:22.9	3:06.6	3:50.8	5:21.8	6:54.3	8:28.4	10:03.1	11:38.3
82.5%	6- 7	2- 3 M	1:23.1	1:44.3	2:27.3	3:12.2	3:57.8	5:31.5	7:06.9	-----	-----	-----
80.0%	8- 9	2- 3 M	1:25.7	1:47.6	2:31.9	3:18.2	4:05.3	5:41.9	-----	-----	-----	-----
77.5%	10-12	1- 2 M	1:28.4	1:51.0	2:36.8	3:24.6	4:13.2	-----	-----	-----	-----	-----
75.0%	13-15	1- 2 M	1:31.4	1:54.7	2:42.0	3:31.4	4:21.6	-----	-----	-----	-----	-----
72.5%	16-18	60-90 S	1:34.5	1:58.7	2:47.6	-----	-----	-----	-----	-----	-----	-----
70.0%	19-21	60-90 S	1:37.9	2:02.9	2:53.6	-----	-----	-----	-----	-----	-----	-----
67.5%	22-24	45-75 S	1:41.5	2:07.5	-----	-----	-----	-----	-----	-----	-----	-----
65.0%	25-29	45-75 S	1:45.4	-----	-----	-----	-----	-----	-----	-----	-----	-----
62.5%	30-35	30-60 S	-----	-----	-----	-----	-----	-----	-----	-----	-----	-----
60.0%	36-40	30-60 S	-----	-----	-----	-----	-----	-----	-----	-----	-----	-----

720 POINT LEVEL PACING TABLE

SPEED	REPS	REST	110 YD	150 YD	165 YD	220 YD	275 YD	330 YD	352 YD	385 YD	440 YD	495 YD
95.0%	0- 1	---	11.3	15.6	17.3	23.5	30.5	38.2	41.4	46.4	54.9	1:03.8
92.5%	1- 2	4- 5 M	11.6	16.1	17.8	24.2	31.3	39.2	42.5	47.6	56.4	1:05.5
90.0%	2- 3	4- 5 M	11.9	16.5	18.3	24.8	32.2	40.3	43.7	49.0	58.0	1:07.3
87.5%	3- 4	3- 4 M	12.3	17.0	18.8	25.5	33.1	41.5	45.0	50.4	59.6	1:09.3
85.0%	4- 5	3- 4 M	12.6	17.5	19.3	26.3	34.1	42.7	46.3	51.8	1:01.4	1:11.3
82.5%	6- 7	2- 3 M	13.0	18.0	19.9	27.1	35.1	44.0	47.7	53.4	1:03.2	1:13.4
80.0%	8- 9	2- 3 M	13.4	18.6	20.5	27.9	36.2	45.4	49.2	55.1	1:05.2	1:15.7
77.5%	10-12	1- 2 M	13.9	19.2	21.2	28.8	37.4	46.8	50.8	56.9	1:07.3	1:18.2
75.0%	13-15	1- 2 M	14.3	19.8	21.9	29.8	38.6	48.4	52.5	58.8	1:09.5	1:20.8
72.5%	16-18	60-90 S	14.8	20.5	22.7	30.8	39.9	50.0	54.3	1:00.8	1:11.9	1:23.6
70.0%	19-21	60-90 S	15.3	21.2	23.5	31.9	41.4	51.8	56.2	1:03.0	1:14.5	1:26.6
67.5%	22-24	45-75 S	15.9	22.0	24.3	33.1	42.9	53.8	58.3	1:05.3	1:17.3	1:29.8
65.0%	25-29	45-75 S	16.5	22.8	25.3	34.4	44.5	55.8	1:00.5	1:07.8	1:20.2	1:33.2
62.5%	30-35	30-60 S	17.2	23.8	26.3	35.7	46.3	58.1	1:03.0	1:10.5	1:23.5	1:37.0
60.0%	36-40	30-60 S	17.9	24.7	27.4	37.2	48.3	1:00.5	1:05.6	1:13.4	1:26.9	-----

SPEED	REPS	REST	550 YD	660 YD	880 YD	1100 YD	1320 YD	1.00 MI	1.25 MI	1.50 MI	1.75 MI	2.00 MI
95.0%	0- 1	---	1:13.0	1:31.7	2:09.5	2:49.0	3:29.2	4:51.6	6:15.6	7:40.9	9:06.9	10:33.2
92.5%	1- 2	4- 5 M	1:15.0	1:34.2	2:13.0	2:53.6	3:34.8	4:59.5	6:25.7	7:53.4	9:21.6	10:50.3
90.0%	2- 3	4- 5 M	1:17.0	1:36.8	2:16.7	2:58.4	3:40.8	5:07.8	6:36.5	8:06.5	9:37.2	11:08.4
87.5%	3- 4	3- 4 M	1:19.2	1:39.5	2:20.6	3:03.5	3:47.1	5:16.6	6:47.8	8:20.4	9:53.7	11:27.5
85.0%	4- 5	3- 4 M	1:21.6	1:42.5	2:24.7	3:08.9	3:53.8	5:25.9	6:59.8	8:35.2	10:11.2	11:47.7
82.5%	6- 7	2- 3 M	1:24.0	1:45.6	2:29.1	3:14.6	4:00.9	5:35.8	7:12.5	-----	-----	-----
80.0%	8- 9	2- 3 M	1:26.7	1:48.9	2:33.8	3:20.7	4:08.4	5:46.3	-----	-----	-----	-----
77.5%	10-12	1- 2 M	1:29.5	1:52.4	2:38.7	3:27.2	4:16.4	-----	-----	-----	-----	-----
75.0%	13-15	1- 2 M	1:32.4	1:56.1	2:44.0	3:34.1	4:25.0	-----	-----	-----	-----	-----
72.5%	16-18	60-90 S	1:35.6	2:00.1	2:49.7	-----	-----	-----	-----	-----	-----	-----
70.0%	19-21	60-90 S	1:39.0	2:04.4	2:55.7	-----	-----	-----	-----	-----	-----	-----
67.5%	22-24	45-75 S	1:42.7	2:09.0	-----	-----	-----	-----	-----	-----	-----	-----
65.0%	25-29	45-75 S	1:46.7	-----	-----	-----	-----	-----	-----	-----	-----	-----
62.5%	30-35	30-60 S	-----	-----	-----	-----	-----	-----	-----	-----	-----	-----
60.0%	36-40	30-60 S	-----	-----	-----	-----	-----	-----	-----	-----	-----	-----

700 POINT LEVEL PACING TABLE
....

SPEED	REPS	REST	110 YD	150 YD	165 YD	220 YD	275 YD	330 YD	352 YD	385 YD	440 YD	495 YD
95.0%	0- 1	----	11.4	15.8	17.5	23.8	30.8	38.6	41.9	46.9	55.5	1:04.5
92.5%	1- 2	4- 5 M	11.7	16.2	17.9	24.4	31.6	39.7	43.0	48.2	57.0	1:06.3
90.0%	2- 3	4- 5 M	12.0	16.7	18.4	25.1	32.5	40.8	44.2	49.5	58.6	1:08.1
87.5%	3- 4	3- 4 M	12.4	17.1	19.0	25.8	33.4	41.9	45.5	50.9	1:00.3	1:10.1
85.0%	4- 5	3- 4 M	12.8	17.6	19.5	26.6	34.4	43.2	46.8	52.4	1:02.1	1:12.1
82.5%	6- 7	2- 3 M	13.1	18.2	20.1	27.4	35.5	44.5	48.2	54.0	1:04.0	1:14.3
80.0%	8- 9	2- 3 M	13.6	18.7	20.7	28.2	36.6	45.9	49.7	55.7	1:06.0	1:16.6
77.5%	10-12	1- 2 M	14.0	19.4	21.4	29.1	37.8	47.3	51.3	57.5	1:08.1	1:19.1
75.0%	13-15	1- 2 M	14.5	20.0	22.1	30.1	39.0	48.9	53.0	59.4	1:10.3	1:21.7
72.5%	16-18	60-90 S	15.0	20.7	22.9	31.1	40.4	50.6	54.9	1:01.5	1:12.8	1:24.6
70.0%	19-21	60-90 S	15.5	21.4	23.7	32.2	41.8	52.4	56.8	1:03.7	1:15.4	1:27.6
67.5%	22-24	45-75 S	16.1	22.2	24.6	33.4	43.3	54.3	58.9	1:06.0	1:18.2	1:30.8
65.0%	25-29	45-75 S	16.7	23.1	25.5	34.7	45.0	56.4	1:01.2	1:08.6	1:21.2	1:34.3
62.5%	30-35	30-60 S	17.3	24.0	26.5	36.1	46.8	58.7	1:03.7	1:11.3	1:24.4	1:38.1
60.0%	36-40	30-60 S	18.1	25.0	27.7	37.6	48.8	1:01.1	1:06.3	1:14.3	1:27.9	-----

SPEED	REPS	REST	550 YD	660 YD	880 YD	1100 YD	1320 YD	1.00 MI	1.25 MI	1.50 MI	1.75 MI	2.00 MI
95.0%	0- 1	---	1:13.9	1:32.8	2:11.1	2:51.2	3:31.9	4:55.5	6:20.6	7:47.1	9:14.3	10:41.8
92.5%	1- 2	4- 5 M	1:15.8	1:35.3	2:14.6	2:55.8	3:37.6	5:03.5	6:30.9	7:59.8	9:29.3	10:59.2
90.0%	2- 3	4- 5 M	1:18.0	1:38.0	2:18.4	3:00.7	3:43.7	5:11.9	6:41.8	8:13.1	9:45.1	11:17.5
87.5%	3- 4	3- 4 M	1:20.2	1:40.8	2:22.3	3:05.9	3:50.1	5:20.8	6:53.2	8:27.2	10:01.8	11:36.8
85.0%	4- 5	3- 4 M	1:22.5	1:43.7	2:26.5	3:11.3	3:56.8	5:30.2	7:05.4	8:42.1	10:19.5	11:57.3
82.5%	6- 7	2- 3 M	1:25.0	1:46.9	2:31.0	3:17.1	4:04.0	5:40.2	7:18.3	8:57.9	-----	-----
80.0%	8- 9	2- 3 M	1:27.7	1:50.2	2:35.7	3:23.3	4:11.6	5:50.9	-----	-----	-----	-----
77.5%	10-12	1- 2 M	1:30.5	1:53.8	2:40.7	3:29.9	4:19.7	-----	-----	-----	-----	-----
75.0%	13-15	1- 2 M	1:33.5	1:57.5	2:46.1	3:36.9	4:28.4	-----	-----	-----	-----	-----
72.5%	16-18	60-90 S	1:36.8	2:01.6	2:51.8	-----	-----	-----	-----	-----	-----	-----
70.0%	19-21	60-90 S	1:40.2	2:05.9	2:57.9	-----	-----	-----	-----	-----	-----	-----
67.5%	22-24	45-75 S	1:43.9	2:10.6	-----	-----	-----	-----	-----	-----	-----	-----
65.0%	25-29	45-75 S	1:47.9	-----	-----	-----	-----	-----	-----	-----	-----	-----
62.5%	30-35	30-60 S	-----	-----	-----	-----	-----	-----	-----	-----	-----	-----
60.0%	36-40	30-60 S	-----	-----	-----	-----	-----	-----	-----	-----	-----	-----

163

680 POINT LEVEL PACING TABLE
••••••••••••••••••••••••••••

SPEED	REPS	REST	110 YD	150 YD	165 YD	220 YD	275 YD	330 YD	352 YD	385 YD	440 YD	495 YD
95.0%	0- 1	---	11.5	15.9	17.6	24.0	31.1	39.0	42.3	47.4	56.2	1:05.3
92.5%	1- 2	4- 5 M	11.8	16.4	18.1	24.7	32.0	40.1	43.5	48.7	57.7	1:07.1
90.0%	2- 3	4- 5 M	12.2	16.8	18.6	25.3	32.9	41.2	44.7	50.1	59.3	1:08.9
87.5%	3- 4	3- 4 M	12.5	17.3	19.2	26.1	33.8	42.4	46.0	51.5	1:01.0	1:10.9
85.0%	4- 5	3- 4 M	12.9	17.8	19.7	26.8	34.8	43.6	47.3	53.0	1:02.8	1:13.0
82.5%	6- 7	2- 3 M	13.3	18.4	20.3	27.6	35.8	45.0	48.8	54.6	1:04.7	1:15.2
80.0%	8- 9	2- 3 M	13.7	18.9	21.0	28.5	37.0	46.4	50.3	56.3	1:06.7	1:17.5
77.5%	10-12	1- 2 M	14.1	19.5	21.6	29.4	38.2	47.9	51.9	58.2	1:08.9	1:20.0
75.0%	13-15	1- 2 M	14.6	20.2	22.3	30.4	39.4	49.5	53.6	1:00.1	1:11.2	1:22.7
72.5%	16-18	60-90 S	15.1	20.9	23.1	31.5	40.8	51.2	55.5	1:02.2	1:13.6	1:25.6
70.0%	19-21	60-90 S	15.6	21.6	23.9	32.6	42.3	53.0	57.5	1:04.4	1:16.2	1:28.6
67.5%	22-24	45-75 S	16.2	22.4	24.8	33.8	43.8	54.9	59.6	1:06.8	1:19.1	1:31.9
65.0%	25-29	45-75 S	16.8	23.3	25.8	35.1	45.5	57.1	1:01.9	1:09.3	1:22.1	1:35.4
62.5%	30-35	30-60 S	17.5	24.2	26.8	36.5	47.3	59.3	1:04.4	1:12.1	1:25.4	1:39.3
60.0%	36-40	30-60 S	18.3	25.2	27.9	38.0	49.3	1:01.8	1:07.0	1:15.1	1:29.0	-----

SPEED	REPS	REST	550 YD	660 YD	880 YD	1100 YD	1320 YD	1.00 MI	1.25 MI	1.50 MI	1.75 MI	2.00 MI
95.0%	0- 1	---	1:14.7	1:33.9	2:12.8	2:53.4	3:34.7	4:59.4	6:25.8	7:53.5	9:21.9	10:50.7
92.5%	1- 2	4- 5 M	1:16.8	1:36.5	2:16.4	2:58.1	3:40.5	5:07.5	6:36.2	8:06.3	9:37.1	11:08.2
90.0%	2- 3	4- 5 M	1:18.9	1:39.2	2:20.1	3:03.1	3:46.6	5:16.1	6:47.2	8:19.8	9:53.1	11:26.8
87.5%	3- 4	3- 4 M	1:21.1	1:42.0	2:24.1	3:08.3	3:53.1	5:25.1	6:58.8	8:34.1	10:10.0	11:46.4
85.0%	4- 5	3- 4 M	1:23.5	1:45.0	2:28.4	3:13.8	3:59.9	5:34.7	7:11.1	8:49.2	10:28.0	12:07.2
82.5%	6- 7	2- 3 M	1:26.1	1:48.2	2:32.9	3:19.7	4:07.2	5:44.8	7:24.2	9:05.3	-----	-----
80.0%	8- 9	2- 3 M	1:28.8	1:51.6	2:37.7	3:25.9	4:14.9	5:55.6	-----	-----	-----	-----
77.5%	10-12	1- 2 M	1:31.6	1:55.2	2:42.7	3:32.6	4:23.2	-----	-----	-----	-----	-----
75.0%	13-15	1- 2 M	1:34.7	1:59.0	2:48.2	3:39.7	4:31.9	-----	-----	-----	-----	-----
72.5%	16-18	60-90 S	1:37.9	2:03.1	2:54.0	3:47.2	-----	-----	-----	-----	-----	-----
70.0%	19-21	60-90 S	1:41.4	2:07.5	3:00.2	-----	-----	-----	-----	-----	-----	-----
67.5%	22-24	45-75 S	1:45.2	2:12.2	-----	-----	-----	-----	-----	-----	-----	-----
65.0%	25-29	45-75 S	1:49.2	-----	-----	-----	-----	-----	-----	-----	-----	-----
62.5%	30-35	30-60 S	1:53.6	-----	-----	-----	-----	-----	-----	-----	-----	-----
60.0%	36-40	30-60 S	-----	-----	-----	-----	-----	-----	-----	-----	-----	-----

660 POINT LEVEL PACING TABLE
....

SPEED	REPS	REST	110 YD	150 YD	165 YD	220 YD	275 YD	330 YD	352 YD	385 YD	440 YD	495 YD
95.0%	0- 1	---	11.6	16.1	17.8	24.3	31.5	39.5	42.8	48.0	56.8	1:06.1
92.5%	1- 2	4- 5 M	12.0	16.5	18.3	24.9	32.3	40.5	44.0	49.3	58.4	1:07.9
90.0%	2- 3	4- 5 M	12.3	17.0	18.8	25.6	33.2	41.7	45.2	50.7	1:00.0	1:09.8
87.5%	3- 4	3- 4 M	12.6	17.5	19.4	26.3	34.2	42.9	46.5	52.1	1:01.7	1:11.7
85.0%	4- 5	3- 4 M	13.0	18.0	19.9	27.1	35.2	44.1	47.9	53.6	1:03.5	1:13.9
82.5%	6- 7	2- 3 M	13.4	18.6	20.5	27.9	36.2	45.5	49.3	55.3	1:05.5	1:16.1
80.0%	8- 9	2- 3 M	13.8	19.1	21.2	28.8	37.4	46.9	50.9	57.0	1:07.5	1:18.5
77.5%	10-12	1- 2 M	14.3	19.7	21.9	29.7	38.6	48.4	52.5	58.8	1:09.7	1:21.0
75.0%	13-15	1- 2 M	14.7	20.4	22.6	30.7	39.9	50.0	54.2	1:00.8	1:12.0	1:23.7
72.5%	16-18	60-90 S	15.3	21.1	23.4	31.8	41.2	51.7	56.1	1:02.9	1:14.5	1:26.6
70.0%	19-21	60-90 S	15.8	21.9	24.2	32.9	42.7	53.6	58.1	1:05.1	1:17.1	1:29.7
67.5%	22-24	45-75 S	16.4	22.7	25.1	34.1	44.3	55.6	1:00.3	1:07.5	1:20.0	1:33.0
65.0%	25-29	45-75 S	17.0	23.5	26.1	35.5	46.0	57.7	1:02.6	1:10.1	1:23.1	1:36.6
62.5%	30-35	30-60 S	17.7	24.5	27.1	36.9	47.8	1:00.0	1:05.1	1:12.9	1:26.4	1:40.4
60.0%	36-40	30-60 S	18.4	25.5	28.2	38.4	49.8	1:02.5	1:07.8	1:16.0	1:30.0	-----

SPEED	REPS	REST	550 YD	660 YD	880 YD	1100 YD	1320 YD	1.00 MI	1.25 MI	1.50 MI	1.75 MI	2.00 MI
95.0%	0- 1	---	1:15.7	1:35.1	2:14.5	2:55.7	3:37.5	5:03.5	6:31.1	8:00.1	9:29.7	10:59.8
92.5%	1- 2	4- 5 M	1:17.7	1:37.7	2:18.1	3:00.4	3:43.4	5:11.7	6:41.6	8:13.0	9:45.1	11:17.6
90.0%	2- 3	4- 5 M	1:19.9	1:40.4	2:21.9	3:05.5	3:49.6	5:20.3	6:52.8	8:26.7	10:01.4	11:36.4
87.5%	3- 4	3- 4 M	1:22.1	1:43.3	2:26.0	3:10.8	3:56.2	5:29.5	7:04.6	8:41.2	10:18.5	11:56.3
85.0%	4- 5	3- 4 M	1:24.6	1:46.3	2:30.3	3:16.4	4:03.1	5:39.2	7:17.1	8:56.5	10:36.7	12:17.4
82.5%	6- 7	2- 3 M	1:27.1	1:49.5	2:34.8	3:22.3	4:10.5	5:49.5	7:30.3	9:12.8	-----	-----
80.0%	8- 9	2- 3 M	1:29.8	1:53.0	2:39.7	3:28.6	4:18.3	6:00.4	-----	-----	-----	-----
77.5%	10-12	1- 2 M	1:32.7	1:56.6	2:44.8	3:35.4	4:26.7	-----	-----	-----	-----	-----
75.0%	13-15	1- 2 M	1:35.8	2:00.5	2:50.3	3:42.5	4:35.5	-----	-----	-----	-----	-----
72.5%	16-18	60-90 S	1:39.1	2:04.6	2:56.2	3:50.2	-----	-----	-----	-----	-----	-----
70.0%	19-21	60-90 S	1:42.7	2:09.1	3:02.5	-----	-----	-----	-----	-----	-----	-----
67.5%	22-24	45-75 S	1:46.5	2:13.9	-----	-----	-----	-----	-----	-----	-----	-----
65.0%	25-29	45-75 S	1:50.6	-----	-----	-----	-----	-----	-----	-----	-----	-----
62.5%	30-35	30-60 S	1:55.0	-----	-----	-----	-----	-----	-----	-----	-----	-----
60.0%	36-40	30-60 S	-----	-----	-----	-----	-----	-----	-----	-----	-----	-----

640 POINT LEVEL PACING TABLE
●●●●●●●●●●●●●●●●●●●●●●●●●●

SPEED	REPS	REST	110 YD	150 YD	165 YD	220 YD	275 YD	330 YD	352 YD	385 YD	440 YD	495 YD
95.0%	0- 1	---	11.8	16.3	18.0	24.5	31.8	39.9	43.3	48.5	57.5	1:06.9
92.5%	1- 2	4- 5 M	12.1	16.7	18.5	25.2	32.7	41.0	44.5	49.9	59.1	1:08.7
90.0%	2- 3	4- 5 M	12.4	17.2	19.0	25.9	33.6	42.1	45.7	51.2	1:00.7	1:10.6
87.5%	3- 4	3- 4 M	12.8	17.7	19.6	26.6	34.5	43.3	47.0	52.7	1:02.5	1:12.6
85.0%	4- 5	3- 4 M	13.1	18.2	20.1	27.4	35.6	44.6	48.4	54.3	1:04.3	1:14.8
82.5%	6- 7	2- 3 M	13.5	18.7	20.7	28.2	36.6	46.0	49.9	55.9	1:06.2	1:17.0
80.0%	8- 9	2- 3 M	14.0	19.3	21.4	29.1	37.8	47.4	51.4	57.7	1:08.3	1:19.4
77.5%	10-12	1- 2 M	14.4	20.0	22.1	30.1	39.0	48.9	53.1	59.5	1:10.5	1:22.0
75.0%	13-15	1- 2 M	14.9	20.6	22.8	31.1	40.3	50.6	54.9	1:01.5	1:12.9	1:24.7
72.5%	16-18	60-90 S	15.4	21.3	23.6	32.1	41.7	52.3	56.8	1:03.6	1:15.4	1:27.6
70.0%	19-21	60-90 S	16.0	22.1	24.4	33.3	43.2	54.2	58.8	1:05.9	1:18.1	1:30.8
67.5%	22-24	45-75 S	16.6	22.9	25.3	34.5	44.8	56.2	1:01.0	1:08.3	1:21.0	1:34.1
65.0%	25-29	45-75 S	17.2	23.8	26.3	35.8	46.5	58.4	1:03.3	1:11.0	1:24.1	1:37.8
62.5%	30-35	30-60 S	17.9	24.7	27.4	37.3	48.4	1:00.7	1:05.8	1:13.8	1:27.4	1:41.7
60.0%	36-40	30-60 S	18.6	25.8	28.5	38.8	50.4	1:03.2	1:08.6	1:16.9	1:31.1	-----

SPEED	REPS	REST	550 YD	660 YD	880 YD	1100 YD	1320 YD	1.00 MI	1.25 MI	1.50 MI	1.75 MI	2.00 MI
95.0%	0- 1	---	1:16.6	1:36.3	2:16.2	2:58.0	3:40.5	5:07.6	6:36.5	8:06.8	9:37.8	11:09.1
92.5%	1- 2	4- 5 M	1:18.7	1:38.9	2:19.9	3:02.8	3:46.4	5:16.0	6:47.2	8:20.0	9:53.4	11:27.2
90.0%	2- 3	4- 5 M	1:20.8	1:41.7	2:23.8	3:07.9	3:52.7	5:24.7	6:58.5	8:33.9	10:09.9	11:46.3
87.5%	3- 4	3- 4 M	1:23.2	1:44.6	2:27.9	3:13.3	3:59.4	5:34.0	7:10.5	8:48.5	10:27.3	12:06.5
85.0%	4- 5	3- 4 M	1:25.6	1:47.7	2:32.2	3:19.0	4:06.4	5:43.8	7:23.1	9:04.1	10:45.7	12:27.9
82.5%	6- 7	2- 3 M	1:28.2	1:50.9	2:36.9	3:25.0	4:13.9	5:54.3	7:36.6	9:20.6	-----	-----
80.0%	8- 9	2- 3 M	1:30.9	1:54.4	2:41.8	3:31.4	4:21.8	6:05.3	-----	-----	-----	-----
77.5%	10-12	1- 2 M	1:33.9	1:58.1	2:47.0	3:38.2	4:30.2	-----	-----	-----	-----	-----
75.0%	13-15	1- 2 M	1:37.0	2:02.0	2:52.5	3:45.5	4:39.3	-----	-----	-----	-----	-----
72.5%	16-18	60-90 S	1:40.4	2:06.2	2:58.5	3:53.3	-----	-----	-----	-----	-----	-----
70.0%	19-21	60-90 S	1:43.9	2:10.7	3:04.9	-----	-----	-----	-----	-----	-----	-----
67.5%	22-24	45-75 S	1:47.8	2:15.6	-----	-----	-----	-----	-----	-----	-----	-----
65.0%	25-29	45-75 S	1:51.9	-----	-----	-----	-----	-----	-----	-----	-----	-----
62.5%	30-35	30-60 S	1:56.4	-----	-----	-----	-----	-----	-----	-----	-----	-----
60.0%	36-40	30-60 S	-----	-----	-----	-----	-----	-----	-----	-----	-----	-----

620 POINT LEVEL PACING TABLE
••••••••••••••••••••••••••••

SPEED	REPS	REST	110 YD	150 YD	165 YD	220 YD	275 YD	330 YD	352 YD	385 YD	440 YD	495 YD
95.0%	0- 1	---	11.9	16.4	18.2	24.8	32.2	40.4	43.8	49.1	58.2	1:07.7
92.5%	1- 2	4- 5 M	12.2	16.9	18.7	25.5	33.0	41.5	45.0	50.4	59.8	1:09.5
90.0%	2- 3	4- 5 M	12.5	17.4	19.2	26.2	34.0	42.6	46.3	51.9	1:01.5	1:11.5
87.5%	3- 4	3- 4 M	12.9	17.9	19.8	26.9	34.9	43.8	47.6	53.3	1:03.2	1:13.5
85.0%	4- 5	3- 4 M	13.3	18.4	20.3	27.7	36.0	45.1	49.0	54.9	1:05.1	1:15.7
82.5%	6- 7	2- 3 M	13.7	18.9	21.0	28.5	37.0	46.5	50.5	56.6	1:07.0	1:18.0
80.0%	8- 9	2- 3 M	14.1	19.5	21.6	29.4	38.2	48.0	52.0	58.3	1:09.1	1:20.4
77.5%	10-12	1- 2 M	14.6	20.2	22.3	30.4	39.4	49.5	53.7	1:00.2	1:11.4	1:23.0
75.0%	13-15	1- 2 M	15.1	20.8	23.1	31.4	40.8	51.2	55.5	1:02.2	1:13.7	1:25.8
72.5%	16-18	60-90 S	15.6	21.6	23.8	32.5	42.2	52.9	57.4	1:04.4	1:16.3	1:28.7
70.0%	19-21	60-90 S	16.1	22.3	24.7	33.6	43.7	54.8	59.5	1:06.7	1:19.0	1:31.9
67.5%	22-24	45-75 S	16.7	23.1	25.6	34.9	45.3	56.8	1:01.7	1:09.1	1:21.9	1:35.3
65.0%	25-29	45-75 S	17.4	24.0	26.6	36.2	47.0	59.0	1:04.0	1:11.8	1:25.1	1:39.0
62.5%	30-35	30-60 S	18.1	25.0	27.7	37.7	48.9	1:01.4	1:06.6	1:14.7	1:28.5	1:42.9
60.0%	36-40	30-60 S	18.8	26.0	28.8	39.2	50.9	1:03.9	1:09.4	1:17.8	1:32.2	-----

SPEED	REPS	REST	550 YD	660 YD	880 YD	1100 YD	1320 YD	1.00 MI	1.25 MI	1.50 MI	1.75 MI	2.00 MI
95.0%	0- 1	---	1:17.5	1:37.6	2:18.0	3:00.4	3:43.5	5:11.9	6:42.1	8:13.7	9:46.0	11:18.8
92.5%	1- 2	4- 5 M	1:19.6	1:40.2	2:21.8	3:05.3	3:49.5	5:20.4	6:53.0	8:27.1	10:01.9	11:37.1
90.0%	2- 3	4- 5 M	1:21.9	1:43.0	2:25.7	3:10.5	3:55.9	5:29.3	7:04.4	8:41.2	10:18.6	11:56.5
87.5%	3- 4	3- 4 M	1:24.2	1:45.9	2:29.9	3:15.9	4:02.6	5:38.7	7:16.6	8:56.1	10:36.3	12:17.0
85.0%	4- 5	3- 4 M	1:26.7	1:49.0	2:34.3	3:21.7	4:09.8	5:48.6	7:29.4	9:11.8	10:55.0	12:38.6
82.5%	6- 7	2- 3 M	1:29.3	1:52.3	2:38.9	3:27.8	4:17.3	5:59.2	7:43.0	9:28.5	-----	-----
80.0%	8- 9	2- 3 M	1:32.1	1:55.9	2:43.9	3:34.3	4:25.4	6:10.4	-----	-----	-----	-----
77.5%	10-12	1- 2 M	1:35.1	1:59.6	2:49.2	3:41.2	4:33.9	-----	-----	-----	-----	-----
75.0%	13-15	1- 2 M	1:38.2	2:03.6	2:54.8	3:48.5	4:43.1	-----	-----	-----	-----	-----
72.5%	16-18	60-90 S	1:41.6	2:07.8	3:00.9	3:56.4	-----	-----	-----	-----	-----	-----
70.0%	19-21	60-90 S	1:45.2	2:12.4	3:07.3	-----	-----	-----	-----	-----	-----	-----
67.5%	22-24	45-75 S	1:49.1	2:17.3	-----	-----	-----	-----	-----	-----	-----	-----
65.0%	25-29	45-75 S	1:53.3	-----	-----	-----	-----	-----	-----	-----	-----	-----
62.5%	30-35	30-60 S	1:57.9	-----	-----	-----	-----	-----	-----	-----	-----	-----
60.0%	36-40	30-60 S	-----	-----	-----	-----	-----	-----	-----	-----	-----	-----

167

600 POINT LEVEL PACING TABLE

SPEED	REPS	REST	110 YD	150 YD	165 YD	220 YD	275 YD	330 YD	352 YD	385 YD	440 YD	495 YD
95.0%	0- 1	---	12.0	16.6	18.4	25.1	32.5	40.9	44.3	49.7	58.9	1:08.6
92.5%	1- 2	4- 5 M	12.3	17.1	18.9	25.7	33.4	42.0	45.5	51.1	1:00.5	1:10.4
90.0%	2- 3	4- 5 M	12.7	17.5	19.4	26.5	34.3	43.1	46.8	52.5	1:02.2	1:12.4
87.5%	3- 4	3- 4 M	13.0	18.0	20.0	27.2	35.3	44.4	48.1	54.0	1:04.0	1:14.4
85.0%	4- 5	3- 4 M	13.4	18.6	20.6	28.0	36.4	45.7	49.6	55.6	1:05.9	1:16.6
82.5%	6- 7	2- 3 M	13.8	19.1	21.2	28.9	37.5	47.0	51.1	57.2	1:07.9	1:18.9
80.0%	8- 9	2- 3 M	14.3	19.7	21.8	29.8	38.6	48.5	52.7	59.0	1:10.0	1:21.4
77.5%	10-12	1- 2 M	14.7	20.4	22.5	30.7	39.9	50.1	54.3	1:00.9	1:12.2	1:24.0
75.0%	13-15	1- 2 M	15.2	21.1	23.3	31.7	41.2	51.8	56.2	1:03.0	1:14.6	1:26.8
72.5%	16-18	60-90 S	15.7	21.8	24.1	32.8	42.6	53.5	58.1	1:05.1	1:17.2	1:29.8
70.0%	19-21	60-90 S	16.3	22.6	25.0	34.0	44.2	55.4	1:00.2	1:07.5	1:20.0	1:33.0
67.5%	22-24	45-75 S	16.9	23.4	25.9	35.3	45.8	57.5	1:02.4	1:10.0	1:22.9	1:36.5
65.0%	25-29	45-75 S	17.5	24.3	26.9	36.6	47.6	59.7	1:04.8	1:12.7	1:26.1	1:40.2
62.5%	30-35	30-60 S	18.3	25.3	28.0	38.1	49.5	1:02.1	1:07.4	1:15.6	1:29.6	1:44.2
60.0%	36-40	30-60 S	19.0	26.3	29.1	39.7	51.5	1:04.7	1:10.2	1:18.7	1:33.3	-----

SPEED	REPS	REST	550 YD	660 YD	880 YD	1100 YD	1320 YD	1.00 MI	1.25 MI	1.50 MI	1.75 MI	2.00 MI
95.0%	0- 1	---	1:18.5	1:38.8	2:19.9	3:02.9	3:46.6	5:16.3	6:47.8	8:20.9	9:54.6	11:28.7
92.5%	1- 2	4- 5 M	1:20.7	1:41.5	2:23.6	3:07.8	3:52.7	5:24.9	6:58.9	8:34.4	10:10.6	11:47.3
90.0%	2- 3	4- 5 M	1:22.9	1:44.3	2:27.6	3:13.1	3:59.2	5:33.9	7:10.5	8:48.7	10:27.6	12:06.9
87.5%	3- 4	3- 4 M	1:25.3	1:47.3	2:31.9	3:18.6	4:06.0	5:43.4	7:22.8	9:03.8	10:45.5	12:27.7
85.0%	4- 5	3- 4 M	1:27.8	1:50.5	2:36.3	3:24.4	4:13.2	5:53.6	7:35.8	9:19.8	11:04.5	12:49.7
82.5%	6- 7	2- 3 M	1:30.4	1:53.8	2:41.1	3:30.6	4:20.9	6:04.3	7:49.6	9:36.8	-----	-----
80.0%	8- 9	2- 3 M	1:33.3	1:57.4	2:46.1	3:37.2	4:29.1	6:15.6	-----	-----	-----	-----
77.5%	10-12	1- 2 M	1:36.3	2:01.1	2:51.5	3:44.2	4:37.7	-----	-----	-----	-----	-----
75.0%	13-15	1- 2 M	1:39.5	2:05.2	2:57.2	3:51.7	4:47.0	-----	-----	-----	-----	-----
72.5%	16-18	60-90 S	1:42.9	2:09.5	3:03.3	3:59.7	-----	-----	-----	-----	-----	-----
70.0%	19-21	60-90 S	1:46.6	2:14.1	3:09.8	-----	-----	-----	-----	-----	-----	-----
67.5%	22-24	45-75 S	1:50.5	2:19.1	-----	-----	-----	-----	-----	-----	-----	-----
65.0%	25-29	45-75 S	1:54.8	-----	-----	-----	-----	-----	-----	-----	-----	-----
62.5%	30-35	30-60 S	1:59.4	-----	-----	-----	-----	-----	-----	-----	-----	-----
60.0%	36-40	30-60 S	-----	-----	-----	-----	-----	-----	-----	-----	-----	-----

580 POINT LEVEL PACING TABLE

SPEED	REPS	REST	110 YD	150 YD	165 YD	220 YD	275 YD	330 YD	352 YD	385 YD	440 YD	495 YD
95.0%	0- 1	---	12.1	16.8	18.6	25.3	32.9	41.3	44.9	50.3	59.7	1:09.4
92.5%	1- 2	4- 5 M	12.5	17.3	19.1	26.0	33.8	42.5	46.1	51.7	1:01.3	1:11.3
90.0%	2- 3	4- 5 M	12.8	17.7	19.6	26.7	34.7	43.6	47.4	53.1	1:03.0	1:13.3
87.5%	3- 4	3- 4 M	13.2	18.2	20.2	27.5	35.7	44.9	48.7	54.6	1:04.8	1:15.4
85.0%	4- 5	3- 4 M	13.6	18.8	20.8	28.3	36.8	46.2	50.1	56.2	1:06.7	1:17.6
82.5%	6- 7	2- 3 M	14.0	19.3	21.4	29.2	37.9	47.6	51.7	57.9	1:08.7	1:19.9
80.0%	8- 9	2- 3 M	14.4	19.9	22.1	30.1	39.1	49.1	53.3	59.7	1:10.8	1:22.4
77.5%	10-12	1- 2 M	14.9	20.6	22.8	31.1	40.3	50.7	55.0	1:01.7	1:13.1	1:25.1
75.0%	13-15	1- 2 M	15.4	21.3	23.5	32.1	41.7	52.4	56.8	1:03.7	1:15.6	1:27.9
72.5%	16-18	60-90 S	15.9	22.0	24.4	33.2	43.1	54.2	58.8	1:05.9	1:18.2	1:31.0
70.0%	19-21	60-90 S	16.5	22.8	25.2	34.4	44.7	56.1	1:00.9	1:08.3	1:21.0	1:34.2
67.5%	22-24	45-75 S	17.1	23.6	26.2	35.7	46.3	58.2	1:03.1	1:10.8	1:24.0	1:37.7
65.0%	25-29	45-75 S	17.7	24.6	27.2	37.0	48.1	1:00.4	1:05.6	1:13.5	1:27.2	1:41.5
62.5%	30-35	30-60 S	18.4	25.5	28.3	38.5	50.0	1:02.8	1:08.2	1:16.5	1:30.7	1:45.5
60.0%	36-40	30-60 S	19.2	26.6	29.4	40.1	52.1	1:05.4	1:11.0	1:19.7	1:34.5	-----

SPEED	REPS	REST	550 YD	660 YD	880 YD	1100 YD	1320 YD	1.00 MI	1.25 MI	1.50 MI	1.75 MI	2.00 MI
95.0%	0- 1	---	1:19.5	1:40.1	2:21.8	3:05.4	3:49.8	5:20.9	6:53.8	8:28.2	10:03.3	11:38.9
92.5%	1- 2	4- 5 M	1:21.7	1:42.8	2:25.6	3:10.4	3:56.0	5:29.5	7:04.9	8:41.9	10:19.6	11:57.8
90.0%	2- 3	4- 5 M	1:24.0	1:45.7	2:29.6	3:15.7	4:02.5	5:38.7	7:16.8	8:56.4	10:36.8	12:17.7
87.5%	3- 4	3- 4 M	1:26.4	1:48.7	2:33.9	3:21.3	4:09.5	5:48.4	7:29.2	9:11.8	10:55.0	12:38.8
85.0%	4- 5	3- 4 M	1:28.9	1:51.9	2:38.4	3:27.2	4:16.8	5:58.6	7:42.4	9:28.0	11:14.3	13:01.1
82.5%	6- 7	2- 3 M	1:31.6	1:55.3	2:43.2	3:33.5	4:24.6	6:09.5	7:56.5	9:45.2	-----	-----
80.0%	8- 9	2- 3 M	1:34.4	1:58.9	2:48.3	3:40.2	4:32.8	6:21.0	-----	-----	-----	-----
77.5%	10-12	1- 2 M	1:37.5	2:02.7	2:53.8	3:47.3	4:41.6	-----	-----	-----	-----	-----
75.0%	13-15	1- 2 M	1:40.7	2:06.8	2:59.6	3:54.9	4:51.0	-----	-----	-----	-----	-----
72.5%	16-18	60-90 S	1:44.2	2:11.2	3:05.8	4:03.0	-----	-----	-----	-----	-----	-----
70.0%	19-21	60-90 S	1:47.9	2:15.9	3:12.4	-----	-----	-----	-----	-----	-----	-----
67.5%	22-24	45-75 S	1:51.9	2:20.9	-----	-----	-----	-----	-----	-----	-----	-----
65.0%	25-29	45-75 S	1:56.2	2:26.3	-----	-----	-----	-----	-----	-----	-----	-----
62.5%	30-35	30-60 S	2:00.9	-----	-----	-----	-----	-----	-----	-----	-----	-----
60.0%	36-40	30-60 S	-----	-----	-----	-----	-----	-----	-----	-----	-----	-----

560 POINT LEVEL PACING TABLE

SPEED	REPS	REST	110 YD	150 YD	165 YD	220 YD	275 YD	330 YD	352 YD	385 YD	440 YD	495 YD
95.0%	0- 1	---	12.3	17.0	18.8	25.6	33.3	41.8	45.4	50.9	1:00.4	1:10.3
92.5%	1- 2	4- 5 M	12.6	17.4	19.3	26.3	34.2	43.0	46.6	52.3	1:02.0	1:12.2
90.0%	2- 3	4- 5 M	12.9	17.9	19.8	27.0	35.1	44.2	47.9	53.8	1:03.8	1:14.2
87.5%	3- 4	3- 4 M	13.3	18.4	20.4	27.8	36.1	45.4	49.3	55.3	1:05.6	1:16.3
85.0%	4- 5	3- 4 M	13.7	19.0	21.0	28.6	37.2	46.7	50.7	56.9	1:07.5	1:18.6
82.5%	6- 7	2- 3 M	14.1	19.6	21.6	29.5	38.3	48.2	52.3	58.6	1:09.6	1:21.0
80.0%	8- 9	2- 3 M	14.6	20.2	22.3	30.4	39.5	49.7	53.9	1:00.5	1:11.7	1:23.5
77.5%	10-12	1- 2 M	15.0	20.8	23.0	31.4	40.8	51.3	55.7	1:02.4	1:14.0	1:26.2
75.0%	13-15	1- 2 M	15.5	21.5	23.8	32.5	42.2	53.0	57.5	1:04.5	1:16.5	1:29.0
72.5%	16-18	60-90 S	16.1	22.2	24.6	33.6	43.6	54.8	59.5	1:06.7	1:19.2	1:32.1
70.0%	19-21	60-90 S	16.6	23.0	25.5	34.8	45.2	56.8	1:01.6	1:09.1	1:22.0	1:35.4
67.5%	22-24	45-75 S	17.3	23.9	26.4	36.1	46.8	58.9	1:03.9	1:11.7	1:25.0	1:38.9
65.0%	25-29	45-75 S	17.9	24.8	27.5	37.4	48.6	1:01.1	1:06.4	1:14.4	1:28.3	1:42.7
62.5%	30-35	30-60 S	18.6	25.8	28.6	38.9	50.6	1:03.6	1:09.0	1:17.4	1:31.8	1:46.9
60.0%	36-40	30-60 S	19.4	26.9	29.8	40.6	52.7	1:06.2	1:11.9	1:20.6	1:35.6	1:51.3

SPEED	REPS	REST	550 YD	660 YD	880 YD	1100 YD	1320 YD	1.00 MI	1.25 MI	1.50 MI	1.75 MI	2.00 MI
95.0%	0- 1	---	1:20.6	1:41.5	2:23.7	3:08.0	3:53.0	5:25.5	6:59.9	8:35.8	10:12.4	11:49.4
92.5%	1- 2	4- 5 M	1:22.7	1:44.2	2:27.6	3:13.1	3:59.3	5:34.3	7:11.2	8:49.7	10:28.9	12:08.6
90.0%	2- 3	4- 5 M	1:25.0	1:47.1	2:31.7	3:18.5	4:06.0	5:43.6	7:23.2	9:04.4	10:46.4	12:28.8
87.5%	3- 4	3- 4 M	1:27.5	1:50.2	2:36.0	3:24.2	4:13.0	5:53.4	7:35.8	9:20.0	11:04.8	12:50.2
85.0%	4- 5	3- 4 M	1:30.0	1:53.4	2:40.6	3:30.2	4:20.5	6:03.8	7:49.3	9:36.4	11:24.4	13:12.9
82.5%	6- 7	2- 3 M	1:32.8	1:56.8	2:45.5	3:36.5	4:28.3	6:14.8	8:03.5	9:53.9	-----	-----
80.0%	8- 9	2- 3 M	1:35.7	2:00.5	2:50.7	3:43.3	4:36.7	6:26.6	-----	-----	-----	-----
77.5%	10-12	1- 2 M	1:38.8	2:04.4	2:56.2	3:50.5	4:45.7	-----	-----	-----	-----	-----
75.0%	13-15	1- 2 M	1:42.1	2:08.5	3:02.0	3:58.2	4:55.2	-----	-----	-----	-----	-----
72.5%	16-18	60-90 S	1:45.6	2:13.0	3:08.3	4:06.4	-----	-----	-----	-----	-----	-----
70.0%	19-21	60-90 S	1:49.3	2:17.7	3:15.0	-----	-----	-----	-----	-----	-----	-----
67.5%	22-24	45-75 S	1:53.4	2:22.8	-----	-----	-----	-----	-----	-----	-----	-----
65.0%	25-29	45-75 S	1:57.8	2:28.3	-----	-----	-----	-----	-----	-----	-----	-----
62.5%	30-35	30-60 S	2:02.5	-----	-----	-----	-----	-----	-----	-----	-----	-----
60.0%	36-40	30-60 S	-----	-----	-----	-----	-----	-----	-----	-----	-----	-----

540 POINT LEVEL PACING TABLE
•••••••••••••••••••••••••••••

SPEED	REPS	REST	110 YD	150 YD	165 YD	220 YD	275 YD	330 YD	352 YD	385 YD	440 YD	495 YD
95.0%	0- 1	---	12.4	17.2	19.0	25.9	33.7	42.3	46.0	51.6	1:01.2	1:11.2
92.5%	1- 2	4- 5 M	12.7	17.6	19.5	26.6	34.6	43.5	47.2	52.9	1:02.8	1:13.1
90.0%	2- 3	4- 5 M	13.1	18.1	20.1	27.3	35.5	44.7	48.5	54.4	1:04.6	1:15.2
87.5%	3- 4	3- 4 M	13.5	18.6	20.6	28.1	36.6	46.0	49.9	56.0	1:06.4	1:17.3
85.0%	4- 5	3- 4 M	13.9	19.2	21.2	29.0	37.6	47.3	51.4	57.6	1:08.4	1:19.6
82.5%	6- 7	2- 3 M	14.3	19.8	21.9	29.8	38.8	48.7	52.9	59.4	1:10.4	1:22.0
80.0%	8- 9	2- 3 M	14.7	20.4	22.6	30.8	40.0	50.3	54.6	1:01.2	1:12.6	1:24.6
77.5%	10-12	1- 2 M	15.2	21.0	23.3	31.8	41.3	51.9	56.3	1:03.2	1:15.0	1:27.3
75.0%	13-15	1- 2 M	15.7	21.7	24.1	32.8	42.7	53.6	58.2	1:05.3	1:17.5	1:30.2
72.5%	16-18	60-90 S	16.2	22.5	24.9	33.9	44.1	55.5	1:00.2	1:07.6	1:20.2	1:33.3
70.0%	19-21	60-90 S	16.8	23.3	25.8	35.2	45.7	57.4	1:02.4	1:10.0	1:23.0	1:36.6
67.5%	22-24	45-75 S	17.4	24.2	26.7	36.5	47.4	59.6	1:04.7	1:12.6	1:26.1	1:40.2
65.0%	25-29	45-75 S	18.1	25.1	27.8	37.9	49.2	1:01.9	1:07.2	1:15.3	1:29.4	1:44.1
62.5%	30-35	30-60 S	18.8	26.1	28.9	39.4	51.2	1:04.3	1:09.9	1:18.4	1:33.0	1:48.2
60.0%	36-40	30-60 S	19.6	27.2	30.1	41.0	53.3	1:07.0	1:12.8	1:21.6	1:36.9	1:52.8

SPEED	REPS	REST	550 YD	660 YD	880 YD	1100 YD	1320 YD	1.00 MI	1.25 MI	1.50 MI	1.75 MI	2.00 MI
95.0%	0- 1	---	1:21.6	1:42.8	2:25.7	3:10.7	3:56.4	5:30.3	7:06.1	8:43.5	10:21.7	12:00.3
92.5%	1- 2	4- 5 M	1:23.8	1:45.6	2:29.7	3:15.9	4:02.8	5:39.3	7:17.7	8:57.7	10:38.5	12:19.7
90.0%	2- 3	4- 5 M	1:26.2	1:48.5	2:33.8	3:21.3	4:09.5	5:48.7	7:29.8	9:12.6	10:56.2	12:40.3
87.5%	3- 4	3- 4 M	1:28.6	1:51.6	2:38.2	3:27.1	4:16.7	5:58.6	7:42.7	9:28.4	11:14.9	13:02.0
85.0%	4- 5	3- 4 M	1:31.2	1:54.9	2:42.9	3:33.1	4:24.2	6:09.2	7:56.3	9:45.1	11:34.8	13:25.0
82.5%	6- 7	2- 3 M	1:34.0	1:58.4	2:47.8	3:39.6	4:32.2	6:20.4	8:10.7	10:02.9	-----	-----
80.0%	8- 9	2- 3 M	1:36.9	2:02.1	2:53.0	3:46.5	4:40.7	6:32.3	-----	-----	-----	-----
77.5%	10-12	1- 2 M	1:40.1	2:06.1	2:58.6	3:53.8	4:49.8	-----	-----	-----	-----	-----
75.0%	13-15	1- 2 M	1:43.4	2:10.3	3:04.6	4:01.6	4:59.4	-----	-----	-----	-----	-----
72.5%	16-18	60-90 S	1:47.0	2:14.7	3:10.9	4:09.9	-----	-----	-----	-----	-----	-----
70.0%	19-21	60-90 S	1:50.8	2:19.6	3:17.8	-----	-----	-----	-----	-----	-----	-----
67.5%	22-24	45-75 S	1:54.9	2:24.7	-----	-----	-----	-----	-----	-----	-----	-----
65.0%	25-29	45-75 S	1:59.3	2:30.3	-----	-----	-----	-----	-----	-----	-----	-----
62.5%	30-35	30-60 S	2:04.1	-----	-----	-----	-----	-----	-----	-----	-----	-----
60.0%	36-40	30-60 S	-----	-----	-----	-----	-----	-----	-----	-----	-----	-----

520 POINT LEVEL PACING TABLE
....

SPEED	REPS	REST	110 YD	150 YD	165 YD	220 YD	275 YD	330 YD	352 YD	385 YD	440 YD	495 YD
95.0%	0- 1	---	12.5	17.4	19.2	26.2	34.1	42.8	46.5	52.2	1:02.0	1:12.1
92.5%	1- 2	4- 5 M	12.9	17.8	19.7	26.9	35.0	44.0	47.8	53.6	1:03.6	1:14.1
90.0%	2- 3	4- 5 M	13.2	18.3	20.3	27.7	36.0	45.2	49.1	55.1	1:05.4	1:16.2
87.5%	3- 4	3- 4 M	13.6	18.8	20.9	28.4	37.0	46.5	50.5	56.7	1:07.3	1:18.3
85.0%	4- 5	3- 4 M	14.0	19.4	21.5	29.3	38.1	47.9	52.0	58.3	1:09.2	1:20.6
82.5%	6- 7	2- 3 M	14.4	20.0	22.1	30.2	39.2	49.3	53.6	1:00.1	1:11.3	1:23.1
80.0%	8- 9	2- 3 M	14.9	20.6	22.8	31.1	40.5	50.9	55.2	1:02.0	1:13.6	1:25.7
77.5%	10-12	1- 2 M	15.4	21.3	23.5	32.1	41.8	52.5	57.0	1:04.0	1:15.9	1:28.4
75.0%	13-15	1- 2 M	15.9	22.0	24.3	33.2	43.2	54.3	58.9	1:06.1	1:18.5	1:31.4
72.5%	16-18	60-90 S	16.4	22.7	25.2	34.3	44.6	56.1	1:01.0	1:08.4	1:21.2	1:34.5
70.0%	19-21	60-90 S	17.0	23.6	26.1	35.6	46.2	58.1	1:03.1	1:10.8	1:24.1	1:37.9
67.5%	22-24	45-75 S	17.6	24.4	27.0	36.9	48.0	1:00.3	1:05.5	1:13.5	1:27.2	1:41.5
65.0%	25-29	45-75 S	18.3	25.4	28.1	38.3	49.8	1:02.6	1:08.0	1:16.3	1:30.6	1:45.4
62.5%	30-35	30-60 S	19.0	26.4	29.2	39.8	51.8	1:05.1	1:10.7	1:19.3	1:34.2	1:49.7
60.0%	36-40	30-60 S	19.8	27.5	30.4	41.5	53.9	1:07.8	1:13.7	1:22.7	1:38.1	1:54.2

SPEED	REPS	REST	550 YD	660 YD	880 YD	1100 YD	1320 YD	1.00 MI	1.25 MI	1.50 MI	1.75 MI	2.00 MI
95.0%	0- 1	---	1:22.7	1:44.2	2:27.8	3:13.5	3:59.9	5:35.3	7:12.6	8:51.6	10:31.3	12:11.4
92.5%	1- 2	4- 5 M	1:25.0	1:47.1	2:31.8	3:18.7	4:06.4	5:44.3	7:24.3	9:05.9	10:48.3	12:31.2
90.0%	2- 3	4- 5 M	1:27.3	1:50.0	2:36.0	3:24.2	4:13.2	5:53.9	7:36.6	9:21.1	11:06.3	12:52.1
87.5%	3- 4	3- 4 M	1:29.8	1:53.2	2:40.4	3:30.1	4:20.4	6:04.0	7:49.7	9:37.1	11:25.4	13:14.1
85.0%	4- 5	3- 4 M	1:32.5	1:56.5	2:45.2	3:36.2	4:28.1	6:14.7	8:03.5	9:54.1	11:45.5	13:37.5
82.5%	6- 7	2- 3 M	1:35.3	2:00.0	2:50.2	3:42.8	4:36.2	6:26.1	8:18.2	10:12.1	-----	-----
80.0%	8- 9	2- 3 M	1:38.2	2:03.8	2:55.5	3:49.7	4:44.8	6:38.1	-----	-----	-----	-----
77.5%	10-12	1- 2 M	1:41.4	2:07.8	3:01.1	3:57.2	4:54.0	-----	-----	-----	-----	-----
75.0%	13-15	1- 2 M	1:44.8	2:12.0	3:07.2	4:05.1	5:03.8	-----	-----	-----	-----	-----
72.5%	16-18	60-90 S	1:48.4	2:16.6	3:13.6	4:13.5	-----	-----	-----	-----	-----	-----
70.0%	19-21	60-90 S	1:52.3	2:21.5	3:20.6	-----	-----	-----	-----	-----	-----	-----
67.5%	22-24	45-75 S	1:56.4	2:26.7	-----	-----	-----	-----	-----	-----	-----	-----
65.0%	25-29	45-75 S	2:00.9	2:32.4	-----	-----	-----	-----	-----	-----	-----	-----
62.5%	30-35	30-60 S	2:05.7	-----	-----	-----	-----	-----	-----	-----	-----	-----
60.0%	36-40	30-60 S	-----	-----	-----	-----	-----	-----	-----	-----	-----	-----

500 POINT LEVEL PACING TABLE

SPEED	REPS	REST	110 YD	150 YD	165 YD	220 YD	275 YD	330 YD	352 YD	385 YD	440 YD	495 YD
95.0%	0- 1	----	12.7	17.5	19.4	26.5	34.5	43.4	47.1	52.9	1:02.8	1:13.1
92.5%	1- 2	4- 5 M	13.0	18.0	20.0	27.2	35.4	44.5	48.4	54.3	1:04.5	1:15.1
90.0%	2- 3	4- 5 M	13.4	18.5	20.5	28.0	36.4	45.8	49.7	55.8	1:06.2	1:17.2
87.5%	3- 4	3- 4 M	13.8	19.1	21.1	28.8	37.4	47.1	51.1	57.4	1:08.1	1:19.4
85.0%	4- 5	3- 4 M	14.2	19.6	21.7	29.6	38.5	48.5	52.6	59.1	1:10.1	1:21.7
82.5%	6- 7	2- 3 M	14.6	20.2	22.4	30.5	39.7	49.9	54.2	1:00.9	1:12.3	1:24.2
80.0%	8- 9	2- 3 M	15.0	20.8	23.1	31.5	40.9	51.5	55.9	1:02.8	1:14.5	1:26.8
77.5%	10-12	1- 2 M	15.5	21.5	23.8	32.5	42.3	53.2	57.7	1:04.8	1:16.9	1:29.6
75.0%	13-15	1- 2 M	16.0	22.2	24.6	33.6	43.7	54.9	59.7	1:07.0	1:19.5	1:32.6
72.5%	16-18	60-90 S	16.6	23.0	25.5	34.7	45.2	56.8	1:01.7	1:09.3	1:22.2	1:35.8
70.0%	19-21	60-90 S	17.2	23.8	26.4	36.0	46.8	58.9	1:03.9	1:11.7	1:25.2	1:39.2
67.5%	22-24	45-75 S	17.8	24.7	27.3	37.3	48.5	1:01.0	1:06.3	1:14.4	1:28.3	1:42.9
65.0%	25-29	45-75 S	18.5	25.6	28.4	38.7	50.4	1:03.4	1:08.8	1:17.3	1:31.7	1:46.8
62.5%	30-35	30-60 S	19.3	26.7	29.5	40.3	52.4	1:05.9	1:11.6	1:20.4	1:35.4	1:51.1
60.0%	36-40	30-60 S	20.1	27.8	30.8	42.0	54.6	1:08.7	1:14.6	1:23.7	1:39.4	1:55.7

SPEED	REPS	REST	550 YD	660 YD	880 YD	1100 YD	1320 YD	1.00 MI	1.25 MI	1.50 MI	1.75 MI	2.00 MI
95.0%	0- 1	----	1:23.8	1:45.7	2:29.9	3:16.3	4:03.4	5:40.4	7:19.3	8:59.8	10:41.1	12:23.0
92.5%	1- 2	4- 5 M	1:26.1	1:48.5	2:33.9	3:21.6	4:10.0	5:49.6	7:31.1	9:14.4	10:58.5	12:43.0
90.0%	2- 3	4- 5 M	1:28.5	1:51.6	2:38.2	3:27.2	4:17.0	5:59.3	7:43.7	9:29.8	11:16.8	13:04.2
87.5%	3- 4	3- 4 M	1:31.0	1:54.8	2:42.7	3:33.1	4:24.3	6:09.5	7:56.9	9:46.1	11:36.1	13:26.6
85.0%	4- 5	3- 4 M	1:33.7	1:58.1	2:47.5	3:39.4	4:32.1	6:20.4	8:11.0	10:03.3	11:56.6	13:50.4
82.5%	6- 7	2- 3 M	1:36.5	2:01.7	2:52.6	3:46.1	4:40.3	6:31.9	8:25.8	10:21.6	-----	-----
80.0%	8- 9	2- 3 M	1:39.6	2:05.5	2:58.0	3:53.1	4:49.1	6:44.2	-----	-----	-----	-----
77.5%	10-12	1- 2 M	1:42.8	2:09.6	3:03.7	4:00.6	4:58.4	-----	-----	-----	-----	-----
75.0%	13-15	1- 2 M	1:46.2	2:13.9	3:09.9	4:08.7	5:08.4	-----	-----	-----	-----	-----
72.5%	16-18	60-90 S	1:49.9	2:18.5	3:16.4	4:17.2	-----	-----	-----	-----	-----	-----
70.0%	19-21	60-90 S	1:53.8	2:23.4	3:23.4	-----	-----	-----	-----	-----	-----	-----
67.5%	22-24	45-75 S	1:58.0	2:28.8	-----	-----	-----	-----	-----	-----	-----	-----
65.0%	25-29	45-75 S	2:02.5	2:34.5	-----	-----	-----	-----	-----	-----	-----	-----
62.5%	30-35	30-60 S	2:07.4	-----	-----	-----	-----	-----	-----	-----	-----	-----
60.0%	36-40	30-60 S	-----	-----	-----	-----	-----	-----	-----	-----	-----	-----

480 POINT LEVEL PACING TABLE
· ·

SPEED	REPS	REST	110 YD	150 YD	165 YD	220 YD	275 YD	330 YD	352 YD	385 YD	440 YD	495 YD
95.0%	0- 1	---	12.8	17.7	19.6	26.8	34.9	43.9	47.7	53.5	1:03.6	1:14.1
92.5%	1- 2	4- 5 M	13.2	18.2	20.2	27.5	35.8	45.1	49.0	55.0	1:05.3	1:16.1
90.0%	2- 3	4- 5 M	13.5	18.7	20.7	28.3	36.8	46.4	50.4	56.5	1:07.1	1:18.2
87.5%	3- 4	3- 4 M	13.9	19.3	21.3	29.1	37.9	47.7	51.8	58.1	1:09.0	1:20.4
85.0%	4- 5	3- 4 M	14.3	19.8	22.0	30.0	39.0	49.1	53.3	59.8	1:11.1	1:22.8
82.5%	6- 7	2- 3 M	14.7	20.4	22.6	30.9	40.2	50.6	54.9	1:01.7	1:13.2	1:25.3
80.0%	8- 9	2- 3 M	15.2	21.1	23.3	31.8	41.4	52.2	56.6	1:03.6	1:15.5	1:28.0
77.5%	10-12	1- 2 M	15.7	21.8	24.1	32.9	42.8	53.8	58.5	1:05.6	1:17.9	1:30.8
75.0%	13-15	1- 2 M	16.2	22.5	24.9	34.0	44.2	55.6	1:00.4	1:07.8	1:20.5	1:33.8
72.5%	16-18	60-90 S	16.8	23.3	25.7	35.1	45.7	57.5	1:02.5	1:10.2	1:23.3	1:37.1
70.0%	19-21	60-90 S	17.4	24.1	26.7	36.4	47.4	59.6	1:04.7	1:12.7	1:26.3	1:40.5
67.5%	22-24	45-75 S	18.0	25.0	27.7	37.7	49.1	1:01.8	1:07.1	1:15.4	1:29.5	1:44.3
65.0%	25-29	45-75 S	18.7	25.9	28.7	39.2	51.0	1:04.2	1:09.7	1:18.3	1:32.9	1:48.3
62.5%	30-35	30-60 S	19.5	27.0	29.9	40.8	53.0	1:06.8	1:12.5	1:21.4	1:36.7	1:52.6
60.0%	36-40	30-60 S	20.3	28.1	31.1	42.5	55.3	1:09.5	1:15.5	1:24.8	1:40.7	1:57.3

SPEED	REPS	REST	550 YD	660 YD	880 YD	1100 YD	1320 YD	1.00 MI	1.25 MI	1.50 MI	1.75 MI	2.00 MI
95.0%	0- 1	---	1:25.0	1:47.2	2:32.1	3:19.2	4:07.1	5:45.6	7:26.1	9:08.4	10:51.4	12:34.9
92.5%	1- 2	4- 5 M	1:27.3	1:50.1	2:36.2	3:24.6	4:13.8	5:55.0	7:38.2	9:23.2	11:09.0	12:55.3
90.0%	2- 3	4- 5 M	1:29.7	1:53.1	2:40.5	3:30.3	4:20.9	6:04.8	7:50.9	9:38.8	11:27.5	13:16.8
87.5%	3- 4	3- 4 M	1:32.3	1:56.4	2:45.1	3:36.3	4:28.3	6:15.2	8:04.4	9:55.4	11:47.2	13:39.6
85.0%	4- 5	3- 4 M	1:35.0	1:59.8	2:50.0	3:42.7	4:36.2	6:26.3	8:18.6	10:12.9	12:08.0	14:03.7
82.5%	6- 7	2- 3 M	1:37.9	2:03.4	2:55.1	3:49.4	4:44.6	6:38.0	8:33.7	10:31.4	-----	-----
80.0%	8- 9	2- 3 M	1:40.9	2:07.3	3:00.6	3:56.6	4:53.5	6:50.4	-----	-----	-----	-----
77.5%	10-12	1- 2 M	1:44.2	2:11.4	3:06.4	4:04.2	5:02.9	-----	-----	-----	-----	-----
75.0%	13-15	1- 2 M	1:47.7	2:15.8	3:12.6	4:12.4	5:13.0	-----	-----	-----	-----	-----
72.5%	16-18	60-90 S	1:51.4	2:20.4	3:19.3	4:21.1	-----	-----	-----	-----	-----	-----
70.0%	19-21	60-90 S	1:55.3	2:25.5	3:26.4	-----	-----	-----	-----	-----	-----	-----
67.5%	22-24	45-75 S	1:59.6	2:30.8	-----	-----	-----	-----	-----	-----	-----	-----
65.0%	25-29	45-75 S	2:04.2	2:36.7	-----	-----	-----	-----	-----	-----	-----	-----
62.5%	30-35	30-60 S	2:09.2	-----	-----	-----	-----	-----	-----	-----	-----	-----
60.0%	36-40	30-60 S	-----	-----	-----	-----	-----	-----	-----	-----	-----	-----

460 POINT LEVEL PACING TABLE

SPEED	REPS	REST	110 YD	150 YD	165 YD	220 YD	275 YD	330 YD	352 YD	385 YD	440 YD	495 YD
95.0%	0- 1	---	12.9	17.9	19.9	27.1	35.3	44.5	48.3	54.2	1:04.4	1:15.1
92.5%	1- 2	4- 5 M	13.3	18.4	20.4	27.9	36.3	45.7	49.6	55.7	1:06.2	1:17.1
90.0%	2- 3	4- 5 M	13.7	18.9	21.0	28.6	37.3	46.9	51.0	57.3	1:08.0	1:19.3
87.5%	3- 4	3- 4 M	14.1	19.5	21.6	29.5	38.4	48.3	52.5	58.9	1:10.0	1:21.5
85.0%	4- 5	3- 4 M	14.5	20.1	22.2	30.3	39.5	49.7	54.0	1:00.6	1:12.0	1:23.9
82.5%	6- 7	2- 3 M	14.9	20.7	22.9	31.2	40.7	51.2	55.6	1:02.5	1:14.2	1:26.5
80.0%	8- 9	2- 3 M	15.4	21.3	23.6	32.2	41.9	52.8	57.4	1:04.4	1:16.5	1:29.2
77.5%	10-12	1- 2 M	15.9	22.0	24.4	33.3	43.3	54.5	59.2	1:06.5	1:19.0	1:32.1
75.0%	13-15	1- 2 M	16.4	22.7	25.2	34.4	44.7	56.3	1:01.2	1:08.7	1:21.6	1:35.1
72.5%	16-18	60-90 S	17.0	23.5	26.0	35.6	46.3	58.3	1:03.3	1:11.1	1:24.4	1:38.4
70.0%	19-21	60-90 S	17.6	24.4	27.0	36.8	47.9	1:00.4	1:05.6	1:13.6	1:27.5	1:41.9
67.5%	22-24	45-75 S	18.2	25.3	28.0	38.2	49.7	1:02.6	1:08.0	1:16.3	1:30.7	1:45.7
65.0%	25-29	45-75 S	18.9	26.2	29.0	39.7	51.6	1:05.0	1:10.6	1:19.3	1:34.2	1:49.8
62.5%	30-35	30-60 S	19.7	27.3	30.2	41.2	53.7	1:07.6	1:13.4	1:22.4	1:37.9	1:54.2
60.0%	36-40	30-60 S	20.5	28.4	31.5	43.0	55.9	1:10.4	1:16.5	1:25.9	1:42.0	1:58.9

SPEED	REPS	REST	550 YD	660 YD	880 YD	1100 YD	1320 YD	1.00 MI	1.25 MI	1.50 MI	1.75 MI	2.00 MI
95.0%	0- 1	---	1:26.2	1:48.7	2:34.3	3:22.2	4:10.9	5:51.0	7:33.2	9:17.2	11:01.9	12:47.1
92.5%	1- 2	4- 5 M	1:28.5	1:51.7	2:38.5	3:27.7	4:17.7	6:00.5	7:45.5	9:32.2	11:19.8	13:07.9
90.0%	2- 3	4- 5 M	1:31.0	1:54.8	2:42.9	3:33.5	4:24.9	6:10.5	7:58.4	9:48.1	11:38.7	13:29.8
87.5%	3- 4	3- 4 M	1:33.6	1:58.0	2:47.6	3:39.6	4:32.4	6:21.1	8:12.1	10:04.9	11:58.6	13:52.9
85.0%	4- 5	3- 4 M	1:36.3	2:01.5	2:52.5	3:46.0	4:40.4	6:32.3	8:26.6	10:22.7	12:19.8	14:17.4
82.5%	6- 7	2- 3 M	1:39.2	2:05.2	2:57.7	3:52.9	4:48.9	6:44.2	8:41.9	10:41.6	-----	-----
80.0%	8- 9	2- 3 M	1:42.3	2:09.1	3:03.3	4:00.2	4:58.0	6:56.8	-----	-----	-----	-----
77.5%	10-12	1- 2 M	1:45.6	2:13.3	3:09.2	4:07.9	5:07.6	-----	-----	-----	-----	-----
75.0%	13-15	1- 2 M	1:49.1	2:17.7	3:15.5	4:16.2	5:17.8	-----	-----	-----	-----	-----
72.5%	16-18	60-90 S	1:52.9	2:22.5	3:22.2	4:25.0	-----	-----	-----	-----	-----	-----
70.0%	19-21	60-90 S	1:56.9	2:27.5	3:29.4	-----	-----	-----	-----	-----	-----	-----
67.5%	22-24	45-75 S	2:01.3	2:33.0	-----	-----	-----	-----	-----	-----	-----	-----
65.0%	25-29	45-75 S	2:05.9	2:38.9	-----	-----	-----	-----	-----	-----	-----	-----
62.5%	30-35	30-60 S	2:11.0	-----	-----	-----	-----	-----	-----	-----	-----	-----
60.0%	36-40	30-60 S	-----	-----	-----	-----	-----	-----	-----	-----	-----	-----

440 POINT LEVEL PACING TABLE

SPEED	REPS	REST	110 YD	150 YD	165 YD	220 YD	275 YD	330 YD	352 YD	385 YD	440 YD	495 YD
95.0%	0- 1	---	13.1	18.2	20.1	27.5	35.8	45.0	48.9	55.0	1:05.3	1:16.1
92.5%	1- 2	4- 5 M	13.5	18.6	20.6	28.2	36.7	46.3	50.3	56.4	1:07.1	1:18.2
90.0%	2- 3	4- 5 M	13.8	19.2	21.2	29.0	37.7	47.5	51.7	58.0	1:08.9	1:20.4
87.5%	3- 4	3- 4 M	14.2	19.7	21.8	29.8	38.8	48.9	53.1	59.7	1:10.9	1:22.7
85.0%	4- 5	3- 4 M	14.6	20.3	22.5	30.7	40.0	50.3	54.7	1:01.4	1:13.0	1:25.1
82.5%	6- 7	2- 3 M	15.1	20.9	23.1	31.6	41.2	51.9	56.4	1:03.3	1:15.2	1:27.7
80.0%	8- 9	2- 3 M	15.6	21.6	23.9	32.6	42.5	53.5	58.1	1:05.3	1:17.6	1:30.4
77.5%	10-12	1- 2 M	16.1	22.3	24.6	33.7	43.8	55.2	1:00.0	1:07.4	1:20.1	1:33.3
75.0%	13-15	1- 2 M	16.6	23.0	25.5	34.8	45.3	57.1	1:02.0	1:09.6	1:22.7	1:36.4
72.5%	16-18	60-90 S	17.2	23.8	26.3	36.0	46.9	59.0	1:04.1	1:12.0	1:25.6	1:39.8
70.0%	19-21	60-90 S	17.8	24.6	27.3	37.3	48.5	1:01.1	1:06.4	1:14.6	1:28.6	1:43.3
67.5%	22-24	45-75 S	18.4	25.5	28.3	38.6	50.3	1:03.4	1:08.9	1:17.3	1:31.9	1:47.2
65.0%	25-29	45-75 S	19.1	26.5	29.4	40.1	52.3	1:05.8	1:11.5	1:20.3	1:35.5	1:51.3
62.5%	30-35	30-60 S	19.9	27.6	30.6	41.7	54.4	1:08.5	1:14.4	1:23.5	1:39.3	1:55.7
60.0%	36-40	30-60 S	20.7	28.7	31.8	43.5	56.6	1:11.3	1:17.5	1:27.0	1:43.4	2:00.6

SPEED	REPS	REST	550 YD	660 YD	880 YD	1100 YD	1320 YD	1.00 MI	1.25 MI	1.50 MI	1.75 MI	2.00 MI
95.0%	0- 1	---	1:27.4	1:50.3	2:36.6	3:25.3	4:14.8	5:56.6	7:40.6	9:26.3	11:12.8	12:59.8
92.5%	1- 2	4- 5 M	1:29.7	1:53.3	2:40.9	3:30.9	4:21.7	6:06.3	7:53.0	9:41.6	11:31.0	13:20.9
90.0%	2- 3	4- 5 M	1:32.2	1:56.4	2:45.3	3:36.8	4:29.0	6:16.4	8:06.2	9:57.7	11:50.2	13:43.2
87.5%	3- 4	3- 4 M	1:34.9	1:59.7	2:50.1	3:42.9	4:36.7	6:27.2	8:20.0	10:14.8	12:10.4	14:06.7
85.0%	4- 5	3- 4 M	1:37.7	2:03.3	2:55.1	3:49.5	4:44.8	6:38.6	8:34.8	10:32.9	12:31.9	14:31.6
82.5%	6- 7	2- 3 M	1:40.6	2:07.0	3:00.4	3:56.5	4:53.4	6:50.7	8:50.4	10:52.1	-----	-----
80.0%	8- 9	2- 3 M	1:43.8	2:11.0	3:06.0	4:03.8	5:02.6	7:03.5	-----	-----	-----	-----
77.5%	10-12	1- 2 M	1:47.1	2:15.2	3:12.0	4:11.7	5:12.4	-----	-----	-----	-----	-----
75.0%	13-15	1- 2 M	1:50.7	2:19.7	3:18.4	4:20.1	5:22.8	-----	-----	-----	-----	-----
72.5%	16-18	60-90 S	1:54.5	2:24.5	3:25.2	4:29.1	-----	-----	-----	-----	-----	-----
70.0%	19-21	60-90 S	1:58.6	2:29.7	3:32.6	-----	-----	-----	-----	-----	-----	-----
67.5%	22-24	45-75 S	2:03.0	2:35.2	-----	-----	-----	-----	-----	-----	-----	-----
65.0%	25-29	45-75 S	2:07.7	2:41.2	-----	-----	-----	-----	-----	-----	-----	-----
62.5%	30-35	30-60 S	2:12.8	-----	-----	-----	-----	-----	-----	-----	-----	-----
60.0%	36-40	30-60 S	-----	-----	-----	-----	-----	-----	-----	-----	-----	-----

420 POINT LEVEL PACING TABLE
••••••••••••••••••••••••••••

SPEED	REPS	REST	110 YD	150 YD	165 YD	220 YD	275 YD	330 YD	352 YD	385 YD	440 YD	495 YD
95.0%	0- 1	---	13.2	18.4	20.3	27.8	36.2	45.6	49.6	55.7	1:06.2	1:17.2
92.5%	1- 2	4- 5 M	13.6	18.9	20.9	28.5	37.2	46.9	50.9	57.2	1:08.0	1:19.3
90.0%	2- 3	4- 5 M	14.0	19.4	21.5	29.3	38.2	48.2	52.3	58.8	1:09.9	1:21.5
87.5%	3- 4	3- 4 M	14.4	19.9	22.1	30.2	39.3	49.5	53.8	1:00.5	1:11.9	1:23.8
85.0%	4- 5	3- 4 M	14.8	20.5	22.7	31.1	40.5	51.0	55.4	1:02.2	1:14.0	1:26.3
82.5%	6- 7	2- 3 M	15.3	21.1	23.4	32.0	41.7	52.5	57.1	1:04.1	1:16.2	1:28.9
80.0%	8- 9	2- 3 M	15.7	21.8	24.2	33.0	43.0	54.2	58.9	1:06.1	1:18.6	1:31.7
77.5%	10-12	1- 2 M	16.2	22.5	24.9	34.1	44.4	55.9	1:00.8	1:08.3	1:21.2	1:34.6
75.0%	13-15	1- 2 M	16.8	23.3	25.8	35.2	45.9	57.8	1:02.8	1:10.5	1:23.9	1:37.8
72.5%	16-18	60-90 S	17.4	24.1	26.7	36.4	47.4	59.8	1:05.0	1:13.0	1:26.8	1:41.2
70.0%	19-21	60-90 S	18.0	24.9	27.6	37.7	49.1	1:01.9	1:07.3	1:15.6	1:29.9	1:44.8
67.5%	22-24	45-75 S	18.6	25.8	28.6	39.1	51.0	1:04.2	1:09.8	1:18.4	1:33.2	1:48.7
65.0%	25-29	45-75 S	19.4	26.8	29.7	40.6	52.9	1:06.7	1:12.5	1:21.4	1:36.8	1:52.8
62.5%	30-35	30-60 S	20.1	27.9	30.9	42.2	55.0	1:09.4	1:15.4	1:24.6	1:40.6	1:57.4
60.0%	36-40	30-60 S	21.0	29.1	32.2	44.0	57.3	1:12.2	1:18.5	1:28.2	1:44.8	2:02.2

SPEED	REPS	REST	550 YD	660 YD	880 YD	1100 YD	1320 YD	1.00 MI	1.25 MI	1.50 MI	1.75 MI	2.00 MI
95.0%	0- 1	---	1:28.6	1:51.9	2:39.0	3:28.5	4:18.9	6:02.4	7:48.1	9:35.7	11:24.0	13:12.9
92.5%	1- 2	4- 5 M	1:31.0	1:54.9	2:43.3	3:34.2	4:25.9	6:12.2	8:00.8	9:51.2	11:42.5	13:34.4
90.0%	2- 3	4- 5 M	1:33.6	1:58.1	2:47.9	3:40.1	4:33.2	6:22.5	8:14.1	10:07.6	12:02.0	13:57.0
87.5%	3- 4	3- 4 M	1:36.2	2:01.5	2:52.7	3:46.4	4:41.1	6:33.4	8:28.3	10:25.0	12:22.7	14:20.9
85.0%	4- 5	3- 4 M	1:39.1	2:05.1	2:57.7	3:53.1	4:49.3	6:45.0	8:43.2	10:43.4	12:44.5	14:46.2
82.5%	6- 7	2- 3 M	1:42.1	2:08.9	3:03.1	4:00.1	4:58.1	6:57.3	8:59.1	11:02.9	-----	-----
80.0%	8- 9	2- 3 M	1:45.3	2:12.9	3:08.8	4:07.6	5:07.4	7:10.3	-----	-----	-----	-----
77.5%	10-12	1- 2 M	1:48.6	2:17.2	3:14.9	4:15.6	5:17.3	-----	-----	-----	-----	-----
75.0%	13-15	1- 2 M	1:52.3	2:21.8	3:21.4	4:24.2	5:27.9	-----	-----	-----	-----	-----
72.5%	16-18	60-90 S	1:56.1	2:26.6	3:28.4	4:33.3	-----	-----	-----	-----	-----	-----
70.0%	19-21	60-90 S	2:00.3	2:31.9	3:35.8	-----	-----	-----	-----	-----	-----	-----
67.5%	22-24	45-75 S	2:04.7	2:37.5	-----	-----	-----	-----	-----	-----	-----	-----
65.0%	25-29	45-75 S	2:09.5	2:43.6	-----	-----	-----	-----	-----	-----	-----	-----
62.5%	30-35	30-60 S	2:14.7	-----	-----	-----	-----	-----	-----	-----	-----	-----
60.0%	36-40	30-60 S	-----	-----	-----	-----	-----	-----	-----	-----	-----	-----

400 POINT LEVEL PACING TABLE
••••••••••••••••••••••••••••••

SPEED	REPS	REST	110 YD	150 YD	165 YD	220 YD	275 YD	330 YD	352 YD	385 YD	440 YD	495 YD
95.0%	0- 1	---	13.4	18.6	20.6	28.1	36.7	46.2	50.2	56.4	1:07.1	1:18.3
92.5%	1- 2	4- 5 M	13.8	19.1	21.1	28.9	37.7	47.5	51.6	58.0	1:08.9	1:20.4
90.0%	2- 3	4- 5 M	14.1	19.6	21.7	29.7	38.7	48.8	53.0	59.6	1:10.9	1:22.7
87.5%	3- 4	3- 4 M	14.5	20.2	22.3	30.5	39.8	50.2	54.5	1:01.3	1:12.9	1:25.0
85.0%	4- 5	3- 4 M	15.0	20.8	23.0	31.4	41.0	51.7	56.2	1:03.1	1:15.0	1:27.5
82.5%	6- 7	2- 3 M	15.4	21.4	23.7	32.4	42.2	53.2	57.9	1:05.0	1:17.3	1:30.2
80.0%	8- 9	2- 3 M	15.9	22.1	24.4	33.4	43.5	54.9	59.7	1:07.0	1:19.7	1:33.0
77.5%	10-12	1- 2 M	16.4	22.8	25.2	34.5	44.9	56.7	1:01.6	1:09.2	1:22.3	1:36.0
75.0%	13-15	1- 2 M	17.0	23.5	26.1	35.6	46.4	58.6	1:03.6	1:11.5	1:25.0	1:39.2
72.5%	16-18	60-90 S	17.6	24.3	27.0	36.9	48.0	1:00.6	1:05.8	1:14.0	1:28.0	1:42.6
70.0%	19-21	60-90 S	18.2	25.2	27.9	38.2	49.8	1:02.7	1:08.2	1:16.6	1:31.1	1:46.3
67.5%	22-24	45-75 S	18.9	26.2	29.0	39.6	51.6	1:05.1	1:10.7	1:19.4	1:34.5	1:50.2
65.0%	25-29	45-75 S	19.6	27.2	30.1	41.1	53.6	1:07.6	1:13.4	1:22.5	1:38.1	1:54.4
62.5%	30-35	30-60 S	20.4	28.2	31.3	42.8	55.7	1:10.3	1:16.4	1:25.8	1:42.0	1:59.0
60.0%	36-40	30-60 S	21.2	29.4	32.6	44.5	58.1	1:13.2	1:19.5	1:29.4	1:46.3	2:04.0

SPEED	REPS	REST	550 YD	660 YD	880 YD	1100 YD	1320 YD	1.00 MI	1.25 MI	1.50 MI	1.75 MI	2.00 MI
95.0%	0- 1	---	1:29.9	1:53.6	2:41.5	3:31.8	4:23.0	6:08.3	7:56.0	9:45.4	11:35.7	13:26.5
92.5%	1- 2	4- 5 M	1:32.3	1:56.7	2:45.8	3:37.6	4:30.1	6:18.3	8:08.8	10:01.2	11:54.5	13:48.3
90.0%	2- 3	4- 5 M	1:34.9	1:59.9	2:50.4	3:43.6	4:37.6	6:28.8	8:22.4	10:17.9	12:14.3	14:11.3
87.5%	3- 4	3- 4 M	1:37.6	2:03.3	2:55.3	3:50.0	4:45.6	6:39.9	8:36.7	10:35.5	12:35.3	14:35.6
85.0%	4- 5	3- 4 M	1:40.5	2:06.9	3:00.5	3:56.8	4:54.0	6:51.7	8:51.9	10:54.2	12:57.5	15:01.4
82.5%	6- 7	2- 3 M	1:43.5	2:10.8	3:05.9	4:03.9	5:02.9	7:04.2	9:08.1	11:14.1	-----	-----
80.0%	8- 9	2- 3 M	1:46.8	2:14.9	3:11.8	4:11.6	5:12.3	7:17.4	-----	-----	-----	-----
77.5%	10-12	1- 2 M	1:50.2	2:19.2	3:17.9	4:19.7	5:22.4	-----	-----	-----	-----	-----
75.0%	13-15	1- 2 M	1:53.9	2:23.9	3:24.5	4:28.3	5:33.2	-----	-----	-----	-----	-----
72.5%	16-18	60-90 S	1:57.8	2:28.8	3:31.6	4:37.6	-----	-----	-----	-----	-----	-----
70.0%	19-21	60-90 S	2:02.0	2:34.1	3:39.1	-----	-----	-----	-----	-----	-----	-----
67.5%	22-24	45-75 S	2:06.6	2:39.9	-----	-----	-----	-----	-----	-----	-----	-----
65.0%	25-29	45-75 S	2:11.4	2:46.0	-----	-----	-----	-----	-----	-----	-----	-----
62.5%	30-35	30-60 S	2:16.7	-----	-----	-----	-----	-----	-----	-----	-----	-----
60.0%	36-40	30-60 S	-----	-----	-----	-----	-----	-----	-----	-----	-----	-----

380 POINT LEVEL PACING TABLE

SPEED	REPS	REST	110 YD	150 YD	165 YD	220 YD	275 YD	330 YD	352 YD	385 YD	440 YD	495 YD
95.0%	0- 1	---	13.6	18.8	20.8	28.5	37.1	46.8	50.9	57.2	1:08.1	1:19.4
92.5%	1- 2	4- 5 M	13.9	19.3	21.4	29.3	38.1	48.1	52.3	58.8	1:09.9	1:21.6
90.0%	2- 3	4- 5 M	14.3	19.8	22.0	30.1	39.2	49.4	53.7	1:00.4	1:11.9	1:23.8
87.5%	3- 4	3- 4 M	14.7	20.4	22.6	30.9	40.3	50.9	55.3	1:02.1	1:13.9	1:26.2
85.0%	4- 5	3- 4 M	15.2	21.0	23.3	31.8	41.5	52.4	56.9	1:04.0	1:16.1	1:28.8
82.5%	6- 7	2- 3 M	15.6	21.7	24.0	32.8	42.8	53.9	58.6	1:05.9	1:18.4	1:31.5
80.0%	8- 9	2- 3 M	16.1	22.3	24.7	33.8	44.1	55.6	1:00.5	1:07.9	1:20.8	1:34.3
77.5%	10-12	1- 2 M	16.6	23.1	25.5	34.9	45.5	57.4	1:02.4	1:10.1	1:23.4	1:37.4
75.0%	13-15	1- 2 M	17.2	23.8	26.4	36.1	47.0	59.3	1:04.5	1:12.5	1:26.2	1:40.6
72.5%	16-18	60-90 S	17.8	24.6	27.3	37.3	48.7	1:01.4	1:06.7	1:15.0	1:29.2	1:44.1
70.0%	19-21	60-90 S	18.4	25.5	28.3	38.7	50.4	1:03.6	1:09.1	1:17.7	1:32.4	1:47.1
67.5%	22-24	45-75 S	19.1	26.5	29.3	40.1	52.3	1:05.9	1:11.7	1:20.5	1:35.8	1:51.8
65.0%	25-29	45-75 S	19.8	27.5	30.4	41.6	54.3	1:08.5	1:14.4	1:23.6	1:39.5	1:56.1
62.5%	30-35	30-60 S	20.6	28.6	31.7	43.3	56.5	1:11.2	1:17.4	1:27.0	1:43.5	2:00.7
60.0%	36-40	30-60 S	21.5	29.8	33.0	45.1	58.8	1:14.2	1:20.6	1:30.6	1:47.8	2:05.8

SPEED	REPS	REST	550 YD	660 YD	880 YD	1100 YD	1320 YD	1.00 MI	1.25 MI	1.50 MI	1.75 MI	2.00 MI
95.0%	0- 1	---	1:31.2	1:55.3	2:44.0	3:35.2	4:27.3	6:14.5	8:04.0	9:55.4	11:47.7	13:40.6
92.5%	1- 2	4- 5 M	1:33.7	1:58.4	2:48.4	3:41.1	4:34.6	6:24.6	8:17.1	10:11.5	12:06.8	14:02.7
90.0%	2- 3	4- 5 M	1:36.3	2:01.7	2:53.1	3:47.2	4:42.2	6:35.3	8:30.9	10:28.5	12:27.0	14:26.1
87.5%	3- 4	3- 4 M	1:39.1	2:05.2	2:58.1	3:53.7	4:50.2	6:46.6	8:45.5	10:46.5	12:48.4	14:50.9
85.0%	4- 5	3- 4 M	1:42.0	2:08.9	3:03.3	4:00.6	4:58.8	6:58.6	9:01.0	11:05.5	13:11.0	15:17.1
82.5%	6- 7	2- 3 M	1:45.1	2:12.8	3:08.9	4:07.9	5:07.8	7:11.2	9:17.4	11:25.6	-----	-----
80.0%	8- 9	2- 3 M	1:48.4	2:16.9	3:14.8	4:15.6	5:17.5	7:24.7	-----	-----	-----	-----
77.5%	10-12	1- 2 M	1:51.8	2:21.3	3:21.0	4:23.9	5:27.7	-----	-----	-----	-----	-----
75.0%	13-15	1- 2 M	1:55.6	2:26.1	3:27.7	4:32.6	5:38.6	-----	-----	-----	-----	-----
72.5%	16-18	60-90 S	1:59.6	2:31.1	3:34.9	4:42.0	-----	-----	-----	-----	-----	-----
70.0%	19-21	60-90 S	2:03.8	2:36.5	3:42.6	-----	-----	-----	-----	-----	-----	-----
67.5%	22-24	45-75 S	2:08.4	2:42.3	-----	-----	-----	-----	-----	-----	-----	-----
65.0%	25-29	45-75 S	2:13.4	2:48.5	-----	-----	-----	-----	-----	-----	-----	-----
62.5%	30-35	30-60 S	2:18.7	-----	-----	-----	-----	-----	-----	-----	-----	-----
60.0%	36-40	30-60 S	-----	-----	-----	-----	-----	-----	-----	-----	-----	-----

360 POINT LEVEL PACING TABLE
•••••••••••••••••••••••••••••

SPEED	REPS	REST	110 YD	150 YD	165 YD	220 YD	275 YD	330 YD	352 YD	385 YD	440 YD	495 YD
95.0%	0- 1	---	13.7	19.0	21.1	28.8	37.6	47.5	51.6	58.0	1:09.0	1:20.6
92.5%	1- 2	4- 5 M	14.1	19.5	21.7	29.6	38.6	48.8	53.0	59.6	1:10.9	1:22.8
90.0%	2- 3	4- 5 M	14.5	20.1	22.3	30.4	39.7	50.1	54.5	1:01.2	1:12.9	1:25.1
87.5%	3- 4	3- 4 M	14.9	20.7	22.9	31.3	40.8	51.5	56.0	1:03.0	1:15.0	1:27.5
85.0%	4- 5	3- 4 M	15.3	21.3	23.6	32.2	42.1	53.1	57.7	1:04.8	1:17.2	1:30.1
82.5%	6- 7	2- 3 M	15.8	21.9	24.3	33.2	43.3	54.7	59.4	1:06.8	1:19.5	1:32.8
80.0%	8- 9	2- 3 M	16.3	22.6	25.0	34.2	44.7	56.4	1:01.3	1:08.9	1:22.0	1:35.7
77.5%	10-12	1- 2 M	16.8	23.3	25.8	35.4	46.1	58.2	1:03.3	1:11.1	1:24.6	1:38.8
75.0%	13-15	1- 2 M	17.4	24.1	26.7	36.5	47.7	1:00.1	1:05.4	1:13.5	1:27.5	1:42.1
72.5%	16-18	60-90 S	18.0	24.9	27.6	37.8	49.3	1:02.2	1:07.6	1:16.0	1:30.5	1:45.6
70.0%	19-21	60-90 S	18.6	25.8	28.6	39.1	51.1	1:04.4	1:10.0	1:18.7	1:33.7	1:49.4
67.5%	22-24	45-75 S	19.3	26.8	29.7	40.6	53.0	1:06.8	1:12.6	1:21.7	1:37.2	1:53.4
65.0%	25-29	45-75 S	20.1	27.8	30.8	42.1	55.0	1:09.4	1:15.4	1:24.8	1:40.9	1:57.8
62.5%	30-35	30-60 S	20.9	28.9	32.0	43.8	57.2	1:12.2	1:18.5	1:28.2	1:45.0	2:02.5
60.0%	36-40	30-60 S	21.7	30.1	33.4	45.7	59.6	1:15.2	1:21.7	1:31.9	1:49.3	2:07.6

SPEED	REPS	REST	550 YD	660 YD	880 YD	1100 YD	1320 YD	1.00 MI	1.25 MI	1.50 MI	1.75 MI	2.00 MI
95.0%	0- 1	---	1:32.6	1:57.1	2:46.6	3:38.8	4:31.8	6:20.9	8:12.4	10:05.8	12:00.2	13:55.1
92.5%	1- 2	4- 5 M	1:35.1	2:00.2	2:51.1	3:44.7	4:39.1	6:31.2	8:25.7	10:22.2	12:19.6	14:17.7
90.0%	2- 3	4- 5 M	1:37.7	2:03.6	2:55.9	3:50.9	4:46.9	6:42.0	8:39.8	10:39.5	12:40.2	14:41.5
87.5%	3- 4	3- 4 M	1:40.5	2:07.1	3:00.9	3:57.5	4:55.1	6:53.5	8:54.6	10:57.7	13:01.9	15:06.7
85.0%	4- 5	3- 4 M	1:43.5	2:10.9	3:06.2	4:04.5	5:03.7	7:05.7	9:10.3	11:17.1	13:24.9	15:33.3
82.5%	6- 7	2- 3 M	1:46.6	2:14.8	3:11.9	4:11.9	5:12.9	7:18.6	9:27.0	11:37.6	-----	-----
80.0%	8- 9	2- 3 M	1:50.0	2:19.0	3:17.9	4:19.8	5:22.7	7:32.3	-----	-----	-----	-----
77.5%	10-12	1- 2 M	1:53.5	2:23.5	3:24.3	4:28.2	5:33.1	-----	-----	-----	-----	-----
75.0%	13-15	1- 2 M	1:57.3	2:28.3	3:31.1	4:37.1	5:44.2	-----	-----	-----	-----	-----
72.5%	16-18	60-90 S	2:01.3	2:33.4	3:38.3	4:46.7	-----	-----	-----	-----	-----	-----
70.0%	19-21	60-90 S	2:05.7	2:38.9	3:46.1	-----	-----	-----	-----	-----	-----	-----
67.5%	22-24	45-75 S	2:10.3	2:44.8	-----	-----	-----	-----	-----	-----	-----	-----
65.0%	25-29	45-75 S	2:15.3	2:51.1	-----	-----	-----	-----	-----	-----	-----	-----
62.5%	30-35	30-60 S	2:20.8	-----	-----	-----	-----	-----	-----	-----	-----	-----
60.0%	36-40	30-60 S	-----	-----	-----	-----	-----	-----	-----	-----	-----	-----

340 POINT LEVEL PACING TABLE

SPEED	REPS	REST	110 YD	150 YD	165 YD	220 YD	275 YD	330 YD	352 YD	385 YD	440 YD	495 YD
95.0%	0- 1	---	13.9	19.3	21.3	29.2	38.1	48.1	52.3	58.8	1:10.1	1:21.8
92.5%	1- 2	4- 5 M	14.3	19.8	21.9	30.0	39.2	49.4	53.7	1:00.4	1:11.9	1:24.0
90.0%	2- 3	4- 5 M	14.7	20.3	22.5	30.8	40.2	50.8	55.2	1:02.1	1:13.9	1:26.3
87.5%	3- 4	3- 4 M	15.1	20.9	23.2	31.7	41.4	52.2	56.8	1:03.9	1:16.1	1:28.8
85.0%	4- 5	3- 4 M	15.5	21.5	23.9	32.6	42.6	53.8	58.5	1:05.8	1:18.3	1:31.4
82.5%	6- 7	2- 3 M	16.0	22.2	24.6	33.6	43.9	55.4	1:00.3	1:07.8	1:20.7	1:34.2
80.0%	8- 9	2- 3 M	16.5	22.9	25.3	34.7	45.3	57.1	1:02.1	1:09.9	1:23.2	1:37.1
77.5%	10-12	1- 2 M	17.0	23.6	26.2	35.8	46.7	59.0	1:04.1	1:12.1	1:25.9	1:40.3
75.0%	13-15	1- 2 M	17.6	24.4	27.0	37.0	48.3	1:01.0	1:06.3	1:14.5	1:28.7	1:43.6
72.5%	16-18	60-90 S	18.2	25.2	28.0	38.3	50.0	1:03.1	1:08.6	1:17.1	1:31.8	1:47.2
70.0%	19-21	60-90 S	18.8	26.1	29.0	39.6	51.7	1:05.3	1:11.0	1:19.9	1:35.1	1:51.0
67.5%	22-24	45-75 S	19.5	27.1	30.0	41.1	53.7	1:07.7	1:13.7	1:22.8	1:38.6	1:55.1
65.0%	25-29	45-75 S	20.3	28.2	31.2	42.7	55.7	1:10.3	1:16.5	1:26.0	1:42.4	1:59.5
62.5%	30-35	30-60 S	21.1	29.3	32.4	44.4	57.9	1:13.1	1:19.5	1:29.4	1:46.5	2:04.3
60.0%	36-40	30-60 S	22.0	30.5	33.8	46.2	1:00.4	1:16.2	1:22.9	1:33.2	1:50.9	2:09.5

SPEED	REPS	REST	550 YD	660 YD	880 YD	1100 YD	1320 YD	1.00 MI	1.25 MI	1.50 MI	1.75 MI	2.00 MI
95.0%	0- 1	---	1:34.0	1:58.9	2:49.3	3:42.4	4:36.4	6:27.5	8:21.1	10:16.6	12:13.1	14:10.2
92.5%	1- 2	4- 5 M	1:36.6	2:02.1	2:53.9	3:48.4	4:43.8	6:37.9	8:34.6	10:33.3	12:32.9	14:33.1
90.0%	2- 3	4- 5 M	1:39.2	2:05.5	2:58.7	3:54.8	4:51.7	6:49.0	8:48.9	10:50.8	12:53.8	14:57.4
87.5%	3- 4	3- 4 M	1:42.1	2:09.1	3:03.8	4:01.5	5:00.1	7:00.7	9:04.0	11:09.4	13:15.9	15:23.0
85.0%	4- 5	3- 4 M	1:45.1	2:12.9	3:09.2	4:08.6	5:08.9	7:13.0	9:20.0	11:29.1	13:39.3	15:50.2
82.5%	6- 7	2- 3 M	1:48.3	2:16.9	3:15.0	4:16.1	5:18.2	7:26.2	9:37.0	11:50.0	------	------
80.0%	8- 9	2- 3 M	1:51.6	2:21.2	3:21.1	4:24.1	5:28.2	7:40.1	7:54.9	------	------	------
77.5%	10-12	1- 2 M	1:55.2	2:25.8	3:27.6	4:32.6	5:38.8	7:54.9	------	------	------	------
75.0%	13-15	1- 2 M	1:59.1	2:30.6	3:34.5	4:41.7	5:50.1	------	------	------	------	------
72.5%	16-18	60-90 S	2:03.2	2:35.8	3:41.9	4:51.4	------	------	------	------	------	------
70.0%	19-21	60-90 S	2:07.6	2:41.4	3:49.8	------	------	------	------	------	------	------
67.5%	22-24	45-75 S	2:12.3	2:47.4	------	------	------	------	------	------	------	------
65.0%	25-29	45-75 S	2:17.4	2:53.8	------	------	------	------	------	------	------	------
62.5%	30-35	30-60 S	2:22.9	------	------	------	------	------	------	------	------	------
60.0%	36-40	30-60 S	------	------	------	------	------	------	------	------	------	------

320 POINT LEVEL PACING TABLE
• •

SPEED	REPS	REST	110 YD	150 YD	165 YD	220 YD	275 YD	330 YD	352 YD	385 YD	440 YD	495 YD
95.0%	0- 1	---	14.1	19.5	21.6	29.6	38.6	48.8	53.1	59.7	1:11.1	1:23.0
92.5%	1- 2	4- 5 M	14.4	20.0	22.2	30.4	39.7	50.1	54.5	1:01.3	1:13.0	1:25.3
90.0%	2- 3	4- 5 M	14.8	20.6	22.8	31.2	40.8	51.5	56.0	1:03.0	1:15.0	1:27.6
87.5%	3- 4	3- 4 M	15.3	21.2	23.5	32.1	41.9	53.0	57.6	1:04.8	1:17.2	1:30.1
85.0%	4- 5	3- 4 M	15.7	21.8	24.2	33.1	43.2	54.5	59.3	1:06.7	1:19.4	1:32.8
82.5%	6- 7	2- 3 M	16.2	22.5	24.9	34.1	44.5	56.2	1:01.1	1:08.7	1:21.9	1:35.6
80.0%	8- 9	2- 3 M	16.7	23.2	25.7	35.1	45.9	57.9	1:03.0	1:10.9	1:24.4	1:38.6
77.5%	10-12	1- 2 M	17.2	23.9	26.5	36.3	47.4	59.8	1:05.1	1:13.2	1:27.1	1:41.8
75.0%	13-15	1- 2 M	17.8	24.7	27.4	37.5	48.9	1:01.8	1:07.2	1:15.6	1:30.0	1:45.2
72.5%	16-18	60-90 S	18.4	25.6	28.3	38.8	50.6	1:03.9	1:09.5	1:18.2	1:33.1	1:48.8
70.0%	19-21	60-90 S	19.1	26.5	29.3	40.1	52.4	1:06.2	1:12.0	1:21.0	1:36.5	1:52.7
67.5%	22-24	45-75 S	19.8	27.4	30.4	41.6	54.4	1:08.7	1:14.7	1:24.0	1:40.0	1:56.9
65.0%	25-29	45-75 S	20.5	28.5	31.6	43.2	56.5	1:11.3	1:17.6	1:27.2	1:43.9	2:01.4
62.5%	30-35	30-60 S	21.4	29.6	32.8	45.0	58.7	1:14.2	1:20.7	1:30.7	1:48.0	2:06.2
60.0%	36-40	30-60 S	22.3	30.9	34.2	46.8	1:01.2	1:17.3	1:24.0	1:34.5	1:52.5	2:11.5

SPEED	REPS	REST	550 YD	660 YD	880 YD	1100 YD	1320 YD	1.00 MI	1.25 MI	1.50 MI	1.75 MI	2.00 MI
95.0%	0- 1	---	1:35.5	2:00.8	2:52.1	3:46.2	4:41.1	6:34.3	8:30.0	10:27.7	12:26.4	14:25.8
92.5%	1- 2	4- 5 M	1:38.0	2:04.1	2:56.8	3:52.3	4:48.7	6:44.9	8:43.8	10:44.7	12:46.6	14:49.2
90.0%	2- 3	4- 5 M	1:40.8	2:07.5	3:01.7	3:58.7	4:56.7	6:56.2	8:58.4	11:02.6	13:07.9	15:13.9
87.5%	3- 4	3- 4 M	1:43.6	2:11.2	3:06.9	4:05.5	5:05.2	7:08.1	9:13.7	11:21.5	13:30.4	15:40.0
85.0%	4- 5	3- 4 M	1:46.7	2:15.0	3:12.4	4:12.8	5:14.2	7:20.7	9:30.0	11:41.6	13:54.2	16:07.6
82.5%	6- 7	2- 3 M	1:49.9	2:19.1	3:18.2	4:20.4	5:23.7	7:34.0	9:47.3	12:02.9	-----	-----
80.0%	8- 9	2- 3 M	1:53.4	2:23.4	3:24.4	4:28.6	5:33.8	7:48.2	-----	-----	-----	-----
77.5%	10-12	1- 2 M	1:57.0	2:28.1	3:31.0	4:37.2	5:44.6	8:03.3	-----	-----	-----	-----
75.0%	13-15	1- 2 M	2:00.9	2:33.0	3:38.0	4:46.5	5:56.1	-----	-----	-----	-----	-----
72.5%	16-18	60-90 S	2:05.1	2:38.3	3:45.5	4:56.3	-----	-----	-----	-----	-----	-----
70.0%	19-21	60-90 S	2:09.5	2:43.9	3:53.6	-----	-----	-----	-----	-----	-----	-----
67.5%	22-24	45-75 S	2:14.3	2:50.0	-----	-----	-----	-----	-----	-----	-----	-----
65.0%	25-29	45-75 S	2:19.5	2:56.6	-----	-----	-----	-----	-----	-----	-----	-----
62.5%	30-35	30-60 S	2:25.1	-----	-----	-----	-----	-----	-----	-----	-----	-----
60.0%	36-40	30-60 S	2:31.1	-----	-----	-----	-----	-----	-----	-----	-----	-----

300 POINT LEVEL PACING TABLE
••••••••••••••••••••••••••••

SPEED	REPS	REST	110 YD	150 YD	165 YD	220 YD	275 YD	330 YD	352 YD	385 YD	440 YD	495 YD
95.0%	0- 1	---	14.2	19.7	21.9	30.0	39.2	49.5	53.8	1:00.5	1:12.1	1:24.3
92.5%	1- 2	4- 5 M	14.6	20.3	22.5	30.8	40.2	50.8	55.3	1:02.2	1:14.1	1:26.6
90.0%	2- 3	4- 5 M	15.0	20.8	23.1	31.6	41.3	52.2	56.8	1:03.9	1:16.2	1:29.0
87.5%	3- 4	3- 4 M	15.4	21.4	23.8	32.5	42.5	53.7	58.4	1:05.7	1:18.3	1:31.5
85.0%	4- 5	3- 4 M	15.9	22.1	24.5	33.5	43.8	55.3	1:00.2	1:07.7	1:20.6	1:34.2
82.5%	6- 7	2- 3 M	16.4	22.7	25.2	34.5	45.1	57.0	1:02.0	1:09.7	1:23.1	1:37.1
80.0%	8- 9	2- 3 M	16.9	23.4	26.0	35.6	46.5	58.8	1:03.9	1:11.9	1:25.7	1:40.1
77.5%	10-12	1- 2 M	17.4	24.2	26.8	36.7	48.0	1:00.7	1:06.0	1:14.2	1:28.4	1:43.3
75.0%	13-15	1- 2 M	18.0	25.0	27.7	38.0	49.6	1:02.7	1:08.2	1:16.7	1:31.4	1:46.8
72.5%	16-18	60-90 S	18.6	25.9	28.7	39.3	51.3	1:04.8	1:10.5	1:19.3	1:34.5	1:50.5
70.0%	19-21	60-90 S	19.3	26.8	29.7	40.7	53.1	1:07.2	1:13.0	1:22.2	1:37.9	1:54.4
67.5%	22-24	45-75 S	20.0	27.8	30.8	42.2	55.1	1:09.6	1:15.8	1:25.2	1:41.5	1:58.6
65.0%	25-29	45-75 S	20.8	28.9	32.0	43.8	57.2	1:12.3	1:18.7	1:28.5	1:45.4	2:03.2
62.5%	30-35	30-60 S	21.6	30.0	33.3	45.6	59.5	1:15.2	1:21.8	1:32.0	1:49.7	2:08.1
60.0%	36-40	30-60 S	22.5	31.3	34.6	47.5	1:02.0	1:18.3	1:25.2	1:35.9	1:54.2	2:13.5

SPEED	REPS	REST	550 YD	660 YD	880 YD	1100 YD	1320 YD	1.00 MI	1.25 MI	1.50 MI	1.75 MI	2.00 MI
95.0%	0- 1	---	1:37.0	2:02.7	2:55.0	3:50.0	4:46.0	6:41.3	8:39.3	10:39.3	12:40.3	14:42.0
92.5%	1- 2	4- 5 M	1:39.6	2:06.1	2:59.7	3:56.3	4:53.8	6:52.2	8:53.4	10:56.6	13:00.9	15:05.8
90.0%	2- 3	4- 5 M	1:42.3	2:09.6	3:04.7	4:02.8	5:01.9	7:03.6	9:08.2	11:14.8	13:22.5	15:31.0
87.5%	3- 4	3- 4 M	1:45.3	2:13.3	3:10.0	4:09.8	5:10.6	7:15.7	9:23.8	11:34.1	13:45.5	15:57.6
85.0%	4- 5	3- 4 M	1:48.4	2:17.2	3:15.6	4:17.1	5:19.7	7:28.6	9:40.4	11:54.5	14:09.8	16:25.7
82.5%	6- 7	2- 3 M	1:51.6	2:21.3	3:21.5	4:24.9	5:29.4	7:42.1	9:58.0	12:16.2	-----	-----
80.0%	8- 9	2- 3 M	1:55.1	2:25.8	3:27.8	4:33.2	5:39.7	7:56.6	-----	-----	-----	-----
77.5%	10-12	1- 2 M	1:58.8	2:30.5	3:34.5	4:42.0	5:50.6	8:12.0	-----	-----	-----	-----
75.0%	13-15	1- 2 M	2:02.8	2:35.5	3:41.7	4:51.4	6:02.3	-----	-----	-----	-----	-----
72.5%	16-18	60-90 S	2:07.0	2:40.8	3:49.3	5:01.4	-----	-----	-----	-----	-----	-----
70.0%	19-21	60-90 S	2:11.6	2:46.6	3:57.5	-----	-----	-----	-----	-----	-----	-----
67.5%	22-24	45-75 S	2:16.4	2:52.8	4:06.3	-----	-----	-----	-----	-----	-----	-----
65.0%	25-29	45-75 S	2:21.7	2:59.4	-----	-----	-----	-----	-----	-----	-----	-----
62.5%	30-35	30-60 S	2:27.4	-----	-----	-----	-----	-----	-----	-----	-----	-----
60.0%	36-40	30-60 S	2:33.5	-----	-----	-----	-----	-----	-----	-----	-----	-----

280 POINT LEVEL PACING TABLE
....

SPEED	REPS	REST	110 YD	150 YD	165 YD	220 YD	275 YD	330 YD	352 YD	385 YD	440 YD	495 YD
95.0%	0- 1	---	14.4	20.0	22.2	30.4	39.7	50.2	54.6	1:01.4	1:13.2	1:25.6
92.5%	1- 2	4- 5 M	14.8	20.5	22.8	31.2	40.8	51.5	56.1	1:03.1	1:15.2	1:27.9
90.0%	2- 3	4- 5 M	15.2	21.1	23.4	32.1	41.9	53.0	57.6	1:04.9	1:17.3	1:30.4
87.5%	3- 4	3- 4 M	15.6	21.7	24.1	33.0	43.1	54.5	59.3	1:06.7	1:19.5	1:33.0
85.0%	4- 5	3- 4 M	16.1	22.4	24.8	33.9	44.4	56.1	1:01.0	1:08.7	1:21.9	1:35.7
82.5%	6- 7	2- 3 M	16.6	23.0	25.5	35.0	45.7	57.8	1:02.9	1:10.7	1:24.3	1:38.6
80.0%	8- 9	2- 3 M	17.1	23.7	26.3	36.1	47.1	59.6	1:04.8	1:13.0	1:27.0	1:41.7
77.5%	10-12	1- 2 M	17.7	24.5	27.2	37.2	48.7	1:01.5	1:06.9	1:15.3	1:29.8	1:44.9
75.0%	13-15	1- 2 M	18.2	25.3	28.1	38.5	50.3	1:03.6	1:09.2	1:17.8	1:32.8	1:48.4
72.5%	16-18	60-90 S	18.9	26.2	29.0	39.8	52.0	1:05.8	1:11.5	1:20.5	1:36.0	1:52.2
70.0%	19-21	60-90 S	19.5	27.1	30.1	41.2	53.9	1:08.1	1:14.1	1:23.4	1:39.4	1:56.2
67.5%	22-24	45-75 S	20.3	28.1	31.2	42.7	55.9	1:10.6	1:16.8	1:26.5	1:43.1	2:00.5
65.0%	25-29	45-75 S	21.1	29.2	32.4	44.4	58.0	1:13.3	1:19.8	1:29.8	1:47.0	2:05.1
62.5%	30-35	30-60 S	21.9	30.4	33.7	46.2	1:00.3	1:16.3	1:23.0	1:33.4	1:51.3	2:10.1
60.0%	36-40	30-60 S	22.8	31.7	35.1	48.1	1:02.8	1:19.5	1:26.5	1:37.3	1:56.0	2:15.6

SPEED	REPS	REST	550 YD	660 YD	880 YD	1100 YD	1320 YD	1.00 MI	1.25 MI	1.50 MI	1.75 MI	2.00 MI
95.0%	0- 1	---	1:38.5	2:04.8	2:58.0	3:54.1	4:51.1	6:48.7	8:49.0	10:51.3	12:54.7	14:58.8
92.5%	1- 2	4- 5 M	1:41.2	2:08.1	3:02.8	4:00.4	4:59.0	6:59.7	9:03.3	11:08.9	13:15.6	15:23.1
90.0%	2- 3	4- 5 M	1:44.0	2:11.7	3:07.9	4:07.1	5:07.3	7:11.4	9:18.3	11:27.5	13:37.7	15:48.7
87.5%	3- 4	3- 4 M	1:46.9	2:15.5	3:13.2	4:14.1	5:16.1	7:23.7	9:34.3	11:47.1	14:01.1	16:15.8
85.0%	4- 5	3- 4 M	1:50.1	2:19.4	3:18.9	4:21.6	5:25.4	7:36.7	9:51.2	12:07.9	14:25.8	16:44.5
82.5%	6- 7	2- 3 M	1:53.4	2:23.7	3:24.9	4:29.5	5:35.2	7:50.6	10:09.1	12:30.0	-----	-----
80.0%	8- 9	2- 3 M	1:57.0	2:28.2	3:31.3	4:38.0	5:45.7	8:05.3	-----	-----	-----	-----
77.5%	10-12	1- 2 M	2:00.7	2:32.9	3:38.2	4:46.9	5:56.9	8:20.9	-----	-----	-----	-----
75.0%	13-15	1- 2 M	2:04.8	2:38.0	3:45.4	4:56.5	6:08.8	-----	-----	-----	-----	-----
72.5%	16-18	60-90 S	2:09.1	2:43.5	3:53.2	5:06.7	-----	-----	-----	-----	-----	-----
70.0%	19-21	60-90 S	2:13.7	2:49.3	4:01.5	-----	-----	-----	-----	-----	-----	-----
67.5%	22-24	45-75 S	2:18.6	2:55.6	4:10.5	-----	-----	-----	-----	-----	-----	-----
65.0%	25-29	45-75 S	2:23.9	3:02.3	-----	-----	-----	-----	-----	-----	-----	-----
62.5%	30-35	30-60 S	2:29.7	-----	-----	-----	-----	-----	-----	-----	-----	-----
60.0%	36-40	30-60 S	2:35.9	-----	-----	-----	-----	-----	-----	-----	-----	-----

260 POINT LEVEL PACING TABLE
••••••••••••••••••••••••••••

SPEED	REPS	REST	110 YD	150 YD	165 YD	220 YD	275 YD	330 YD	352 YD	385 YD	440 YD	495 YD
95.0%	0- 1	---	14.6	20.3	22.4	30.8	40.2	50.9	55.4	1:02.4	1:14.4	1:27.0
92.5%	1- 2	4- 5 M	15.0	20.8	23.1	31.6	41.3	52.3	56.9	1:04.0	1:16.4	1:29.3
90.0%	2- 3	4- 5 M	15.4	21.4	23.7	32.5	42.5	53.7	58.5	1:05.8	1:18.5	1:31.8
87.5%	3- 4	3- 4 M	15.8	22.0	24.4	33.4	43.7	55.3	1:00.2	1:07.7	1:20.7	1:34.4
85.0%	4- 5	3- 4 M	16.3	22.6	25.1	34.4	45.0	56.9	1:01.9	1:09.7	1:23.1	1:37.2
82.5%	6- 7	2- 3 M	16.8	23.3	25.9	35.4	46.3	58.6	1:03.8	1:11.8	1:25.6	1:40.1
80.0%	8- 9	2- 3 M	17.3	24.1	26.7	36.5	47.8	1:00.5	1:05.8	1:14.1	1:28.3	1:43.3
77.5%	10-12	1- 2 M	17.9	24.8	27.5	37.7	49.3	1:02.4	1:07.9	1:16.4	1:31.2	1:46.6
75.0%	13-15	1- 2 M	18.5	25.7	28.4	39.0	51.0	1:04.5	1:10.2	1:19.0	1:34.2	1:50.2
72.5%	16-18	60-90 S	19.1	26.5	29.4	40.3	52.7	1:06.7	1:12.6	1:21.7	1:37.5	1:54.0
70.0%	19-21	60-90 S	19.8	27.5	30.5	41.8	54.6	1:09.1	1:15.2	1:24.6	1:40.9	1:58.0
67.5%	22-24	45-75 S	20.5	28.5	31.6	43.3	56.6	1:11.7	1:18.0	1:27.8	1:44.7	2:02.4
65.0%	25-29	45-75 S	21.3	29.6	32.8	45.0	58.8	1:14.4	1:21.0	1:31.1	1:48.7	2:07.1
62.5%	30-35	30-60 S	22.2	30.8	34.1	46.8	1:01.2	1:17.4	1:24.2	1:34.8	1:53.0	2:12.2
60.0%	36-40	30-60 S	23.1	32.1	35.5	48.7	1:03.7	1:20.6	1:27.7	1:38.7	1:57.8	2:17.7

SPEED	REPS	REST	550 YD	660 YD	880 YD	1100 YD	1320 YD	1.00 MI	1.25 MI	1.50 MI	1.75 MI	2.00 MI
95.0%	0- 1	---	1:40.1	2:06.8	3:01.1	3:58.2	4:56.4	6:56.2	8:59.0	11:03.8	13:09.7	15:16.2
92.5%	1- 2	4- 5 M	1:42.8	2:10.3	3:06.0	4:04.7	5:04.4	7:07.5	9:13.5	11:21.7	13:31.0	15:41.0
90.0%	2- 3	4- 5 M	1:45.6	2:13.9	3:11.1	4:11.5	5:12.9	7:19.4	9:28.9	11:40.7	13:53.5	16:07.1
87.5%	3- 4	3- 4 M	1:48.7	2:17.7	3:16.6	4:18.7	5:21.8	7:31.9	9:45.2	12:00.7	14:17.3	16:34.8
85.0%	4- 5	3- 4 M	1:51.9	2:21.8	3:22.4	4:26.3	5:31.3	7:45.2	10:02.4	12:21.9	14:42.6	17:04.0
82.5%	6- 7	2- 3 M	1:55.2	2:26.1	3:28.5	4:34.3	5:41.3	7:59.3	10:20.6	12:44.3	-----	-----
80.0%	8- 9	2- 3 M	1:58.8	2:30.6	3:35.0	4:42.9	5:52.0	8:14.3	10:40.0	-----	-----	-----
77.5%	10-12	1- 2 M	2:02.7	2:35.5	3:41.9	4:52.0	6:03.3	8:30.2	-----	-----	-----	-----
75.0%	13-15	1- 2 M	2:06.8	2:40.7	3:49.3	5:01.8	6:15.5	-----	-----	-----	-----	-----
72.5%	16-18	60-90 S	2:11.1	2:46.2	3:57.2	5:12.2	-----	-----	-----	-----	-----	-----
70.0%	19-21	60-90 S	2:15.8	2:52.1	4:05.7	-----	-----	-----	-----	-----	-----	-----
67.5%	22-24	45-75 S	2:20.9	2:58.5	4:14.8	-----	-----	-----	-----	-----	-----	-----
65.0%	25-29	45-75 S	2:26.3	3:05.4	-----	-----	-----	-----	-----	-----	-----	-----
62.5%	30-35	30-60 S	2:32.1	-----	-----	-----	-----	-----	-----	-----	-----	-----
60.0%	36-40	30-60 S	2:38.5	-----	-----	-----	-----	-----	-----	-----	-----	-----

240 POINT LEVEL PACING TABLE
•••••••••••••••••••••••••••••

SPEED	REPS	REST	110 YD	150 YD	165 YD	220 YD	275 YD	330 YD	352 YD	385 YD	440 YD	495 YD
95.0%	0- 1	---	14.8	20.5	22.7	31.2	40.8	51.7	56.2	1:03.3	1:15.5	1:28.4
92.5%	1- 2	4- 5 M	15.2	21.1	23.4	32.0	41.9	53.1	57.8	1:05.0	1:17.6	1:30.8
90.0%	2- 3	4- 5 M	15.6	21.7	24.0	32.9	43.1	54.5	59.4	1:06.8	1:19.7	1:33.3
87.5%	3- 4	3- 4 M	16.0	22.3	24.7	33.9	44.3	56.1	1:01.1	1:08.7	1:22.0	1:35.9
85.0%	4- 5	3- 4 M	16.5	22.9	25.4	34.9	45.6	57.7	1:02.8	1:10.8	1:24.4	1:38.8
82.5%	6- 7	2- 3 M	17.0	23.6	26.2	35.9	47.0	59.5	1:04.8	1:12.9	1:27.0	1:41.8
80.0%	8- 9	2- 3 M	17.5	24.4	27.0	37.0	48.5	1:01.3	1:06.8	1:15.2	1:29.7	1:44.9
77.5%	10-12	1- 2 M	18.1	25.2	27.9	38.2	50.0	1:03.3	1:08.9	1:17.6	1:32.6	1:48.3
75.0%	13-15	1- 2 M	18.7	26.0	28.8	39.5	51.7	1:05.4	1:11.2	1:20.2	1:35.7	1:51.9
72.5%	16-18	60-90 S	19.4	26.9	29.8	40.9	53.5	1:07.7	1:13.7	1:23.0	1:39.0	1:55.8
70.0%	19-21	60-90 S	20.0	27.8	30.9	42.3	55.4	1:10.1	1:16.3	1:25.9	1:42.5	1:59.9
67.5%	22-24	45-75 S	20.8	28.9	32.0	43.9	57.4	1:12.7	1:19.1	1:29.1	1:46.3	2:04.4
65.0%	25-29	45-75 S	21.6	30.0	33.2	45.6	59.7	1:15.5	1:22.2	1:32.5	1:50.4	2:09.1
62.5%	30-35	30-60 S	22.5	31.2	34.6	47.4	1:02.0	1:18.5	1:25.5	1:36.2	1:54.8	2:14.3
60.0%	36-40	30-60 S	23.4	32.5	36.0	49.4	1:04.6	1:21.8	1:29.0	1:40.2	1:59.6	2:19.9

SPEED	REPS	REST	550 YD	660 YD	880 YD	1100 YD	1320 YD	1.00 MI	1.25 MI	1.50 MI	1.75 MI	2.00 MI
95.0%	0- 1	---	1:41.7	2:09.0	3:04.2	4:02.6	5:01.9	7:04.1	9:09.3	11:16.7	13:25.2	15:34.4
92.5%	1- 2	4- 5 M	1:44.5	2:12.5	3:09.2	4:09.1	5:10.0	7:15.6	9:24.2	11:35.0	13:47.0	15:59.7
90.0%	2- 3	4- 5 M	1:47.4	2:16.2	3:14.5	4:16.0	5:18.7	7:27.7	9:39.9	11:54.3	14:09.9	16:26.3
87.5%	3- 4	3- 4 M	1:50.4	2:20.0	3:20.0	4:23.3	5:27.8	7:40.5	9:56.4	12:14.7	14:34.2	16:54.5
85.0%	4- 5	3- 4 M	1:53.7	2:24.2	3:25.9	4:31.1	5:37.4	7:54.0	10:14.0	12:36.3	14:59.9	17:24.3
82.5%	6- 7	2- 3 M	1:57.1	2:28.5	3:32.2	4:39.3	5:47.6	8:08.4	10:32.6	12:59.3	-----	-----
80.0%	8- 9	2- 3 M	2:00.8	2:33.2	3:38.8	4:48.0	5:58.5	8:23.7	10:52.3	-----	-----	-----
77.5%	10-12	1- 2 M	2:04.7	2:38.1	3:45.9	4:57.3	6:10.0	8:39.9	-----	-----	-----	-----
75.0%	13-15	1- 2 M	2:08.8	2:43.4	3:53.4	5:07.2	6:22.4	-----	-----	-----	-----	-----
72.5%	16-18	60-90 S	2:13.3	2:49.0	4:01.4	5:17.8	-----	-----	-----	-----	-----	-----
70.0%	19-21	60-90 S	2:18.1	2:55.1	4:10.1	-----	-----	-----	-----	-----	-----	-----
67.5%	22-24	45-75 S	2:23.2	3:01.5	4:19.3	-----	-----	-----	-----	-----	-----	-----
65.0%	25-29	45-75 S	2:28.7	3:08.5	-----	-----	-----	-----	-----	-----	-----	-----
62.5%	30-35	30-60 S	2:34.6	-----	-----	-----	-----	-----	-----	-----	-----	-----
60.0%	36-40	30-60 S	2:41.1	-----	-----	-----	-----	-----	-----	-----	-----	-----

220 POINT LEVEL PACING TABLE
••••••••••••••••••••••••••••

SPEED	REPS	REST	110 YD	150 YD	165 YD	220 YD	275 YD	330 YD	352 YD	385 YD	440 YD	495 YD
95.0%	0- 1	---	15.0	20.8	23.0	31.6	41.4	52.4	57.1	1:04.3	1:16.7	1:29.8
92.5%	1- 2	4- 5 M	15.4	21.4	23.7	32.5	42.5	53.8	58.6	1:06.0	1:18.8	1:32.2
90.0%	2- 3	4- 5 M	15.8	21.9	24.3	33.4	43.7	55.3	1:00.3	1:07.9	1:21.0	1:34.8
87.5%	3- 4	3- 4 M	16.2	22.6	25.0	34.3	45.0	56.9	1:02.0	1:09.8	1:23.3	1:37.5
85.0%	4- 5	3- 4 M	16.7	23.2	25.8	35.3	46.3	58.6	1:03.8	1:11.4	1:25.8	1:40.4
82.5%	6- 7	2- 3 M	17.2	23.9	26.5	36.4	47.7	1:00.4	1:05.7	1:14.0	1:28.4	1:43.4
80.0%	8- 9	2- 3 M	17.8	24.7	27.4	37.6	49.2	1:02.3	1:07.8	1:16.3	1:31.1	1:46.6
77.5%	10-12	1- 2 M	18.3	25.5	28.3	38.8	50.8	1:04.3	1:10.0	1:18.8	1:34.1	1:50.1
75.0%	13-15	1- 2 M	19.0	26.3	29.2	40.1	52.4	1:06.4	1:12.3	1:21.4	1:37.2	1:53.8
72.5%	16-18	60-90 S	19.6	27.2	30.2	41.4	54.3	1:08.7	1:14.8	1:24.2	1:40.6	1:57.7
70.0%	19-21	60-90 S	20.3	28.2	31.3	42.9	56.2	1:11.2	1:17.5	1:27.2	1:44.1	2:01.9
67.5%	22-24	45-75 S	21.1	29.3	32.4	44.5	58.3	1:13.8	1:20.3	1:30.5	1:48.0	2:06.4
65.0%	25-29	45-75 S	21.9	30.4	33.7	46.2	1:00.5	1:16.6	1:23.4	1:34.0	1:52.2	2:11.3
62.5%	30-35	30-60 S	22.7	31.6	35.0	48.1	1:02.9	1:19.7	1:26.8	1:37.7	1:56.6	2:16.5
60.0%	36-40	30-60 S	23.7	32.9	36.5	50.1	1:05.6	1:23.0	1:30.4	1:41.8	2:01.5	2:22.2

SPEED	REPS	REST	550 YD	660 YD	880 YD	1100 YD	1320 YD	1.00 MI	1.25 MI	1.50 MI	1.75 MI	2.00 MI
95.0%	0- 1	---	1:43.4	2:11.2	3:07.6	4:07.0	5:07.6	7:12.3	9:20.1	11:30.2	13:41.4	15:53.3
92.5%	1- 2	4- 5 M	1:46.2	2:14.8	3:12.6	4:13.7	5:15.9	7:24.0	9:35.3	11:48.8	14:03.6	16:19.1
90.0%	2- 3	4- 5 M	1:49.2	2:18.5	3:18.0	4:20.8	5:24.6	7:36.3	9:51.3	12:08.5	14:27.0	16:46.3
87.5%	3- 4	3- 4 M	1:52.3	2:22.5	3:23.6	4:28.2	5:33.9	7:49.4	10:08.2	12:29.3	14:51.8	17:15.0
85.0%	4- 5	3- 4 M	1:55.6	2:26.7	3:29.6	4:36.1	5:43.7	8:03.2	10:26.0	12:51.4	15:18.0	17:45.5
82.5%	6- 7	2- 3 M	1:59.1	2:31.1	3:36.0	4:44.5	5:54.2	8:17.8	10:45.0	13:14.8	-----	-----
80.0%	8- 9	2- 3 M	2:02.8	2:35.8	3:42.7	4:53.3	6:05.2	8:33.4	11:05.2	-----	-----	-----
77.5%	10-12	1- 2 M	2:06.8	2:40.8	3:49.9	5:02.8	6:17.0	8:49.9	-----	-----	-----	-----
75.0%	13-15	1- 2 M	2:11.0	2:46.2	3:57.6	5:12.9	6:29.6	-----	-----	-----	-----	-----
72.5%	16-18	60-90 S	2:15.5	2:51.9	4:05.8	5:23.7	-----	-----	-----	-----	-----	-----
70.0%	19-21	60-90 S	2:20.4	2:58.1	4:14.5	-----	-----	-----	-----	-----	-----	-----
67.5%	22-24	45-75 S	2:25.6	3:04.7	4:24.0	-----	-----	-----	-----	-----	-----	-----
65.0%	25-29	45-75 S	2:31.2	3:11.8	-----	-----	-----	-----	-----	-----	-----	-----
62.5%	30-35	30-60 S	2:37.2	3:19.4	-----	-----	-----	-----	-----	-----	-----	-----
60.0%	36-40	30-60 S	2:43.7	-----	-----	-----	-----	-----	-----	-----	-----	-----

200 POINT LEVEL PACING TABLE
•••••••••••••••••••••••••••••

SPEED	REPS	REST	110 YD	150 YD	165 YD	220 YD	275 YD	330 YD	352 YD	385 YD	440 YD	495 YD
95.0%	0- 1	---	15.2	21.1	23.4	32.1	42.0	53.2	58.0	1:05.3	1:18.0	1:31.3
92.5%	1- 2	4- 5 M	15.6	21.6	24.0	32.9	43.1	54.7	59.5	1:07.1	1:20.1	1:33.8
90.0%	2- 3	4- 5 M	16.0	22.2	24.7	33.8	44.3	56.2	1:01.2	1:08.9	1:22.3	1:36.4
87.5%	3- 4	3- 4 M	16.5	22.9	25.4	34.8	45.6	57.8	1:02.9	1:10.9	1:24.7	1:39.1
85.0%	4- 5	3- 4 M	16.9	23.5	26.1	35.8	46.9	59.5	1:04.8	1:13.0	1:27.1	1:42.0
82.5%	6- 7	2- 3 M	17.5	24.3	26.9	36.9	48.4	1:01.3	1:06.7	1:15.2	1:29.8	1:45.1
80.0%	8- 9	2- 3 M	18.0	25.0	27.7	38.1	49.9	1:03.2	1:08.8	1:17.5	1:32.6	1:48.4
77.5%	10-12	1- 2 M	18.6	25.8	28.6	39.3	51.5	1:05.2	1:11.0	1:20.0	1:35.6	1:51.9
75.0%	13-15	1- 2 M	19.2	26.7	29.6	40.6	53.2	1:07.4	1:13.4	1:22.7	1:38.8	1:55.6
72.5%	16-18	60-90 S	19.9	27.6	30.6	42.0	55.0	1:09.7	1:15.9	1:25.6	1:42.2	1:59.6
70.0%	19-21	60-90 S	20.6	28.6	31.7	43.5	57.0	1:12.2	1:18.7	1:28.6	1:45.8	2:03.9
67.5%	22-24	45-75 S	21.3	29.7	32.9	45.1	59.1	1:14.9	1:21.6	1:31.9	1:49.7	2:08.5
65.0%	25-29	45-75 S	22.2	30.8	34.1	46.9	1:01.4	1:17.8	1:24.7	1:35.4	1:54.0	2:13.4
62.5%	30-35	30-60 S	23.0	32.0	35.5	48.7	1:03.8	1:20.9	1:28.1	1:39.2	1:58.5	2:18.8
60.0%	36-40	30-60 S	24.0	33.4	37.0	50.8	1:06.5	1:24.3	1:31.8	1:43.4	2:03.5	2:24.6

SPEED	REPS	REST	550 YD	660 YD	880 YD	1100 YD	1320 YD	1.00 MI	1.25 MI	1.50 MI	1.75 MI	2.00 MI
95.0%	0- 1	---	1:45.2	2:13.5	3:11.0	4:11.7	5:13.5	7:20.8	9:31.4	11:44.2	13:58.2	16:13.0
92.5%	1- 2	4- 5 M	1:48.0	2:17.1	3:16.1	4:18.5	5:21.9	7:32.7	9:46.8	12:03.2	14:20.9	16:39.3
90.0%	2- 3	4- 5 M	1:51.0	2:20.9	3:21.6	4:25.7	5:30.9	7:45.3	10:03.1	12:23.3	14:44.8	17:07.0
87.5%	3- 4	3- 4 M	1:54.2	2:25.0	3:27.4	4:33.2	5:40.3	7:58.6	10:20.3	12:44.6	15:10.0	17:36.4
85.0%	4- 5	3- 4 M	1:57.5	2:29.2	3:33.5	4:41.3	5:50.3	8:12.7	10:38.6	13:07.0	15:36.8	18:07.5
82.5%	6- 7	2- 3 M	2:01.1	2:33.7	3:39.9	4:49.8	6:01.0	8:27.6	10:57.9	13:30.9	-----	-----
80.0%	8- 9	2- 3 M	2:04.9	2:38.6	3:46.8	4:58.9	6:12.2	8:43.5	11:18.5	-----	-----	-----
77.5%	10-12	1- 2 M	2:08.9	2:43.7	3:54.1	5:08.5	6:24.2	9:00.4	-----	-----	-----	-----
75.0%	13-15	1- 2 M	2:13.2	2:49.1	4:01.9	5:18.8	6:37.0	-----	-----	-----	-----	-----
72.5%	16-18	60-90 S	2:17.8	2:55.0	4:10.3	5:29.8	-----	-----	-----	-----	-----	-----
70.0%	19-21	60-90 S	2:22.7	3:01.2	4:19.2	-----	-----	-----	-----	-----	-----	-----
67.5%	22-24	45-75 S	2:28.0	3:07.9	4:28.8	-----	-----	-----	-----	-----	-----	-----
65.0%	25-29	45-75 S	2:33.7	3:15.1	-----	-----	-----	-----	-----	-----	-----	-----
62.5%	30-35	30-60 S	2:39.9	3:22.9	-----	-----	-----	-----	-----	-----	-----	-----
60.0%	36-40	30-60 S	2:46.5	-----	-----	-----	-----	-----	-----	-----	-----	-----

180 POINT LEVEL PACING TABLE

SPEED	REPS	REST	110 YD	150 YD	165 YD	220 YD	275 YD	330 YD	352 YD	385 YD	440 YD	495 YD
95.0%	0- 1	---	15.4	21.4	23.7	32.5	42.6	54.0	58.9	1:06.3	1:19.3	1:32.8
92.5%	1- 2	4- 5 M	15.8	21.9	24.3	33.4	43.8	55.5	1:00.5	1:08.1	1:21.4	1:35.3
90.0%	2- 3	4- 5 M	16.2	22.5	25.0	34.3	45.0	57.0	1:02.1	1:10.0	1:23.7	1:38.0
87.5%	3- 4	3- 4 M	16.7	23.2	25.7	35.3	46.3	58.7	1:03.9	1:12.0	1:26.1	1:40.8
85.0%	4- 5	3- 4 M	17.2	23.9	26.5	36.3	47.6	1:00.4	1:05.8	1:14.1	1:28.6	1:43.8
82.5%	6- 7	2- 3 M	17.7	24.6	27.3	37.4	49.1	1:02.2	1:07.8	1:16.4	1:31.3	1:46.9
80.0%	8- 9	2- 3 M	18.2	25.4	28.1	38.6	50.6	1:04.2	1:09.9	1:18.8	1:34.1	1:50.2
77.5%	10-12	1- 2 M	18.8	26.2	29.0	39.9	52.2	1:06.2	1:12.2	1:21.3	1:37.2	1:53.8
75.0%	13-15	1- 2 M	19.5	27.0	30.0	41.2	54.0	1:08.5	1:14.6	1:24.0	1:40.4	1:57.6
72.5%	16-18	60-90 S	20.1	28.0	31.0	42.6	55.9	1:10.8	1:17.1	1:26.9	1:43.9	2:01.6
70.0%	19-21	60-90 S	20.8	29.0	32.1	44.1	57.8	1:13.3	1:19.9	1:30.0	1:47.6	2:06.0
67.5%	22-24	45-75 S	21.6	30.1	33.3	45.8	1:00.0	1:16.1	1:22.8	1:33.4	1:51.5	2:10.7
65.0%	25-29	45-75 S	22.5	31.2	34.6	47.5	1:02.3	1:19.0	1:26.0	1:36.9	1:55.8	2:15.7
62.5%	30-35	30-60 S	23.3	32.5	36.0	49.4	1:04.8	1:22.1	1:29.5	1:40.8	2:00.5	2:21.1
60.0%	36-40	30-60 S	24.3	33.8	37.5	51.5	1:07.5	1:25.6	1:33.2	1:45.0	2:05.5	2:27.0

SPEED	REPS	REST	550 YD	660 YD	880 YD	1100 YD	1320 YD	1.00 MI	1.25 MI	1.50 MI	1.75 MI	2.00 MI
95.0%	0- 1	----	1:47.0	2:15.9	3:14.5	4:16.5	5:19.6	7:29.7	9:43.1	11:58.8	14:15.7	16:33.5
92.5%	1- 2	4- 5 M	1:49.9	2:19.6	3:19.8	4:23.4	5:28.2	7:41.8	9:58.8	12:18.2	14:38.9	17:00.3
90.0%	2- 3	4- 5 M	1:52.9	2:23.5	3:25.3	4:30.7	5:37.3	7:54.6	10:15.5	12:38.7	15:03.3	17:28.7
87.5%	3- 4	3- 4 M	1:56.2	2:27.6	3:31.2	4:38.5	5:47.0	8:08.2	10:33.0	13:00.4	15:03.3	17:28.7
85.0%	4- 5	3- 4 M	1:59.6	2:31.9	3:37.4	4:46.7	5:57.2	8:22.6	10:51.7	13:23.3	15:56.4	18:30.4
82.5%	6- 7	2- 3 M	2:03.2	2:36.5	3:44.0	4:55.4	6:08.0	8:37.8	11:11.4	13:47.7	-----	-----
80.0%	8- 9	2- 3 M	2:07.1	2:41.4	3:51.0	5:04.6	6:19.5	8:54.0	11:32.4	13:47.7	-----	-----
77.5%	10-12	1- 2 M	2:11.1	2:46.6	3:58.5	5:14.4	6:31.7	9:11.2	-----	-----	-----	-----
75.0%	13-15	1- 2 M	2:15.5	2:52.1	4:06.4	5:24.9	6:44.8	-----	-----	-----	-----	-----
72.5%	16-18	60-90 S	2:20.2	2:58.1	4:14.9	5:36.1	-----	-----	-----	-----	-----	-----
70.0%	19-21	60-90 S	2:25.2	3:04.4	4:24.0	-----	-----	-----	-----	-----	-----	-----
67.5%	22-24	45-75 S	2:30.6	3:11.3	4:33.8	-----	-----	-----	-----	-----	-----	-----
65.0%	25-29	45-75 S	2:36.4	3:18.6	-----	-----	-----	-----	-----	-----	-----	-----
62.5%	30-35	30-60 S	2:42.6	3:26.6	-----	-----	-----	-----	-----	-----	-----	-----
60.0%	36-40	30-60 S	2:49.4	-----	-----	-----	-----	-----	-----	-----	-----	-----

160 POINT LEVEL PACING TABLE
• •

SPEED	REPS	REST	110 YD	150 YD	165 YD	220 YD	275 YD	330 YD	352 YD	385 YD	440 YD	495 YD
95.0%	0- 1	---	15.6	21.6	24.0	33.0	43.3	54.9	59.8	1:07.4	1:20.6	1:34.4
92.5%	1- 2	4- 5 M	16.0	22.2	24.7	33.9	44.4	56.4	1:01.4	1:09.2	1:22.8	1:37.0
90.0%	2- 3	4- 5 M	16.4	22.9	25.3	34.8	45.7	57.9	1:03.1	1:11.2	1:25.1	1:39.7
87.5%	3- 4	3- 4 M	16.9	23.5	26.1	35.8	47.0	59.6	1:04.9	1:13.2	1:27.5	1:42.5
85.0%	4- 5	3- 4 M	17.4	24.2	26.8	36.9	48.4	1:01.3	1:06.8	1:15.3	1:30.1	1:45.5
82.5%	6- 7	2- 3 M	17.9	24.9	27.6	38.0	49.8	1:03.2	1:08.9	1:17.6	1:32.8	1:48.7
80.0%	8- 9	2- 3 M	18.5	25.7	28.5	39.2	51.4	1:05.2	1:11.0	1:20.0	1:35.7	1:52.1
77.5%	10-12	1- 2 M	19.1	26.5	29.4	40.4	53.0	1:07.3	1:13.3	1:22.6	1:38.8	1:55.8
75.0%	13-15	1- 2 M	19.7	27.4	30.4	41.8	54.8	1:09.5	1:15.7	1:25.4	1:42.1	1:59.6
72.5%	16-18	60-90 S	20.4	28.4	31.5	43.2	56.7	1:11.9	1:18.4	1:28.3	1:45.6	2:03.7
70.0%	19-21	60-90 S	21.1	29.4	32.6	44.8	58.7	1:14.5	1:21.1	1:31.5	1:49.4	2:08.2
67.5%	22-24	45-75 S	21.9	30.5	33.8	46.4	1:00.9	1:17.2	1:24.2	1:34.9	1:53.4	2:12.9
65.0%	25-29	45-75 S	22.8	31.6	35.1	48.2	1:03.2	1:20.2	1:27.4	1:38.5	1:57.8	2:18.0
62.5%	30-35	30-60 S	23.7	32.9	36.5	50.1	1:05.8	1:23.4	1:30.9	1:42.5	2:02.5	2:23.5
60.0%	36-40	30-60 S	24.7	34.3	38.0	52.2	1:08.5	1:26.9	1:34.7	1:46.7	2:07.6	2:29.5

SPEED	REPS	REST	550 YD	660 YD	880 YD	1100 YD	1320 YD	1.00 MI	1.25 MI	1.50 MI	1.75 MI	2.00 MI
95.0%	0- 1	---	1:48.9	2:18.4	3:18.2	4:21.5	5:26.0	7:38.9	9:55.2	12:14.0	14:34.0	16:54.9
92.5%	1- 2	4- 5 M	1:51.8	2:22.1	3:23.6	4:28.6	5:34.8	7:51.3	10:11.3	12:33.8	14:57.6	17:22.3
90.0%	2- 3	4- 5 M	1:54.9	2:26.1	3:29.2	4:36.0	5:44.1	8:04.4	10:28.3	12:54.8	15:22.6	17:51.3
87.5%	3- 4	3- 4 M	1:58.2	2:30.2	3:35.2	4:43.9	5:53.9	8:18.2	10:46.3	13:16.9	15:48.9	18:21.9
85.0%	4- 5	3- 4 M	2:01.7	2:34.7	3:41.5	4:52.3	6:04.3	8:32.9	11:05.3	13:40.3	16:16.8	18:54.3
82.5%	6- 7	2- 3 M	2:05.4	2:39.3	3:48.3	5:01.1	6:15.3	8:48.4	11:25.4	14:05.2	-----	-----
80.0%	8- 9	2- 3 M	2:09.3	2:44.3	3:55.4	5:10.5	6:27.1	9:04.9	11:46.8	-----	-----	-----
77.5%	10-12	1- 2 M	2:13.5	2:49.6	4:03.0	5:20.6	6:39.6	9:22.5	-----	-----	-----	-----
75.0%	13-15	1- 2 M	2:17.9	2:55.3	4:11.1	5:31.2	6:52.9	-----	-----	-----	-----	-----
72.5%	16-18	60-90 S	2:22.7	3:01.3	4:19.7	5:42.7	-----	-----	-----	-----	-----	-----
70.0%	19-21	60-90 S	2:27.8	3:07.8	4:29.0	-----	-----	-----	-----	-----	-----	-----
67.5%	22-24	45-75 S	2:33.2	3:14.8	4:39.0	-----	-----	-----	-----	-----	-----	-----
65.0%	25-29	45-75 S	2:39.1	3:22.2	-----	-----	-----	-----	-----	-----	-----	-----
62.5%	30-35	30-60 S	2:45.5	3:30.3	-----	-----	-----	-----	-----	-----	-----	-----
60.0%	36-40	30-60 S	2:52.4	-----	-----	-----	-----	-----	-----	-----	-----	-----

140 POINT LEVEL PACING TABLE
• •

SPEED	REPS	REST	110 YD	150 YD	165 YD	220 YD	275 YD	330 YD	352 YD	385 YD	440 YD	495 YD
95.0%	0- 1	----	15.8	21.9	24.3	33.5	43.9	55.8	1:00.8	1:08.5	1:21.9	1:36.1
92.5%	1- 2	4- 5 M	16.2	22.5	25.0	34.4	45.1	57.3	1:02.4	1:10.4	1:24.2	1:38.7
90.0%	2- 3	4- 5 M	16.7	23.2	25.7	35.3	46.4	58.9	1:04.1	1:12.3	1:26.5	1:41.4
87.5%	3- 4	3- 4 M	17.1	23.8	26.4	36.3	47.7	1:00.5	1:06.0	1:14.4	1:29.0	1:44.3
85.0%	4- 5	3- 4 M	17.6	24.5	27.2	37.4	49.1	1:02.3	1:07.9	1:16.6	1:31.6	1:47.4
82.5%	6- 7	2- 3 M	18.2	25.3	28.0	38.5	50.6	1:04.2	1:10.0	1:18.9	1:34.4	1:50.6
80.0%	8- 9	2- 3 M	18.7	26.1	28.9	39.7	52.2	1:06.2	1:12.1	1:21.4	1:37.3	1:54.1
77.5%	10-12	1- 2 M	19.3	26.9	29.8	41.0	53.8	1:08.3	1:14.5	1:24.0	1:40.5	1:57.8
75.0%	13-15	1- 2 M	20.0	27.8	30.8	42.4	55.6	1:10.6	1:17.0	1:26.8	1:43.8	2:01.7
72.5%	16-18	60-90 S	20.7	28.8	31.9	43.9	57.6	1:13.1	1:19.6	1:29.8	1:47.4	2:05.9
70.0%	19-21	60-90 S	21.4	29.8	33.0	45.4	59.6	1:15.7	1:22.5	1:33.0	1:51.2	2:10.4
67.5%	22-24	45-75 S	22.2	30.9	34.3	47.1	1:01.8	1:18.5	1:25.5	1:36.4	1:55.3	2:15.2
65.0%	25-29	45-75 S	23.1	32.1	35.6	48.9	1:04.2	1:21.5	1:28.8	1:40.1	1:59.8	2:20.4
62.5%	30-35	30-60 S	24.0	33.4	37.0	50.9	1:06.8	1:24.7	1:32.4	1:44.1	2:04.6	2:26.0
60.0%	36-40	30-60 S	25.0	34.8	38.5	53.0	1:09.5	1:28.3	1:36.2	1:48.5	2:09.8	2:32.1

SPEED	REPS	REST	550 YD	660 YD	880 YD	1100 YD	1320 YD	1.00 MI	1.25 MI	1.50 MI	1.75 MI	2.00 MI
95.0%	0- 1	----	1:50.8	2:20.9	3:22.1	4:26.7	5:32.6	7:48.5	10:07.9	12:29.9	14:53.1	17:17.2
92.5%	1- 2	4- 5 M	1:53.8	2:24.7	3:27.5	4:33.9	5:41.6	8:01.1	10:24.4	12:50.1	15:17.2	17:45.2
90.0%	2- 3	4- 5 M	1:57.0	2:28.8	3:33.3	4:41.5	5:51.1	8:14.5	10:41.7	13:11.5	15:42.7	18:14.8
87.5%	3- 4	3- 4 M	2:00.3	2:33.0	3:39.4	4:49.6	6:01.1	8:28.6	11:00.0	13:34.1	16:09.6	18:46.1
85.0%	4- 5	3- 4 M	2:03.9	2:37.5	3:45.8	4:58.1	6:11.7	8:43.6	11:19.5	13:58.1	16:38.2	19:19.2
82.5%	6- 7	2- 3 M	2:07.6	2:42.3	3:52.7	5:07.1	6:23.0	8:59.5	11:40.0	14:23.5	-----	-----
80.0%	8- 9	2- 3 M	2:11.6	2:47.4	3:59.9	5:16.7	6:34.9	9:16.3	12:01.9	-----	-----	-----
77.5%	10-12	1- 2 M	2:15.8	2:52.8	4:07.7	5:26.9	6:47.7	9:34.3	-----	-----	-----	-----
75.0%	13-15	1- 2 M	2:20.4	2:58.5	4:15.9	5:37.8	7:01.3	-----	-----	-----	-----	-----
72.5%	16-18	60-90 S	2:25.2	3:04.7	4:24.8	5:49.5	-----	-----	-----	-----	-----	-----
70.0%	19-21	60-90 S	2:30.4	3:11.3	4:34.2	6:02.0	-----	-----	-----	-----	-----	-----
67.5%	22-24	45-75 S	2:36.0	3:18.4	4:44.4	-----	-----	-----	-----	-----	-----	-----
65.0%	25-29	45-75 S	2:42.0	3:26.0	-----	-----	-----	-----	-----	-----	-----	-----
62.5%	30-35	30-60 S	2:48.4	3:34.2	-----	-----	-----	-----	-----	-----	-----	-----
60.0%	36-40	30-60 S	2:55.5	-----	-----	-----	-----	-----	-----	-----	-----	-----

120 POINT LEVEL PACING TABLE
••••••••••••••••••••••••••••

SPEED	REPS	REST	110 YD	150 YD	165 YD	220 YD	275 YD	330 YD	352 YD	385 YD	440 YD	495 YD
95.0%	0- 1	---	16.0	22.3	24.7	34.0	44.6	56.7	1:01.8	1:09.7	1:23.4	1:37.8
92.5%	1- 2	4- 5 M	16.4	22.9	25.4	34.9	45.8	58.2	1:03.4	1:11.5	1:25.6	1:40.4
90.0%	2- 3	4- 5 M	16.9	23.5	26.1	35.9	47.1	59.8	1:05.2	1:13.5	1:28.0	1:43.2
87.5%	3- 4	3- 4 M	17.4	24.2	26.8	36.9	48.4	1:01.5	1:07.0	1:15.6	1:30.5	1:46.2
85.0%	4- 5	3- 4 M	17.9	24.9	27.6	38.0	49.8	1:03.3	1:09.0	1:17.9	1:33.2	1:49.3
82.5%	6- 7	2- 3 M	18.4	25.6	28.4	39.1	51.4	1:05.2	1:11.1	1:20.2	1:36.0	1:52.6
80.0%	8- 9	2- 3 M	19.0	26.4	29.3	40.3	53.0	1:07.3	1:13.3	1:22.7	1:39.0	1:56.1
77.5%	10-12	1- 2 M	19.6	27.3	30.3	41.6	54.7	1:09.4	1:15.7	1:25.4	1:42.2	1:59.9
75.0%	13-15	1- 2 M	20.3	28.2	31.3	43.0	56.5	1:11.8	1:18.2	1:28.2	1:45.6	2:03.9
72.5%	16-18	60-90 S	21.0	29.2	32.4	44.5	58.4	1:14.2	1:20.9	1:31.3	1:49.2	2:08.1
70.0%	19-21	60-90 S	21.7	30.2	33.5	46.1	1:00.5	1:16.9	1:23.8	1:34.5	1:53.1	2:12.7
67.5%	22-24	45-75 S	22.5	31.3	34.7	47.8	1:02.8	1:19.7	1:26.9	1:38.0	1:57.3	2:17.6
65.0%	25-29	45-75 S	23.4	32.5	36.1	49.6	1:05.2	1:22.8	1:30.3	1:41.8	2:01.8	2:22.9
62.5%	30-35	30-60 S	24.3	33.8	37.5	51.6	1:07.8	1:26.1	1:33.9	1:45.9	2:06.7	2:28.6
60.0%	36-40	30-60 S	25.3	35.2	39.1	53.8	1:10.6	1:29.7	1:37.8	1:50.3	2:12.0	2:34.8

SPEED	REPS	REST	550 YD	660 YD	880 YD	1100 YD	1320 YD	1.00 MI	1.25 MI	1.50 MI	1.75 MI	2.00 MI
95.0%	0- 1	---	1:52.8	2:23.6	3:26.0	4:32.1	5:39.5	7:58.5	10:21.2	12:46.4	15:13.0	17:40.5
92.5%	1- 2	4- 5 M	1:55.9	2:27.5	3:31.6	4:39.5	5:48.7	8:11.4	10:38.0	13:07.1	15:37.7	18:09.2
90.0%	2- 3	4- 5 M	1:59.1	2:31.6	3:37.5	4:47.3	5:58.4	8:25.1	10:55.7	13:29.0	16:03.8	18:39.5
87.5%	3- 4	3- 4 M	2:02.5	2:35.9	3:43.7	4:55.5	6:08.6	8:39.5	11:14.4	13:52.1	16:31.3	19:11.4
85.0%	4- 5	3- 4 M	2:06.1	2:40.5	3:50.3	5:04.2	6:19.4	8:54.8	11:34.3	14:16.6	17:00.4	19:45.3
82.5%	6- 7	2- 3 M	2:09.9	2:45.4	3:57.3	5:13.4	6:30.9	9:11.0	11:55.3	14:42.5	-----	-----
80.0%	8- 9	2- 3 M	2:14.0	2:50.5	4:04.7	5:23.2	6:43.1	9:28.2	12:17.7	-----	-----	-----
77.5%	10-12	1- 2 M	2:18.3	2:56.0	4:12.6	5:33.6	6:56.2	9:46.5	-----	-----	-----	-----
75.0%	13-15	1- 2 M	2:22.9	3:01.9	4:21.0	5:44.7	7:10.0	-----	-----	-----	-----	-----
72.5%	16-18	60-90 S	2:27.8	3:08.2	4:30.0	5:56.6	-----	-----	-----	-----	-----	-----
70.0%	19-21	60-90 S	2:33.1	3:14.9	4:39.6	6:09.3	-----	-----	-----	-----	-----	-----
67.5%	22-24	45-75 S	2:38.8	3:22.1	4:50.0	-----	-----	-----	-----	-----	-----	-----
65.0%	25-29	45-75 S	2:44.9	3:29.9	-----	-----	-----	-----	-----	-----	-----	-----
62.5%	30-35	30-60 S	2:51.5	3:38.3	-----	-----	-----	-----	-----	-----	-----	-----
60.0%	36-40	30-60 S	2:58.6	-----	-----	-----	-----	-----	-----	-----	-----	-----

100 POINT LEVEL PACING TABLE
....

SPEED	REPS	REST	110 YD	150 YD	165 YD	220 YD	275 YD	330 YD	352 YD	385 YD	440 YD	495 YD
95.0%	0- 1	---	16.2	22.6	25.0	34.5	45.3	57.6	1:02.8	1:10.8	1:24.8	1:39.6
92.5%	1- 2	4- 5 M	16.7	23.2	25.7	35.4	46.5	59.1	1:04.5	1:12.8	1:27.1	1:42.2
90.0%	2- 3	4- 5 M	17.1	23.8	26.4	36.4	47.8	1:00.8	1:06.3	1:14.8	1:29.5	1:45.1
87.5%	3- 4	3- 4 M	17.6	24.5	27.2	37.4	49.2	1:02.5	1:08.2	1:16.9	1:32.1	1:48.1
85.0%	4- 5	3- 4 M	18.1	25.2	28.0	38.5	50.6	1:04.4	1:10.2	1:19.2	1:34.8	1:51.3
82.5%	6- 7	2- 3 M	18.7	26.0	28.8	39.7	52.2	1:06.3	1:12.3	1:21.6	1:37.7	1:54.6
80.0%	8- 9	2- 3 M	19.3	26.8	29.7	40.9	53.8	1:08.4	1:14.6	1:24.1	1:40.7	1:58.2
77.5%	10-12	1- 2 M	19.9	27.7	30.7	42.3	55.5	1:10.6	1:17.0	1:26.8	1:44.0	2:02.0
75.0%	13-15	1- 2 M	20.6	28.6	31.7	43.7	57.4	1:12.9	1:19.5	1:29.7	1:47.5	2:06.1
72.5%	16-18	60-90 S	21.3	29.6	32.8	45.2	59.4	1:15.5	1:22.3	1:32.8	1:51.2	2:10.4
70.0%	19-21	60-90 S	22.0	30.6	34.0	46.8	1:01.5	1:18.1	1:25.2	1:36.1	1:55.1	2:15.1
67.5%	22-24	45-75 S	22.8	31.8	35.3	48.5	1:03.8	1:21.0	1:28.4	1:39.7	1:59.4	2:20.1
65.0%	25-29	45-75 S	23.7	33.0	36.6	50.4	1:06.2	1:24.2	1:31.8	1:43.5	2:04.0	2:25.5
62.5%	30-35	30-60 S	24.7	34.3	38.1	52.4	1:08.9	1:27.5	1:35.4	1:47.7	2:08.9	2:31.3
60.0%	36-40	30-60 S	25.7	35.8	39.7	54.6	1:11.7	1:31.2	1:39.4	1:52.2	2:14.3	2:37.6

SPEED	REPS	REST	550 YD	660 YD	880 YD	1100 YD	1320 YD	1.00 MI	1.25 MI	1.50 MI	1.75 MI	2.00 MI
95.0%	0- 1	---	1:54.9	2:26.4	3:30.2	4:37.8	5:46.7	8:08.9	10:35.0	13:03.7	15:33.9	18:05.0
92.5%	1- 2	4- 5 M	1:58.0	2:30.3	3:35.9	4:45.3	5:56.1	8:22.1	10:52.2	13:24.9	15:59.1	18:34.3
90.0%	2- 3	4- 5 M	2:01.3	2:34.5	3:41.9	4:53.2	6:06.0	8:36.1	11:10.3	13:47.3	16:25.8	19:05.2
87.5%	3- 4	3- 4 M	2:04.8	2:38.9	3:48.2	5:01.6	6:16.4	8:50.8	11:29.5	14:10.9	16:53.9	19:37.9
85.0%	4- 5	3- 4 M	2:08.4	2:43.6	3:54.9	5:10.5	6:27.5	9:06.4	11:49.7	14:35.9	17:23.7	20:12.6
82.5%	6- 7	2- 3 M	2:12.3	2:48.5	4:02.0	5:19.9	6:39.2	9:23.0	12:11.2	15:02.5	-----	-----
80.0%	8- 9	2- 3 M	2:16.5	2:53.8	4:09.6	5:29.9	6:51.7	9:40.6	12:34.1	-----	-----	-----
77.5%	10-12	1- 2 M	2:20.9	2:59.4	4:17.6	5:40.5	7:05.0	9:59.3	-----	-----	-----	-----
75.0%	13-15	1- 2 M	2:25.6	3:05.4	4:26.2	5:51.9	7:19.1	-----	-----	-----	-----	-----
72.5%	16-18	60-90 S	2:30.6	3:11.8	4:35.4	6:04.0	7:34.3	-----	-----	-----	-----	-----
70.0%	19-21	60-90 S	2:36.0	3:18.6	4:45.2	6:17.0	-----	-----	-----	-----	-----	-----
67.5%	22-24	45-75 S	2:41.7	3:26.0	4:55.8	-----	-----	-----	-----	-----	-----	-----
65.0%	25-29	45-75 S	2:48.0	3:33.9	-----	-----	-----	-----	-----	-----	-----	-----
62.5%	30-35	30-60 S	2:54.7	3:42.5	-----	-----	-----	-----	-----	-----	-----	-----
60.0%	36-40	30-60 S	3:02.0	-----	-----	-----	-----	-----	-----	-----	-----	-----

80 POINT LEVEL PACING TABLE
●●●●●●●●●●●●●●●●●●●●●●●●●●●

SPEED	REPS	REST	110 YD	150 YD	165 YD	220 YD	275 YD	330 YD	352 YD	385 YD	440 YD	495 YD
95.0%	0- 1	---	16.5	22.9	25.4	35.0	46.0	58.5	1:03.8	1:12.1	1:26.3	1:41.4
92.5%	1- 2	4- 5 M	16.9	23.5	26.1	35.9	47.3	1:00.1	1:05.6	1:14.0	1:28.7	1:44.1
90.0%	2- 3	4- 5 M	17.4	24.2	26.8	36.9	48.6	1:01.8	1:07.4	1:16.1	1:31.1	1:47.0
87.5%	3- 4	3- 4 M	17.9	24.9	27.6	38.0	50.0	1:03.6	1:09.3	1:18.3	1:33.8	1:50.1
85.0%	4- 5	3- 4 M	18.4	25.6	28.4	39.1	51.4	1:05.4	1:11.4	1:20.6	1:36.5	1:53.3
82.5%	6- 7	2- 3 M	18.9	26.4	29.3	40.3	53.0	1:07.4	1:13.5	1:23.0	1:39.4	1:56.7
80.0%	8- 9	2- 3 M	19.5	27.2	30.2	41.6	54.7	1:09.5	1:15.8	1:25.6	1:42.5	2:00.4
77.5%	10-12	1- 2 M	20.2	28.1	31.2	42.9	56.4	1:11.8	1:18.3	1:28.3	1:45.8	2:04.3
75.0%	13-15	1- 2 M	20.8	29.0	32.2	44.3	58.3	1:14.2	1:20.9	1:31.3	1:49.4	2:08.4
72.5%	16-18	60-90 S	21.6	30.0	33.3	45.9	1:00.3	1:16.7	1:23.7	1:34.4	1:53.1	2:12.9
70.0%	19-21	60-90 S	22.3	31.1	34.5	47.5	1:02.5	1:19.4	1:26.6	1:37.8	1:57.2	2:17.6
67.5%	22-24	45-75 S	23.2	32.2	35.8	49.3	1:04.8	1:22.4	1:29.9	1:41.4	2:01.5	2:22.7
65.0%	25-29	45-75 S	24.1	33.5	37.1	51.2	1:07.3	1:25.6	1:33.3	1:45.3	2:06.2	2:28.2
62.5%	30-35	30-60 S	25.0	34.8	38.6	53.2	1:10.0	1:29.0	1:37.0	1:49.6	2:11.3	2:34.1
60.0%	36-40	30-60 S	26.1	36.3	40.2	55.4	1:12.9	1:32.7	1:41.0	1:54.1	2:16.7	2:40.5

SPEED	REPS	REST	550 YD	660 YD	880 YD	1100 YD	1320 YD	1.00 MI	1.25 MI	1.50 MI	1.75 MI	2.00 MI
95.0%	0- 1	---	1:57.1	2:29.2	3:34.5	4:43.7	5:54.2	8:19.8	10:49.5	13:21.9	15:55.7	18:30.5
92.5%	1- 2	4- 5 M	2:00.3	2:33.3	3:40.3	4:51.3	6:03.8	8:33.3	11:07.1	13:43.5	16:21.5	19:00.5
90.0%	2- 3	4- 5 M	2:03.6	2:37.5	3:46.4	4:59.4	6:13.9	8:47.6	11:25.6	14:06.4	16:48.8	19:32.2
87.5%	3- 4	3- 4 M	2:07.1	2:42.0	3:52.9	5:08.0	6:24.6	9:02.7	11:45.2	14:30.6	17:17.6	20:05.7
85.0%	4- 5	3- 4 M	2:10.9	2:46.8	3:59.7	5:17.1	6:35.9	9:18.6	12:05.9	14:56.2	17:48.1	20:41.2
82.5%	6- 7	2- 3 M	2:14.8	2:51.8	4:07.0	5:26.7	6:47.9	9:35.6	12:27.9	15:23.3	-----	-----
80.0%	8- 9	2- 3 M	2:19.0	2:57.2	4:14.7	5:36.9	7:00.6	9:53.5	12:51.3	-----	-----	-----
77.5%	10-12	1- 2 M	2:23.5	3:02.9	4:22.9	5:47.7	7:14.2	10:12.7	-----	-----	-----	-----
75.0%	13-15	1- 2 M	2:28.3	3:09.0	4:31.7	5:59.3	7:28.7	-----	-----	-----	-----	-----
72.5%	16-18	60-90 S	2:33.4	3:15.5	4:41.1	6:11.7	7:44.1	-----	-----	-----	-----	-----
70.0%	19-21	60-90 S	2:38.9	3:22.5	4:51.1	6:25.0	-----	-----	-----	-----	-----	-----
67.5%	22-24	45-75 S	2:44.8	3:30.0	5:01.9	-----	-----	-----	-----	-----	-----	-----
65.0%	25-29	45-75 S	2:51.1	3:38.1	-----	-----	-----	-----	-----	-----	-----	-----
62.5%	30-35	30-60 S	2:58.0	3:46.8	-----	-----	-----	-----	-----	-----	-----	-----
60.0%	36-40	30-60 S	3:05.4	-----	-----	-----	-----	-----	-----	-----	-----	-----

60 POINT LEVEL PACING TABLE

SPEED	REPS	REST	110 YD	150 YD	165 YD	220 YD	275 YD	330 YD	352 YD	385 YD	440 YD	495 YD
95.0%	0- 1	----	16.7	23.2	25.8	35.5	46.8	59.5	1:04.9	1:13.3	1:27.9	1:43.3
92.5%	1- 2	4- 5 M	17.1	23.9	26.5	36.5	48.0	1:01.1	1:06.7	1:15.3	1:30.3	1:46.1
90.0%	2- 3	4- 5 M	17.6	24.5	27.2	37.5	49.4	1:02.8	1:08.5	1:17.4	1:32.8	1:49.0
87.5%	3- 4	3- 4 M	18.1	25.2	28.0	38.6	50.8	1:04.6	1:10.5	1:19.6	1:35.5	1:52.1
85.0%	4- 5	3- 4 M	18.7	26.0	28.8	39.7	52.3	1:06.5	1:12.6	1:22.0	1:38.3	1:55.4
82.5%	6- 7	2- 3 M	19.2	26.8	29.7	40.9	53.9	1:08.6	1:14.8	1:24.5	1:41.2	1:58.9
80.0%	8- 9	2- 3 M	19.8	27.6	30.6	42.2	55.5	1:10.7	1:17.1	1:27.1	1:44.4	2:02.7
77.5%	10-12	1- 2 M	20.5	28.5	31.6	43.6	57.3	1:13.0	1:19.6	1:29.9	1:47.8	2:06.6
75.0%	13-15	1- 2 M	21.1	29.4	32.7	45.0	59.2	1:15.4	1:22.3	1:32.9	1:51.4	2:10.8
72.5%	16-18	60-90 S	21.9	30.5	33.8	46.6	1:01.3	1:18.0	1:25.1	1:36.1	1:55.2	2:15.3
70.0%	19-21	60-90 S	22.7	31.5	35.0	48.2	1:03.5	1:20.8	1:28.1	1:39.5	1:59.3	2:20.2
67.5%	22-24	45-75 S	23.5	32.7	36.3	50.0	1:05.8	1:23.8	1:31.4	1:43.2	2:03.7	2:25.4
65.0%	25-29	45-75 S	24.4	34.0	37.7	51.9	1:08.4	1:27.0	1:34.9	1:47.2	2:08.5	2:31.0
62.5%	30-35	30-60 S	25.4	35.3	39.2	54.0	1:11.1	1:30.5	1:38.7	1:51.5	2:13.6	2:37.0
60.0%	36-40	30-60 S	26.4	36.8	40.8	56.3	1:14.0	1:34.3	1:42.8	1:56.1	2:19.2	2:43.5

SPEED	REPS	REST	550 YD	660 YD	880 YD	1100 YD	1320 YD	1.00 MI	1.25 MI	1.50 MI	1.75 MI	2.00 MI
95.0%	0- 1	----	1:59.3	2:32.2	3:39.0	4:49.8	6:02.0	8:31.2	11:04.6	13:40.8	16:18.5	18:57.3
92.5%	1- 2	4- 5 M	2:02.6	2:36.3	3:44.9	4:57.7	6:11.8	8:45.0	11:22.6	14:03.0	16:45.0	19:28.0
90.0%	2- 3	4- 5 M	2:06.0	2:40.7	3:51.2	5:05.9	6:22.2	8:59.6	11:41.6	14:26.4	17:12.9	20:00.5
87.5%	3- 4	3- 4 M	2:09.6	2:45.3	3:57.8	5:14.7	6:33.1	9:15.1	12:01.6	14:51.2	17:42.4	20:34.8
85.0%	4- 5	3- 4 M	2:13.4	2:50.1	4:04.8	5:23.9	6:44.6	9:31.4	12:22.8	15:17.4	18:13.7	21:11.1
82.5%	6- 7	2- 3 M	2:17.4	2:55.3	4:12.2	5:33.7	6:56.9	9:48.7	12:45.4	15:45.2	-----	-----
80.0%	8- 9	2- 3 M	2:21.7	3:00.8	4:20.1	5:44.2	7:09.9	10:07.1	13:09.3	-----	-----	-----
77.5%	10-12	1- 2 M	2:26.3	3:06.6	4:28.4	5:55.3	7:23.8	10:26.7	-----	-----	-----	-----
75.0%	13-15	1- 2 M	2:31.2	3:12.8	4:37.4	6:07.1	7:38.6	-----	-----	-----	-----	-----
72.5%	16-18	60-90 S	2:36.4	3:19.5	4:47.0	6:19.8	7:54.4	-----	-----	-----	-----	-----
70.0%	19-21	60-90 S	2:42.0	3:26.6	4:57.2	6:33.3	-----	-----	-----	-----	-----	-----
67.5%	22-24	45-75 S	2:48.0	3:34.2	5:08.2	-----	-----	-----	-----	-----	-----	-----
65.0%	25-29	45-75 S	2:54.4	3:42.5	-----	-----	-----	-----	-----	-----	-----	-----
62.5%	30-35	30-60 S	3:01.4	3:51.4	-----	-----	-----	-----	-----	-----	-----	-----
60.0%	36-40	30-60 S	3:09.0	-----	-----	-----	-----	-----	-----	-----	-----	-----

40 POINT LEVEL PACING TABLE
· ·

SPEED	REPS	REST	110 YD	150 YD	165 YD	220 YD	275 YD	330 YD	352 YD	385 YD	440 YD	495 YD
95.0%	0- 1	---	16.9	23.6	26.2	36.1	47.5	1:00.6	1:06.1	1:14.7	1:29.6	1:45.3
92.5%	1- 2	4- 5 M	17.4	24.2	26.9	37.1	48.8	1:02.2	1:07.9	1:16.7	1:32.0	1:48.1
90.0%	2- 3	4- 5 M	17.9	24.9	27.6	38.1	50.2	1:03.9	1:09.7	1:18.8	1:34.5	1:51.1
87.5%	3- 4	3- 4 M	18.4	25.6	28.4	39.2	51.6	1:05.7	1:11.7	1:21.1	1:37.2	1:54.3
85.0%	4- 5	3- 4 M	18.9	26.4	29.3	40.3	53.1	1:07.7	1:13.9	1:23.4	1:40.1	1:57.7
82.5%	6- 7	2- 3 M	19.5	27.2	30.2	41.6	54.7	1:09.7	1:16.1	1:26.0	1:43.1	2:01.2
80.0%	8- 9	2- 3 M	20.1	28.0	31.1	42.9	56.5	1:11.9	1:18.5	1:28.7	1:46.3	2:05.0
77.5%	10-12	1- 2 M	20.8	28.9	32.1	44.3	58.3	1:14.2	1:21.0	1:31.5	1:49.8	2:09.0
75.0%	13-15	1- 2 M	21.5	29.9	33.2	45.7	1:00.2	1:16.7	1:23.7	1:34.6	1:53.4	2:13.3
72.5%	16-18	60-90 S	22.2	30.9	34.3	47.3	1:02.3	1:19.4	1:26.6	1:37.8	1:57.3	2:17.9
70.0%	19-21	60-90 S	23.0	32.0	35.5	49.0	1:04.5	1:22.2	1:29.7	1:41.3	2:01.5	2:22.9
67.5%	22-24	45-75 S	23.8	33.2	36.9	50.8	1:06.9	1:25.2	1:33.0	1:45.1	2:06.0	2:28.2
65.0%	25-29	45-75 S	24.8	34.5	38.3	52.8	1:09.5	1:28.5	1:36.6	1:49.1	2:10.9	2:33.9
62.5%	30-35	30-60 S	25.7	35.9	39.8	54.9	1:12.3	1:32.0	1:40.4	1:53.5	2:16.1	2:40.0
60.0%	36-40	30-60 S	26.8	37.4	41.5	57.2	1:15.3	1:35.9	1:44.6	1:58.2	2:21.8	2:46.7

SPEED	REPS	REST	550 YD	660 YD	880 YD	1100 YD	1320 YD	1.00 MI	1.25 MI	1.50 MI	1.75 MI	2.00 MI
95.0%	0- 1	---	2:01.7	2:35.3	3:43.7	4:56.2	6:10.2	8:43.2	11:20.5	14:00.7	16:42.5	19:25.4
92.5%	1- 2	4- 5 M	2:05.0	2:39.5	3:49.7	5:04.2	6:20.3	8:57.3	11:38.9	14:23.4	17:09.6	19:56.9
90.0%	2- 3	4- 5 M	2:08.5	2:44.0	3:56.1	5:12.7	6:30.8	9:12.2	11:58.3	14:47.4	17:38.2	20:30.2
87.5%	3- 4	3- 4 M	2:12.1	2:48.6	4:02.8	5:21.6	6:42.0	9:28.0	12:18.8	15:12.8	18:08.5	21:05.3
85.0%	4- 5	3- 4 M	2:16.0	2:53.6	4:10.0	5:31.1	6:53.8	9:44.7	12:40.6	15:39.6	18:40.5	21:42.5
82.5%	6- 7	2- 3 M	2:20.1	2:58.9	4:17.6	5:41.1	7:06.3	10:02.4	13:03.6	16:08.1	-----	-----
80.0%	8- 9	2- 3 M	2:24.5	3:04.5	4:25.6	5:51.8	7:19.7	10:21.3	13:28.1	-----	-----	-----
77.5%	10-12	1- 2 M	2:29.2	3:10.4	4:34.2	6:03.1	7:33.8	10:41.3	-----	-----	-----	-----
75.0%	13-15	1- 2 M	2:34.1	3:16.8	4:43.3	6:15.2	7:49.0	-----	-----	-----	-----	-----
72.5%	16-18	60-90 S	2:39.5	3:23.5	4:53.1	6:28.2	8:05.1	-----	-----	-----	-----	-----
70.0%	19-21	60-90 S	2:45.2	3:30.8	5:03.6	6:42.0	-----	-----	-----	-----	-----	-----
67.5%	22-24	45-75 S	2:51.3	3:38.6	5:14.8	-----	-----	-----	-----	-----	-----	-----
65.0%	25-29	45-75 S	2:57.9	3:47.0	-----	-----	-----	-----	-----	-----	-----	-----
62.5%	30-35	30-60 S	3:05.0	3:56.1	-----	-----	-----	-----	-----	-----	-----	-----
60.0%	36-40	30-60 S	3:12.7	-----	-----	-----	-----	-----	-----	-----	-----	-----

196

20 POINT LEVEL PACING TABLE

SPEED	REPS	REST	110 YD	150 YD	165 YD	220 YD	275 YD	330 YD	352 YD	385 YD	440 YD	495 YD
95.0%	0- 1	---	17.2	24.0	26.6	36.7	48.3	1:01.6	1:07.3	1:16.0	1:31.2	1:47.3
92.5%	1- 2	4- 5 M	17.7	24.6	27.3	37.7	49.6	1:03.3	1:09.1	1:18.1	1:33.7	1:50.2
90.0%	2- 3	4- 5 M	18.1	25.3	28.1	38.7	51.0	1:05.0	1:11.0	1:20.2	1:36.3	1:53.3
87.5%	3- 4	3- 4 M	18.7	26.0	28.9	39.8	52.5	1:06.9	1:13.0	1:22.5	1:39.1	1:56.5
85.0%	4- 5	3- 4 M	19.2	26.8	29.7	41.0	54.0	1:08.9	1:15.2	1:25.0	1:42.0	1:59.9
82.5%	6- 7	2- 3 M	19.8	27.6	30.6	42.2	55.7	1:11.0	1:17.4	1:27.5	1:45.1	2:03.6
80.0%	8- 9	2- 3 M	20.4	28.4	31.6	43.6	57.4	1:13.2	1:19.9	1:30.3	1:48.4	2:07.4
77.5%	10-12	1- 2 M	21.1	29.4	32.6	45.0	59.2	1:15.5	1:22.4	1:33.2	1:51.9	2:11.6
75.0%	13-15	1- 2 M	21.8	30.3	33.7	46.5	1:01.2	1:18.1	1:25.2	1:36.3	1:55.6	2:15.9
72.5%	16-18	60-90 S	22.5	31.4	34.8	48.1	1:03.3	1:20.7	1:28.1	1:39.6	1:59.6	2:20.6
70.0%	19-21	60-90 S	23.3	32.5	36.1	49.8	1:05.6	1:23.6	1:31.3	1:43.2	2:03.8	2:25.6
67.5%	22-24	45-75 S	24.2	33.7	37.4	51.6	1:08.0	1:26.7	1:34.7	1:47.0	2:08.4	2:31.0
65.0%	25-29	45-75 S	25.1	35.0	38.9	53.6	1:10.6	1:30.1	1:38.3	1:51.1	2:13.4	2:36.9
62.5%	30-35	30-60 S	26.1	36.4	40.4	55.8	1:13.5	1:33.7	1:42.2	1:55.5	2:18.7	2:43.1
60.0%	36-40	30-60 S	27.2	37.9	42.1	58.1	1:16.5	1:37.6	1:46.5	2:00.4	2:24.5	2:49.9

SPEED	REPS	REST	550 YD	660 YD	880 YD	1100 YD	1320 YD	1.00 MI	1.25 MI	1.50 MI	1.75 MI	2.00 MI
95.0%	0- 1	---	2:04.1	2:38.6	3:48.6	5:02.9	6:18.8	8:55.7	11:37.2	14:21.6	17:07.7	19:55.0
92.5%	1- 2	4- 5 M	2:07.5	2:42.9	3:54.7	5:11.1	6:29.1	9:10.2	11:56.0	14:44.9	17:35.5	20:27.3
90.0%	2- 3	4- 5 M	2:11.0	2:47.4	4:01.3	5:19.8	6:39.9	9:25.4	12:15.9	15:09.5	18:04.8	21:01.3
87.5%	3- 4	3- 4 M	2:14.8	2:52.2	4:08.2	5:28.9	6:51.3	9:41.6	12:36.9	15:35.4	18:35.8	21:37.4
85.0%	4- 5	3- 4 M	2:18.7	2:57.2	4:15.5	5:38.6	7:03.4	9:58.7	12:59.2	16:03.0	19:08.6	22:15.5
82.5%	6- 7	2- 3 M	2:22.9	3:02.6	4:23.2	5:48.8	7:16.2	10:16.8	13:22.8	16:32.1	-----	-----
80.0%	8- 9	2- 3 M	2:27.4	3:08.3	4:31.4	5:59.7	7:29.9	10:36.1	13:47.9	-----	-----	-----
77.5%	10-12	1- 2 M	2:32.2	3:14.4	4:40.2	6:11.3	7:44.4	10:56.6	-----	-----	-----	-----
75.0%	13-15	1- 2 M	2:37.2	3:20.9	4:49.5	6:23.7	7:59.8	-----	-----	-----	-----	-----
72.5%	16-18	60-90 S	2:42.7	3:27.8	4:59.5	6:37.0	8:16.4	-----	-----	-----	-----	-----
70.0%	19-21	60-90 S	2:48.5	3:35.2	5:10.2	6:51.1	-----	-----	-----	-----	-----	-----
67.5%	22-24	45-75 S	2:54.7	3:43.2	5:21.7	-----	-----	-----	-----	-----	-----	-----
65.0%	25-29	45-75 S	3:01.4	3:51.8	-----	-----	-----	-----	-----	-----	-----	-----
62.5%	30-35	30-60 S	3:08.7	4:01.0	-----	-----	-----	-----	-----	-----	-----	-----
60.0%	36-40	30-60 S	3:16.5	-----	-----	-----	-----	-----	-----	-----	-----	-----

0 POINT LEVEL PACING TABLE
· ·

SPEED	REPS	REST	110 YD	150 YD	165 YD	220 YD	275 YD	330 YD	352 YD	385 YD	440 YD	495 YD
95.0%	0- 1	---	17.5	24.3	27.0	37.3	49.2	1:02.7	1:08.5	1:17.4	1:33.0	1:49.5
92.5%	1- 2	4- 5 M	17.9	25.0	27.7	38.3	50.5	1:04.4	1:10.3	1:19.5	1:35.5	1:52.4
90.0%	2- 3	4- 5 M	18.4	25.7	28.5	39.3	51.9	1:06.2	1:12.3	1:21.7	1:38.2	1:55.5
87.5%	3- 4	3- 4 M	18.9	26.4	29.3	40.5	53.4	1:08.1	1:14.3	1:24.1	1:41.0	1:58.8
85.0%	4- 5	3- 4 M	19.5	27.2	30.2	41.7	54.9	1:10.1	1:16.5	1:26.5	1:43.9	2:02.3
82.5%	6- 7	2- 3 M	20.1	28.0	31.1	42.9	56.6	1:12.2	1:18.9	1:29.2	1:47.1	2:06.0
80.0%	8- 9	2- 3 M	20.7	28.9	32.1	44.3	58.4	1:14.5	1:21.3	1:32.0	1:50.4	2:10.0
77.5%	10-12	1- 2 M	21.4	29.8	33.1	45.7	1:00.3	1:16.9	1:23.9	1:34.9	1:54.0	2:14.2
75.0%	13-15	1- 2 M	22.1	30.8	34.2	47.2	1:02.3	1:19.4	1:26.7	1:38.1	1:57.8	2:18.6
72.5%	16-18	60-90 S	22.9	31.9	35.4	48.8	1:04.4	1:22.2	1:29.7	1:41.5	2:01.9	2:23.4
70.0%	19-21	60-90 S	23.7	33.0	36.6	50.6	1:06.7	1:25.1	1:32.9	1:45.1	2:06.2	2:28.5
67.5%	22-24	45-75 S	24.6	34.2	38.0	52.5	1:09.2	1:28.3	1:36.4	1:49.0	2:10.9	2:34.0
65.0%	25-29	45-75 S	25.5	35.5	39.5	54.5	1:11.8	1:31.7	1:40.1	1:53.2	2:15.9	2:40.0
62.5%	30-35	30-60 S	26.5	37.0	41.0	56.7	1:14.7	1:35.3	1:44.1	1:57.7	2:21.4	2:46.4
60.0%	36-40	30-60 S	27.6	38.5	42.8	59.0	1:17.8	1:39.3	1:48.4	2:02.6	2:27.3	2:53.3

SPEED	REPS	REST	550 YD	660 YD	880 YD	1100 YD	1320 YD	1.00 MI	1.25 MI	1.50 MI	1.75 MI	2.00 MI
95.0%	0- 1	---	2:06.7	2:41.9	3:53.7	5:10.0	6:27.8	9:08.8	11:54.6	14:43.5	17:34.2	20:26.0
92.5%	1- 2	4- 5 M	2:10.1	2:46.3	4:00.0	5:18.3	6:38.3	9:23.6	12:14.0	15:07.4	18:02.7	20:59.2
90.0%	2- 3	4- 5 M	2:13.7	2:50.9	4:06.7	5:27.2	6:49.4	9:39.3	12:34.4	15:32.6	18:32.8	21:34.2
87.5%	3- 4	3- 4 M	2:17.5	2:55.8	4:13.7	5:36.5	7:01.1	9:55.8	12:55.9	15:59.3	19:04.6	22:11.1
85.0%	4- 5	3- 4 M	2:21.6	3:01.0	4:21.2	5:46.4	7:13.4	10:13.4	13:18.7	16:27.5	19:38.2	22:50.3
82.5%	6- 7	2- 3 M	2:25.9	3:06.5	4:29.1	5:56.9	7:26.6	10:32.0	13:42.9	16:57.4	-----	-----
80.0%	8- 9	2- 3 M	2:30.4	3:12.3	4:37.5	6:08.1	7:40.5	10:51.7	14:08.6	-----	-----	-----
77.5%	10-12	1- 2 M	2:35.3	3:18.5	4:46.4	6:19.9	7:55.4	11:12.7	-----	-----	-----	-----
75.0%	13-15	1- 2 M	2:40.4	3:25.1	4:56.0	6:32.6	8:11.2	-----	-----	-----	-----	-----
72.5%	16-18	60-90 S	2:46.0	3:32.2	5:06.2	6:46.1	8:28.2	-----	-----	-----	-----	-----
70.0%	19-21	60-90 S	2:51.9	3:39.8	5:17.1	7:00.7	-----	-----	-----	-----	-----	-----
67.5%	22-24	45-75 S	2:58.3	3:47.9	5:28.9	-----	-----	-----	-----	-----	-----	-----
65.0%	25-29	45-75 S	3:05.1	3:56.7	5:41.5	-----	-----	-----	-----	-----	-----	-----
62.5%	30-35	30-60 S	3:12.5	4:06.2	-----	-----	-----	-----	-----	-----	-----	-----
60.0%	36-40	30-60 S	3:20.6	4:16.4	-----	-----	-----	-----	-----	-----	-----	-----

Table 5: Per Mile Average Tables

The per mile average tables given on the following pages are similar to the scoring tables in that the point level is printed in the left column and the other columns are headed by distances. The entries in the distance columns are per mile average times for the respective point level.

These tables are employed as an aid to determine the proper pace for continuous running training. The athlete determines his point level from the scoring tables (Table 1a, 1b, 1c) and then refers to this table to read the per mile average at his point level for the distance to be run. This is the 100% speed (all out effort) for the distance to be run; the athlete refers to the reduced speed tables to determine the desired percentage speed for the run. Figure 7.2 shows this process visually.

SCORING TABLES
PER MILE AVERAGES FOR LONG DISTANCE RUNNING
●●

POINTS	5.00 MI	6.00 MI	7.00 MI	8.00 MI	9.00 MI	10.00 MI	11.00 MI	12.00 MI	13.00 MI	14.00 MI
1050	4:22.7	4:25.9	4:28	4:31	4:33	4:35	4:37	4:38	4:40	4:41
1040	4:24.2	4:27.4	4:30	4:32	4:34	4:36	4:38	4:40	4:41	4:43
1030	4:25.7	4:29.0	4:31	4:34	4:36	4:38	4:40	4:41	4:43	4:44
1020	4:27.2	4:30.5	4:33	4:35	4:38	4:40	4:41	4:43	4:44	4:46
1010	4:28.7	4:32.1	4:35	4:37	4:39	4:41	4:43	4:45	4:46	4:48
1000	4:30.3	4:33.6	4:36	4:39	4:41	4:43	4:45	4:46	4:48	4:49
990	4:31.8	4:35.2	4:38	4:40	4:42	4:45	4:46	4:48	4:50	4:51
980	4:33.4	4:36.8	4:39	4:42	4:44	4:46	4:48	4:50	4:51	4:53
970	4:35.0	4:38.5	4:41	4:44	4:46	4:48	4:50	4:51	4:53	4:54
960	4:36.6	4:40.1	4:43	4:45	4:48	4:50	4:52	4:53	4:55	4:56
950	4:38.3	4:41.8	4:44	4:47	4:49	4:51	4:53	4:55	4:57	4:58
940	4:39.9	4:43.5	4:46	4:49	4:51	4:53	4:55	4:57	4:58	5:00
930	4:41.6	4:45.2	4:48	4:51	4:53	4:55	4:57	4:59	5:00	5:02
920	4:43.3	4:46.9	4:50	4:52	4:55	4:57	4:59	5:00	5:02	5:04
910	4:45.0	4:48.7	4:51	4:54	4:56	4:59	5:01	5:02	5:04	5:05
900	4:46.8	4:50.4	4:53	4:56	4:58	5:01	5:02	5:04	5:06	5:07
890	4:48.6	4:52.2	4:55	4:58	5:00	5:02	5:04	5:06	5:08	5:09
880	4:50.3	4:54.1	4:57	5:00	5:02	5:04	5:06	5:08	5:10	5:11
870	4:52.2	4:55.9	4:59	5:01	5:04	5:06	5:08	5:10	5:12	5:13
860	4:54.0	4:57.8	5:01	5:03	5:06	5:08	5:10	5:12	5:14	5:15
850	4:55.8	4:59.6	5:02	5:05	5:08	5:10	5:12	5:14	5:16	5:17
840	4:57.7	5:01.6	5:04	5:07	5:10	5:12	5:14	5:16	5:18	5:19
830	4:59.6	5:03.5	5:06	5:09	5:12	5:14	5:16	5:18	5:20	5:21
820	5:01.6	5:05.5	5:08	5:11	5:14	5:16	5:18	5:20	5:22	5:24
810	5:03.5	5:07.4	5:10	5:13	5:16	5:18	5:20	5:22	5:24	5:26
800	5:05.5	5:09.4	5:12	5:15	5:18	5:20	5:23	5:24	5:26	5:28
790	5:07.5	5:11.5	5:14	5:18	5:20	5:23	5:25	5:27	5:28	5:30
780	5:09.5	5:13.6	5:17	5:20	5:22	5:25	5:27	5:29	5:31	5:32
770	5:11.6	5:15.6	5:19	5:22	5:24	5:27	5:29	5:31	5:33	5:35
760	5:13.7	5:17.8	5:21	5:24	5:27	5:29	5:31	5:33	5:35	5:37
750	5:15.8	5:19.9	5:23	5:26	5:29	5:31	5:34	5:36	5:37	5:39
740	5:17.9	5:22.1	5:25	5:28	5:31	5:34	5:36	5:38	5:40	5:42

SCORING TABLES
PER MILE AVERAGES FOR LONG DISTANCE RUNNING
•••

POINTS	5.00 MI	6.00 MI	7.00 MI	8.00 MI	9.00 MI	10.00 MI	11.00 MI	12.00 MI	13.00 MI	14.00 MI
730	5:20.1	5:24.3	5:28	5:31	5:33	5:36	5:38	5:40	5:42	5:44
720	5:22.3	5:26.5	5:30	5:33	5:36	5:38	5:41	5:43	5:45	5:46
710	5:24.5	5:28.8	5:32	5:35	5:38	5:41	5:43	5:45	5:47	5:49
700	5:26.8	5:31.1	5:34	5:38	5:40	5:43	5:46	5:47	5:49	5:51
690	5:29.1	5:33.5	5:37	5:40	5:43	5:46	5:48	5:50	5:52	5:54
680	5:31.4	5:35.8	5:39	5:43	5:45	5:48	5:50	5:53	5:54	5:56
670	5:33.8	5:38.2	5:42	5:45	5:48	5:51	5:53	5:55	5:57	5:59
660	5:36.2	5:40.7	5:44	5:47	5:50	5:53	5:56	5:58	6:00	6:02
650	5:38.6	5:43.1	5:47	5:50	5:53	5:56	5:58	6:00	6:02	6:04
640	5:41.1	5:45.6	5:49	5:53	5:56	5:58	6:01	6:03	6:05	6:07
630	5:43.6	5:48.2	5:52	5:55	5:58	6:01	6:04	6:06	6:08	6:10
620	5:46.1	5:50.8	5:54	5:58	6:01	6:04	6:06	6:08	6:11	6:13
610	5:48.7	5:53.4	5:57	6:01	6:04	6:07	6:09	6:11	6:13	6:15
600	5:51.3	5:56.1	6:00	6:03	6:06	6:09	6:12	6:14	6:16	6:18
590	5:53.9	5:58.8	6:02	6:06	6:09	6:12	6:15	6:17	6:19	6:21
580	5:56.6	6:01.5	6:05	6:09	6:12	6:15	6:18	6:20	6:22	6:24
570	5:59.4	6:04.3	6:08	6:12	6:15	6:18	6:21	6:23	6:25	6:27
560	6:02.1	6:07.1	6:11	6:15	6:18	6:21	6:24	6:26	6:28	6:30
550	6:05.0	6:10.0	6:14	6:18	6:21	6:24	6:27	6:29	6:31	6:33
540	6:07.8	6:12.9	6:17	6:21	6:24	6:27	6:30	6:32	6:34	6:37
530	6:10.7	6:15.9	6:20	6:24	6:27	6:30	6:33	6:35	6:38	6:40
520	6:13.7	6:18.9	6:23	6:27	6:30	6:33	6:36	6:39	6:41	6:43
510	6:16.7	6:21.9	6:26	6:30	6:33	6:37	6:39	6:42	6:44	6:46
500	6:19.7	6:25.0	6:29	6:33	6:37	6:40	6:43	6:45	6:48	6:50
490	6:22.8	6:28.2	6:32	6:36	6:40	6:43	6:46	6:49	6:51	6:53
480	6:26.0	6:31.4	6:36	6:40	6:43	6:47	6:50	6:52	6:54	6:57
470	6:29.2	6:34.7	6:39	6:43	6:47	6:50	6:53	6:56	6:58	7:00
460	6:32.5	6:38.0	6:42	6:47	6:50	6:54	6:57	6:59	7:02	7:04
450	6:35.8	6:41.4	6:46	6:50	6:54	6:57	7:00	7:03	7:05	7:08
440	6:39.1	6:44.8	6:49	6:54	6:57	7:01	7:04	7:06	7:09	7:11
430	6:42.6	6:48.3	6:53	6:57	7:01	7:04	7:08	7:10	7:13	7:15
420	6:46.1	6:51.9	6:56	7:01	7:05	7:08	7:11	7:14	7:17	7:19

POINTS	5.00 MI	6.00 MI	7.00 MI	8.00 MI	9.00 MI	10.00 MI	11.00 MI	12.00 MI	13.00 MI	14.00 MI
410	6:49.6	6:55.5	7:00	7:05	7:08	7:12	7:15	7:18	7:21	7:23
400	6:53.2	6:59.2	7:04	7:08	7:12	7:16	7:19	7:22	7:25	7:27
390	6:56.9	7:02.9	7:08	7:12	7:16	7:20	7:23	7:26	7:29	7:31
380	7:00.6	7:06.7	7:12	7:16	7:20	7:24	7:27	7:30	7:33	7:35
370	7:04.4	7:10.6	7:16	7:20	7:24	7:28	7:31	7:34	7:37	7:40
360	7:08.3	7:14.6	7:20	7:24	7:28	7:32	7:36	7:38	7:41	7:44
350	7:12.3	7:18.6	7:24	7:28	7:33	7:36	7:40	7:43	7:46	7:48
340	7:16.3	7:22.7	7:28	7:33	7:37	7:41	7:44	7:47	7:50	7:53
330	7:20.4	7:26.9	7:32	7:37	7:41	7:45	7:49	7:52	7:55	7:57
320	7:24.6	7:31.2	7:36	7:41	7:46	7:50	7:53	7:56	7:59	8:02
310	7:28.8	7:35.5	7:41	7:46	7:50	7:54	7:58	8:01	8:04	8:07
300	7:33.2	7:40.0	7:45	7:50	7:55	7:59	8:03	8:06	8:09	8:12
290	7:37.6	7:44.5	7:50	7:55	8:00	8:04	8:08	8:11	8:14	8:17
280	7:42.1	7:49.1	7:55	8:00	8:04	8:09	8:12	8:16	8:19	8:22
270	7:46.7	7:53.8	7:59	8:05	8:09	8:14	8:17	8:21	8:24	8:27
260	7:51.4	7:58.6	8:04	8:10	8:14	8:19	8:23	8:26	8:29	8:32
250	7:56.2	8:03.5	8:09	8:15	8:20	8:24	8:28	8:31	8:35	8:38
240	8:01.1	8:08.5	8:14	8:20	8:25	8:29	8:33	8:37	8:40	8:43
230	8:06.1	8:13.6	8:20	8:25	8:30	8:35	8:39	8:42	8:46	8:49
220	8:11.2	8:18.8	8:25	8:31	8:36	8:40	8:44	8:48	8:51	8:54
210	8:16.4	8:24.1	8:30	8:36	8:41	8:46	8:50	8:54	8:57	9:00
200	8:21.7	8:29.5	8:36	8:42	8:47	8:52	8:56	9:00	9:03	9:06
190	8:27.1	8:35.1	8:41	8:47	8:53	8:58	9:02	9:06	9:09	9:12
180	8:32.7	8:40.7	8:47	8:53	8:59	9:04	9:08	9:12	9:15	9:19
170	8:38.3	8:46.5	8:53	8:59	9:05	9:10	9:14	9:18	9:22	9:25
160	8:44.1	8:52.5	8:59	9:05	9:11	9:16	9:21	9:24	9:28	9:32
150	8:50.1	8:58.5	9:05	9:12	9:17	9:22	9:27	9:31	9:35	9:38
140	8:56.1	9:04.7	9:12	9:18	9:24	9:29	9:34	9:38	9:42	9:45
130	9:02.3	9:11.1	9:18	9:25	9:31	9:36	9:41	9:45	9:49	9:52
120	9:08.7	9:17.6	9:25	9:32	9:37	9:43	9:48	9:52	9:56	10:00
110	9:15.2	9:24.2	9:32	9:38	9:44	9:50	9:55	9:59	10:03	10:07
100	9:21.8	9:31.0	9:39	9:46	9:52	9:57	10:02	10:07	10:11	10:15

POINTS	5.00 MI	6.00 MI	7.00 MI	8.00 MI	9.00 MI	10.00 MI	11.00 MI	12.00 MI	13.00 MI	14.00 MI
90	9:28.6	9:38.0	9:46	9:53	9:59	10:05	10:10	10:14	10:18	10:22
80	9:35.6	9:45.2	9:53	10:00	10:06	10:12	10:17	10:22	10:26	10:30
70	9:42.8	9:52.5	10:00	10:08	10:14	10:20	10:25	10:30	10:34	10:39
60	9:50.1	10:00.0	10:08	10:16	10:22	10:28	10:34	10:38	10:43	10:47
50	9:57.7	10:07.7	10:16	10:24	10:30	10:36	10:42	10:47	10:51	10:56
40	10:05.4	10:15.7	10:24	10:32	10:39	10:45	10:50	10:55	11:00	11:04
30	10:13.3	10:23.8	10:32	10:40	10:47	10:54	10:59	11:04	11:09	11:13
20	10:21.4	10:32.1	10:41	10:49	10:56	11:03	11:08	11:13	11:18	11:23
10	10:29.8	10:40.7	10:50	10:58	11:05	11:12	11:18	11:23	11:28	11:32
0	10:38.4	10:49.5	10:59	11:07	11:14	11:21	11:27	11:33	11:38	11:42

SCORING TABLES
PER MILE AVERAGES FOR EXTRA-LONG DISTANCE RUNNING
●●●

POINTS	15.00 MI	16.00 MI	18.00 MI	20.00 MI	23.00 MI	25.00 MI	MARATHON	28.00 MI	30.00 MI	32.00 MI
1050	4:42	4:43	4:46	4:48	4:51	4:52	4:54	4:55	4:57	4:59
1040	4:44	4:45	4:47	4:49	4:52	4:54	4:55	4:57	4:59	5:00
1030	4:45	4:47	4:49	4:51	4:54	4:56	4:57	4:59	5:00	5:02
1020	4:47	4:48	4:51	4:53	4:56	4:58	4:59	5:00	5:02	5:04
1010	4:49	4:50	4:52	4:54	4:57	4:59	5:01	5:02	5:04	5:06
1000	4:50	4:52	4:54	4:56	4:59	5:01	5:02	5:04	5:06	5:07
990	4:52	4:53	4:56	4:58	5:01	5:03	5:04	5:06	5:08	5:09
980	4:54	4:55	4:58	5:00	5:03	5:05	5:06	5:08	5:09	5:11
970	4:56	4:57	4:59	5:02	5:05	5:07	5:08	5:10	5:11	5:13
960	4:58	4:59	5:01	5:03	5:06	5:08	5:10	5:11	5:13	5:15
950	4:59	5:01	5:03	5:05	5:08	5:10	5:12	5:13	5:15	5:17
940	5:01	5:02	5:05	5:07	5:10	5:12	5:14	5:15	5:17	5:19
930	5:03	5:04	5:07	5:09	5:12	5:14	5:16	5:17	5:19	5:21
920	5:05	5:06	5:09	5:11	5:14	5:16	5:17	5:19	5:21	5:23
910	5:07	5:08	5:11	5:13	5:16	5:18	5:19	5:21	5:23	5:25
900	5:09	5:10	5:12	5:15	5:18	5:20	5:21	5:23	5:25	5:27
890	5:11	5:12	5:14	5:17	5:20	5:22	5:24	5:25	5:27	5:29
880	5:13	5:14	5:16	5:19	5:22	5:24	5:26	5:27	5:29	5:31
870	5:15	5:16	5:19	5:21	5:24	5:26	5:28	5:30	5:31	5:33
860	5:17	5:18	5:21	5:23	5:26	5:28	5:30	5:32	5:34	5:36
850	5:19	5:20	5:23	5:25	5:28	5:31	5:32	5:34	5:36	5:38
840	5:21	5:22	5:25	5:27	5:31	5:33	5:34	5:36	5:38	5:40
830	5:23	5:24	5:27	5:29	5:33	5:35	5:36	5:38	5:40	5:42
820	5:25	5:26	5:29	5:32	5:35	5:37	5:39	5:41	5:43	5:45
810	5:27	5:29	5:31	5:34	5:37	5:39	5:41	5:43	5:45	5:47
800	5:29	5:31	5:33	5:36	5:40	5:42	5:43	5:45	5:47	5:49
790	5:32	5:33	5:36	5:38	5:42	5:44	5:46	5:48	5:50	5:52
780	5:34	5:35	5:38	5:41	5:44	5:46	5:48	5:50	5:52	5:54
770	5:36	5:38	5:40	5:43	5:47	5:49	5:50	5:52	5:54	5:57
760	5:38	5:40	5:43	5:45	5:49	5:51	5:53	5:55	5:57	5:59
750	5:41	5:42	5:45	5:48	5:51	5:54	5:55	5:57	5:59	6:02
740	5:43	5:45	5:47	5:50	5:54	5:56	5:58	6:00	6:02	6:04

PER MILE AVERAGES FOR EXTRA-LONG DISTANCE RUNNING
●●

POINTS	15.00 MI	16.00 MI	18.00 MI	20.00 MI	23.00 MI	25.00 MI	MARATHON	28.00 MI	30.00 MI	32.00 MI
730	5:45	5:47	5:50	5:53	5:56	5:59	6:00	6:02	6:04	6:07
720	5:48	5:49	5:52	5:55	5:59	6:01	6:03	6:05	6:07	6:09
710	5:50	5:52	5:55	5:58	6:01	6:04	6:05	6:08	6:10	6:12
700	5:53	5:54	5:57	6:00	6:04	6:06	6:08	6:10	6:12	6:15
690	5:55	5:57	6:00	6:03	6:07	6:09	6:11	6:13	6:15	6:17
680	5:58	6:00	6:03	6:05	6:09	6:12	6:14	6:16	6:18	6:20
670	6:01	6:02	6:05	6:08	6:12	6:15	6:16	6:19	6:21	6:23
660	6:03	6:05	6:08	6:11	6:15	6:17	6:19	6:21	6:24	6:26
650	6:06	6:08	6:11	6:14	6:18	6:20	6:22	6:24	6:26	6:29
640	6:09	6:10	6:14	6:16	6:21	6:23	6:25	6:27	6:29	6:32
630	6:11	6:13	6:16	6:19	6:23	6:26	6:28	6:30	6:32	6:35
620	6:14	6:16	6:19	6:22	6:26	6:29	6:31	6:33	6:35	6:38
610	6:17	6:19	6:22	6:25	6:29	6:32	6:34	6:36	6:39	6:41
600	6:20	6:22	6:25	6:28	6:32	6:35	6:37	6:39	6:42	6:44
590	6:23	6:25	6:28	6:31	6:35	6:38	6:40	6:42	6:45	6:47
580	6:26	6:28	6:31	6:34	6:39	6:41	6:43	6:46	6:48	6:51
570	6:29	6:31	6:34	6:37	6:42	6:44	6:46	6:49	6:51	6:54
560	6:32	6:34	6:37	6:41	6:45	6:48	6:50	6:52	6:55	6:57
550	6:35	6:37	6:41	6:44	6:48	6:51	6:53	6:55	6:58	7:01
540	6:38	6:40	6:44	6:47	6:52	6:54	6:56	6:59	7:01	7:04
530	6:42	6:44	6:47	6:50	6:55	6:58	7:00	7:02	7:05	7:08
520	6:45	6:47	6:50	6:54	6:58	7:01	7:03	7:06	7:08	7:11
510	6:48	6:50	6:54	6:57	7:02	7:05	7:07	7:09	7:12	7:15
500	6:52	6:54	6:57	7:01	7:05	7:08	7:10	7:13	7:16	7:19
490	6:55	6:57	7:01	7:04	7:09	7:12	7:14	7:17	7:20	7:22
480	6:59	7:01	7:04	7:08	7:13	7:16	7:18	7:21	7:23	7:26
470	7:02	7:04	7:08	7:12	7:17	7:20	7:22	7:24	7:27	7:30
460	7:06	7:08	7:12	7:15	7:20	7:23	7:26	7:28	7:31	7:34
450	7:10	7:12	7:16	7:19	7:24	7:27	7:29	7:32	7:35	7:38
440	7:14	7:16	7:19	7:23	7:28	7:31	7:33	7:36	7:39	7:42
430	7:17	7:19	7:23	7:27	7:32	7:35	7:38	7:40	7:43	7:46
420	7:21	7:23	7:27	7:31	7:36	7:40	7:42	7:45	7:48	7:51

PER MILE AVERAGES FOR EXTRA-LONG DISTANCE RUNNING

• •

POINTS	15.00 MI	16.00 MI	18.00 MI	20.00 MI	23.00 MI	25.00 MI	MARATHON	28.00 MI	30.00 MI	32.00 MI
410	7:25	7:27	7:31	7:35	7:40	7:44	7:46	7:49	7:52	7:55
400	7:29	7:31	7:36	7:39	7:45	7:48	7:50	7:53	7:56	7:59
390	7:33	7:36	7:40	7:44	7:49	7:52	7:55	7:58	8:01	8:04
380	7:38	7:40	7:44	7:48	7:53	7:57	7:59	8:02	8:05	8:08
370	7:42	7:44	7:48	7:52	7:58	8:01	8:04	8:07	8:10	8:13
360	7:46	7:49	7:53	7:57	8:02	8:06	8:08	8:11	8:15	8:18
350	7:51	7:53	7:57	8:01	8:07	8:11	8:13	8:16	8:19	8:23
340	7:55	7:58	8:02	8:06	8:12	8:15	8:18	8:21	8:24	8:28
330	8:00	8:02	8:07	8:11	8:17	8:20	8:23	8:26	8:29	8:33
320	8:05	8:07	8:12	8:16	8:22	8:25	8:28	8:31	8:35	8:38
310	8:09	8:12	8:16	8:21	8:27	8:30	8:33	8:36	8:40	8:43
300	8:14	8:17	8:21	8:26	8:32	8:36	8:38	8:42	8:45	8:49
290	8:19	8:22	8:27	8:31	8:37	8:41	8:44	8:47	8:50	8:54
280	8:24	8:27	8:32	8:36	8:42	8:46	8:49	8:53	8:56	9:00
270	8:30	8:32	8:37	8:42	8:48	8:52	8:55	8:58	9:02	9:05
260	8:35	8:38	8:42	8:47	8:53	8:57	9:00	9:04	9:07	9:11
250	8:40	8:43	8:48	8:53	8:59	9:03	9:06	9:10	9:13	9:17
240	8:46	8:49	8:54	8:58	9:05	9:09	9:12	9:16	9:19	9:23
230	8:52	8:54	8:59	9:04	9:11	9:15	9:18	9:22	9:26	9:30
220	8:57	9:00	9:05	9:10	9:17	9:21	9:24	9:28	9:32	9:36
210	9:03	9:06	9:11	9:16	9:23	9:28	9:31	9:34	9:38	9:42
200	9:09	9:12	9:18	9:23	9:30	9:34	9:37	9:41	9:45	9:49
190	9:16	9:18	9:24	9:29	9:36	9:41	9:44	9:48	9:52	9:56
180	9:22	9:25	9:30	9:36	9:43	9:47	9:50	9:54	9:59	10:03
170	9:28	9:31	9:37	9:42	9:50	9:54	9:57	10:01	10:06	10:10
160	9:35	9:38	9:44	9:49	9:57	10:01	10:04	10:09	10:13	10:17
150	9:42	9:45	9:51	9:56	10:04	10:08	10:12	10:16	10:20	10:25
140	9:49	9:52	9:58	10:03	10:11	10:16	10:19	10:24	10:28	10:32
130	9:56	9:59	10:05	10:11	10:19	10:23	10:27	10:31	10:36	10:40
120	10:03	10:06	10:12	10:18	10:26	10:31	10:35	10:39	10:44	10:48
110	10:10	10:14	10:20	10:26	10:34	10:39	10:43	10:47	10:52	10:57
100	10:18	10:22	10:28	10:34	10:42	10:47	10:51	10:56	11:00	11:05

SCORING TABLES
PER MILE AVERAGES FOR EXTRA-LONG DISTANCE RUNNING
....

POINTS	15.00 MI	16.00 MI	18.00 MI	20.00 MI	23.00 MI	25.00 MI	MARATHON	28.00 MI	30.00 MI	32.00 MI
90	10:26	10:29	10:36	10:42	10:50	10:56	10:59	11:04	11:09	11:14
80	10:34	10:38	10:44	10:50	10:59	11:04	11:08	11:13	11:18	11:23
70	10:42	10:46	10:53	10:59	11:08	11:13	11:17	11:22	11:27	11:32
60	10:51	10:54	11:01	11:08	11:17	11:22	11:26	11:31	11:36	11:41
50	10:59	11:03	11:10	11:17	11:26	11:31	11:35	11:40	11:46	11:51
40	11:08	11:12	11:19	11:26	11:35	11:41	11:45	11:50	11:56	12:01
30	11:17	11:21	11:29	11:35	11:45	11:51	11:55	12:00	12:06	12:11
20	11:27	11:31	11:38	11:45	11:55	12:01	12:05	12:11	12:16	12:22
10	11:37	11:41	11:48	11:55	12:05	12:11	12:16	12:21	12:27	12:33
0	11:47	11:51	11:58	12:06	12:16	12:22	12:26	12:32	12:38	12:44

Metric Unit Tables

This section contains essentially the same information as the English Unit Tables, except all distances are given in meters. The description preceding each table of the English Unit Tables is applicable here except for references to English distances which should be read as metric distances. The decision to publish both English and metric unit tables is based simply on the fact that the two systems are in common use in the world. Runners in the U.S. and other "English" countries can refer to the English Unit Tables, while most of Europe and other "metric" countries can refer to the Metric Unit Tables.

Table 1a of the Metric Unit Tables gives the performance rating (point level) for the classical metric racing distances, while Table 1b gives the same point levels for the non-classical metric racing distances, and Table 1c gives the long metric distances. Table 2 gives the intermediate times for constant speed runs, based on a 400 meter pace. Table 3 gives reduced speed percentages for continuous running training, based on the one kilometer pace. Finally, Table 4 presents the pacing tables for metric interval distances.

Short summaries of how to use the tables are given in French and in German on the next few pages.

Short Summary in French

TABLES MÉTRIQUES

Cette partie contient essentiellement les mêmes données que les tables en mesures anglaises (pages 119 à 207), mais cette fois les distances sont en mètres. La description précédant les tables en mesures anglaises est applicable ici, mais les références aux distances anglaises sont à lire en distances métriques.

Il n'est pas nécessaire de savoir l'anglais pour se servir de ces tables. Un court exposé du mode d'emploi suit ci-dessous, de même que la traduction de tous les termes anglais employés dans les tables.

De la page 223 à la page 226, les Tables de Scores ("Scoring Tables") 1A des Tables Métriques ("Metric Unit Tables") donnent l'evaluation des performances sous forme d'un certain nombre de points par rapport aux distances classiques dans le système métrique ("Classical Metric Racing Distances"). L'abréviation MT indique le mètre.

La table 1B (de la page 227 à la page 230) donne le nombre de points correspondant aux distances mètriques inusitées ("Non-Classical Metric Racing Distances") et la table 1C donne les points pour les courses de fond dans le même système métrique ("Long Metric Racing Distances").

La table 2 (de la page 235 à la page 238) donne les temps intermédiaires pour des courses à train régulier ("Intermediate Times for Constant Speed Runs") établis à partir d'un régime de 400 mètres.

La table 3 (de la page 239 à la page 240) est celle des vitesses réduites pour un entraînement à train constante ("Reduced Speeds for Continuous Running Training") basée sur le train au Kilométre. "Per kilometer average" signifie la moyenne au kilomètre.

La table 4 (de la page 241—) présente les tables de train pour des courses répétées sur des distances métriques. Chaque page contient une table pour un certain nombre de points, designée comme "Point Level Pacing Table." "Speed" signifie vitesse; "Reps" est une abréviation de répétition; "Rest" signifie repos ou pause.

RÉSUMÉ

Cet ouvrage indique à l'entraîneur et à l'athlète ce qu'ils veulent apprendre de la méthode d'entraînement sectionné. Il donne la vitesse, la distance et le nombre d'échauffements, ainsi que le temps de repos entre chaque effort. De plus, il indique les vitesses et les distances recommandées pour des échauffements répétés au-delà de ce qui est généralement entendu par entraînement "sectionné." Ceci a été rendu possible grâce a l'emploi d'un ordinateur. L'ouvrage présente des programmes d'entraînement quotidien pour des coureurs de toutes spécialitiés et de tous calibres, du coureur de vitesse au coureur de fond et du novice au coureur de classe internationale. Que le coureur ait battu un record mondial ou qu'il soit simplement débutant, ce livre lui fournit une grande variété de programmes d'entraînment preparés spécialement à son intention.

Ces programmes sont présentés sous forme de tabulations de temps pour les distances couvertes par l'athlète à l'entraînement. Pour chaque distance et chaque temps, un certain nombre de répétitions est suggéré, ainsi que l'intervalle de repos nécessaire après chaque effort' Une seule table de vitesses et de distances est présentée pour chaque niveau de performance. Nous appellerons ces tables "tables de train."

Les tables sont préparées pour différents niveaux de performance allant de 3'30" à 5'23" au 1500

211

mètres. Le niveau des performances est mesuré à l'aide d'une table qui fournit les points correspondant à la capacité du coureur. Cette capacité une fois établie, on peut sélectionner la table d'entraînement qui fournit une source d'intensité équivalente à la capacité des programmes d'entraînement.

Le grand nombre de tables, chacune contenant 15 temps (vitesses) différents pour 20 distances, a été facilité par l'emploi de l'ordinateur. A cet effet, on a rangé dans la mémoire de l'ordinateur une description des relations entre les variables d'un entraînement "sectionné": vitesse, distance, nombre d'efforts et pauses. Cette description (programmation) a permi de calculer une série d'entraînements correspondant à chaque niveau de capacité.

La caractéristique la plus importante de ces tables est qu'elles fournissent à l'entraîneur et à l'athlète un programme d'entraînement sur mesure, taillé selon la capacité de chaque coureur.

Chaque coureur, qu'il soit ou non au mieux de sa forme, est capable de couvrir la distance choisie en un certain temps. Le temps de sa performance est une indication de sa condition physique et de sa capacité de suivre un entraînement. L'emploi d'une table proportionelle est une façon de comparer le niveau de performance à celui d'un coureur dont les possibilités se situent à un niveau différent. La table donne un certain nombre de points selon le temps de la performance dans une course du même type. La table des points qui sert à mesurer la performance est donnée sous la nomenclature 1a, 1b et 1c.

Il est facile de se servir de la table de performances. Il suffit d'y trouver le temps réalisé et de se reporter à la colonne gauche pour y lire le nombre de points correspondant à la distance desirée. Ce nombre de points détermine la capacité relative de l'athlète par rapport aux autres niveaux ou classes. Il faut remarquer que la capacité relative est exprimée en points quelle que soit la distance parcourue par l'athlète.

Le coureur ayant réalise un 400 mètres en 51'6/10, un 800 en 2'', un 1500 en 4'' 9'8/10 ou un 5000 en 15'' 43' 1/10, est considéré comme appartenant au niveau ou à la classe des 760 points. Quand le terme "performance équivalente" est employé, il faut se souvenir que ces performances sont considérées comme étant de niveau égal pour toutes les distances. Un coureur doit accomplir une seule performance au niveau des 760 points pour être considéré comme appartenant à cette classe. Cependant, des distances *presque* égales peuvent être rapportées, pour un *seul* athléte, aux distances les plus proches de celles qu'il couvre en compétition.

Le nombre de points indique aussi la capacité d'un athléte à suivre un entraînement donné. C'est l'application de la table des points est de la plus grande importance quand on se sert des tables de régime. Comme des facteurs autres que la condition physique et la capacité d'un coureur influent sur la performance, il n'est pas nécessaire que les temps donnés dans la table d'évaluation correspondent *exactement* à celui de l'essai. Comme une indication générale de la capacité de l'athlète suffit, la table des points n'est établie que de dix en dix points.

Les tables de régime sont données de 30 en 30 points, de 1050 à 540. De cette façon, l'évaluation de la performance en vue de l'entraînement doit se sitner à une quinzaine de points du score exact pour une performance particuliére. *Il est important qu'il y ait une relation directe entre le niveau de performance de l'athléte et sa capacité a suivre un entraînement "sectionné."* La table d'évaluation donne une mesure de cette capacité. La table des temps donnée a chaque niveau de points est établie en vue de la capacité du coureur dont la performance correspond au nombre de points de la table des temps. C'est le principe fondamental du système d'ordination.

La recommandation la plus importante dans l'emploi des tables de régime est de choisir celle qui convient le mieux a la capacité du coureur. Ayant établi son niveau de points a partir de la table d'évaluation, le coureur qui désire obtenir un programme d'entraînement n'aura qu'a trouver la table de train qui correspond le mieux à son niveau de points parmi la série de tables proposées.

Il est important de noter que *les temps fournis par les tables de régime sont données pour un départ lancé.* Ceci est plus important pour les sprint que pour les distances supérieures à 400 mètres. D'autre part, chaque course est considérée comme commençant au milieu d'une piste de 400 mètres, c'est-à-dire que la moitié d'un 100 mètres se trouve dans la tournant.

La sélection des tables de train doit se faire à partir d'un essai plutôt qu'à partir d'un but qu'on se

213

propose. Les tables de temps sont basées sur la performance réalisée à l'entraînement, s'appuyant sur le résultat de l'essai pour mesurer sa capacité. La performance visée apparaîtra au cours de programme de conditionnement. Au fur et a mesure de ses progrès, le coureur pourra choisir une table de niveau plus élevé, selon les données de ses performances à l'entraînement ou en compétition.

Chaque table de régime comprend les données nécessaires à la préparation de n'importe quel type d'entraînement "sectionné." Ces tables peuvent être employées par tout athlète, du commençant au champion du monde. A l'aide du ces tables, l'athlète sera à même d'individualiser son entraînement et pourra progresser selon ses propres moyens. De plus, ces tables permettent de définir et classer plus précisément les différents types d'entraînement. Le programme d'entraînement général peut alors être conçu et structuré en detail.

Les Temps Intermédiaires pour Courses à Vitesse Constante (Table 2) donnent les temps pour des distances intermédiaires à train régulier. On veut souvent savoir en quel temps on devrait courir une certaine distance, par exemple 250 ou 500 mètres à train régulier, ce qu'on exprime généralement en secondes/400 mètres. Par exemple, un coureur couvrant les 200 mètres en 30 secondes pour un 400 mètres en de 60 secondes.

Dans l'entraînement sectionnée, un coureur desire couvrir une fraction quelconque d'une distance de compétition, au train de compétition. Si l'athlète désire couvrir un certain nombre de fois 250 mètres au train de 2'' au 800, c'est-à-dire 400 mètres en 60 secondes, les tables de vitesse constante donnent le temps désiré: 37' 5/10.

Par exemple, si un athlète désire courir une série de 250 mètres au train de 400 mètres en 66 secondes, la colonne des 250 mètres lui fournit un temps de 41' 3/10 pour le régime selectionné.

La Table de Vitesse Réduite pour un Entraînement à Course Constante (Table 3) donne le temps au kilomètre pour realiser une vitesse proportionnelle particulière basée sur la meilleure performance moyenne au kilomètre. Ce genre de table rend service pour l'entraînement à train régulier suivi généralement par les coureurs de fond, mais aussi, dans une certaine mesure, par toutes sortes de coureurs, y compris les sprinters, en-dehors de la saison sportive.

Supposons qu'un athlète puisse parcourir 10 kilomètres en 30 minutes avec un effort de 100%, c'est-à-dire a un régime de 3 minutes au kilomètre. S'il veut courir 10 kilomètres à 85%, il devra parcourir chaque kilomètre en 3'' 32' 8/10. Pour courir à une vitesse de 85% au kilomètre, il devra courir chaque kilomètre dans le temps indiqué dans la colonne des 85% pour obtenir la moyenne au kilomètre de son meilleur temps sur 15 kilomètres.

Les quatre tables de cette partie de l'ouvrage permettront à chaque coureur s'entraînant sur une piste de 400 mètres de se servir du système développé par l'ordinateur.

Les coureurs en-deça du niveau de performance des 400 points peuvent se servir de la 4e table de train en mesures anglaises pour un entraînement sectionné sur une piste de 400 mètres. La différence des temps pour les 400 mètres correspondants n'est pas très importante pour la plupart des distances courues "en sectionné." Les temps peuvent donc être presque directement suivis si l'on note les distances correspondantes:

yards:	100	165	220	275	330	385	440	495	550	660	880
mètres:	100	150	200	250	300	350	400	450	500	600	800

1100	1320	1760 (Un Mille)
1000	1200	1600

Pour ceux qui désirent des temps plus précis, le système métrique correspondant peut être obtenu en soustrayant 0,34 seconde pour chaque minute du temps indiqué pour chaque course. Ainsi, un mile en 5'' correspond à un 1600 mètres en 5'' moins 5 fois 0,34 seconde, c'est-à-dire 4'' 58' 3/10. Un 880 yards en 3'' correspond à un 800 mètres en 2' 59'', et deux miles en 11' 20'' correspondent à 3200 mètres en 11'' 16' 2/10. La plupart des coureurs ne sont pas capables de contrôler leur train à ce point de précision

(0,3 seconde par minute), de sorte que les temps par rapport aux distances en yards peuvent être employés sans se soucier de ces différences minimes.

Short Summary in German

METRIK-TABELLEN

Dieser Teil enthält im wesentlichen dieselbe Auskunft wie die englischen Metrik-Tabellen (Seite 119 bis 207), nur dass alle Entfernungen metrisch angegeben sind. Die Beschreibung, die jede Tabelle der englischen Metrik-Tabelle vorangeht, ist hier anwendbar, nur dass Verweisungen auf englische Entfernungen als metrische Entfernungen gelesen werden sollte.

Englischkenntnisse sind nicht nötig, um diese Tabellen zu gebrauchen. Eine kurze Übersicht folgt, wie man dieses System zu benützen hat. Übersetzungen von allen englischen Wörtern der verschiedenen Tabellen werden auch gegeben werden.

Anschreibetafeln ("Scoring Tables" auf englisch) 1A der Metrik-Tabellen ("Metric Unit Tables" auf englisch) geben auf Seite 223 bis 226 die Bewertungen der Leistungen (anders bekannt als Punkthöhen, "point levels") für die klassischen metrischen Rennentfernungen ("Classical Metric Racing Distances" auf englisch). "Points" bedeuten Punkte. "MT" bedeutet Meter.

Tabelle 1B (Seite 227 bis 230 gibt dieselbe Punkthöhe für die nicht klassischen metrischen Rennentfernungen ("Non-Classical Racing Distances") und Tabelle 1C gibt die langen metrischen Rennentfernungen

("Long Metric Racing Distances").

Tabelle 2 (Seite 235 bis 238) gibt die dazwischen liegenden Zeiten für die gleichbleibenden Schnelligkeits-Rennen ("Intermediate Times for Constant Speed Runs") die auf einen 400 Meter-Gang basiert ist.

Tabelle 3 (Seite 239 bis 240) ist eine Tabelle von reduzierten Zeiten für anhaltendes Renntraining ("Continuous Running Training"), die auf einen Kilometer-Gang basiert ist. "Per Kilometer Average" bedeutet je Durchscnittskilometer.

Tabelle 4 (Seite 241–) ist die Gang-Tabelle für wiederholtes Rennen zu metrisch periodischen Entfernungen. Jede Seite enthält eine Tabelle für eine besondere Punkthöhe. Diese Tabelle heisst Punkthöhe Gang-Tabelle ("Point Level Pacing Table"). "Speed" bedeutet Schnelligkeit. "Reps" ist eine Abkürzung für Wiederholungen; "Rest" bedeutet Ruhepause; "MT" bedeutet Meter.

EINE KURZE ÜBERSICHT

Dieses Buch wird dem Leichtathletik-Coach und dem Läufer behilflich sein, indem es die periodische Methode des Trainings erklärt. Hier wird gegeben, wie schnell, wie weit, wiewiele Wiederholungen zu machen, und wiewiele Ruhepause zwischen verschiedenen Rennen zu nehmen. Hier wird auch gegeben, Schnelligkeiten und Entfernungen, die ferner des gewöhnlichen periodischen Trainings sind. Die Hilfe von einem Computer hat dies möglich gemacht. Es enthält täglich Leibesübungen-Programme für Läufer von jeglichen Fähigkeiten in jeglichen Wettkämpfen. Es gibt Programme für Sprinter oder Langstreckenläufer, für Weltmeister oder Anfänger. Dieses Buch enthält verschiedene Programme, die besonders hier für jede Gruppe verschiedener Läufer entworfen worden sind.

Diese Leibesübungen sind in Form einer Tabellarisierung der Zeiten für jede der Entfernungen, die man in einem Training-Programm zu benützen hat, dargestellt. Mit jeder Zeit und Entfernung ist eine vorgeschlagene Anzahl von Wiederholungen und die empfohlene nach jedem Rennen nötige Ruhepause gegeben, so dass die Leibesübungen richtig vollziehen können. Eine einzige, vollständige Tabelle von Zeiten und Entfernungen ist mit jeder Ebene der Fähigkeit dargestellt. Diese Tabellen werden hernach Gang-Tabellen heissen.

Tabelle für verschiedene Ebene der Fähigkeiten sind gegeben—in der Anreihung einer Leistung von 3:30 für 1500 Meter bis zu einer Leistung von 5:23 für 1500 Meter. Die Höhe der Leistung wird durch eine gekürzte Anschreibetafel gegeben, die eine Punkthöhe entsprechen der Fähigkeit des Läufers anzeigt. Nachdem man die Höhe der Leistung weiss, kann man die Gang-Tabelle auswählen, die das richtige Leibesübungen-Programm angibt.

Die grosse Zahl der Tabellen (jede enthält 15 verschiedene Zeiten für 20 verschiedene Entfernungen) wurde durch einen modernen elektronischen Computer möglich gemacht. Um diese zu erreichen, wurde einem Computer die Beschreibung für Beziehungen zwischen Veränderlichungen in einer Leibesübung gegeben: Schnelligkeit, Entfernung, Wiederholungen und Ruhepausen. Diese Beschreibung hat die entsprechenden Leibesübungen für alle Ebene der Fähigkeiten hergegeben.

Das wichtigste Merkmal der Tabellen ist die Tatsache, dass sie den Coach oder den Läufer selbst in den Stand setzen, dass er das richtige Programm für die Fähigkeit des Athleten auswählen kann.

Jeder konkurrierende Läufer kann seine gewählte Entfernung in einer bestimmten Zeit leisten, wenn er auch nicht gut in Form ist. Seine Leistungszeit zeigt seine jetzige Kondition und seine Fähigkeiten. Man Kann seine Kondition und Fähigkeiten als seine *Leistungshöhe* bezeichnen. Die Kenntnis seiner Leistungshöhe ist hier wichtig, weil sie Bezug auf seine Fähigkeit, eine Leibesübung durchzuführen, hat. Man kann auch eine Ausgleichensanschreibetafel benutzen, um seine Leistungshöhe mit einem Läufer in einer anderen Gruppe zu vergleichen. Die Anschreibetafel bigt eine Punkthöhe, die auf die Leistungszeit einer Veranstaltung basiert ist. Diese Anschreibetafel wird in Tabellen 1a, 1b, 1c in diesem Teil des Buches gegeben.

Das Gebruach dieser Leistungsanschreibetafel ist verhältnismässig einfach. Man sucht seine geleistete Zeit in der Tabelle für die entsprechende Entfernung einfach aus; dann kann man seine Punkthöhe in der linken Reihe finden. Diese Punkthöhe zeigt die entsprechende Fähigkeit des Athleten in Vergleich zu allen anderen Punkthöhen. Zu bemerken ist, dass die entsprechende Fähigkeit als eine Punkthöhe angegeben ist, abgesehen von der Entfernung, die gerannt worden ist.

Jemand, der 400 Meter in 51.6 Sekunden läufen kann, 800 Meter in 2:00, 1500 Meter in 4:09.8, oder 5000 Meter in 15:43.1, heisst ein 760 Punkt-Läufer ("760 point level runner"). Wenn der Ausdruck "entsprechende Leistungen" angewendet ist, muss man immer wahrnehmen, dass diese als gleiche Leistungshöhen für alle Entfernungen sind. Ein Läufer braucht nur *eine* 760 Punkthöhe zu leisten, um einen 760 Punkt-Läufer zu sein. Fast gleiche Entfernungen können aber für *einen* Athleten als die gleiche gelten.

Die Punkthöhe zeigt auch die Fähigkeit eines Läufers, Leibesübungen zu lesiten. Diese Anwendung der Anschreibetafel ist wichtig in Gebrauch der Gang-Tabellen. Weil andere Faktoren ausser Gesundheitszustand und Fähigkeit auf die Leistung wirken, ist es *nicht* so wichtig, das die in der Tabelle gegebenen Zeiten *genau* mit der Zeit der ersten Probe übereinstimmen. Was nötig ist, ist eine Angabe auf die jetzige Fähigkeit des Athleten. Deswegen ist die Anschreibetafel mit 10 Punkt Stufen gedruckt.

Die Gang-Tabellen gaben in 30 Punkt-Abständen die Punkthöhen von 540 Punkten bis 1050 Punkt einer besonderen Leistung zu sein. *Das Wichtig ste hier ist die direket Beziehung zwichen der Leistungshöhe eines Athleten und seine Fähigkeit, Übungen durchzuführen.* Die Leistungshöhetabelle zeigt die Fähigkeit eines Läufers. Die zur jeden Punkthöhe gegebenen Zeittabelle ist für die Fähigkeite eines Läufers bestimmt, dessen Leistung die Punkthöhe der Zeittabelle anpasst. Das ist das grundlegende Prinzip des Computersystems.

Das Wichtigste beim Gebrauch der Gang-Tabellen is die Auswahl der Tabelle, die die Fähigkeit des Läufers am besten anpasst. Ein Läufer hat seine Punkthöhe in der Leistungshöhetabelle gefunden. Er will die Richtlinien seiner Übungen jetzt festellen. Er sucht seine Gang-Tabelle aus der ganzen Reihe einfach aus, die am mähesten zu seiner Punkthöhe steht. Wichtig ist, *alle die in der Gang-Tabellen gegebenen Zeiten nehmen einer Rennstart an.* Diese Tatsache ist wichtiger für die Kürzeren Entfernungen als für die 400 Meter und andere längere Entfernungen. Wir nehmen auch an, der Läufer fängt in der Mitte einer 400 Meter Rennbahn an; d.h., die Hälfte der 100 Meter Entfernung liegt auf der Kurve.

Es ist hier unentbehrlich, dass die Auswahl der Gang-Tabelle auf eine tatsächlich durchgeführte Liestung basiert ist, und nicht auf irgendien Zeil. Die Zeittabellen sind auf die jetzige Fähigkeit eines Athleten basiert; wir nehmen an, dass die Zeit der Probe die Fähigkeit zeigt. Seine Möglichkeit als Läufer wird sich zeigen, indem er übt. Wenn er sich verbessert hat, kann er eine höhere Gang-Tabelle auswählen, die seine durchgeführte Leistung entspricht.

Jede Gang-Tabelle enthält die nötige Information für fast alle mögliche Leibesübungen, die ein Läufer durchführen könnte. Jeder Athlet, ob er Anfänger oder Weltmeister ist, kann diese Tabellen gebrauchen. Mit Hilfe dieser Tabellen kann der Athlet sein persönliches Trainingprogramm feststellen und kann sich seiner eigenen Fähigkeiten gemäss weiternetwickeln. Noch ein Vorteil der Gang-Tabellen ist, dass man die verschiedenen Arten von Training genauer difinieren kann. Das Gesamttrainingprogramm kann daher ausführlicher beschreiben und geplant werden.

Die dazwischen liegenden Zeiten für die gleichbleibenden Schnelligkeits-Rennen (Tabelle 2) geben die Zeiten für die dazwischen liegenden Entfernungen zu einer gleichbleibenden Zeit (Gang). Man will oft wissen, zu welcher Zeit er eine ungewöhnlichen Entfernung, z.B. 250 Meter oder 500 Meter, rennen sollte. Wir geben als Beispiel einen Läufer, der mit einem 60 Sekunden-Gang für 200 Meter in 30 Sekunden rennt.

In dem periodischen Training will man oft nur ein Teil seiner gewöhnlichen Entfernung rennen, aber mit demselben Renngang. Ein Athlet, zum Beispiel, der 800 Meter in 2:00 rennen kann, will vielleicht einige Wiederholungen von 250 Metern zu demselben Gang rennen. (Die 800 Meter Tabelle mit einem Gang von 2:00 ist hier als die 400 Meter mit einem 60 Sekunden-Gang gegeben.) Die Tabelle zeigt die gewünschte Zeit für 250 Meter mit einem 400 Meter Gang zu 60 Sekunden (37.5 Sekunden).

Noch einem Beispiel: wenn der Athlet 250 Meter mit einem 400 Meter Gang zu 66 Sekunden rennen will, sieht er in der 250 Meter Reihe eine Zeit von 41.3 Sekunden.

Die Tabelle von reduzierten Zeiten für anhaltendes Rennen (Tabelle 3) gibt die Zeit pro Kilometer, die ein Läufer leisten sollte, um einen besonderen Durchschnitt der besten Zeit von dem Läufer zu erreichen. Diese Tabelle ist hier vorteilhaft für das anhaltende Rennen eines Langstreckenläufers. Am anfang des Trainingprogramms, wenn alle Athleten längere Entfernungen rennen, ist diese Tabelle auch gut.

Wenn ein Athlet zum Beispiel 10 Kilometer in 30 Minuten mit einer 100% Anstrengung rennen kann, müsste er jetzt jedes Kilometer in 3:32.8 rennen, wenn er 10 Kilometer mit 85% Anstrengung rennen wollte. Um 15 Kilometer mit einer 85% Anstrengung zu rennen, müsste er jedes Kilometer mit dem in der 85% Reihe gegebenen Gang rennen. Die Reihe, worin er seine Zeit aussucht, entspricht seine beste 15 Kilometer Zeit.

Die vier Tabellen in diesem Teil des Buches wird jeden Läufer, der auf eine 400 Meter Rennbahn läuft, in den Stand sitzen, dieses Computersystems zu gebrauchen.

Läufer, die eine Leistung unter der 400 Punkthöhe durchführen, können die englischen Tabellen (Tabelle 4) für ihre Leibesübungen auf eine 400 Meter Rennbahn benützen. Der Unterschied zwischen den Zeiten sind für die meisten Entfernungen nicht wesentlich. Die für Yards gegebenen Zeiten kann der Athlet direkt benützen, indem er die entsprechende Entfernung aussucht:

Yards:	100	165	220	275	330	385	440	495	550	660	880
Meter:	100	150	200	250	300	350	400	450	500	600	800

	1100	1320	1760 (Meile)
	1000	1200	1600

Diejenigen, die eine genauere Zeit wollen, können die entsprechende metrische Zeit selbst rechnen. Man braucht nur 0.34 Sekunden von jeder in der Tabelle gegeben Minute subrrahieren. Eine in 5 Minuten geläufene Meile entspricht daher 1600 Meter in 5:00 weniger 5 x .34 Sekunden oder 4:58.3. 800 Yards in 3:00 entspricht 3200 Meter in 11:16.2. Die meisten Läufer können direkt gebraucht werden, ohne Aufsicht auf diese kleinen Unterschiede.

POINTS	100 MT	200 MT	400 MT	800 MT	1500 MT	3000 MT	5000 MT	10000 MT	20.00 KM	MARATHON
1150	9.45	19.1	42.4	1:37.2	3:20.4	7:12.9	12:29.6	26:08.0	54:42	2:01:29
1140	9.48	19.2	42.6	1:37.7	3:21.4	7:15.2	12:33.5	26:16.4	54:59	2:02:09
1130	9.52	19.3	42.8	1:38.1	3:22.4	7:17.5	12:37.5	26:24.9	55:17	2:02:49
1120	9.56	19.4	43.0	1:38.6	3:23.5	7:19.8	12:41.6	26:33.4	55:35	2:03:30
1110	9.60	-------	43.2	1:39.1	3:24.5	7:22.1	12:45.7	26:42.1	55:54	2:04:11
1100	9.64	19.5	43.4	1:39.6	3:25.6	7:24.5	12:49.8	26:50.9	56:12	2:04:53
1090	9.68	19.6	43.6	1:40.1	3:26.7	7:26.9	12:54.0	26:59.8	56:31	2:05:36
1080	9.72	19.7	43.8	1:40.6	3:27.8	7:29.3	12:58.2	27:08.7	56:50	2:06:18
1070	9.76	19.8	44.0	1:41.1	3:28.9	7:31.7	13:02.5	27:17.8	57:09	2:07:02
1060	9.80	19.9	44.2	1:41.6	3:30.0	7:34.2	13:06.8	27:27.0	57:29	2:07:45
1050	9.84	20.0	44.5	1:42.2	3:31.1	7:36.7	13:11.2	27:36.2	57:49	2:08:30
1040	9.89	-------	44.7	1:42.7	3:32.2	7:39.2	13:15.6	27:45.6	58:08	2:09:14
1030	9.93	20.1	44.9	1:43.2	3:33.4	7:41.8	13:20.1	27:55.1	58:29	2:10:00
1020	9.97	20.2	45.1	1:43.8	3:34.5	7:44.3	13:24.6	28:04.7	58:49	2:10:46
1010	10.01	20.3	45.3	1:44.3	3:35.7	7:46.9	13:29.2	28:14.4	59:09	2:11:32
1000	10.06	20.4	45.5	1:44.9	3:36.9	7:49.6	13:33.8	28:24.2	59:30	2:12:19
990	10.10	20.5	45.8	1:45.4	3:38.1	7:52.2	13:38.5	28:34.1	59:51	2:13:06
980	10.14	20.6	46.0	1:46.0	3:39.3	7:54.9	13:43.2	28:44.1	1:00:13	2:13:54
970	10.19	20.7	46.2	1:46.6	3:40.5	7:57.7	13:48.0	28:54.3	1:00:34	2:14:43
960	10.23	20.8	46.5	1:47.1	3:41.8	8:00.4	13:52.8	29:04.6	1:00:56	2:15:32
950	10.28	20.9	46.7	1:47.7	3:43.0	8:03.2	13:57.7	29:15.0	1:01:18	2:16:22
940	10.32	21.0	46.9	1:48.3	3:44.3	8:06.0	14:02.7	29:25.5	1:01:41	2:17:12
930	10.37	21.1	47.2	1:48.9	3:45.6	8:08.9	14:07.7	29:36.2	1:02:03	2:18:04
920	10.41	21.2	47.4	1:49.5	3:46.8	8:11.8	14:12.8	29:47.0	1:02:26	2:18:55
910	10.46	21.3	47.6	1:50.1	3:48.2	8:14.7	14:17.9	29:57.9	1:02:49	2:19:48
900	10.51	21.4	47.9	1:50.7	3:49.5	8:17.7	14:23.1	30:08.9	1:03:13	2:20:41
890	10.56	21.5	48.1	1:51.3	3:50.8	8:20.6	14:28.3	30:20.1	1:03:37	2:21:34
880	10.60	21.6	48.4	1:52.0	3:52.2	8:23.7	14:33.7	30:31.4	1:04:01	2:22:29
870	10.65	21.7	48.6	1:52.6	3:53.6	8:26.7	14:39.1	30:42.9	1:04:25	2:23:24
860	10.70	21.8	48.9	1:53.2	3:54.9	8:29.8	14:44.5	30:54.5	1:04:50	2:24:20
850	10.75	21.9	49.2	1:53.9	3:56.3	8:33.0	14:50.0	31:06.3	1:05:15	2:25:16
840	10.80	22.0	49.4	1:54.5	3:57.8	8:36.2	14:55.6	31:18.2	1:05:40	2:26:13

POINTS	100 MT	200 MT	400 MT	800 MT	1500 MT	3000 MT	5000 MT	10000 MT	20.00 KM	MARATHON
830	10.85	22.1	49.7	1:55.2	3:59.2	8:39.4	15:01.3	31:30.3	1:06:06	2:27:11
820	10.90	22.2	50.0	1:55.9	4:00.7	8:42.7	15:07.1	31:42.5	1:06:32	2:28:10
810	10.95	22.3	50.2	1:56.5	4:02.1	8:46.0	15:12.9	31:54.9	1:06:58	2:29:10
800	11.00	22.4	50.5	1:57.2	4:03.6	8:49.3	15:18.8	32:07.4	1:07:25	2:30:10
790	11.05	22.5	50.8	1:57.9	4:05.1	8:52.7	15:24.7	32:20.1	1:07:52	2:31:11
780	11.11	22.6	51.0	1:58.6	4:06.7	8:56.1	15:30.8	32:33.0	1:08:19	2:32:13
770	11.16	22.8	51.3	1:59.3	4:08.2	8:59.6	15:36.9	32:46.0	1:08:47	2:33:16
760	11.21	22.9	51.6	2:00.1	4:09.8	9:03.1	15:43.1	32:59.3	1:09:15	2:34:20
750	11.27	23.0	51.9	2:00.8	4:11.4	9:06.7	15:49.4	33:12.7	1:09:44	2:35:25
740	11.32	23.1	52.2	2:01.5	4:13.0	9:10.3	15:55.7	33:26.3	1:10:13	2:36:30
730	11.38	23.2	52.5	2:02.3	4:14.6	9:14.0	16:02.2	33:40.0	1:10:42	2:37:37
720	11.43	23.3	52.8	2:03.0	4:16.3	9:17.7	16:08.7	33:54.0	1:11:12	2:38:44
710	11.49	23.5	53.1	2:03.8	4:17.9	9:21.4	16:15.4	34:08.1	1:11:42	2:39:53
700	11.55	23.6	53.4	2:04.6	4:19.6	9:25.3	16:22.1	34:22.5	1:12:13	2:41:02
690	11.60	23.7	53.7	2:05.4	4:21.4	9:29.1	16:28.9	34:37.1	1:12:44	2:42:13
680	11.66	23.8	54.0	2:06.2	4:23.1	9:33.0	16:35.8	34:51.8	1:13:15	2:43:24
670	11.72	23.9	54.3	2:07.0	4:24.9	9:37.0	16:42.8	35:06.8	1:13:47	2:44:37
660	11.78	24.1	54.7	2:07.8	4:26.7	9:41.0	16:49.9	35:22.0	1:14:20	2:45:50
650	11.84	24.2	55.0	2:08.6	4:28.5	9:45.1	16:57.2	35:37.4	1:14:53	2:47:05
640	11.90	24.3	55.3	2:09.5	4:30.3	9:49.3	17:04.5	35:53.0	1:15:26	2:48:21
630	11.96	24.5	55.6	2:10.3	4:32.2	9:53.5	17:11.9	36:08.9	1:16:00	2:49:38
620	12.02	24.6	56.0	2:11.2	4:34.0	9:57.7	17:19.4	36:25.0	1:16:35	2:50:56
610	12.08	24.7	56.3	2:12.0	4:36.0	10:02.1	17:27.1	36:41.4	1:17:10	2:52:15
600	12.15	24.9	56.7	2:12.9	4:37.9	10:06.4	17:34.8	36:57.9	1:17:45	2:53:36
590	12.21	25.0	57.0	2:13.8	4:39.9	10:10.9	17:42.7	37:14.8	1:18:21	2:54:58
580	12.27	25.1	57.4	2:14.7	4:41.9	10:15.4	17:50.7	37:31.9	1:18:58	2:56:21
570	12.34	25.3	57.7	2:15.6	4:43.9	10:20.0	17:58.8	37:49.3	1:19:35	2:57:45
560	12.40	25.4	58.1	2:16.6	4:46.0	10:24.7	18:07.0	38:06.9	1:20:13	2:59:11
550	12.47	25.6	58.4	2:17.5	4:48.0	10:29.4	18:15.4	38:24.8	1:20:51	3:00:39
540	12.54	25.7	58.8	2:18.5	4:50.1	10:34.2	18:23.9	38:43.0	1:21:30	3:02:07
530	12.61	25.9	59.2	2:19.4	4:52.3	10:39.0	18:32.5	39:01.5	1:22:10	3:03:37
520	12.67	26.0	59.6	2:20.4	4:54.5	10:44.0	18:41.2	39:20.3	1:22:50	3:05:09

POINTS	100 MT	200 MT	400 MT	800 MT	1500 MT	3000 MT	5000 MT	10000 MT	20.00 KM	MARATHON
510	12.74	26.1	59.9	2:21.4	4:56.7	10:49.0	18:50.1	39:39.3	1:23:31	3:06:42
500	12.81	26.3	1:00.3	2:22.4	4:58.9	10:54.1	18:59.2	39:58.7	1:24:12	3:08:17
490	12.88	26.5	1:00.7	2:23.5	5:01.2	10:59.3	19:08.3	40:18.4	1:24:55	3:09:53
480	12.95	26.6	1:01.1	2:24.5	5:03.5	11:04.6	19:17.7	40:38.5	1:25:38	3:11:32
470	13.03	26.8	1:01.5	2:25.6	5:05.9	11:09.9	19:27.2	40:58.9	1:26:21	3:13:11
460	13.10	26.9	1:01.9	2:26.6	5:08.3	11:15.3	19:36.8	41:19.6	1:27:06	3:14:53
450	13.17	27.1	1:02.4	2:27.7	5:10.7	11:20.9	19:46.6	41:40.7	1:27:51	3:16:36
440	13.25	27.2	1:02.8	2:28.8	5:13.1	11:26.5	19:56.6	42:02.1	1:28:37	3:18:21
430	13.32	27.4	1:03.2	2:30.0	5:15.6	11:32.2	20:06.7	42:23.9	1:29:24	3:20:08
420	13.40	27.6	1:03.6	2:31.1	5:18.2	11:38.0	20:17.0	42:46.1	1:30:12	3:21:57
410	13.48	27.7	1:04.1	2:32.3	5:20.8	11:43.9	20:27.5	43:08.6	1:31:00	3:23:48
400	13.56	27.9	1:04.5	2:33.4	5:23.4	11:49.9	20:38.2	43:31.6	1:31:50	3:25:41
390	13.63	28.1	1:05.0	2:34.6	5:26.1	11:56.0	20:49.0	43:55.0	1:32:40	3:27:36
380	13.71	28.3	1:05.4	2:35.8	5:28.8	12:02.2	21:00.1	44:18.8	1:33:31	3:29:34
370	13.80	28.4	1:05.9	2:37.1	5:31.5	12:08.6	21:11.3	44:43.0	1:34:24	3:31:33
360	13.88	28.6	1:06.4	2:38.3	5:34.3	12:15.0	21:22.8	45:07.7	1:35:17	3:33:35
350	13.96	28.8	1:06.9	2:39.6	5:37.2	12:21.5	21:34.4	45:32.9	1:36:11	3:35:39
340	14.04	29.0	1:07.3	2:40.9	5:40.1	12:28.2	21:46.3	45:58.5	1:37:06	3:37:46
330	14.13	29.2	1:07.8	2:42.2	5:43.1	12:35.0	21:58.4	46:24.6	1:38:02	3:39:55
320	14.22	29.3	1:08.3	2:43.5	5:46.1	12:41.9	22:10.7	46:51.2	1:39:00	3:42:06
310	14.30	29.5	1:08.8	2:44.9	5:49.1	12:49.0	22:23.3	47:18.3	1:39:58	3:44:21
300	14.39	29.7	1:09.3	2:46.3	5:52.2	12:56.1	22:36.0	47:46.0	1:40:58	3:46:38
290	14.48	29.9	1:09.9	2:47.7	5:55.4	13:03.4	22:49.1	48:14.1	1:41:59	3:48:58
280	14.57	30.1	1:10.4	2:49.1	5:58.6	13:10.9	23:02.4	48:42.9	1:43:01	3:51:21
270	14.66	30.3	1:10.9	2:50.5	6:01.9	13:18.5	23:15.9	49:12.2	1:44:05	3:53:46
260	14.75	30.5	1:11.5	2:52.0	6:05.3	13:26.2	23:29.7	49:42.1	1:45:09	3:56:15
250	14.85	30.7	1:12.0	2:53.5	6:08.7	13:34.1	23:43.8	50:12.7	1:46:15	3:58:47
240	14.94	30.9	1:12.6	2:55.1	6:12.1	13:42.1	23:58.2	50:43.8	1:47:23	4:01:23
230	15.04	31.1	1:13.2	2:56.6	6:15.7	13:50.3	24:12.8	51:15.6	1:48:32	4:04:02
220	15.14	31.4	1:13.8	2:58.2	6:19.3	13:58.7	24:27.8	51:48.1	1:49:42	4:06:44
210	15.23	31.6	1:14.3	2:59.8	6:23.0	14:07.2	24:43.1	52:21.3	1:50:54	4:09:30
200	15.33	31.8	1:14.9	3:01.4	6:26.7	14:15.9	24:58.7	52:55.2	1:52:08	4:12:20

POINTS	100 MT	200 MT	400 MT	800 MT	1500 MT	3000 MT	5000 MT	10000 MT	20.00 KM	MARATHON
190	15.44	32.0	1:15.6	3:03.1	6:30.5	14:24.8	25:14.6	53:29.8	1:53:23	4:15:13
180	15.54	32.3	1:16.2	3:04.8	6:34.4	14:33.9	25:30.9	54:05.2	1:54:40	4:18:11
170	15.64	32.5	1:16.8	3:06.6	6:38.4	14:43.2	25:47.5	54:41.4	1:55:59	4:21:13
160	15.75	32.7	1:17.4	3:08.3	6:42.5	14:52.7	26:04.5	55:18.4	1:57:19	4:24:19
150	15.85	33.0	1:18.1	3:10.1	6:46.6	15:02.4	26:21.9	55:56.3	1:58:41	4:27:29
140	15.96	33.2	1:18.8	3:12.0	6:50.8	15:12.2	26:39.7	56:35.0	2:00:06	4:30:45
130	16.07	33.4	1:19.4	3:13.8	6:55.1	15:22.4	26:57.8	57:14.6	2:01:32	4:34:05
120	16.18	33.7	1:20.1	3:15.7	6:59.6	15:32.7	27:16.4	57:55.2	2:03:00	4:37:30
110	16.30	33.9	1:20.8	3:17.7	7:04.1	15:43.3	27:35.4	58:36.7	2:04:31	4:41:00
100	16.41	34.2	1:21.5	3:19.7	7:08.7	15:54.1	27:54.9	59:19.2	2:06:04	4:44:36
90	16.53	34.5	1:22.2	3:21.7	7:13.4	16:05.1	28:14.8	1:00:02.8	2:07:39	4:48:17
80	16.65	34.7	1:23.0	3:23.8	7:18.2	16:16.5	28:35.2	1:00:47.4	2:09:17	4:52:04
70	16.76	35.0	1:23.7	3:25.9	7:23.1	16:28.1	28:56.2	1:01:33.2	2:10:57	4:55:57
60	16.89	35.3	1:24.5	3:28.0	7:28.1	16:39.9	29:17.6	1:02:20.2	2:12:40	4:59:56
50	17.01	35.5	1:25.3	3:30.2	7:33.2	16:52.1	29:39.5	1:03:08.3	2:14:25	5:04:02
40	17.13	35.8	1:26.1	3:32.5	7:38.5	17:04.6	30:02.0	1:03:57.7	2:16:13	5:08:15
30	17.26	36.1	1:26.9	3:34.8	7:43.9	17:17.3	30:25.1	1:04:48.4	2:18:05	5:12:34
20	17.39	36.4	1:27.7	3:37.1	7:49.4	17:30.4	30:48.8	1:05:40.5	2:19:59	5:17:01
10	17.52	36.7	1:28.5	3:39.5	7:55.0	17:43.8	31:13.1	1:06:34.0	2:21:56	5:21:36
0	17.65	37.0	1:29.4	3:42.0	8:00.8	17:57.6	31:38.1	1:07:28.9	2:23:57	5:26:19

●●

POINTS	50 MT	80 MT	300 MT	350 MT	500 MT	1000 MT	1200 MT	2400 MT	3200 MT	4800 MT
1150	5.18	7.72	30.1	36.1	55.7	2:06.1	2:35.5	5:39.1	7:44.4	11:57.7
1140	5.20	7.75	30.2	36.3	56.0	2:06.8	2:36.3	5:40.8	7:46.8	12:01.5
1130	5.22	7.78	30.3	36.5	56.2	2:07.4	2:37.1	5:42.6	7:49.3	12:05.3
1120	5.24	7.81	30.5	36.6	56.5	2:08.0	2:37.9	5:44.4	7:51.8	12:09.2
1110	5.26	7.84	30.6	36.8	56.8	2:08.7	2:38.7	5:46.2	7:54.3	12:13.1
1100	5.28	7.87	30.8	37.0	57.0	2:09.3	2:39.5	5:48.0	7:56.8	12:17.1
1090	5.30	7.91	30.9	37.1	57.3	2:10.0	2:40.3	5:49.9	7:59.4	12:21.1
1080	5.33	7.94	31.0	37.3	57.6	2:10.7	2:41.1	5:51.8	8:02.0	12:25.1
1070	5.35	7.97	31.2	37.5	57.9	2:11.4	2:42.0	5:53.7	8:04.6	12:29.2
1060	5.37	8.01	31.3	37.7	58.2	2:12.0	2:42.8	5:55.6	8:07.3	12:33.3
1050	5.39	8.04	31.5	37.8	58.5	2:12.7	2:43.7	5:57.5	8:09.9	12:37.5
1040	5.41	8.07	31.6	38.0	58.7	2:13.4	2:44.6	5:59.5	8:12.7	12:41.8
1030	5.44	8.11	31.8	38.2	59.0	2:14.1	2:45.4	6:01.5	8:15.4	12:46.0
1020	5.46	8.14	31.9	38.4	59.3	2:14.8	2:46.3	6:03.5	8:18.2	12:50.4
1010	5.48	8.18	32.0	38.6	59.6	2:15.6	2:47.2	6:05.5	8:21.0	12:54.7
1000	5.51	8.21	32.2	38.8	59.9	2:16.3	2:48.1	6:07.5	8:23.8	12:59.1
990	5.53	8.25	32.4	38.9	1:00.2	2:17.0	2:49.1	6:09.6	8:26.7	13:03.6
980	5.55	8.28	32.5	39.1	1:00.5	2:17.8	2:50.0	6:11.7	8:29.6	13:08.1
970	5.58	8.32	32.7	39.3	1:00.8	2:18.5	2:50.9	6:13.8	8:32.5	13:12.7
960	5.60	8.35	32.8	39.5	1:01.2	2:19.3	2:51.9	6:16.0	8:35.4	13:17.4
950	5.63	8.39	33.0	39.7	1:01.5	2:20.0	2:52.8	6:18.1	8:38.4	13:22.0
940	5.65	8.43	33.1	39.9	1:01.8	2:20.8	2:53.8	6:20.3	8:41.5	13:26.8
930	5.68	8.47	33.3	40.1	1:02.1	2:21.6	2:54.8	6:22.5	8:44.5	13:31.6
920	5.70	8.50	33.5	40.3	1:02.5	2:22.4	2:55.8	6:24.8	8:47.7	13:36.4
910	5.73	8.54	33.6	40.5	1:02.8	2:23.2	2:56.8	6:27.0	8:50.8	13:41.3
900	5.75	8.58	33.8	40.7	1:03.1	2:24.0	2:57.8	6:29.3	8:54.0	13:46.3
890	5.78	8.62	34.0	40.9	1:03.5	2:24.8	2:58.8	6:31.7	8:57.2	13:51.3
880	5.80	8.66	34.1	41.1	1:03.8	2:25.7	2:59.8	6:34.0	9:00.4	13:56.4
870	5.83	8.70	34.3	41.3	1:04.1	2:26.5	3:00.9	6:36.4	9:03.7	14:01.6
860	5.86	8.74	34.5	41.6	1:04.5	2:27.3	3:02.0	6:38.8	9:07.1	14:06.8
850	5.88	8.78	34.6	41.8	1:04.8	2:28.2	3:03.0	6:41.2	9:10.5	14:12.1
840	5.91	8.82	34.8	42.0	1:05.2	2:29.1	3:04.1	6:43.7	9:13.9	14:17.5

POINTS	50 MT	80 MT	300 MT	350 MT	500 MT	1000 MT	1200 MT	2400 MT	3200 MT	4800 MT
830	5.94	8.86	35.0	42.2	1:05.6	2:30.0	3:05.2	6:46.2	9:17.3	14:22.9
820	5.96	8.90	35.2	42.4	1:05.9	2:30.8	3:06.3	6:48.7	9:20.9	14:28.4
810	5.99	8.94	35.4	42.7	1:06.3	2:31.7	3:07.5	6:51.3	9:24.4	14:33.9
800	6.02	8.98	35.5	42.9	1:06.7	2:32.7	3:08.6	6:53.9	9:28.0	14:39.6
790	6.05	9.02	35.7	43.1	1:07.0	2:33.6	3:09.7	6:56.5	9:31.6	14:45.3
780	6.08	9.07	35.9	43.3	1:07.4	2:34.5	3:10.9	6:59.2	9:35.3	14:51.0
770	6.11	9.11	36.1	43.6	1:07.8	2:35.5	3:12.1	7:01.9	9:39.1	14:56.9
760	6.13	9.15	36.3	43.8	1:08.2	2:36.4	3:13.3	7:04.6	9:42.9	15:02.8
750	6.16	9.20	36.5	44.1	1:08.6	2:37.4	3:14.5	7:07.4	9:46.7	15:08.8
740	6.19	9.24	36.7	44.3	1:09.0	2:38.4	3:15.7	7:10.2	9:50.6	15:14.9
730	6.22	9.29	36.9	44.5	1:09.4	2:39.4	3:17.0	7:13.0	9:54.5	15:21.1
720	6.25	9.33	37.1	44.8	1:09.8	2:40.4	3:18.2	7:15.9	9:58.5	15:27.4
710	6.28	9.38	37.3	45.0	1:10.2	2:41.4	3:19.5	7:18.8	10:02.6	15:33.7
700	6.31	9.42	37.5	45.3	1:10.6	2:42.4	3:20.8	7:21.7	10:06.7	15:40.1
690	6.35	9.47	37.7	45.6	1:11.1	2:43.5	3:22.1	7:24.7	10:10.8	15:46.6
680	6.38	9.52	37.9	45.8	1:11.5	2:44.5	3:23.4	7:27.8	10:15.0	15:53.3
670	6.41	9.56	38.1	46.1	1:11.9	2:45.6	3:24.8	7:30.9	10:19.3	16:00.0
660	6.44	9.61	38.3	46.3	1:12.4	2:46.7	3:26.2	7:34.0	10:23.6	16:06.8
650	6.47	9.66	38.6	46.6	1:12.8	2:47.8	3:27.5	7:37.1	10:28.0	16:13.7
640	6.51	9.71	38.8	46.9	1:13.2	2:48.9	3:28.9	7:40.3	10:32.5	16:20.6
630	6.54	9.76	39.0	47.2	1:13.7	2:50.0	3:30.3	7:43.6	10:37.0	16:27.7
620	6.57	9.81	39.2	47.4	1:14.2	2:51.2	3:31.8	7:46.9	10:41.6	16:34.9
610	6.61	9.86	39.4	47.7	1:14.6	2:52.3	3:33.2	7:50.2	10:46.2	16:42.2
600	6.64	9.91	39.7	48.0	1:15.1	2:53.5	3:34.7	7:53.6	10:51.0	16:49.7
590	6.67	9.96	39.9	48.3	1:15.6	2:54.7	3:36.2	7:57.1	10:55.8	16:57.2
580	6.71	10.01	40.1	48.6	1:16.1	2:55.9	3:37.7	8:00.6	11:00.6	17:04.8
570	6.74	10.06	40.4	48.9	1:16.6	2:57.1	3:39.3	8:04.1	11:05.5	17:12.6
560	6.78	10.12	40.6	49.2	1:17.0	2:58.4	3:40.8	8:07.7	11:10.6	17:20.4
550	6.81	10.17	40.9	49.5	1:17.6	2:59.6	3:42.4	8:11.4	11:15.6	17:28.4
540	6.85	10.23	41.1	49.8	1:18.1	3:00.9	3:44.0	8:15.1	11:20.8	17:36.5
530	6.89	10.28	41.4	50.1	1:18.6	3:02.2	3:45.7	8:18.8	11:26.0	17:44.8
520	6.92	10.34	41.6	50.4	1:19.1	3:03.5	3:47.3	8:22.6	11:31.4	17:53.2

POINTS	50 MT	80 MT	300 MT	350 MT	500 MT	1000 MT	1200 MT	2400 MT	3200 MT	4800 MT
510	6.96	10.39	41.9	50.7	1:19.6	3:04.9	3:49.0	8:26.5	11:36.8	18:01.7
500	7.00	10.45	42.1	51.0	1:20.2	3:06.2	3:50.7	8:30.5	11:42.3	18:10.3
490	7.04	10.51	42.4	51.4	1:20.7	3:07.6	3:52.4	8:34.5	11:47.8	18:19.1
480	7.08	10.56	42.6	51.7	1:21.3	3:09.0	3:54.2	8:38.5	11:53.5	18:28.0
470	7.11	10.62	42.9	52.0	1:21.8	3:10.4	3:56.0	8:42.7	11:59.3	18:37.1
460	7.15	10.68	43.2	52.4	1:22.4	3:11.9	3:57.8	8:46.9	12:05.1	18:46.3
450	7.19	10.74	43.5	52.7	1:23.0	3:13.3	3:59.6	8:51.1	12:11.1	18:55.7
440	7.23	10.80	43.7	53.1	1:23.6	3:14.8	4:01.5	8:55.5	12:17.1	19:05.2
430	7.27	10.86	44.0	53.4	1:24.2	3:16.3	4:03.4	8:59.9	12:23.2	19:14.9
420	7.32	10.92	44.3	53.8	1:24.8	3:17.8	4:05.3	9:04.3	12:29.5	19:24.7
410	7.36	10.99	44.6	54.1	1:25.4	3:19.4	4:07.3	9:08.9	12:35.8	19:34.7
400	7.40	11.05	44.9	54.5	1:26.0	3:21.0	4:09.2	9:13.5	12:42.3	19:44.9
390	7.44	11.11	45.2	54.9	1:26.6	3:22.6	4:11.3	9:18.2	12:48.9	19:55.3
380	7.49	11.18	45.5	55.2	1:27.2	3:24.2	4:13.3	9:23.0	12:55.6	20:05.9
370	7.53	11.24	45.8	55.6	1:27.9	3:25.8	4:15.4	9:27.9	13:02.4	20:16.6
360	7.57	11.31	46.1	56.0	1:28.5	3:27.5	4:17.5	9:32.8	13:09.3	20:27.6
350	7.62	11.38	46.4	56.4	1:29.2	3:29.2	4:19.7	9:37.9	13:16.4	20:38.7
340	7.66	11.45	46.7	56.8	1:29.9	3:31.0	4:21.9	9:43.0	13:23.5	20:50.0
330	7.71	11.51	47.0	57.2	1:30.6	3:32.7	4:24.1	9:48.2	13:30.9	21:01.6
320	7.76	11.58	47.4	57.6	1:31.3	3:34.5	4:26.4	9:53.6	13:38.3	21:13.4
310	7.80	11.65	47.7	58.0	1:32.0	3:36.4	4:28.7	9:59.0	13:45.9	21:25.4
300	7.85	11.73	48.0	58.5	1:32.7	3:38.2	4:31.0	10:04.5	13:53.6	21:37.6
290	7.90	11.80	48.4	58.9	1:33.4	3:40.1	4:33.4	10:10.1	14:01.5	21:50.0
280	7.95	11.87	48.7	59.3	1:34.2	3:42.0	4:35.9	10:15.8	14:09.5	22:02.7
270	8.00	11.95	49.1	59.8	1:34.9	3:44.0	4:38.3	10:21.7	14:17.7	22:15.7
260	8.05	12.02	49.4	1:00.2	1:35.7	3:46.0	4:40.9	10:27.6	14:26.0	22:28.9
250	8.10	12.10	49.8	1:00.7	1:36.5	3:48.0	4:43.4	10:33.7	14:34.5	22:42.3
240	8.15	12.17	50.2	1:01.1	1:37.3	3:50.1	4:46.1	10:39.9	14:43.2	22:56.1
230	8.20	12.25	50.5	1:01.6	1:38.1	3:52.2	4:48.7	10:46.2	14:52.0	23:10.1
220	8.25	12.33	50.9	1:02.1	1:38.9	3:54.3	4:51.4	10:52.6	15:01.0	23:24.4
210	8.30	12.41	51.3	1:02.5	1:39.7	3:56.5	4:54.2	10:59.1	15:10.2	23:39.0
200	8.36	12.49	51.7	1:03.0	1:40.6	3:58.7	4:57.0	11:05.8	15:19.6	23:53.9

●●

POINTS	50 MT	80 MT	300 MT	350 MT	500 MT	1000 MT	1200 MT	2400 MT	3200 MT	4800 MT
190	8.41	12.57	52.1	1:03.5	1:41.4	4:01.0	4:59.9	11:12.6	15:29.2	24:09.1
180	8.47	12.65	52.5	1:04.0	1:42.3	4:03.3	5:02.8	11:19.6	15:39.0	24:24.6
170	8.52	12.74	52.9	1:04.5	1:43.2	4:05.6	5:05.8	11:26.7	15:49.0	24:40.5
160	8.58	12.82	53.3	1:05.1	1:44.1	4:08.0	5:08.9	11:34.0	15:59.2	24:56.8
150	8.64	12.91	53.7	1:05.6	1:45.0	4:10.5	5:12.0	11:41.4	16:09.6	25:13.3
140	8.69	13.00	54.1	1:06.1	1:45.9	4:13.0	5:15.1	11:49.0	16:20.3	25:30.3
130	8.75	13.09	54.6	1:06.7	1:46.9	4:15.5	5:18.4	11:56.7	16:31.2	25:47.7
120	8.81	13.18	55.0	1:07.2	1:47.9	4:18.1	5:21.7	12:04.6	16:42.3	26:05.4
110	8.87	13.27	55.4	1:07.8	1:48.9	4:20.8	5:25.0	12:12.7	16:53.7	26:23.6
100	8.94	13.36	55.9	1:08.4	1:49.9	4:23.5	5:28.5	12:21.0	17:05.4	26:42.2
90	9.00	13.45	56.4	1:09.0	1:50.9	4:26.2	5:32.0	12:29.5	17:17.3	27:01.2
80	9.06	13.55	56.8	1:09.6	1:51.9	4:29.1	5:35.6	12:38.1	17:29.6	27:20.7
70	9.12	13.64	57.3	1:10.2	1:53.0	4:31.9	5:39.3	12:47.0	17:42.1	27:40.6
60	9.19	13.74	57.8	1:10.8	1:54.1	4:34.9	5:43.0	12:56.0	17:54.9	28:01.1
50	9.26	13.84	58.3	1:11.4	1:55.2	4:37.9	5:46.9	13:05.3	18:08.0	28:22.0
40	9.32	13.94	58.8	1:12.1	1:56.3	4:41.0	5:50.8	13:14.8	18:21.4	28:43.5
30	9.39	14.04	59.3	1:12.7	1:57.5	4:44.1	5:54.8	13:24.6	18:35.2	29:05.6
20	9.46	14.15	59.8	1:13.4	1:58.6	4:47.3	5:58.9	13:34.6	18:49.3	29:28.2
10	9.53	14.25	1:00.3	1:14.0	1:59.8	4:50.6	6:03.1	13:44.8	19:03.8	29:51.4
0	9.60	14.36	1:00.9	1:14.7	2:01.1	4:54.0	6:07.4	13:55.3	19:18.7	30:15.2

POINTS	6.00 KM	8.00 KM	12.00 KM	15.00 KM	20.00 KM	25.00 KM	30.00 KM	40.00 KM	MARATHON	50.00 KM
1150	15:10.0	20:36.0	31:44	40:16	54:42	1:09:21	1:24:13	1:54:36	2:01:29	2:25:54
1140	15:14.8	20:42.6	31:54	40:29	54:59	1:09:43	1:24:40	1:55:14	2:02:09	2:26:42
1130	15:19.7	20:49.2	32:05	40:42	55:17	1:10:06	1:25:08	1:55:52	2:02:49	2:27:31
1120	15:24.6	20:56.0	32:15	40:55	55:35	1:10:30	1:25:37	1:56:31	2:03:30	2:28:20
1110	15:29.6	21:02.8	32:26	41:09	55:54	1:10:53	1:26:05	1:57:10	2:04:11	2:29:10
1100	15:34.7	21:09.7	32:36	41:22	56:12	1:11:17	1:26:34	1:57:49	2:04:53	2:30:00
1090	15:39.8	21:16.6	32:47	41:36	56:31	1:11:40	1:27:03	1:58:29	2:05:36	2:30:51
1080	15:44.9	21:23.7	32:58	41:50	56:50	1:12:05	1:27:32	1:59:09	2:06:18	2:31:43
1070	15:50.1	21:30.8	33:09	42:04	57:09	1:12:29	1:28:02	1:59:50	2:07:02	2:32:35
1060	15:55.4	21:38.0	33:20	42:18	57:29	1:12:54	1:28:32	2:00:31	2:07:45	2:33:28
1050	16:00.7	21:45.2	33:32	42:33	57:49	1:13:19	1:29:03	2:01:13	2:08:30	2:34:21
1040	16:06.1	21:52.6	33:43	42:47	58:08	1:13:44	1:29:34	2:01:55	2:09:14	2:35:15
1030	16:11.5	22:00.0	33:55	43:02	58:29	1:14:10	1:30:05	2:02:38	2:10:00	2:36:10
1020	16:17.1	22:07.6	34:06	43:17	58:49	1:14:36	1:30:36	2:03:21	2:10:46	2:37:05
1010	16:22.6	22:15.2	34:18	43:32	59:09	1:15:02	1:31:08	2:04:05	2:11:32	2:38:01
1000	16:28.3	22:22.9	34:30	43:47	59:30	1:15:28	1:31:41	2:04:49	2:12:19	2:38:58
990	16:34.0	22:30.7	34:42	44:02	59:51	1:15:55	1:32:13	2:05:34	2:13:06	2:39:55
980	16:39.7	22:38.5	34:54	44:18	1:00:13	1:16:22	1:32:46	2:06:19	2:13:54	2:40:53
970	16:45.6	22:46.5	35:07	44:34	1:00:34	1:16:50	1:33:20	2:07:05	2:14:43	2:41:51
960	16:51.5	22:54.6	35:19	44:50	1:00:56	1:17:18	1:33:54	2:07:51	2:15:32	2:42:51
950	16:57.4	23:02.7	35:32	45:06	1:01:18	1:17:46	1:34:28	2:08:38	2:16:22	2:43:51
940	17:03.5	23:11.0	35:45	45:22	1:01:41	1:18:14	1:35:03	2:09:26	2:17:12	2:44:52
930	17:09.6	23:19.3	35:58	45:39	1:02:03	1:18:43	1:35:38	2:10:14	2:18:04	2:45:53
920	17:15.8	23:27.8	36:11	45:56	1:02:26	1:19:12	1:36:14	2:11:03	2:18:55	2:46:56
910	17:22.0	23:36.4	36:24	46:13	1:02:49	1:19:42	1:36:50	2:11:52	2:19:48	2:47:59
900	17:28.4	23:45.0	36:38	46:30	1:03:13	1:20:12	1:37:26	2:12:42	2:20:41	2:49:03
890	17:34.8	23:53.8	36:51	46:47	1:03:37	1:20:42	1:38:03	2:13:33	2:21:34	2:50:08
880	17:41.3	24:02.7	37:05	47:05	1:04:01	1:21:13	1:38:40	2:14:24	2:22:29	2:51:13
870	17:47.8	24:11.7	37:19	47:23	1:04:25	1:21:44	1:39:18	2:15:16	2:23:24	2:52:20
860	17:54.5	24:20.8	37:33	47:41	1:04:50	1:22:15	1:39:57	2:16:08	2:24:20	2:53:27
850	18:01.2	24:30.0	37:48	47:59	1:05:15	1:22:47	1:40:36	2:17:02	2:25:16	2:54:35
840	18:08.1	24:39.3	38:02	48:18	1:05:40	1:23:20	1:41:15	2:17:56	2:26:13	2:55:44

POINTS	6.00 KM	8.00 KM	12.00 KM	15.00 KM	20.00 KM	25.00 KM	30.00 KM	40.00 KM	MARATHON	50.00 KM
830	18:15.0	24:48.8	38:17	48:36	1:06:06	1:23:52	1:41:55	2:18:50	2:27:11	2:56:54
820	18:22.0	24:58.4	38:32	48:55	1:06:32	1:24:25	1:42:35	2:19:46	2:28:10	2:58:05
810	18:29.1	25:08.1	38:47	49:15	1:06:58	1:24:59	1:43:16	2:20:42	2:29:10	2:59:17
800	18:36.3	25:17.9	39:02	49:34	1:07:25	1:25:33	1:43:58	2:21:39	2:30:10	3:00:30
790	18:43.5	25:27.9	39:18	49:54	1:07:52	1:26:08	1:44:40	2:22:36	2:31:11	3:01:44
780	18:50.9	25:37.9	39:34	50:14	1:08:19	1:26:42	1:45:22	2:23:35	2:32:13	3:02:59
770	18:58.4	25:48.2	39:49	50:34	1:08:47	1:27:18	1:46:06	2:24:34	2:33:16	3:04:15
760	19:05.9	25:58.5	40:06	50:55	1:09:15	1:27:54	1:46:50	2:25:34	2:34:20	3:05:32
750	19:13.6	26:09.0	40:22	51:16	1:09:44	1:28:30	1:47:34	2:26:35	2:35:25	3:06:50
740	19:21.4	26:19.7	40:39	51:37	1:10:13	1:29:07	1:48:19	2:27:37	2:36:30	3:08:09
730	19:29.3	26:30.5	40:55	51:58	1:10:42	1:29:45	1:49:05	2:28:39	2:37:37	3:09:29
720	19:37.2	26:41.4	41:12	52:20	1:11:12	1:30:23	1:49:51	2:29:43	2:38:44	3:10:51
710	19:45.3	26:52.5	41:30	52:42	1:11:42	1:31:01	1:50:38	2:30:47	2:39:53	3:12:13
700	19:53.5	27:03.7	41:47	53:05	1:12:13	1:31:40	1:51:26	2:31:53	2:41:02	3:13:37
690	20:01.9	27:15.1	42:05	53:27	1:12:44	1:32:20	1:52:14	2:32:59	2:42:13	3:15:02
680	20:10.3	27:26.7	42:23	53:50	1:13:15	1:33:00	1:53:03	2:34:07	2:43:24	3:16:28
670	20:18.9	27:38.4	42:41	54:14	1:13:47	1:33:41	1:53:53	2:35:15	2:44:37	3:17:56
660	20:27.5	27:50.3	43:00	54:37	1:14:20	1:34:22	1:54:43	2:36:24	2:45:50	3:19:25
650	20:36.4	28:02.4	43:19	55:01	1:14:53	1:35:04	1:55:35	2:37:35	2:47:05	3:20:55
640	20:45.3	28:14.6	43:38	55:26	1:15:26	1:35:47	1:56:27	2:38:46	2:48:21	3:22:27
630	20:54.4	28:27.0	43:57	55:51	1:16:00	1:36:30	1:57:19	2:39:58	2:49:38	3:24:00
620	21:03.5	28:39.6	44:17	56:16	1:16:35	1:37:14	1:58:13	2:41:12	2:50:56	3:25:34
610	21:12.9	28:52.4	44:37	56:41	1:17:10	1:37:59	1:59:08	2:42:27	2:52:15	3:27:10
600	21:22.3	29:05.4	44:57	57:07	1:17:45	1:38:44	2:00:03	2:43:43	2:53:36	3:28:48
590	21:32.0	29:18.6	45:18	57:33	1:18:21	1:39:30	2:00:59	2:45:00	2:54:58	3:30:27
580	21:41.7	29:32.0	45:39	58:00	1:18:58	1:40:17	2:01:56	2:46:18	2:56:21	3:32:07
570	21:51.6	29:45.6	46:00	58:27	1:19:35	1:41:04	2:02:54	2:47:38	2:57:45	3:33:49
560	22:01.7	29:59.3	46:21	58:55	1:20:13	1:41:52	2:03:53	2:48:59	2:59:11	3:35:33
550	22:11.9	30:13.4	46:43	59:23	1:20:51	1:42:41	2:04:53	2:50:21	3:00:39	3:37:19
540	22:22.3	30:27.6	47:05	59:51	1:21:30	1:43:31	2:05:53	2:51:44	3:02:07	3:39:06
530	22:32.8	30:42.0	47:28	1:00:20	1:22:10	1:44:22	2:06:55	2:53:09	3:03:37	3:40:55
520	22:43.5	30:56.7	47:51	1:00:49	1:22:50	1:45:13	2:07:58	2:54:36	3:05:09	3:42:46

POINTS	6.00 KM	8.00 KM	12.00 KM	15.00 KM	20.00 KM	25.00 KM	30.00 KM	40.00 KM	MARATHON	50.00 KM
510	22:54.4	31:11.6	48:14	1:01:19	1:23:31	1:46:05	2:09:02	2:56:03	3:06:42	3:44:38
500	23:05.4	31:26.8	48:38	1:01:50	1:24:12	1:46:58	2:10:07	2:57:33	3:08:17	3:46:33
490	23:16.6	31:42.2	49:02	1:02:20	1:24:55	1:47:52	2:11:13	2:59:03	3:09:53	3:48:30
480	23:28.0	31:57.9	49:27	1:02:52	1:25:38	1:48:47	2:12:20	3:00:36	3:11:32	3:50:28
470	23:39.6	32:13.8	49:52	1:03:24	1:26:21	1:49:43	2:13:28	3:02:10	3:13:11	3:52:29
460	23:51.4	32:30.0	50:17	1:03:56	1:27:06	1:50:40	2:14:38	3:03:45	3:14:53	3:54:32
450	24:03.4	32:46.5	50:43	1:04:29	1:27:51	1:51:38	2:15:48	3:05:22	3:16:36	3:56:37
440	24:15.6	33:03.2	51:09	1:05:03	1:28:37	1:52:37	2:17:00	3:07:01	3:18:21	3:58:44
430	24:28.0	33:20.2	51:36	1:05:37	1:29:24	1:53:37	2:18:14	3:08:42	3:20:08	4:00:53
420	24:40.6	33:37.6	52:03	1:06:11	1:30:12	1:54:38	2:19:28	3:10:25	3:21:57	4:03:05
410	24:53.4	33:55.2	52:30	1:06:47	1:31:00	1:55:40	2:20:44	3:12:09	3:23:48	4:05:19
400	25:06.5	34:13.1	52:58	1:07:23	1:31:50	1:56:43	2:22:01	3:13:56	3:25:41	4:07:36
390	25:19.8	34:31.4	53:27	1:07:59	1:32:40	1:57:47	2:23:20	3:15:44	3:27:36	4:09:56
380	25:33.3	34:50.0	53:56	1:08:37	1:33:31	1:58:53	2:24:40	3:17:34	3:29:34	4:12:18
370	25:47.1	35:08.9	54:26	1:09:15	1:34:24	2:00:00	2:26:02	3:19:27	3:31:33	4:14:42
360	26:01.1	35:28.2	54:56	1:09:53	1:35:17	2:01:08	2:27:25	3:21:22	3:33:35	4:17:10
350	26:15.3	35:47.8	55:27	1:10:33	1:36:11	2:02:17	2:28:50	3:23:18	3:35:39	4:19:40
340	26:29.9	36:07.8	55:58	1:11:13	1:37:06	2:03:28	2:30:16	3:25:18	3:37:46	4:22:14
330	26:44.7	36:28.2	56:30	1:11:54	1:38:02	2:04:40	2:31:44	3:27:19	3:39:55	4:24:50
320	26:59.7	36:48.9	57:03	1:12:36	1:39:00	2:05:53	2:33:14	3:29:23	3:42:06	4:27:30
310	27:15.1	37:10.1	57:36	1:13:18	1:39:58	2:07:08	2:34:46	3:31:29	3:44:21	4:30:12
300	27:30.8	37:31.6	58:10	1:14:02	1:40:58	2:08:25	2:36:20	3:33:38	3:46:38	4:32:59
290	27:46.7	37:53.6	58:44	1:14:46	1:41:59	2:09:43	2:37:55	3:35:50	3:48:58	4:35:48
280	28:03.0	38:16.0	59:20	1:15:31	1:43:01	2:11:02	2:39:32	3:38:04	3:51:21	4:38:41
270	28:19.6	38:38.9	59:55	1:16:17	1:44:05	2:12:23	2:41:12	3:40:22	3:53:46	4:41:38
260	28:36.5	39:02.2	1:00:32	1:17:04	1:45:09	2:13:46	2:42:53	3:42:42	3:56:15	4:44:39
250	28:53.8	39:26.0	1:01:10	1:17:52	1:46:15	2:15:11	2:44:37	3:45:05	3:58:47	4:47:43
240	29:11.4	39:50.3	1:01:48	1:18:41	1:47:23	2:16:37	2:46:23	3:47:31	4:01:23	4:50:51
230	29:29.4	40:15.1	1:02:27	1:19:31	1:48:32	2:18:06	2:48:11	3:50:00	4:04:02	4:54:04
220	29:47.7	40:40.4	1:03:07	1:20:22	1:49:42	2:19:36	2:50:02	3:52:33	4:06:44	4:57:21
210	30:06.5	41:06.2	1:03:47	1:21:15	1:50:54	2:21:08	2:51:55	3:55:09	4:09:30	5:00:42
200	30:25.6	41:32.6	1:04:29	1:22:08	1:52:08	2:22:42	2:53:50	3:57:49	4:12:20	5:04:08

● ●

POINTS	6.00 KM	8.00 KM	12.00 KM	15.00 KM	20.00 KM	25.00 KM	30.00 KM	40.00 KM	MARATHON	50.00 KM
190	30:45.1	41:59.6	1:05:11	1:23:02	1:53:23	2:24:19	2:55:48	4:00:32	4:15:13	5:07:39
180	31:05.1	42:27.1	1:05:55	1:23:58	1:54:40	2:25:58	2:57:49	4:03:19	4:18:11	5:11:15
170	31:25.5	42:55.3	1:06:39	1:24:55	1:55:59	2:27:38	2:59:53	4:06:10	4:21:13	5:14:56
160	31:46.4	43:24.1	1:07:25	1:25:54	1:57:19	2:29:22	3:02:00	4:09:05	4:24:19	5:18:42
150	32:07.7	43:53.5	1:08:11	1:26:53	1:58:41	2:31:07	3:04:09	4:12:05	4:27:29	5:22:33
140	32:29.5	44:23.6	1:08:59	1:27:54	2:00:06	2:32:55	3:06:22	4:15:08	4:30:45	5:26:30
130	32:51.8	44:54.5	1:09:47	1:28:57	2:01:32	2:34:46	3:08:38	4:18:16	4:34:05	5:30:33
120	33:14.6	45:26.0	1:10:37	1:30:01	2:03:00	2:36:40	3:10:57	4:21:29	4:37:30	5:34:43
110	33:38.0	45:58.3	1:11:28	1:31:06	2:04:31	2:38:36	3:13:20	4:24:47	4:41:00	5:38:58
100	34:01.9	46:31.3	1:12:20	1:32:14	2:06:04	2:40:35	3:15:46	4:28:10	4:44:36	5:43:20
90	34:26.3	47:05.2	1:13:14	1:33:23	2:07:39	2:42:38	3:18:16	4:31:38	4:48:17	5:47:49
80	34:51.4	47:39.9	1:14:09	1:34:33	2:09:17	2:44:43	3:20:50	4:35:11	4:52:04	5:52:25
70	35:17.1	48:15.4	1:15:05	1:35:46	2:10:57	2:46:52	3:23:28	4:38:50	4:55:57	5:57:09
60	35:43.4	48:51.9	1:16:03	1:37:00	2:12:40	2:49:04	3:26:10	4:42:35	4:59:56	6:02:00
50	36:10.4	49:29.3	1:17:02	1:38:16	2:14:25	2:51:19	3:28:57	4:46:26	5:04:02	6:06:59
40	36:38.1	50:07.6	1:18:03	1:39:34	2:16:13	2:53:39	3:31:48	4:50:24	5:08:15	6:12:07
30	37:06.5	50:47.0	1:19:05	1:40:55	2:18:05	2:56:02	3:34:44	4:54:28	5:12:34	6:17:23
20	37:35.6	51:27.4	1:20:09	1:42:17	2:19:59	2:58:29	3:37:45	4:58:39	5:17:01	6:22:48
10	38:05.5	52:08.8	1:21:15	1:43:42	2:21:56	3:01:00	3:40:50	5:02:57	5:21:36	6:28:23
0	38:36.2	52:51.4	1:22:23	1:45:09	2:23:57	3:03:36	3:44:02	5:07:23	5:26:19	6:34:08

INTERMEDIATE TIMES FOR CONSTANT SPEED RUNS

....

400 M	100 M	150 M	200 M	250 M	300 M	350 M	450 M	500 M	600 M	700 M
43.0	10.8	16.1	21.5	26.9	32.3	37.6	48.4	53.8	1:04.5	1:15.3
44.0	11.0	16.5	22.0	27.5	33.0	38.5	49.5	55.0	1:06.0	1:17.0
45.0	11.3	16.9	22.5	28.1	33.8	39.4	50.6	56.3	1:07.5	1:18.8
46.0	11.5	17.3	23.0	28.8	34.5	40.3	51.8	57.5	1:09.0	1:20.5
47.0	11.8	17.6	23.5	29.4	35.3	41.1	52.9	58.8	1:10.5	1:22.3
48.0	12.0	18.0	24.0	30.0	36.0	42.0	54.0	1:00.0	1:12.0	1:24.0
49.0	12.3	18.4	24.5	30.6	36.8	42.9	55.1	1:01.3	1:13.5	1:25.8
50.0	12.5	18.8	25.0	31.3	37.5	43.8	56.3	1:02.5	1:15.0	1:27.5
51.0	12.8	19.1	25.5	31.9	38.3	44.6	57.4	1:03.8	1:16.5	1:29.3
52.0	13.0	19.5	26.0	32.5	39.0	45.5	58.5	1:05.0	1:18.0	1:31.0
53.0	13.3	19.9	26.5	33.1	39.8	46.4	59.6	1:06.3	1:19.5	1:32.8
54.0	13.5	20.3	27.0	33.8	40.5	47.3	1:00.8	1:07.5	1:21.0	1:34.5
55.0	13.8	20.6	27.5	34.4	41.3	48.1	1:01.9	1:08.8	1:22.5	1:36.3
56.0	14.0	21.0	28.0	35.0	42.0	49.0	1:03.0	1:10.0	1:24.0	1:38.0
57.0	14.3	21.4	28.5	35.6	42.8	49.9	1:04.1	1:11.3	1:25.5	1:39.8
58.0	14.5	21.8	29.0	36.3	43.5	50.8	1:05.3	1:12.5	1:27.0	1:41.5
59.0	14.8	22.1	29.5	36.9	44.3	51.6	1:06.4	1:13.8	1:28.5	1:43.3
1:00.0	15.0	22.5	30.0	37.5	45.0	52.5	1:07.5	1:15.0	1:30.0	1:45.0
1:01.0	15.3	22.9	30.5	38.1	45.8	53.4	1:08.6	1:16.3	1:31.5	1:46.8
1:02.0	15.5	23.3	31.0	38.8	46.5	54.3	1:09.8	1:17.5	1:33.0	1:48.5
1:03.0	15.8	23.6	31.5	39.4	47.3	55.1	1:10.9	1:18.8	1:34.5	1:50.3
1:04.0	16.0	24.0	32.0	40.0	48.0	56.0	1:12.0	1:20.0	1:36.0	1:52.0
1:05.0	16.3	24.4	32.5	40.6	48.8	56.9	1:13.1	1:21.3	1:37.5	1:53.8
1:06.0	16.5	24.8	33.0	41.3	49.5	57.8	1:14.3	1:22.5	1:39.0	1:55.5
1:07.0	16.8	25.1	33.5	41.9	50.3	58.6	1:15.4	1:23.8	1:40.5	1:57.3
1:08.0	17.0	25.5	34.0	42.5	51.0	59.5	1:16.5	1:25.0	1:42.0	1:59.0
1:09.0	17.3	25.9	34.5	43.1	51.8	1:00.4	1:17.6	1:26.3	1:43.5	2:00.8

INTERMEDIATE TIMES FOR CONSTANT SPEED RUNS
. . . .

400 M	100 M	150 M	200 M	250 M	300 M	350 M	450 M	500 M	600 M	700 M
1:10.0	17.5	26.3	35.0	43.8	52.5	1:01.3	1:18.8	1:27.5	1:45.0	2:02.5
1:11.0	17.8	26.6	35.5	44.4	53.3	1:02.1	1:19.9	1:28.8	1:46.5	2:04.3
1:12.0	18.0	27.0	36.0	45.0	54.0	1:03.0	1:21.C	1:30.0	1:48.0	2:06.0
1:13.0	18.3	27.4	36.5	45.6	54.8	1:03.9	1:22.1	1:31.3	1:49.5	2:C7.8
1:14.0	18.5	27.8	37.C	46.3	55.5	1:04.8	1:23.3	1:32.5	1:51.0	2:09.5
1:15.0	18.8	28.1	37.5	46.9	56.3	1:05.6	1:24.4	1:33.8	1:52.5	2:11.3
1:16.0	19.0	28.5	38.0	47.5	57.0	1:06.5	1:25.5	1:35.0	1:54.0	2:13.0
1:17.0	19.3	28.9	38.5	48.1	57.8	1:07.4	1:26.6	1:36.3	1:55.5	2:14.8
1:18.0	19.5	29.3	39.0	48.8	58.5	1:08.3	1:27.8	1:37.5	1:57.0	2:16.5
1:19.0	19.8	29.6	39.5	49.4	59.3	1:09.1	1:28.9	1:38.8	1:58.5	2:18.3
1:20.0	20.0	30.0	40.0	50.0	1:00.0	1:10.0	1:30.C	1:40.0	2:00.0	2:20.0
1:21.0	20.3	30.4	40.5	50.6	1:00.8	1:10.9	1:31.1	1:41.3	2:01.5	2:21.8
1:22.0	20.5	30.8	41.0	51.3	1:01.5	1:11.8	1:32.3	1:42.5	2:03.0	2:23.5
1:23.0	20.8	31.1	41.5	51.9	1:02.3	1:12.6	1:33.4	1:43.8	2:04.5	2:25.3
1:24.0	21.0	31.5	42.0	52.5	1:03.0	1:13.5	1:34.5	1:45.0	2:06.0	2:27.0
1:25.0	21.3	31.9	42.5	53.1	1:03.8	1:14.4	1:35.6	1:46.3	2:07.5	2:28.8
1:26.0	21.5	32.3	43.0	53.8	1:04.5	1:15.3	1:36.8	1:47.5	2:09.0	2:30.5
1:27.0	21.8	32.6	43.5	54.4	1:05.3	1:16.1	1:37.9	1:48.8	2:10.5	2:32.3
1:28.0	22.0	33.0	44.0	55.0	1:06.0	1:17.0	1:39.C	1:50.0	2:12.0	2:34.0
1:29.0	22.3	33.4	44.5	55.6	1:06.8	1:17.9	1:40.1	1:51.3	2:13.5	2:35.8
1:30.0	22.5	33.8	45.0	56.3	1:07.5	1:18.8	1:41.3	1:52.5	2:15.0	2:37.5
1:31.0	22.8	34.1	45.5	56.9	1:08.3	1:19.6	1:42.4	1:53.8	2:16.5	2:39.3
1:32.0	23.0	34.5	46.0	57.5	1:09.0	1:20.5	1:43.5	1:55.0	2:18.0	2:41.0
1:33.0	23.3	34.9	46.5	58.1	1:09.8	1:21.4	1:44.6	1:56.3	2:19.5	2:42.8
1:34.0	23.5	35.3	47.0	58.8	1:10.5	1:22.3	1:45.8	1:57.5	2:21.0	2:44.5
1:35.0	23.8	35.6	47.5	59.4	1:11.3	1:23.1	1:46.9	1:58.8	2:22.5	2:46.3
1:36.0	24.0	36.0	48.0	1:00.0	1:12.0	1:24.0	1:48.C	2:00.0	2:24.0	2:48.0

INTERMEDIATE TIMES FOR CONSTANT SPEED RUNS
•••

400 M	800 M	900 M	1000 M	1200 M	1500 M	1600 M	2000 M	2400 M	2800 M	3200 M
43.0	1:26.0	1:36.8	1:47.5	2:09.0	2:41.3	2:52.0	3:35.0	4:18.0	5:01.0	5:44.0
44.0	1:28.0	1:39.0	1:50.0	2:12.0	2:45.0	2:56.0	3:40.0	4:24.0	5:08.0	5:52.0
45.0	1:30.0	1:41.3	1:52.5	2:15.0	2:48.8	3:00.0	3:45.0	4:30.0	5:15.0	6:00.0
46.0	1:32.0	1:43.5	1:55.0	2:18.0	2:52.5	3:04.0	3:50.C	4:36.0	5:22.0	6:08.0
47.0	1:34.0	1:45.8	1:57.5	2:21.0	2:56.3	3:08.0	3:55.C	4:42.0	5:29.0	6:16.0
48.0	1:36.0	1:48.0	2:00.0	2:24.0	3:00.0	3:12.0	4:00.0	4:48.0	5:36.0	6:24.0
49.0	1:38.0	1:50.3	2:02.5	2:27.0	3:03.8	3:16.0	4:05.C	4:54.0	5:43.0	6:32.0
50.0	1:40.0	1:52.5	2:05.0	2:30.0	3:07.5	3:20.0	4:10.C	5:00.0	5:50.0	6:40.0
51.0	1:42.0	1:54.8	2:07.5	2:33.0	3:11.3	3:24.0	4:15.C	5:06.0	5:57.0	6:48.0
52.0	1:44.0	1:57.0	2:10.0	2:36.0	3:15.0	3:28.0	4:20.C	5:12.0	6:04.0	6:56.0
53.0	1:46.0	1:59.3	2:12.5	2:39.0	3:18.8	3:32.0	4:25.0	5:18.0	6:11.0	7:04.0
54.0	1:48.0	2:01.5	2:15.0	2:42.0	3:22.5	3:36.0	4:30.0	5:24.0	6:18.0	7:12.0
55.0	1:50.0	2:03.8	2:17.5	2:45.0	3:26.3	3:40.0	4:35.C	5:30.0	6:25.0	7:20.0
56.C	1:52.0	2:06.0	2:20.0	2:48.0	3:30.0	3:44.0	4:40.0	5:36.0	6:32.0	7:28.0
57.0	1:54.0	2:08.3	2:22.5	2:51.0	3:33.8	3:48.0	4:45.0	5:42.0	6:39.0	7:36.0
58.0	1:56.C	2:10.5	2:25.0	2:54.0	3:37.5	3:52.0	4:50.0	5:48.0	6:46.0	7:44.0
59.0	1:58.0	2:12.8	2:27.5	2:57.0	3:41.3	3:56.0	4:55.0	5:54.0	6:53.0	7:52.0
1:00.0	2:00.0	2:15.0	2:30.0	3:00.0	3:45.0	4:00.0	5:00.C	6:00.0	7:00.0	8:00.0
1:01.0	2:02.0	2:17.3	2:32.5	3:03.0	3:48.8	4:04.0	5:05.0	6:06.0	7:07.0	8:08.0
1:02.0	2:04.0	2:19.5	2:35.C	3:06.0	3:52.5	4:C8.0	5:10.C	6:12.0	7:14.0	8:16.0
1:03.0	2:06.0	2:21.8	2:37.5	3:09.0	3:56.3	4:12.0	5:15.0	6:18.0	7:21.0	8:24.0
1:04.0	2:08.0	2:24.0	2:4C.0	3:12.0	4:00.0	4:16.0	5:20.0	6:24.0	7:28.0	8:32.0
1:05.0	2:10.0	2:26.3	2:42.5	3:15.0	4:03.8	4:20.0	5:25.C	6:30.0	7:35.0	8:40.0
1:06.0	2:12.0	2:28.5	2:45.0	3:18.0	4:07.5	4:24.0	5:30.C	6:36.0	7:42.0	8:48.0
1:07.0	2:14.0	2:30.8	2:47.5	3:21.0	4:11.3	4:28.0	5:35.C	6:42.0	7:49.0	8:56.0
1:C8.0	2:16.0	2:33.0	2:50.0	3:24.0	4:15.0	4:32.0	5:40.C	6:48.0	7:56.0	9:04.0
1:09.0	2:18.0	2:35.3	2:52.5	3:27.0	4:18.8	4:36.0	5:45.0	6:54.0	8:03.0	9:12.0

INTERMEDIATE TIMES FOR CONSTANT SPEED RUNS

400 M	800 M	900 M	1000 M	1200 M	1500 M	1600 M	2000 M	2400 M	2800 M	3200 M
1:10.0	2:20.0	2:37.5	2:55.0	3:30.0	4:22.5	4:40.0	5:50.0	7:00.0	8:10.0	9:20.0
1:11.0	2:22.0	2:39.8	2:57.5	3:33.0	4:26.3	4:44.0	5:55.0	7:06.0	8:17.0	9:28.0
1:12.0	2:24.0	2:42.0	3:00.0	3:36.0	4:30.0	4:48.0	6:00.C	7:12.0	8:24.C	9:36.0
1:13.0	2:26.0	2:44.3	3:02.5	3:39.0	4:33.8	4:52.0	6:05.0	7:18.0	8:31.0	9:44.0
1:14.0	2:28.0	2:46.5	3:05.0	3:42.0	4:37.5	4:56.0	6:10.C	7:24.0	8:38.0	9:52.0
1:15.0	2:30.0	2:48.8	3:07.5	3:45.0	4:41.3	5:00.0	6:15.C	7:30.0	8:45.0	0:00.0
1:16.C	2:32.C	2:51.0	3:10.0	3:48.0	4:45.0	5:04.0	6:20.0	7:36.0	8:52.0	0:08.0
1:17.0	2:34.0	2:53.3	3:12.5	3:51.0	4:48.8	5:08.0	6:25.0	7:42.0	8:59.0	0:16.0
1:18.0	2:36.0	2:55.5	3:15.0	3:54.0	4:52.5	5:12.0	6:30.0	7:48.0	9:06.0	0:24.0
1:19.0	2:38.0	2:57.8	3:17.5	3:57.0	4:56.3	5:16.0	6:35.0	7:54.0	9:13.0	0:32.0
1:20.0	2:40.0	3:00.0	3:20.0	4:00.0	5:00.0	5:20.0	6:40.C	8:00.0	9:20.0	0:40.0
1:21.0	2:42.0	3:02.3	3:22.5	4:03.0	5:03.8	5:24.0	6:45.0	8:06.0	9:27.0	0:48.0
1:22.0	2:44.0	3:04.5	3:25.0	4:06.0	5:07.5	5:28.C	6:50.C	8:12.0	9:34.0	0:56.0
1:23.0	2:46.0	3:06.8	3:27.5	4:09.0	5:11.3	5:32.0	6:55.0	8:18.0	9:41.0	1:04.0
1:24.0	2:48.0	3:09.0	3:30.0	4:12.0	5:15.0	5:36.0	7:00.0	8:24.0	9:48.0	1:12.0
1:25.0	2:50.0	3:11.3	3:32.5	4:15.0	5:18.8	5:40.0	7:05.C	8:30.0	9:55.0	1:20.0
1:26.0	2:52.0	3:13.5	3:35.0	4:18.0	5:22.5	5:44.0	7:10.0	8:36.0	0:02.0	1:28.0
1:27.0	2:54.0	3:15.8	3:37.5	4:21.0	5:26.3	5:48.0	7:15.C	8:42.0	0:09.0	1:36.0
1:28.0	2:56.0	3:18.0	3:40.0	4:24.0	5:30.0	5:52.0	7:20.C	8:48.0	0:16.0	1:44.0
1:29.0	2:58.0	3:20.3	3:42.5	4:27.0	5:33.8	5:56.0	7:25.0	8:54.0	0:23.0	1:52.0
1:30.0	3:00.0	3:22.5	3:45.0	4:30.0	5:37.5	6:00.0	7:30.C	9:00.0	0:30.0	2:00.0
1:31.0	3:02.0	3:24.8	3:47.5	4:33.0	5:41.3	6:04.0	7:35.C	9:06.0	0:37.0	2:08.0
1:32.0	3:04.0	3:27.0	3:50.0	4:36.0	5:45.0	6:08.0	7:40.C	9:12.0	0:44.0	2:16.0
1:33.0	3:06.0	3:29.3	3:52.5	4:39.0	5:48.8	6:12.0	7:45.C	9:18.0	0:51.0	2:24.0
1:34.0	3:08.0	3:31.5	3:55.0	4:42.0	5:52.5	6:16.0	7:50.C	9:24.0	0:58.0	2:32.0
1:35.0	3:10.0	3:33.8	3:57.5	4:45.0	5:56.3	6:20.0	7:55.C	9:30.0	1:05.0	2:40.0
1:36.0	3:12.0	3:36.0	4:00.0	4:48.0	6:00.0	6:24.0	8:00.0	9:36.0	1:12.0	2:48.0

TABLE OF REDUCED SPEEDS FOR CONTINUOUS RUNNING TRAINING
....

PER KILOMETER AVERAGE

100.0 %	97.5 %	95.0 %	92.5 %	90.0 %	87.5 %	85.0 %	82.5 %	80.0 %
2:30.0	2:33.8	2:37.9	2:42.2	2:46.7	2:51.4	2:56.5	3:01.8	3:07.5
2:33.0	2:36.9	2:41.1	2:45.4	2:50.0	2:54.9	3:00.0	3:05.5	3:11.3
2:36.0	2:40.0	2:44.2	2:48.6	2:53.3	2:58.3	3:03.5	3:09.1	3:15.0
2:39.0	2:43.1	2:47.4	2:51.9	2:56.7	3:01.7	3:07.1	3:12.7	3:18.8
2:42.0	2:46.2	2:50.5	2:55.1	3:00.0	3:05.1	3:10.6	3:16.4	3:22.5
2:45.0	2:49.2	2:53.7	2:58.4	3:03.3	3:08.6	3:14.1	3:20.0	3:26.3
2:48.0	2:52.3	2:56.8	3:01.6	3:06.7	3:12.0	3:17.6	3:23.6	3:30.0
2:51.0	2:55.4	3:00.0	3:04.9	3:10.0	3:15.4	3:21.2	3:27.3	3:33.8
2:54.0	2:58.5	3:03.2	3:08.1	3:13.3	3:18.9	3:24.7	3:30.9	3:37.5
2:57.0	3:01.5	3:06.3	3:11.4	3:16.7	3:22.3	3:28.2	3:34.5	3:41.3
3:00.0	3:04.6	3:09.5	3:14.6	3:20.0	3:25.7	3:31.8	3:38.2	3:45.0
3:03.0	3:07.7	3:12.6	3:17.8	3:23.3	3:29.1	3:35.3	3:41.8	3:48.8
3:06.0	3:10.8	3:15.8	3:21.1	3:26.7	3:32.6	3:38.8	3:45.5	3:52.5
3:09.0	3:13.8	3:18.9	3:24.3	3:30.0	3:36.0	3:42.4	3:49.1	3:56.3
3:12.0	3:16.9	3:22.1	3:27.6	3:33.3	3:39.4	3:45.9	3:52.7	4:00.0
3:15.0	3:20.0	3:25.3	3:30.8	3:36.7	3:42.9	3:49.4	3:56.4	4:03.8
3:18.0	3:23.1	3:28.4	3:34.1	3:40.0	3:46.3	3:52.9	4:00.0	4:07.5
3:21.0	3:26.2	3:31.6	3:37.3	3:43.3	3:49.7	3:56.5	4:03.6	4:11.3
3:24.0	3:29.2	3:34.7	3:40.5	3:46.7	3:53.1	4:00.0	4:07.3	4:15.0
3:27.0	3:32.3	3:37.9	3:43.8	3:50.0	3:56.6	4:03.5	4:10.9	4:18.8
3:30.0	3:35.4	3:41.1	3:47.0	3:53.3	4:00.0	4:07.1	4:14.5	4:22.5
3:33.0	3:38.5	3:44.2	3:50.3	3:56.7	4:03.4	4:10.6	4:18.2	4:26.3
3:36.0	3:41.5	3:47.4	3:53.5	4:00.0	4:06.9	4:14.1	4:21.8	4:30.0
3:39.0	3:44.6	3:50.5	3:56.8	4:03.3	4:10.3	4:17.6	4:25.5	4:33.8
3:42.0	3:47.7	3:53.7	4:00.0	4:06.7	4:13.7	4:21.2	4:29.1	4:37.5

TABLE OF REDUCED SPEEDS FOR CONTINUOUS RUNNING TRAINING
. . . .

PER KILOMETER AVERAGE

100.0 %	97.5 %	95.0 %	92.5 %	90.0 %	87.5 %	85.0 %	82.5 %	80.0 %
3:45.0	3:50.8	3:56.8	4:03.2	4:10.0	4:17.1	4:24.7	4:32.7	4:41.3
3:48.0	3:53.8	4:00.0	4:06.5	4:13.3	4:20.6	4:28.2	4:36.4	4:45.0
3:51.0	3:56.9	4:03.2	4:09.7	4:16.7	4:24.0	4:31.8	4:40.0	4:48.8
3:54.0	4:00.0	4:06.3	4:13.0	4:20.0	4:27.4	4:35.3	4:43.6	4:52.5
3:57.0	4:03.1	4:09.5	4:16.2	4:23.3	4:30.9	4:38.8	4:47.3	4:56.3
4:00.0	4:06.2	4:12.6	4:19.5	4:26.7	4:34.3	4:42.4	4:50.9	5:00.0
4:03.0	4:09.2	4:15.8	4:22.7	4:30.0	4:37.7	4:45.9	4:54.5	5:03.8
4:06.0	4:12.3	4:18.9	4:25.9	4:33.3	4:41.1	4:49.4	4:58.2	5:07.5
4:09.0	4:15.4	4:22.1	4:29.2	4:36.7	4:44.6	4:52.9	5:01.8	5:11.3
4:12.0	4:18.5	4:25.3	4:32.4	4:40.0	4:48.0	4:56.5	5:05.5	5:15.0
4:15.0	4:21.5	4:28.4	4:35.7	4:43.3	4:51.4	5:00.0	5:09.1	5:18.8
4:18.0	4:24.6	4:31.6	4:38.9	4:46.7	4:54.9	5:03.5	5:12.7	5:22.5
4:21.0	4:27.7	4:34.7	4:42.2	4:50.0	4:58.3	5:07.1	5:16.4	5:26.3
4:24.0	4:30.8	4:37.9	4:45.4	4:53.3	5:01.7	5:10.6	5:20.0	5:30.0
4:27.0	4:33.8	4:41.1	4:48.6	4:56.7	5:05.1	5:14.1	5:23.6	5:33.8
4:30.0	4:36.9	4:44.2	4:51.9	5:00.0	5:08.6	5:17.6	5:27.3	5:37.5
4:33.0	4:40.0	4:47.4	4:55.1	5:03.3	5:12.0	5:21.2	5:30.9	5:41.3
4:36.0	4:43.1	4:50.5	4:58.4	5:06.7	5:15.4	5:24.7	5:34.5	5:45.0
4:39.0	4:46.2	4:53.7	5:01.6	5:10.0	5:18.9	5:28.2	5:38.2	5:48.8
4:42.0	4:49.2	4:56.8	5:04.9	5:13.3	5:22.3	5:31.8	5:41.8	5:52.5
4:45.0	4:52.3	5:00.0	5:08.1	5:16.7	5:25.7	5:35.3	5:45.5	5:56.3
4:48.0	4:55.4	5:03.2	5:11.4	5:20.0	5:29.1	5:38.8	5:49.1	6:00.0
4:51.0	4:58.5	5:06.3	5:14.6	5:23.3	5:32.6	5:42.4	5:52.7	6:03.8
4:54.0	5:01.5	5:09.5	5:17.8	5:26.7	5:36.0	5:45.9	5:56.4	6:07.5
4:57.0	5:04.6	5:12.6	5:21.1	5:30.0	5:39.4	5:49.4	6:00.0	6:11.3

1050 POINT LEVEL PACING TABLE

SPEED	REPS	REST	100 MT	150 MT	200 MT	250 MT	300 MT	350 MT	400 MT	450 MT	500 MT	600 MT
95.0%	0- 1	---	9.7	14.8	20.0	25.8	32.2	38.9	45.9	53.1	1:00.7	1:15.9
92.5%	1- 2	4- 5 M	9.9	15.2	20.5	26.5	33.0	40.0	47.1	54.6	1:02.3	1:18.0
90.0%	2- 3	4- 5 M	10.2	15.6	21.1	27.2	33.9	41.1	48.4	56.1	1:04.0	1:20.2
87.5%	3- 4	3- 4 M	10.5	16.0	21.7	28.0	34.9	42.2	49.8	57.7	1:05.9	1:22.4
85.0%	4- 5	3- 4 M	10.8	16.5	22.3	28.8	35.9	43.5	51.3	59.4	1:07.8	1:24.9
82.5%	6- 7	2- 3 M	11.1	17.0	23.0	29.7	37.0	44.8	52.8	1:01.2	1:09.9	1:27.4
80.0%	8- 9	2- 3 M	11.5	17.5	23.7	30.6	38.2	46.2	54.5	1:03.1	1:12.0	1:30.2
77.5%	10-12	1- 2 M	11.9	18.1	24.5	31.6	39.4	47.7	56.2	1:05.1	1:14.4	1:33.1
75.0%	13-15	1- 2 M	12.3	18.7	25.3	32.6	40.7	49.3	58.1	1:07.3	1:16.8	1:36.2
72.5%	16-18	60-90 S	12.7	19.3	26.2	33.8	42.1	51.0	1:00.1	1:09.6	1:19.5	1:39.5
70.0%	19-21	60-90 S	13.1	20.0	27.1	35.0	43.6	52.8	1:02.3	1:12.1	1:22.3	1:43.1
67.5%	22-24	45-75 S	13.6	20.8	28.1	36.3	45.3	54.8	1:04.6	1:14.8	1:25.4	1:46.9
65.0%	25-29	45-75 S	14.1	21.6	29.2	37.7	47.0	56.9	1:07.1	1:17.7	1:28.7	-----
62.5%	30-35	30-60 S	14.7	22.4	30.4	39.2	48.9	59.1	1:09.7	1:20.8	-----	-----
60.0%	36-40	30-60 S	15.3	23.4	31.6	40.8	50.9	1:01.6	-----	-----	-----	-----

SPEED	REPS	REST	700 MT	800 MT	1000 MT	1200 MT	1500 MT	1600 MT	2000 MT	2400 MT	2800 MT	3200 MT
95.0%	0- 1	---	1:31.4	1:46.7	2:18.9	2:51.6	3:41.5	3:58.5	5:06.5	6:15.6	7:25.2	8:35.0
92.5%	1- 2	4- 5 M	1:33.8	1:49.6	2:22.7	2:56.2	3:47.4	4:04.9	5:14.8	6:25.8	7:37.2	8:49.0
90.0%	2- 3	4- 5 M	1:36.5	1:52.7	2:26.7	3:01.1	3:53.8	4:11.7	5:23.5	6:36.5	7:49.9	9:03.7
87.5%	3- 4	3- 4 M	1:39.2	1:55.9	2:30.8	3:06.3	4:00.4	4:18.9	5:32.8	6:47.8	8:03.4	9:19.2
85.0%	4- 5	3- 4 M	1:42.1	1:59.3	2:35.3	3:11.7	4:07.5	4:26.5	5:42.5	6:59.8	8:17.6	9:35.6
82.5%	6- 7	2- 3 M	1:45.2	2:02.9	2:40.0	3:17.5	4:15.0	4:34.6	5:52.9	-----	-----	-----
80.0%	8- 9	2- 3 M	1:48.5	2:06.8	2:45.0	3:23.7	4:23.0	4:43.2	-----	-----	-----	-----
77.5%	10-12	1- 2 M	1:52.0	2:10.9	2:50.3	3:30.3	-----	-----	-----	-----	-----	-----
75.0%	13-15	1- 2 M	1:55.7	2:15.2	2:56.0	-----	-----	-----	-----	-----	-----	-----
72.5%	16-18	60-90 S	1:59.7	2:19.9	-----	-----	-----	-----	-----	-----	-----	-----
70.0%	19-21	60-90 S	2:04.0	-----	-----	-----	-----	-----	-----	-----	-----	-----
67.5%	22-24	45-75 S	-----	-----	-----	-----	-----	-----	-----	-----	-----	-----
65.0%	25-29	45-75 S	-----	-----	-----	-----	-----	-----	-----	-----	-----	-----
62.5%	30-35	30-60 S	-----	-----	-----	-----	-----	-----	-----	-----	-----	-----
60.0%	36-40	30-60 S	-----	-----	-----	-----	-----	-----	-----	-----	-----	-----

1020 POINT LEVEL PACING TABLE

SPEED	REPS	REST	100 MT	150 MT	200 MT	250 MT	300 MT	350 MT	400 MT	450 MT	500 MT	600 MT
95.0%	0- 1	---	9.8	14.9	20.3	26.1	32.6	39.5	46.6	53.9	1:01.6	1:17.1
92.5%	1- 2	4- 5 M	10.1	15.4	20.8	26.8	33.5	40.5	47.8	55.4	1:03.2	1:19.2
90.0%	2- 3	4- 5 M	10.3	15.8	21.4	27.6	34.4	41.7	49.1	56.9	1:05.0	1:21.4
87.5%	3- 4	3- 4 M	10.6	16.2	22.0	28.4	35.4	42.8	50.5	58.6	1:06.9	1:23.7
85.0%	4- 5	3- 4 M	10.9	16.7	22.6	29.2	36.4	44.1	52.0	1:00.3	1:08.8	1:26.2
82.5%	6- 7	2- 3 M	11.3	17.2	23.3	30.1	37.5	45.4	53.6	1:02.1	1:10.9	1:28.8
80.0%	8- 9	2- 3 M	11.6	17.8	24.0	31.0	38.7	46.9	55.3	1:04.0	1:13.1	1:31.6
77.5%	10-12	1- 2 M	12.0	18.3	24.8	32.0	40.0	48.4	57.1	1:06.1	1:15.5	1:34.5
75.0%	13-15	1- 2 M	12.4	18.9	25.7	33.1	41.3	50.0	59.0	1:08.3	1:18.0	1:37.7
72.5%	16-18	60-90 S	12.8	19.6	26.5	34.2	42.7	51.7	1:01.0	1:10.7	1:20.7	1:41.0
70.0%	19-21	60-90 S	13.3	20.3	27.5	35.5	44.2	53.6	1:03.2	1:13.2	1:23.6	1:44.6
67.5%	22-24	45-75 S	13.8	21.0	28.5	36.8	45.9	55.5	1:05.5	1:15.9	1:26.7	1:48.5
65.0%	25-29	45-75 S	14.3	21.8	29.6	38.2	47.7	57.7	1:08.0	1:18.8	1:30.0	-----
62.5%	30-35	30-60 S	14.9	22.7	30.8	39.7	49.6	1:00.0	1:10.8	1:22.0	-----	-----
60.0%	36-40	30-60 S	15.5	23.7	32.1	41.4	51.6	1:02.5	-----	-----	-----	-----

SPEED	REPS	REST	700 MT	800 MT	1000 MT	1200 MT	1500 MT	1600 MT	2000 MT	2400 MT	2800 MT	3200 MT
95.0%	0- 1	---	1:32.8	1:48.4	2:21.1	2:54.3	3:45.1	4:02.4	5:11.5	6:21.9	7:32.6	8:43.7
92.5%	1- 2	4- 5 M	1:35.3	1:51.4	2:25.0	2:59.0	3:51.2	4:08.9	5:20.0	6:32.2	7:44.9	8:57.8
90.0%	2- 3	4- 5 M	1:38.0	1:54.4	2:29.0	3:04.0	3:57.6	4:15.8	5:28.9	6:43.1	7:57.8	9:12.8
87.5%	3- 4	3- 4 M	1:40.8	1:57.7	2:33.2	3:09.3	4:04.4	4:23.1	5:38.3	6:54.6	8:11.4	9:28.6
85.0%	4- 5	3- 4 M	1:43.7	2:01.2	2:37.8	3:14.8	4:11.6	4:30.9	5:48.2	7:06.8	8:25.9	9:45.3
82.5%	6- 7	2- 3 M	1:46.9	2:04.8	2:42.5	3:20.7	4:19.2	4:39.1	5:58.8	-----	-----	-----
80.0%	8- 9	2- 3 M	1:50.2	2:08.7	2:47.6	3:27.0	4:27.3	4:47.8	-----	-----	-----	-----
77.5%	10-12	1- 2 M	1:53.8	2:12.9	2:53.0	3:33.7	-----	-----	-----	-----	-----	-----
75.0%	13-15	1- 2 M	1:57.5	2:17.3	2:58.8	-----	-----	-----	-----	-----	-----	-----
72.5%	16-18	60-90 S	2:01.6	2:22.1	-----	-----	-----	-----	-----	-----	-----	-----
70.0%	19-21	60-90 S	2:05.9	-----	-----	-----	-----	-----	-----	-----	-----	-----
67.5%	22-24	45-75 S	-----	-----	-----	-----	-----	-----	-----	-----	-----	-----
65.0%	25-29	45-75 S	-----	-----	-----	-----	-----	-----	-----	-----	-----	-----
62.5%	30-35	30-60 S	-----	-----	-----	-----	-----	-----	-----	-----	-----	-----
60.0%	36-40	30-60 S	-----	-----	-----	-----	-----	-----	-----	-----	-----	-----

990 PCINT LEVEL PACING TABLE

SPEED	REPS	REST	100 MT	150 MT	200 MT	250 MT	300 MT	350 MT	400 MT	450 MT	500 MT	600 MT
95.0%	0- 1	---	9.9	15.1	20.5	26.5	33.1	40.0	47.2	54.7	1:02.5	1:18.3
92.5%	1- 2	4- 5 M	10.2	15.6	21.1	27.2	34.0	41.1	48.5	56.2	1:04.2	1:20.4
90.0%	2- 3	4- 5 M	10.5	16.0	21.7	28.0	34.9	42.3	49.9	57.8	1:06.0	1:22.6
87.5%	3- 4	3- 4 M	10.8	16.4	22.3	28.8	35.9	43.5	51.3	59.4	1:07.9	1:25.0
85.0%	4- 5	3- 4 M	11.1	16.9	22.9	29.6	37.0	44.7	52.8	1:01.2	1:09.9	1:27.5
82.5%	6- 7	2- 3 M	11.4	17.4	23.6	30.5	38.1	46.1	54.4	1:03.0	1:12.0	1:30.2
80.0%	8- 9	2- 3 M	11.8	18.0	24.4	31.5	39.3	47.5	56.1	1:05.0	1:14.2	1:33.0
77.5%	10-12	1- 2 M	12.2	18.6	25.2	32.5	40.5	49.1	57.9	1:07.1	1:16.6	1:36.0
75.0%	13-15	1- 2 M	12.6	19.2	26.0	33.6	41.9	50.7	59.8	1:09.3	1:19.2	1:39.2
72.5%	16-18	60-90 S	13.0	19.8	26.9	34.7	43.3	52.5	1:01.9	1:11.7	1:21.9	1:42.6
70.0%	19-21	60-90 S	13.5	20.6	27.9	35.9	44.9	54.3	1:04.1	1:14.3	1:24.8	1:46.3
67.5%	22-24	45-75 S	14.0	21.3	28.9	37.3	46.5	56.3	1:06.5	1:17.0	1:28.0	1:50.2
65.0%	25-29	45-75 S	14.5	22.1	30.0	38.7	48.3	58.5	1:09.0	1:20.0	1:31.4	-----
62.5%	30-35	30-60 S	15.1	23.0	31.2	40.3	50.3	1:00.9	1:11.8	1:23.2	-----	-----
60.0%	36-40	30-60 S	15.7	24.0	32.5	41.9	52.4	1:03.4	-----	-----	-----	-----

SPEED	REPS	REST	700 MT	8CO MT	1000 MT	1200 MT	1500 MT	1600 MT	2000 MT	2400 MT	2800 MT	3200 MT
95.0%	0- 1	---	1:34.3	1:50.1	2:23.4	2:57.2	3:48.8	4:06.4	5:16.8	6:28.3	7:40.3	8:52.6
92.5%	1- 2	4- 5 M	1:36.8	1:53.1	2:27.3	3:02.0	3:55.0	4:13.1	5:25.3	6:38.8	7:52.8	9:07.0
90.0%	2- 3	4- 5 M	1:39.5	1:56.3	2:31.4	3:07.0	4:01.5	4:20.1	5:34.4	6:49.9	8:05.9	9:22.2
87.5%	3- 4	3- 4 M	1:42.3	1:59.6	2:35.7	3:12.4	4:08.4	4:27.5	5:43.9	7:01.6	8:19.8	9:38.3
85.0%	4- 5	3- 4 M	1:45.3	2:03.1	2:40.3	3:18.0	4:15.7	4:35.4	5:54.0	7:14.0	8:34.5	9:55.3
82.5%	6- 7	2- 3 M	1:48.5	2:06.8	2:45.2	3:24.0	4:23.5	4:43.7	6:04.8	-----	-----	-----
80.0%	8- 9	2- 3 M	1:51.9	2:10.8	2:50.3	3:30.4	4:31.7	4:52.6	-----	-----	-----	-----
77.5%	10-12	1- 2 M	1:55.5	2:15.0	2:55.8	3:37.2	-----	-----	-----	-----	-----	-----
75.0%	13-15	1- 2 M	1:59.4	2:19.5	3:01.7	-----	-----	-----	-----	-----	-----	-----
72.5%	16-18	60-90 S	2:03.5	2:24.3	-----	-----	-----	-----	-----	-----	-----	-----
70.0%	19-21	60-90 S	2:07.9	-----	-----	-----	-----	-----	-----	-----	-----	-----
67.5%	22-24	45-75 S	-----	-----	-----	-----	-----	-----	-----	-----	-----	-----
65.0%	25-29	45-75 S	-----	-----	-----	-----	-----	-----	-----	-----	-----	-----
62.5%	30-35	30-60 S	-----	-----	-----	-----	-----	-----	-----	-----	-----	-----
60.0%	36-40	30-60 S	-----	-----	-----	-----	-----	-----	-----	-----	-----	-----

243

960 POINT LEVEL PACING TABLE
....

SPEED	REPS	REST	100 MT	150 MT	200 MT	250 MT	300 MT	350 MT	400 MT	450 MT	500 MT	600 MT
95.0%	0- 1	---	10.1	15.3	20.8	26.9	33.5	40.6	48.0	55.6	1:03.5	1:19.5
92.5%	1- 2	4- 5 M	10.3	15.8	21.4	27.6	34.5	41.7	49.2	57.1	1:05.2	1:21.7
90.0%	2- 3	4- 5 M	10.6	16.2	22.0	28.4	35.4	42.9	50.6	58.7	1:07.0	1:23.9
87.5%	3- 4	3- 4 M	10.9	16.7	22.6	29.2	36.4	44.1	52.1	1:00.3	1:08.9	1:26.3
85.0%	4- 5	3- 4 M	11.2	17.2	23.3	30.0	37.5	45.4	53.6	1:02.1	1:10.9	1:28.9
82.5%	6- 7	2- 3 M	11.6	17.7	24.0	30.9	38.6	46.8	55.2	1:04.0	1:13.1	1:31.6
80.0%	8- 9	2- 3 M	11.9	18.2	24.7	31.9	39.8	48.2	56.9	1:06.0	1:15.4	1:34.4
77.5%	10-12	1- 2 M	12.3	18.8	25.5	32.9	41.1	49.8	58.8	1:08.1	1:17.8	1:37.5
75.0%	13-15	1- 2 M	12.7	19.4	26.4	34.0	42.5	51.5	1:00.7	1:10.4	1:20.4	1:40.7
72.5%	16-18	60-90 S	13.2	20.1	27.3	35.2	44.0	53.2	1:02.8	1:12.8	1:23.2	1:44.2
70.0%	19-21	60-90 S	13.6	20.8	28.2	36.5	45.5	55.1	1:05.1	1:15.4	1:26.1	1:47.9
67.5%	22-24	45-75 S	14.1	21.6	29.3	37.8	47.2	57.2	1:07.5	1:18.2	1:29.3	1:51.9
65.0%	25-29	45-75 S	14.7	22.4	30.4	39.3	49.0	59.4	1:10.1	1:21.2	1:32.8	-----
62.5%	30-35	30-60 S	15.3	23.3	31.6	40.8	51.0	1:01.8	1:12.9	1:24.5	-----	-----
60.0%	36-40	30-60 S	15.9	24.3	32.9	42.5	53.1	1:04.3	-----	-----	-----	-----

SPEED	REPS	REST	700 MT	800 MT	1000 MT	1200 MT	1500 MT	1600 MT	2000 MT	2400 MT	2800 MT	3200 MT
95.0%	0- 1	---	1:35.8	1:51.9	2:25.8	3:00.1	3:52.7	4:10.6	5:22.2	6:35.0	7:48.3	9:01.8
92.5%	1- 2	4- 5 M	1:38.4	1:55.0	2:29.7	3:05.0	3:58.9	4:17.3	5:30.9	6:45.7	8:00.9	9:16.5
90.0%	2- 3	4- 5 M	1:41.1	1:58.1	2:33.9	3:10.1	4:05.6	4:24.5	5:40.1	6:56.9	8:14.3	9:31.9
87.5%	3- 4	3- 4 M	1:44.0	2:01.5	2:38.3	3:15.6	4:12.6	4:32.0	5:49.8	7:08.9	8:28.4	9:48.3
85.0%	4- 5	3- 4 M	1:47.0	2:05.1	2:42.9	3:21.3	4:20.0	4:40.0	6:00.1	7:21.5	8:43.4	10:05.6
82.5%	6- 7	2- 3 M	1:50.3	2:08.9	2:47.9	3:27.4	4:27.9	4:48.5	6:11.0	-----	-----	-----
80.0%	8- 9	2- 3 M	1:53.7	2:12.9	2:53.1	3:33.9	4:36.3	4:57.5	-----	-----	-----	-----
77.5%	10-12	1- 2 M	1:57.4	2:17.2	2:58.7	3:40.8	-----	-----	-----	-----	-----	-----
75.0%	13-15	1- 2 M	2:01.3	2:21.8	3:04.7	-----	-----	-----	-----	-----	-----	-----
72.5%	16-18	60-90 S	2:05.5	2:26.7	-----	-----	-----	-----	-----	-----	-----	-----
70.0%	19-21	60-90 S	2:10.0	-----	-----	-----	-----	-----	-----	-----	-----	-----
67.5%	22-24	45-75 S	-----	-----	-----	-----	-----	-----	-----	-----	-----	-----
65.0%	25-29	45-75 S	-----	-----	-----	-----	-----	-----	-----	-----	-----	-----
62.5%	30-35	30-60 S	-----	-----	-----	-----	-----	-----	-----	-----	-----	-----
60.0%	36-40	30-60 S	-----	-----	-----	-----	-----	-----	-----	-----	-----	-----

930 POINT LEVEL PACING TABLE
•••••••••••••••••••••••••••••

SPEED	REPS	REST	100 MT	150 MT	200 MT	250 MT	300 MT	350 MT	400 MT	450 MT	500 MT	600 MT
95.0%	0- 1	---	10.2	15.6	21.1	27.2	34.0	41.2	48.7	56.4	1:04.5	1:20.8
92.5%	1- 2	4- 5 M	10.5	16.0	21.7	28.0	35.0	42.3	50.0	58.0	1:06.2	1:23.0
90.0%	2- 3	4- 5 M	10.8	16.4	22.3	28.8	35.9	43.5	51.4	59.6	1:08.1	1:25.3
87.5%	3- 4	3- 4 M	11.1	16.9	22.9	29.6	37.0	44.8	52.9	1:01.3	1:10.0	1:27.7
85.0%	4- 5	3- 4 M	11.4	17.4	23.6	30.4	38.0	46.1	54.4	1:03.1	1:12.1	1:30.3
82.5%	6- 7	2- 3 M	11.7	17.9	24.3	31.4	39.2	47.5	56.1	1:05.2	1:14.2	1:33.0
80.0%	8- 9	2- 3 M	12.1	18.5	25.0	32.3	40.4	49.0	57.8	1:07.0	1:16.6	1:36.0
77.5%	10-12	1- 2 M	12.5	19.1	25.9	33.4	41.7	50.5	59.7	1:09.2	1:19.0	1:39.1
75.0%	13-15	1- 2 M	12.9	19.7	26.7	34.5	43.1	52.2	1:01.7	1:11.5	1:21.7	1:42.4
72.5%	16-18	60-90 S	13.3	20.4	27.6	35.7	44.6	54.0	1:03.8	1:14.0	1:24.5	1:45.9
70.0%	19-21	60-90 S	13.8	21.1	28.6	37.0	46.2	56.0	1:06.1	1:16.6	1:27.5	1:49.7
67.5%	22-24	45-75 S	14.3	21.9	29.7	38.3	47.9	58.0	1:08.5	1:19.4	1:30.7	1:53.7
65.0%	25-29	45-75 S	14.9	22.7	30.8	39.8	49.7	1:00.3	1:11.2	1:22.5	1:34.2	-----
62.5%	30-35	30-60 S	15.5	23.6	32.1	41.4	51.7	1:02.7	1:14.0	1:25.8	-----	-----
60.0%	36-40	30-60 S	16.1	24.6	33.4	43.1	53.9	1:05.3	-----	-----	-----	-----

SPEED	REPS	REST	700 MT	800 MT	1000 MT	1200 MT	1500 MT	1600 MT	2000 MT	2400 MT	2800 MT	3200 MT
95.0%	0- 1	---	1:37.3	1:53.8	2:28.2	3:03.2	3:56.6	4:14.9	5:27.8	6:41.9	7:56.5	9:11.4
92.5%	1- 2	4- 5 M	1:40.0	1:56.8	2:32.2	3:08.1	4:03.0	4:21.7	5:36.6	6:52.8	8:09.4	9:26.3
90.0%	2- 3	4- 5 M	1:42.7	2:00.1	2:36.5	3:13.3	4:09.8	4:29.0	5:46.0	7:04.2	8:23.0	9:42.0
87.5%	3- 4	3- 4 M	1:45.7	2:03.5	2:40.9	3:18.9	4:16.9	4:36.7	5:55.9	7:16.4	8:37.3	9:58.7
85.0%	4- 5	3- 4 M	1:48.8	2:07.2	2:45.7	3:24.7	4:24.5	4:44.8	6:06.3	7:29.2	8:52.6	10:16.3
82.5%	6- 7	2- 3 M	1:52.1	2:11.0	2:50.7	3:30.9	4:32.5	4:53.5	6:17.4	-----	-----	-----
80.0%	8- 9	2- 3 M	1:55.6	2:15.1	2:56.0	3:37.5	4:41.0	5:02.6	-----	-----	-----	-----
77.5%	10-12	1- 2 M	1:59.3	2:19.5	3:01.7	3:44.5	-----	-----	-----	-----	-----	-----
75.0%	13-15	1- 2 M	2:03.3	2:24.1	3:07.8	-----	-----	-----	-----	-----	-----	-----
72.5%	16-18	60-90 S	2:07.5	2:29.1	-----	-----	-----	-----	-----	-----	-----	-----
70.0%	19-21	60-90 S	2:12.1	-----	-----	-----	-----	-----	-----	-----	-----	-----
67.5%	22-24	45-75 S	-----	-----	-----	-----	-----	-----	-----	-----	-----	-----
65.0%	25-29	45-75 S	-----	-----	-----	-----	-----	-----	-----	-----	-----	-----
62.5%	30-35	30-60 S	-----	-----	-----	-----	-----	-----	-----	-----	-----	-----
60.0%	36-40	30-60 S	-----	-----	-----	-----	-----	-----	-----	-----	-----	-----

900 POINT LEVEL PACING TABLE

SPEED	REPS	REST	100 MT	150 MT	200 MT	250 MT	300 MT	350 MT	400 MT	450 MT	500 MT	600 MT
95.0%	0- 1	---	10.3	15.8	21.4	27.6	34.5	41.9	49.4	57.3	1:05.5	1:22.1
92.5%	1- 2	4- 5 M	10.6	16.2	22.0	28.4	35.5	43.0	50.8	58.9	1:07.3	1:24.3
90.0%	2- 3	4- 5 M	10.9	16.6	22.6	29.2	36.5	44.2	52.2	1:00.5	1:09.1	1:26.7
87.5%	3- 4	3- 4 M	11.2	17.1	23.2	30.0	37.5	45.4	53.7	1:02.2	1:11.1	1:29.2
85.0%	4- 5	3- 4 M	11.5	17.6	23.9	30.9	38.6	46.8	55.3	1:04.1	1:13.2	1:31.8
82.5%	6- 7	2- 3 M	11.9	18.2	24.6	31.8	39.8	48.2	56.9	1:06.0	1:15.4	1:34.6
80.0%	8- 9	2- 3 M	12.3	18.7	25.4	32.8	41.0	49.7	58.7	1:08.1	1:17.8	1:37.5
77.5%	10-12	1- 2 M	12.7	19.3	26.2	33.9	42.3	51.3	1:00.6	1:10.3	1:20.3	1:40.7
75.0%	13-15	1- 2 M	13.1	20.0	27.1	35.0	43.7	53.0	1:02.6	1:12.6	1:23.0	1:44.0
72.5%	16-18	60-90 S	13.5	20.7	28.0	36.2	45.3	54.8	1:04.8	1:15.1	1:25.8	1:47.6
70.0%	19-21	60-90 S	14.0	21.4	29.0	37.5	46.9	56.8	1:07.1	1:17.8	1:28.9	1:51.5
67.5%	22-24	45-75 S	14.5	22.2	30.1	38.9	48.6	58.9	1:09.6	1:20.7	1:32.2	1:55.6
65.0%	25-29	45-75 S	15.1	23.0	31.3	40.4	50.5	1:01.2	1:12.3	1:23.8	1:35.7	-----
62.5%	30-35	30-60 S	15.7	24.0	32.5	42.0	52.5	1:03.6	1:15.1	1:27.1	-----	-----
60.0%	36-40	30-60 S	16.3	25.0	33.9	43.8	54.7	1:06.3	1:18.3	-----	-----	-----

SPEED	REPS	REST	700 MT	800 MT	1000 MT	1200 MT	1500 MT	1600 MT	2000 MT	2400 MT	2800 MT	3200 MT
95.0%	0- 1	---	1:38.9	1:55.7	2:30.7	3:06.3	4:00.8	4:19.3	5:33.6	6:49.1	8:05.0	9:21.3
92.5%	1- 2	4- 5 M	1:41.6	1:58.8	2:34.8	3:11.3	4:07.3	4:26.3	5:42.6	7:00.1	8:18.1	9:36.5
90.0%	2- 3	4- 5 M	1:44.4	2:02.1	2:39.1	3:16.7	4:14.1	4:33.7	5:52.1	7:11.8	8:32.0	9:52.5
87.5%	3- 4	3- 4 M	1:47.4	2:05.6	2:43.7	3:22.3	4:21.4	4:41.5	6:02.2	7:24.1	8:46.6	10:09.4
85.0%	4- 5	3- 4 M	1:50.6	2:09.3	2:48.5	3:28.2	4:29.1	4:49.8	6:12.8	7:37.2	9:02.1	10:27.4
82.5%	6- 7	2- 3 M	1:53.9	2:13.2	2:53.6	3:34.5	4:37.2	4:58.6	6:24.1	-----	-----	-----
80.0%	8- 9	2- 3 M	1:57.5	2:17.4	2:59.0	3:41.2	4:45.9	5:07.9	-----	-----	-----	-----
77.5%	10-12	1- 2 M	2:01.3	2:21.8	3:04.8	3:48.4	-----	-----	-----	-----	-----	-----
75.0%	13-15	1- 2 M	2:05.3	2:26.5	3:10.9	-----	-----	-----	-----	-----	-----	-----
72.5%	16-18	60-90 S	2:09.6	2:31.6	-----	-----	-----	-----	-----	-----	-----	-----
70.0%	19-21	60-90 S	2:14.3	-----	-----	-----	-----	-----	-----	-----	-----	-----
67.5%	22-24	45-75 S	-----	-----	-----	-----	-----	-----	-----	-----	-----	-----
65.0%	25-29	45-75 S	-----	-----	-----	-----	-----	-----	-----	-----	-----	-----
62.5%	30-35	30-60 S	-----	-----	-----	-----	-----	-----	-----	-----	-----	-----
60.0%	36-40	30-60 S	-----	-----	-----	-----	-----	-----	-----	-----	-----	-----

SPEED	REPS	REST	100 MT	150 MT	200 MT	250 MT	300 MT	350 MT	400 MT	450 MT	500 MT	600 MT
95.0%	0- 1	---	10.5	16.0	21.7	28.0	35.1	42.5	50.2	58.2	1:06.6	1:23.5
92.5%	1- 2	4- 5 M	10.7	16.4	22.3	28.8	36.0	43.7	51.6	59.8	1:08.4	1:25.7
90.0%	2- 3	4- 5 M	11.0	16.9	22.9	29.6	37.0	44.9	53.0	1:01.5	1:10.3	1:28.1
87.5%	3- 4	3- 4 M	11.4	17.4	23.6	30.4	38.1	46.1	54.5	1:03.2	1:12.3	1:30.6
85.0%	4- 5	3- 4 M	11.7	17.9	24.2	31.3	39.2	47.5	56.1	1:05.1	1:14.4	1:33.3
82.5%	6- 7	2- 3 M	12.1	18.4	25.0	32.3	40.4	48.9	57.8	1:07.1	1:16.7	1:36.1
80.0%	8- 9	2- 3 M	12.4	19.0	25.8	33.3	41.6	50.5	59.6	1:09.2	1:19.0	1:39.1
77.5%	10-12	1- 2 M	12.8	19.6	26.6	34.4	43.0	52.1	1:01.6	1:11.4	1:21.6	1:42.3
75.0%	13-15	1- 2 M	13.3	20.3	27.5	35.5	44.4	53.8	1:03.6	1:13.8	1:24.3	1:45.7
72.5%	16-18	60-90 S	13.7	21.0	28.4	36.7	45.9	55.7	1:05.8	1:16.3	1:27.2	1:49.4
70.0%	19-21	60-90 S	14.2	21.7	29.4	38.1	47.6	57.7	1:08.1	1:19.0	1:30.3	1:53.3
67.5%	22-24	45-75 S	14.7	22.5	30.5	39.5	49.3	59.8	1:10.7	1:22.0	1:33.7	1:57.5
65.0%	25-29	45-75 S	15.3	23.4	31.7	41.0	51.2	1:02.1	1:13.4	1:25.1	1:37.3	-----
62.5%	30-35	30-60 S	15.9	24.3	33.0	42.6	53.3	1:04.6	1:16.3	1:28.5	-----	-----
60.0%	36-40	30-60 S	16.6	25.3	34.4	44.4	55.5	1:07.3	1:19.5	-----	-----	-----

SPEED	REPS	REST	700 MT	800 MT	1000 MT	1200 MT	1500 MT	1600 MT	2000 MT	2400 MT	2800 MT	3200 MT
95.0%	0- 1	---	1:40.6	1:57.6	2:33.4	3:09.6	4:05.0	4:23.9	5:39.6	6:56.5	8:13.9	9:31.6
92.5%	1- 2	4- 5 M	1:43.3	2:00.8	2:37.5	3:14.7	4:11.7	4:31.1	5:48.7	7:07.7	8:27.2	9:47.0
90.0%	2- 3	4- 5 M	1:46.2	2:04.2	2:41.9	3:20.1	4:18.6	4:38.6	5:58.4	7:19.6	8:41.3	10:03.4
87.5%	3- 4	3- 4 M	1:49.2	2:07.7	2:46.5	3:25.8	4:26.0	4:46.5	6:08.7	7:32.2	8:56.2	10:20.6
85.0%	4- 5	3- 4 M	1:52.4	2:11.5	2:51.4	3:31.9	4:33.9	4:55.0	6:19.5	7:45.5	9:12.0	10:38.8
82.5%	6- 7	2- 3 M	1:55.8	2:15.5	2:56.6	3:38.3	4:42.2	5:03.9	6:31.0	-----	-----	-----
80.0%	8- 9	2- 3 M	1:59.5	2:19.7	3:02.1	3:45.1	4:51.0	5:13.4	-----	-----	-----	-----
77.5%	10-12	1- 2 M	2:03.3	2:24.2	3:08.0	3:52.4	-----	-----	-----	-----	-----	-----
75.0%	13-15	1- 2 M	2:07.4	2:29.0	3:14.2	-----	-----	-----	-----	-----	-----	-----
72.5%	16-18	60-90 S	2:11.8	2:34.1	-----	-----	-----	-----	-----	-----	-----	-----
70.0%	19-21	60-90 S	2:16.5	2:39.6	-----	-----	-----	-----	-----	-----	-----	-----
67.5%	22-24	45-75 S	-----	-----	-----	-----	-----	-----	-----	-----	-----	-----
65.0%	25-29	45-75 S	-----	-----	-----	-----	-----	-----	-----	-----	-----	-----
62.5%	30-35	30-60 S	-----	-----	-----	-----	-----	-----	-----	-----	-----	-----
60.0%	36-40	30-60 S	-----	-----	-----	-----	-----	-----	-----	-----	-----	-----

840 POINT LEVEL PACING TABLE

SPEED	REPS	REST	100 MT	150 MT	200 MT	250 MT	300 MT	350 MT	400 MT	450 MT	500 MT	600 MT
95.0%	0- 1	---	10.6	16.2	22.0	28.5	35.6	43.2	51.0	59.2	1:07.7	1:24.9
92.5%	1- 2	4- 5 M	10.9	16.7	22.6	29.2	36.6	44.3	52.4	1:00.8	1:09.5	1:27.2
90.0%	2- 3	4- 5 M	11.2	17.1	23.2	30.0	37.6	45.6	53.8	1:02.5	1:11.4	1:29.6
87.5%	3- 4	3- 4 M	11.5	17.6	23.9	30.9	38.6	46.9	55.4	1:04.3	1:13.5	1:32.2
85.0%	4- 5	3- 4 M	11.9	18.1	24.6	31.8	39.8	48.2	57.0	1:06.2	1:15.6	1:34.9
82.5%	6- 7	2- 3 M	12.2	18.7	25.3	32.8	41.0	49.7	58.7	1:08.2	1:17.9	1:37.8
80.0%	8- 9	2- 3 M	12.6	19.3	26.1	33.8	42.3	51.3	1:00.6	1:10.3	1:20.4	1:40.8
77.5%	10-12	1- 2 M	13.0	19.9	27.0	34.9	43.6	52.9	1:02.5	1:12.6	1:22.9	1:44.1
75.0%	13-15	1- 2 M	13.4	20.5	27.9	36.0	45.1	54.7'	1:04.6	1:15.0	1:25.7	1:47.5
72.5%	16-18	60-90 S	13.9	21.2	28.8	37.3	46.6	56.6	1:06.8	1:17.6	1:28.7	1:51.2
70.0%	19-21	60-90 S	14.4	22.0	29.9	38.6	48.3	58.6	1:09.2	1:20.3	1:31.8	1:55.2
67.5%	22-24	45-75 S	14.9	22.8	31.0	40.1	50.1	1:00.8	1:11.8	1:23.3	1:35.2	1:59.5
65.0%	25-29	45-75 S	15.5	23.7	32.2	41.6	52.0	1:03.1	1:14.6	1:26.5	1:38.9	-----
62.5%	30-35	30-60 S	16.1	24.6	33.5	43.3	54.1	1:05.6	1:17.5	1:30.0	-----	-----
60.0%	36-40	30-60 S	16.8	25.7	34.8	45.1	56.4	1:08.3	1:20.8	-----	-----	-----

SPEED	REPS	REST	700 MT	800 MT	1000 MT	1200 MT	1500 MT	1600 MT	2000 MT	2400 MT	2800 MT	3200 MT
95.0%	0- 1	---	1:42.3	1:59.7	2:36.1	3:13.0	4:09.5	4:28.7	5:45.8	7:04.2	8:23.0	9:42.3
92.5%	1- 2	4- 5 M	1:45.1	2:02.9	2:40.3	3:18.2	4:16.2	4:36.0	5:55.1	7:15.6	8:36.6	9:58.0
90.0%	2- 3	4- 5 M	1:48.0	2:06.3	2:44.7	3:23.7	4:23.3	4:43.6	6:05.0	7:27.7	8:51.0	10:14.6
87.5%	3- 4	3- 4 M	1:51.1	2:09.9	2:49.4	3:29.5	4:30.8	4:51.7	6:15.4	7:40.5	9:06.1	10:32.2
85.0%	4- 5	3- 4 M	1:54.4	2:13.7	2:54.4	3:35.7	4:38.8	5:00.3	6:26.5	7:54.1	9:22.2	10:50.8
82.5%	6- 7	2- 3 M	1:57.8	2:17.8	2:59.7	3:42.2	4:47.2	5:09.4	6:38.2	-----	-----	-----
80.0%	8- 9	2- 3 M	2:01.5	2:22.1	3:05.3	3:49.1	4:56.2	5:19.1	-----	-----	-----	-----
77.5%	10-12	1- 2 M	2:05.4	2:26.7	3:11.3	3:56.5	-----	-----	-----	-----	-----	-----
75.0%	13-15	1- 2 M	2:09.6	2:31.6	3:17.7	-----	-----	-----	-----	-----	-----	-----
72.5%	16-18	60-90 S	2:14.1	2:36.8	-----	-----	-----	-----	-----	-----	-----	-----
70.0%	19-21	60-90 S	2:18.9	2:42.4	-----	-----	-----	-----	-----	-----	-----	-----
67.5%	22-24	45-75 S	-----	-----	-----	-----	-----	-----	-----	-----	-----	-----
65.0%	25-29	45-75 S	-----	-----	-----	-----	-----	-----	-----	-----	-----	-----
62.5%	30-35	30-60 S	-----	-----	-----	-----	-----	-----	-----	-----	-----	-----
60.0%	36-40	30-60 S	-----	-----	-----	-----	-----	-----	-----	-----	-----	-----

810 POINT LEVEL PACING TABLE

SPEED	REPS	REST	100 MT	150 MT	200 MT	250 MT	300 MT	350 MT	400 MT	450 MT	500 MT	600 MT
95.0%	0- 1	---	10.8	16.4	22.3	28.9	36.1	43.9	51.8	1:00.2	1:08.8	1:26.3
92.5%	1- 2	4- 5 M	11.1	16.9	22.9	29.7	37.1	45.0	53.2	1:01.8	1:10.7	1:28.7
90.0%	2- 3	4- 5 M	11.4	17.4	23.6	30.5	38.2	46.3	54.7	1:03.5	1:12.6	1:31.1
87.5%	3- 4	3- 4 M	11.7	17.9	24.2	31.4	39.2	47.6	56.3	1:05.3	1:14.7	1:33.7
85.0%	4- 5	3- 4 M	12.0	18.4	25.0	32.3	40.4	49.0	57.9	1:07.2	1:16.9	1:36.5
82.5%	6- 7	2- 3 M	12.4	18.9	25.7	33.3	41.6	50.5	59.7	1:09.3	1:19.2	1:39.4
80.0%	8- 9	2- 3 M	12.8	19.5	26.5	34.3	42.9	52.1	1:01.6	1:11.4	1:21.7	1:42.5
77.5%	10-12	1- 2 M	13.2	20.2	27.4	35.4	44.3	53.8	1:03.5	1:13.8	1:24.3	1:45.8
75.0%	13-15	1- 2 M	13.6	20.8	28.3	36.6	45.8	55.5	1:05.7	1:16.2	1:27.1	1:49.4
72.5%	16-18	60-90 S	14.1	21.6	29.3	37.9	47.4	57.5	1:07.9	1:18.8	1:30.1	1:53.1
70.0%	19-21	60-90 S	14.6	22.3	30.3	39.2	49.1	59.5	1:10.4	1:21.7	1:33.4	1:57.2
67.5%	22-24	45-75 S	15.1	23.2	31.4	40.7	50.9	1:01.7	1:13.0	1:24.7	1:36.8	2:01.5
65.0%	25-29	45-75 S	15.7	24.0	32.6	42.2	52.8	1:04.1	1:15.8	1:27.9	1:40.6	-----
62.5%	30-35	30-60 S	16.4	25.0	33.9	43.9	54.9	1:06.7	1:18.8	1:31.5	-----	-----
60.0%	36-40	30-60 S	17.0	26.0	35.4	45.7	57.2	1:09.4	1:22.1	-----	-----	-----

SPEED	REPS	REST	700 MT	800 MT	1000 MT	1200 MT	1500 MT	1600 MT	2000 MT	2400 MT	2800 MT	3200 MT
95.0%	0- 1	---	1:44.1	2:01.8	2:38.9	3:16.5	4:14.0	4:33.7	5:52.2	7:12.1	8:32.5	9:53.3
92.5%	1- 2	4- 5 M	1:46.9	2:05.1	2:43.1	3:21.8	4:20.9	4:41.1	6:01.8	7:23.8	8:46.4	10:09.3
90.0%	2- 3	4- 5 M	1:49.9	2:08.5	2:47.7	3:27.4	4:28.2	4:48.9	6:11.8	7:36.1	9:01.0	10:26.3
87.5%	3- 4	3- 4 M	1:53.0	2:12.2	2:52.5	3:33.3	4:35.8	4:57.1	6:22.4	7:49.2	9:16.5	10:44.2
85.0%	4- 5	3- 4 M	1:56.4	2:16.1	2:57.5	3:39.6	4:43.9	5:05.9	6:33.7	8:03.0	9:32.8	11:03.1
82.5%	6- 7	2- 3 M	1:59.9	2:20.2	3:02.9	3:46.2	4:52.5	5:15.1	6:45.6	-----	-----	-----
80.0%	8- 9	2- 3 M	2:03.6	2:24.6	3:08.6	3:53.3	5:01.7	5:25.0	-----	-----	-----	-----
77.5%	10-12	1- 2 M	2:07.6	2:29.3	3:14.7	4:00.8	-----	-----	-----	-----	-----	-----
75.0%	13-15	1- 2 M	2:11.9	2:34.2	3:21.2	-----	-----	-----	-----	-----	-----	-----
72.5%	16-18	60-90 S	2:16.4	2:39.6	-----	-----	-----	-----	-----	-----	-----	-----
70.0%	19-21	60-90 S	2:21.3	2:45.3	-----	-----	-----	-----	-----	-----	-----	-----
67.5%	22-24	45-75 S	-----	-----	-----	-----	-----	-----	-----	-----	-----	-----
65.0%	25-29	45-75 S	-----	-----	-----	-----	-----	-----	-----	-----	-----	-----
62.5%	30-35	30-60 S	-----	-----	-----	-----	-----	-----	-----	-----	-----	-----
60.0%	36-40	30-60 S	-----	-----	-----	-----	-----	-----	-----	-----	-----	-----

780 POINT LEVEL PACING TABLE
·······························

SPEED	REPS	REST	100 MT	150 MT	200 MT	250 MT	300 MT	350 MT	400 MT	450 MT	500 MT	600 MT
95.0%	0- 1	---	10.9	16.7	22.7	29.3	36.7	44.6	52.7	1:01.2	1:10.0	1:27.8
92.5%	1- 2	4- 5 M	11.2	17.1	23.3	30.1	37.7	45.8	54.1	1:02.8	1:11.9	1:30.2
90.0%	2- 3	4- 5 M	11.5	17.6	23.9	31.0	38.8	47.0	55.6	1:04.6	1:13.9	1:32.7
87.5%	3- 4	3- 4 M	11.8	18.1	24.6	31.8	39.9	48.4	57.2	1:06.4	1:16.0	1:35.4
85.0%	4- 5	3- 4 M	12.2	18.7	25.3	32.8	41.0	49.8	58.9	1:08.4	1:18.2	1:38.2
82.5%	6- 7	2- 3 M	12.6	19.2	26.1	33.8	42.3	51.3	1:00.7	1:10.4	1:20.6	1:41.2
80.0%	8- 9	2- 3 M	13.0	19.8	26.9	34.8	43.6	52.9	1:02.6	1:12.6	1:23.1	1:44.3
77.5%	10-12	1- 2 M	13.4	20.5	27.8	36.0	45.0	54.6	1:04.6	1:15.0	1:25.8	1:47.7
75.0%	13-15	1- 2 M	13.8	21.1	28.7	37.2	46.5	56.4	1:06.7	1:17.5	1:28.6	1:51.3
72.5%	16-18	60-90 S	14.3	21.9	29.7	38.4	48.1	58.4	1:09.1	1:20.2	1:31.7	1:55.1
70.0%	19-21	60-90 S	14.8	22.6	30.8	39.8	49.8	1:00.5	1:11.5	1:23.0	1:35.0	1:59.2
67.5%	22-24	45-75 S	15.4	23.5	31.9	41.3	51.7	1:02.7	1:14.2	1:26.1	1:38.5	2:03.6
65.0%	25-29	45-75 S	16.0	24.4	33.1	42.9	53.7	1:05.1	1:17.0	1:29.4	1:42.3	-----
62.5%	30-35	30-60 S	16.6	25.4	34.5	44.6	55.8	1:07.7	1:20.1	1:33.0	-----	-----
60.0%	36-40	30-60 S	17.3	26.4	35.9	46.4	58.1	1:10.6	1:23.4	-----	-----	-----

SPEED	REPS	REST	700 MT	800 MT	1000 MT	1200 MT	1500 MT	1600 MT	2000 MT	2400 MT	2800 MT	3200 MT
95.0%	0- 1	---	1:45.9	2:04.0	2:41.7	3:20.1	4:18.8	4:38.8	5:58.9	7:20.4	8:42.4	10:04.8
92.5%	1- 2	4- 5 M	1:48.8	2:07.3	2:46.1	3:25.5	4:25.8	4:46.3	6:08.6	7:32.3	8:56.5	10:21.1
90.0%	2- 3	4- 5 M	1:51.8	2:10.8	2:50.7	3:31.2	4:33.2	4:54.3	6:18.9	7:44.9	9:11.4	10:38.4
87.5%	3- 4	3- 4 M	1:55.0	2:14.6	2:55.6	3:37.2	4:41.0	5:02.7	6:29.7	7:58.2	9:27.2	10:56.6
85.0%	4- 5	3- 4 M	1:58.4	2:18.5	3:00.8	3:43.6	4:49.2	5:11.6	6:41.2	8:12.2	9:43.9	11:16.0
82.5%	6- 7	2- 3 M	2:02.0	2:22.7	3:06.3	3:50.4	4:58.0	5:21.0	6:53.3	-----	-----	-----
80.0%	8- 9	2- 3 M	2:05.8	2:27.2	3:12.1	3:57.6	5:07.3	5:31.1	-----	-----	-----	-----
77.5%	10-12	1- 2 M	2:09.9	2:31.9	3:18.3	4:05.3	-----	-----	-----	-----	-----	-----
75.0%	13-15	1- 2 M	2:14.2	2:37.0	3:24.9	4:13.4	-----	-----	-----	-----	-----	-----
72.5%	16-18	60-90 S	2:18.8	2:42.4	-----	-----	-----	-----	-----	-----	-----	-----
70.0%	19-21	60-90 S	2:23.8	2:48.2	-----	-----	-----	-----	-----	-----	-----	-----
67.5%	22-24	45-75 S	-----	-----	-----	-----	-----	-----	-----	-----	-----	-----
65.0%	25-29	45-75 S	-----	-----	-----	-----	-----	-----	-----	-----	-----	-----
62.5%	30-35	30-60 S	-----	-----	-----	-----	-----	-----	-----	-----	-----	-----
60.0%	36-40	30-60 S	-----	-----	-----	-----	-----	-----	-----	-----	-----	-----

250

750 POINT LEVEL PACING TABLE

SPEED	REPS	REST	100 MT	150 MT	200 MT	250 MT	300 MT	350 MT	400 MT	450 MT	500 MT	600 MT
95.0%	0- 1	---	11.1	16.9	23.0	29.8	37.3	45.3	53.6	1:02.2	1:11.2	1:29.4
92.5%	1- 2	4- 5 M	11.4	17.4	23.6	30.6	38.3	46.5	55.0	1:03.9	1:13.1	1:31.8
90.0%	2- 3	4- 5 M	11.7	17.9	24.3	31.4	39.4	47.8	56.6	1:05.7	1:15.1	1:34.4
87.5%	3- 4	3- 4 M	12.0	18.4	25.0	32.3	40.5	49.2	58.2	1:07.6	1:17.3	1:37.1
85.0%	4- 5	3- 4 M	12.4	18.9	25.7	33.3	41.7	50.6	59.9	1:09.5	1:19.6	1:39.9
82.5%	6- 7	2- 3 M	12.7	19.5	26.5	34.3	43.0	52.2	1:01.7	1:11.7	1:22.0	1:43.0
80.0%	8- 9	2- 3 M	13.1	20.1	27.3	35.4	44.3	53.8	1:03.6	1:13.9	1:24.5	1:46.2
77.5%	10-12	1- 2 M	13.6	20.8	28.2	36.5	45.7	55.5	1:05.7	1:16.3	1:27.3	1:49.6
75.0%	13-15	1- 2 M	14.0	21.5	29.1	37.7	47.3	57.4	1:07.9	1:18.8	1:30.2	1:53.3
72.5%	16-18	60-90 S	14.5	22.2	30.1	39.0	48.9	59.4	1:10.2	1:21.5	1:33.3	1:57.2
70.0%	19-21	60-90 S	15.0	23.0	31.2	40.4	50.6	1:01.5	1:12.7	1:24.4	1:36.6	2:01.3
67.5%	22-24	45-75 S	15.6	23.8	32.4	41.9	52.5	1:03.7	1:15.4	1:27.6	1:40.2	2:05.8
65.0%	25-29	45-75 S	16.2	24.8	33.6	43.5	54.5	1:06.2	1:18.3	1:30.9	1:44.0	-----
62.5%	30-35	30-60 S	16.8	25.7	35.0	45.3	56.7	1:08.8	1:21.4	1:34.6	-----	-----
60.0%	36-40	30-60 S	17.5	26.8	36.4	47.2	59.1	1:11.7	1:24.8	-----	-----	-----

SPEED	REPS	REST	700 MT	800 MT	1000 MT	1200 MT	1500 MT	1600 MT	2000 MT	2400 MT	2800 MT	3200 MT
95.0%	0- 1	---	1:47.9	2:06.2	2:44.8	3:23.8	4:23.7	4:44.1	6:05.9	7:29.0	8:52.7	10:16.7
92.5%	1- 2	4- 5 M	1:50.8	2:09.6	2:49.2	3:29.4	4:30.9	4:51.8	6:15.8	7:41.2	9:07.1	10:33.4
90.0%	2- 3	4- 5 M	1:53.9	2:13.2	2:53.9	3:35.2	4:38.4	4:59.9	6:26.2	7:54.0	9:22.3	10:51.0
87.5%	3- 4	3- 4 M	1:57.1	2:17.0	2:58.9	3:41.3	4:46.3	5:08.5	6:37.3	8:07.5	9:38.3	11:09.6
85.0%	4- 5	3- 4 M	2:00.5	2:21.1	3:04.1	3:47.8	4:54.8	5:17.6	6:48.9	8:21.8	9:55.4	11:29.3
82.5%	6- 7	2- 3 M	2:04.2	2:25.3	3:09.7	3:54.7	5:03.7	5:27.2	7:01.3	-----	-----	-----
80.0%	8- 9	2- 3 M	2:08.1	2:29.9	3:15.6	4:02.1	5:13.2	5:37.4	-----	-----	-----	-----
77.5%	10-12	1- 2 M	2:12.2	2:34.7	3:22.0	4:09.9	-----	-----	-----	-----	-----	-----
75.0%	13-15	1- 2 M	2:16.6	2:39.9	3:28.7	4:18.2	-----	-----	-----	-----	-----	-----
72.5%	16-18	60-90 S	2:21.3	2:45.4	-----	-----	-----	-----	-----	-----	-----	-----
70.0%	19-21	60-90 S	2:26.4	2:51.3	-----	-----	-----	-----	-----	-----	-----	-----
67.5%	22-24	45-75 S	-----	-----	-----	-----	-----	-----	-----	-----	-----	-----
65.0%	25-29	45-75 S	-----	-----	-----	-----	-----	-----	-----	-----	-----	-----
62.5%	30-35	30-60 S	-----	-----	-----	-----	-----	-----	-----	-----	-----	-----
60.0%	36-40	30-60 S	-----	-----	-----	-----	-----	-----	-----	-----	-----	-----

720 POINT LEVEL PACING TABLE

SPEED	REPS	REST	100 MT	150 MT	200 MT	250 MT	300 MT	350 MT	400 MT	450 MT	500 MT	600 MT
95.0%	0- 1	---	11.2	17.2	23.4	30.3	37.9	46.0	54.5	1:03.3	1:12.4	1:31.0
92.5%	1- 2	4- 5 M	11.5	17.7	24.0	31.1	38.9	47.3	56.0	1:05.0	1:14.4	1:33.5
90.0%	2- 3	4- 5 M	11.9	18.1	24.7	31.9	40.0	48.6	57.5	1:06.8	1:16.5	1:36.1
87.5%	3- 4	3- 4 M	12.2	18.7	25.4	32.9	41.2	50.0	59.2	1:08.7	1:18.6	1:38.8
85.0%	4- 5	3- 4 M	12.6	19.2	26.1	33.8	42.4	51.5	1:00.9	1:10.8	1:21.0	1:41.7
82.5%	6- 7	2- 3 M	12.9	19.8	26.9	34.8	43.7	53.0	1:02.8	1:12.9	1:23.4	1:44.8
80.0%	8- 9	2- 3 M	13.3	20.4	27.7	35.9	45.0	54.7	1:04.7	1:15.2	1:26.0	1:48.1
77.5%	10-12	1- 2 M	13.8	21.1	28.6	37.1	46.5	56.4	1:06.8	1:17.6	1:28.8	1:51.6
75.0%	13-15	1- 2 M	14.2	21.8	29.6	38.3	48.0	58.3	1:09.0	1:20.2	1:31.8	1:55.3
72.5%	16-18	60-90 S	14.7	22.5	30.6	39.6	49.7	1:00.3	1:11.4	1:22.9	1:34.9	1:59.3
70.0%	19-21	60-90 S	15.2	23.3	31.7	41.1	51.5	1:02.5	1:14.0	1:25.9	1:38.3	2:03.5
67.5%	22-24	45-75 S	15.8	24.2	32.9	42.6	53.4	1:04.8	1:16.7	1:29.1	1:42.0	2:08.1
65.0%	25-29	45-75 S	16.4	25.1	34.1	44.2	55.4	1:07.3	1:19.6	1:32.5	1:45.9	-----
62.5%	30-35	30-60 S	17.1	26.1	35.5	46.0	57.6	1:10.0	1:22.8	1:36.2	-----	-----
60.0%	36-40	30-60 S	17.8	27.2	37.0	47.9	1:00.0	1:12.9	1:26.3	-----	-----	-----

SPEED	REPS	REST	700 MT	800 MT	1000 MT	1200 MT	1500 MT	1600 MT	2000 MT	2400 MT	2800 MT	3200 MT
95.0%	0- 1	---	1:49.8	2:08.6	2:47.9	3:27.8	4:28.9	4:49.7	6:13.1	7:38.0	9:03.4	10:29.2
92.5%	1- 2	4- 5 M	1:52.8	2:12.0	2:52.4	3:33.4	4:36.1	4:57.5	6:23.2	7:50.3	9:18.1	10:46.2
90.0%	2- 3	4- 5 M	1:55.9	2:15.7	2:57.2	3:39.3	4:43.8	5:05.8	6:33.8	8:03.4	9:33.6	11:04.1
87.5%	3- 4	3- 4 M	1:59.3	2:19.6	3:02.3	3:45.6	4:51.9	5:14.5	6:45.1	8:17.2	9:49.9	11:23.1
85.0%	4- 5	3- 4 M	2:02.8	2:23.7	3:07.6	3:52.2	5:00.5	5:23.8	6:57.0	8:31.8	10:07.3	11:43.2
82.5%	6- 7	2- 3 M	2:06.5	2:28.0	3:13.3	3:59.2	5:09.6	5:33.6	7:09.7	8:47.3	-----	-----
80.0%	8- 9	2- 3 M	2:10.4	2:32.7	3:19.4	4:06.7	5:19.3	5:44.0	-----	-----	-----	-----
77.5%	10-12	1- 2 M	2:14.6	2:37.6	3:25.8	4:14.7	5:29.6	-----	-----	-----	-----	-----
75.0%	13-15	1- 2 M	2:19.1	2:42.8	3:32.6	4:23.2	-----	-----	-----	-----	-----	-----
72.5%	16-18	60-90 S	2:23.9	2:48.5	-----	-----	-----	-----	-----	-----	-----	-----
70.0%	19-21	60-90 S	2:29.1	2:54.5	-----	-----	-----	-----	-----	-----	-----	-----
67.5%	22-24	45-75 S	-----	-----	-----	-----	-----	-----	-----	-----	-----	-----
65.0%	25-29	45-75 S	-----	-----	-----	-----	-----	-----	-----	-----	-----	-----
62.5%	30-35	30-60 S	-----	-----	-----	-----	-----	-----	-----	-----	-----	-----
60.0%	36-40	30-60 S	-----	-----	-----	-----	-----	-----	-----	-----	-----	-----

690 POINT LEVEL PACING TABLE
••••••••••••••••••••••••••

SPEED	REPS	REST	100 MT	150 MT	200 MT	250 MT	300 MT	350 MT	400 MT	450 MT	500 MT	600 MT
95.0%	0- 1	---	11.4	17.4	23.7	30.7	38.5	46.8	55.4	1:04.4	1:13.7	1:32.7
92.5%	1- 2	4- 5 M	11.7	17.9	24.4	31.6	39.6	48.1	56.9	1:06.2	1:15.7	1:35.2
90.0%	2- 3	4- 5 M	12.0	18.4	25.0	32.5	40.7	49.4	58.5	1:08.0	1:17.8	1:37.8
87.5%	3- 4	3- 4 M	12.4	18.9	25.8	33.4	41.8	50.8	1:00.2	1:09.9	1:20.1	1:40.6
85.0%	4- 5	3- 4 M	12.7	19.5	26.5	34.4	43.1	52.3	1:02.0	1:12.0	1:22.4	1:43.6
82.5%	6- 7	2- 3 M	13.1	20.1	27.3	35.4	44.4	53.9	1:03.8	1:14.2	1:24.9	1:46.7
80.0%	8- 9	2- 3 M	13.5	20.7	28.2	36.5	45.8	55.6	1:05.8	1:16.5	1:27.6	1:50.1
77.5%	10-12	1- 2 M	14.0	21.4	29.1	37.7	47.2	57.4	1:08.0	1:19.0	1:30.4	1:53.6
75.0%	13-15	1- 2 M	14.4	22.1	30.1	38.9	48.8	59.3	1:10.2	1:21.6	1:33.4	1:57.4
72.5%	16-18	60-90 S	14.9	22.9	31.1	40.3	50.5	1:01.4	1:12.6	1:24.4	1:36.6	2:01.5
70.0%	19-21	60-90 S	15.5	23.7	32.2	41.7	52.3	1:03.6	1:15.2	1:27.4	1:40.1	2:05.8
67.5%	22-24	45-75 S	16.0	24.6	33.4	43.3	54.2	1:05.9	1:18.0	1:30.7	1:43.8	2:10.5
65.0%	25-29	45-75 S	16.7	25.5	34.7	44.9	56.3	1:08.4	1:21.0	1:34.2	1:47.8	-----
62.5%	30-35	30-60 S	17.3	26.5	36.1	46.7	58.6	1:11.2	1:24.3	1:37.9	1:52.1	-----
60.0%	36-40	30-60 S	18.1	27.6	37.6	48.7	1:01.0	1:14.1	1:27.8	-----	-----	-----

SPEED	REPS	REST	700 MT	800 MT	1000 MT	1200 MT	1500 MT	1600 MT	2000 MT	2400 MT	2800 MT	3200 MT
95.0%	0- 1	---	1:51.9	2:11.0	2:51.1	3:31.8	4:34.2	4:55.5	6:20.6	7:47.3	9:14.5	10:42.1
92.5%	1- 2	4- 5 M	1:54.9	2:14.5	2:55.7	3:37.5	4:41.6	5:03.4	6:30.9	7:59.9	9:29.5	10:59.5
90.0%	2- 3	4- 5 M	1:58.1	2:18.3	3:00.6	3:43.6	4:49.4	5:11.9	6:41.8	8:13.2	9:45.3	11:17.8
87.5%	3- 4	3- 4 M	2:01.5	2:22.2	3:05.8	3:50.0	4:57.7	5:20.8	6:53.3	8:27.3	10:02.0	11:37.1
85.0%	4- 5	3- 4 M	2:05.1	2:26.4	3:11.2	3:56.7	5:06.5	5:30.2	7:05.4	8:42.2	10:19.7	11:57.6
82.5%	6- 7	2- 3 M	2:08.8	2:30.8	3:17.0	4:03.9	5:15.7	5:40.2	7:18.3	8:58.1	-----	-----
80.0%	8- 9	2- 3 M	2:12.9	2:35.5	3:23.2	4:11.5	5:25.6	5:50.8	-----	-----	-----	-----
77.5%	10-12	1- 2 M	2:17.2	2:40.6	3:29.8	4:19.7	5:36.1	-----	-----	-----	-----	-----
75.0%	13-15	1- 2 M	2:21.7	2:45.9	3:36.7	4:28.3	-----	-----	-----	-----	-----	-----
72.5%	16-18	60-90 S	2:26.6	2:51.6	3:44.2	-----	-----	-----	-----	-----	-----	-----
70.0%	19-21	60-90 S	2:31.9	2:57.8	-----	-----	-----	-----	-----	-----	-----	-----
67.5%	22-24	45-75 S	-----	-----	-----	-----	-----	-----	-----	-----	-----	-----
65.0%	25-29	45-75 S	-----	-----	-----	-----	-----	-----	-----	-----	-----	-----
62.5%	30-35	30-60 S	-----	-----	-----	-----	-----	-----	-----	-----	-----	-----
60.0%	36-40	30-60 S	-----	-----	-----	-----	-----	-----	-----	-----	-----	-----

660 PCINT LEVEL PACING TABLE
. . . .

SPEED	REPS	REST	100 MT	150 MT	200 MT	250 MT	300 MT	350 MT	400 MT	450 MT	500 MT	600 MT
95.0%	0- 1	---	11.6	17.7	24.1	31.2	39.2	47.6	56.4	1:05.6	1:15.1	1:34.4
92.5%	1- 2	4- 5 M	11.9	18.2	24.8	32.1	40.2	48.9	57.9	1:07.4	1:17.1	1:37.0
90.0%	2- 3	4- 5 M	12.2	18.7	25.4	33.0	41.4	50.3	59.6	1:09.2	1:19.3	1:39.7
87.5%	3- 4	3- 4 M	12.6	19.2	26.2	33.9	42.5	51.7	1:01.3	1:11.2	1:21.5	1:42.5
85.0%	4- 5	3- 4 M	12.9	19.8	26.9	34.9	43.8	53.2	1:03.1	1:13.3	1:23.9	1:45.5
82.5%	6- 7	2- 3 M	13.3	20.4	27.8	36.0	45.1	54.9	1:05.0	1:15.5	1:26.5	1:48.7
80.0%	8- 9	2- 3 M	13.7	21.0	28.6	37.1	46.5	56.6	1:07.0	1:17.9	1:29.2	1:52.1
77.5%	10-12	1- 2 M	14.2	21.7	29.5	38.3	48.0	58.4	1:09.2	1:20.4	1:32.0	1:55.8
75.0%	13-15	1- 2 M	14.7	22.4	30.5	39.6	49.6	1:00.3	1:11.5	1:23.1	1:35.1	1:59.6
72.5%	16-18	60-90 S	15.2	23.2	31.6	40.9	51.4	1:02.4	1:13.9	1:25.9	1:38.4	2:03.7
70.0%	19-21	60-90 S	15.7	24.0	32.7	42.4	53.2	1:04.7	1:16.6	1:29.0	1:41.9	2:08.2
67.5%	22-24	45-75 S	16.3	24.9	33.9	44.0	55.2	1:07.0	1:19.4	1:32.3	1:45.7	2:12.9
65.0%	25-29	45-75 S	16.9	25.9	35.2	45.7	57.3	1:09.6	1:22.5	1:35.9	1:49.7	-----
62.5%	30-35	30-60 S	17.6	26.9	36.6	47.5	59.6	1:12.4	1:25.8	1:39.7	1:54.1	-----
60.0%	36-40	30-60 S	18.3	28.1	38.2	49.5	1:02.0	1:15.4	1:29.3	-----	-----	-----

SPEED	REPS	REST	700 MT	800 MT	1000 MT	1200 MT	1500 MT	1600 MT	2000 MT	2400 MT	2800 MT	3200 MT
95.0%	0- 1	---	1:54.0	2:13.5	2:54.5	3:36.0	4:39.8	5:01.5	6:28.5	7:57.0	9:26.1	10:55.6
92.5%	1- 2	4- 5 M	1:57.1	2:17.1	2:59.2	3:41.9	4:47.3	5:09.6	6:39.0	8:09.9	9:41.4	11:13.3
90.0%	2- 3	4- 5 M	2:00.4	2:20.9	3:04.2	3:48.1	4:55.3	5:18.2	6:50.1	8:23.5	9:57.5	11:32.0
87.5%	3- 4	3- 4 M	2:03.8	2:25.0	3:09.4	3:54.6	5:03.7	5:27.3	7:01.8	8:37.9	10:14.6	11:51.8
85.0%	4- 5	3- 4 M	2:07.4	2:29.2	3:15.0	4:01.5	5:12.7	5:36.9	7:14.2	8:53.1	10:32.7	12:12.7
82.5%	6- 7	2- 3 M	2:11.3	2:33.7	3:20.9	4:08.8	5:22.1	5:47.1	7:27.3	9:09.2	-----	-----
80.0%	8- 9	2- 3 M	2:15.4	2:38.5	3:27.2	4:16.6	5:32.2	5:58.0	-----	-----	-----	-----
77.5%	10-12	1- 2 M	2:19.8	2:43.7	3:33.9	4:24.8	5:42.9	-----	-----	-----	-----	-----
75.0%	13-15	1- 2 M	2:24.4	2:49.1	3:41.0	4:33.7	-----	-----	-----	-----	-----	-----
72.5%	16-18	60-90 S	2:29.4	2:54.9	3:48.6	-----	-----	-----	-----	-----	-----	-----
70.0%	19-21	60-90 S	2:34.8	3:01.2	-----	-----	-----	-----	-----	-----	-----	-----
67.5%	22-24	45-75 S	-----	-----	-----	-----	-----	-----	-----	-----	-----	-----
65.0%	25-29	45-75 S	-----	-----	-----	-----	-----	-----	-----	-----	-----	-----
62.5%	30-35	30-60 S	-----	-----	-----	-----	-----	-----	-----	-----	-----	-----
60.0%	36-40	30-60 S	-----	-----	-----	-----	-----	-----	-----	-----	-----	-----

630 POINT LEVEL PACING TABLE
....

SPEED	REPS	REST	100 MT	150 MT	200 MT	250 MT	300 MT	350 MT	400 MT	450 MT	500 MT	600 MT
95.0%	0- 1	---	11.8	18.0	24.5	31.8	39.9	48.5	57.4	1:06.8	1:16.5	1:36.2
92.5%	1- 2	4- 5 M	12.1	18.5	25.2	32.6	40.9	49.8	59.0	1:08.6	1:18.6	1:38.8
90.0%	2- 3	4- 5 M	12.4	19.0	25.9	33.5	42.1	51.2	1:00.6	1:10.5	1:20.7	1:41.6
87.5%	3- 4	3- 4 M	12.8	19.5	26.6	34.5	43.3	52.6	1:02.4	1:12.5	1:23.0	1:44.5
85.0%	4- 5	3- 4 M	13.1	20.1	27.4	35.5	44.5	54.2	1:04.2	1:14.6	1:25.5	1:47.6
82.5%	6- 7	2- 3 M	13.5	20.7	28.2	36.6	45.9	55.8	1:06.1	1:16.9	1:28.1	1:50.8
80.0%	8- 9	2- 3 M	14.0	21.4	29.1	37.7	47.3	57.6	1:08.2	1:19.3	1:30.8	1:54.3
77.5%	10-12	1- 2 M	14.4	22.1	30.0	38.9	48.9	59.4	1:10.4	1:21.9	1:33.8	1:58.0
75.0%	13-15	1- 2 M	14.9	22.8	31.0	40.2	50.5	1:01.4	1:12.7	1:24.6	1:36.9	2:01.9
72.5%	16-18	60-90 S	15.4	23.6	32.1	41.6	52.2	1:03.5	1:15.3	1:27.5	1:40.2	2:06.1
70.0%	19-21	60-90 S	15.9	24.4	33.2	43.1	54.1	1:05.8	1:17.9	1:30.6	1:43.8	2:10.6
67.5%	22-24	45-75 S	16.5	25.3	34.5	44.7	56.1	1:08.2	1:20.8	1:34.0	1:47.7	2:15.5
65.0%	25-29	45-75 S	17.2	26.3	35.8	46.4	58.3	1:10.9	1:23.9	1:37.6	1:51.8	-----
62.5%	30-35	30-60 S	17.9	27.4	37.2	48.3	1:00.6	1:13.7	1:27.3	1:41.5	1:56.3	-----
60.0%	36-40	30-60 S	18.6	28.5	38.8	50.3	1:03.1	1:16.8	1:30.9	-----	-----	-----

SPEED	REPS	REST	700 MT	800 MT	1000 MT	1200 MT	1500 MT	1600 MT	2000 MT	2400 MT	2800 MT	3200 MT
95.0%	0- 1	---	1:56.2	2:16.1	2:58.0	3:40.4	4:45.5	5:07.7	6:36.6	8:07.1	9:38.1	11:09.6
92.5%	1- 2	4- 5 M	1:59.4	2:19.8	3:02.8	3:46.4	4:53.3	5:16.0	6:47.4	8:20.2	9:53.8	11:27.7
90.0%	2- 3	4- 5 M	2:02.7	2:23.7	3:07.9	3:52.7	5:01.4	5:24.8	6:58.7	8:34.1	10:10.3	11:46.8
87.5%	3- 4	3- 4 M	2:06.2	2:27.8	3:13.2	3:59.3	5:10.0	5:34.1	7:10.6	8:48.8	10:27.7	12:07.0
85.0%	4- 5	3- 4 M	2:09.9	2:32.2	3:18.9	4:06.4	5:19.1	5:43.9	7:23.3	9:04.4	10:46.2	12:28.4
82.5%	6- 7	2- 3 M	2:13.9	2:36.8	3:25.0	4:13.8	5:28.8	5:54.3	7:36.7	9:20.9	-----	-----
80.0%	8- 9	2- 3 M	2:18.0	2:41.7	3:31.4	4:21.8	5:39.1	6:05.4	-----	-----	-----	-----
77.5%	10-12	1- 2 M	2:22.5	2:46.9	3:38.2	4:30.2	5:50.0	-----	-----	-----	-----	-----
75.0%	13-15	1- 2 M	2:27.2	2:52.4	3:45.4	4:39.2	-----	-----	-----	-----	-----	-----
72.5%	16-18	60-90 S	2:32.3	2:58.4	3:53.2	-----	-----	-----	-----	-----	-----	-----
70.0%	19-21	60-90 S	2:37.8	3:04.8	-----	-----	-----	-----	-----	-----	-----	-----
67.5%	22-24	45-75 S	2:43.6	-----	-----	-----	-----	-----	-----	-----	-----	-----
65.0%	25-29	45-75 S	-----	-----	-----	-----	-----	-----	-----	-----	-----	-----
62.5%	30-35	30-60 S	-----	-----	-----	-----	-----	-----	-----	-----	-----	-----
60.0%	36-40	30-60 S	-----	-----	-----	-----	-----	-----	-----	-----	-----	-----

600 POINT LEVEL PACING TABLE

SPEED	REPS	REST	100 MT	150 MT	200 MT	250 MT	300 MT	350 MT	400 MT	450 MT	500 MT	600 MT
95.0%	0- 1	---	11.9	18.3	24.9	32.3	40.6	49.3	58.5	1:08.0	1:17.9	1:38.1
92.5%	1- 2	4- 5 M	12.3	18.8	25.6	33.2	41.6	50.7	1:00.1	1:09.9	1:20.0	1:40.8
90.0%	2- 3	4- 5 M	12.6	19.3	26.3	34.1	42.8	52.1	1:01.7	1:11.8	1:22.3	1:43.6
87.5%	3- 4	3- 4 M	13.0	19.9	27.0	35.1	44.0	53.6	1:03.5	1:13.9	1:24.6	1:46.5
85.0%	4- 5	3- 4 M	13.3	20.4	27.8	36.1	45.3	55.1	1:05.4	1:16.0	1:27.1	1:49.7
82.5%	6- 7	2- 3 M	13.7	21.1	28.7	37.2	46.7	56.8	1:07.3	1:18.3	1:29.8	1:53.0
80.0%	8- 9	2- 3 M	14.2	21.7	29.6	38.4	48.2	58.6	1:09.5	1:20.8	1:32.6	1:56.5
77.5%	10-12	1- 2 M	14.6	22.4	30.5	39.6	49.7	1:00.5	1:11.7	1:23.4	1:35.5	2:00.3
75.0%	13-15	1- 2 M	15.1	23.2	31.5	40.9	51.4	1:02.5	1:14.1	1:26.2	1:38.7	2:04.3
72.5%	16-18	60-90 S	15.6	24.0	32.6	42.3	53.1	1:04.7	1:16.6	1:29.1	1:42.1	2:08.6
70.0%	19-21	60-90 S	16.2	24.8	33.8	43.8	55.0	1:07.0	1:19.4	1:32.3	1:45.8	2:13.2
67.5%	22-24	45-75 S	16.8	25.7	35.0	45.5	57.1	1:09.4	1:22.3	1:35.7	1:49.7	2:18.1
65.0%	25-29	45-75 S	17.4	26.7	36.4	47.2	59.3	1:12.1	1:25.5	1:39.4	1:53.9	2:23.4
62.5%	30-35	30-60 S	18.1	27.8	37.8	49.1	1:01.6	1:15.0	1:28.9	1:43.4	1:58.5	-----
60.0%	36-40	30-60 S	18.9	28.9	39.4	51.1	1:04.2	1:18.1	1:32.6	-----	-----	-----

SPEED	REPS	REST	700 MT	800 MT	1000 MT	1200 MT	1500 MT	1600 MT	2000 MT	2400 MT	2800 MT	3200 MT
95.0%	0- 1	---	1:58.5	2:18.9	3:01.6	3:45.0	4:51.6	5:14.2	6:45.1	8:17.6	9:50.7	11:24.3
92.5%	1- 2	4- 5 M	2:01.8	2:22.6	3:06.5	3:51.1	4:59.4	5:22.7	6:56.1	8:31.1	10:06.7	11:42.8
90.0%	2- 3	4- 5 M	2:05.1	2:26.6	3:11.7	3:57.5	5:07.8	5:31.7	7:07.7	8:45.3	10:23.6	12:02.3
87.5%	3- 4	3- 4 M	2:08.7	2:30.8	3:17.2	4:04.3	5:16.6	5:41.2	7:19.9	9:00.3	10:41.4	12:23.0
85.0%	4- 5	3- 4 M	2:12.5	2:35.2	3:23.0	4:11.5	5:25.9	5:51.2	7:32.8	9:16.2	11:00.2	12:44.8
82.5%	6- 7	2- 3 M	2:16.5	2:39.9	3:29.2	4:19.1	5:35.7	6:01.8	7:46.5	9:33.0	-----	-----
80.0%	8- 9	2- 3 M	2:20.8	2:44.9	3:35.7	4:27.2	5:46.2	6:13.1	-----	-----	-----	-----
77.5%	10-12	1- 2 M	2:25.3	2:50.2	3:42.6	4:35.8	5:57.4	-----	-----	-----	-----	-----
75.0%	13-15	1- 2 M	2:30.2	2:55.9	3:50.1	4:45.0	-----	-----	-----	-----	-----	-----
72.5%	16-18	60-90 S	2:35.3	3:02.0	3:58.0	-----	-----	-----	-----	-----	-----	-----
70.0%	19-21	60-90 S	2:40.9	3:08.5	-----	-----	-----	-----	-----	-----	-----	-----
67.5%	22-24	45-75 S	2:46.8	-----	-----	-----	-----	-----	-----	-----	-----	-----
65.0%	25-29	45-75 S	-----	-----	-----	-----	-----	-----	-----	-----	-----	-----
62.5%	30-35	30-60 S	-----	-----	-----	-----	-----	-----	-----	-----	-----	-----
60.0%	36-40	30-60 S	-----	-----	-----	-----	-----	-----	-----	-----	-----	-----

570 POINT LEVEL PACING TABLE
••••••••••••••••••••••••••••••

SPEED	REPS	REST	100 MT	150 MT	200 MT	250 MT	300 MT	350 MT	400 MT	450 MT	500 MT	600 MT
95.0%	0- 1	---	12.1	18.6	25.3	32.9	41.3	50.2	59.6	1:09.3	1:19.4	1:40.1
92.5%	1- 2	4- 5 M	12.5	19.1	26.0	33.7	42.4	51.6	1:01.2	1:11.2	1:21.6	1:42.8
90.0%	2- 3	4- 5 M	12.8	19.6	26.7	34.7	43.6	53.0	1:02.9	1:13.2	1:23.9	1:45.6
87.5%	3- 4	3- 4 M	13.2	20.2	27.5	35.7	44.8	54.5	1:04.7	1:15.3	1:26.3	1:48.6
85.0%	4- 5	3- 4 M	13.5	20.8	28.3	36.7	46.1	56.2	1:06.6	1:17.5	1:28.8	1:51.8
82.5%	6- 7	2- 3 M	14.0	21.4	29.1	37.8	47.5	57.9	1:08.6	1:19.8	1:31.5	1:55.2
80.0%	8- 9	2- 3 M	14.4	22.1	30.1	39.0	49.0	59.7	1:10.7	1:22.3	1:34.3	1:58.8
77.5%	10-12	1- 2 M	14.9	22.8	31.0	40.3	50.6	1:01.6	1:13.0	1:25.0	1:37.4	2:02.7
75.0%	13-15	1- 2 M	15.4	23.5	32.1	41.6	52.3	1:03.6	1:15.5	1:27.8	1:40.6	2:06.7
72.5%	16-18	60-90 S	15.9	24.3	33.2	43.1	54.1	1:05.8	1:18.1	1:30.8	1:44.1	2:11.1
70.0%	19-21	60-90 S	16.5	25.2	34.3	44.6	56.0	1:08.2	1:20.9	1:34.1	1:47.8	2:15.8
67.5%	22-24	45-75 S	17.1	26.1	35.6	46.2	58.1	1:10.7	1:23.8	1:37.6	1:51.8	2:20.8
65.0%	25-29	45-75 S	17.7	27.2	37.0	48.0	1:00.3	1:13.4	1:27.1	1:41.3	1:56.1	2:26.2
62.5%	30-35	30-60 S	18.4	28.2	38.5	49.9	1:02.7	1:16.4	1:30.6	1:45.4	2:00.8	-----
60.0%	36-40	30-60 S	19.2	29.4	40.1	52.0	1:05.3	1:19.6	1:34.3	1:49.8	-----	-----

SPEED	REPS	REST	700 MT	800 MT	1000 MT	1200 MT	1500 MT	1600 MT	2000 MT	2400 MT	2800 MT	3200 MT
95.0%	0- 1	---	2:00.9	2:21.7	3:05.4	3:49.8	4:57.8	5:21.0	6:54.0	8:28.6	10:03.9	11:39.6
92.5%	1- 2	4- 5 M	2:04.2	2:25.5	3:10.4	3:56.0	5:05.9	5:29.7	7:05.2	8:42.4	10:20.2	11:58.5
90.0%	2- 3	4- 5 M	2:07.7	2:29.6	3:15.7	4:02.6	5:14.4	5:38.8	7:17.0	8:56.9	10:37.5	12:18.5
87.5%	3- 4	3- 4 M	2:11.3	2:33.9	3:21.3	4:09.5	5:23.4	5:48.5	7:29.5	9:12.2	10:55.7	12:39.6
85.0%	4- 5	3- 4 M	2:15.2	2:38.4	3:27.2	4:16.8	5:32.9	5:58.8	7:42.7	9:28.5	11:14.9	13:01.9
82.5%	6- 7	2- 3 M	2:19.3	2:43.2	3:33.5	4:24.6	5:43.0	6:09.7	7:56.8	9:45.7	-----	-----
80.0%	8- 9	2- 3 M	2:23.6	2:48.3	3:40.2	4:32.9	5:53.7	6:21.2	-----	-----	-----	-----
77.5%	10-12	1- 2 M	2:28.3	2:53.7	3:47.3	4:41.7	6:05.1	-----	-----	-----	-----	-----
75.0%	13-15	1- 2 M	2:33.2	2:59.5	3:54.9	4:51.1	-----	-----	-----	-----	-----	-----
72.5%	16-18	60-90 S	2:38.5	3:05.7	4:03.0	-----	-----	-----	-----	-----	-----	-----
70.0%	19-21	60-90 S	2:44.1	3:12.3	-----	-----	-----	-----	-----	-----	-----	-----
67.5%	22-24	45-75 S	2:50.2	-----	-----	-----	-----	-----	-----	-----	-----	-----
65.0%	25-29	45-75 S	-----	-----	-----	-----	-----	-----	-----	-----	-----	-----
62.5%	30-35	30-60 S	-----	-----	-----	-----	-----	-----	-----	-----	-----	-----
60.0%	36-40	30-60 S	-----	-----	-----	-----	-----	-----	-----	-----	-----	-----

540 POINT LEVEL PACING TABLE

SPEED	REPS	REST	100 MT	150 MT	200 MT	250 MT	300 MT	350 MT	400 MT	450 MT	500 MT	600 MT
95.0%	0- 1	---	12.3	18.9	25.7	33.4	42.0	51.2	1:00.7	1:10.7	1:21.0	1:42.1
92.5%	1- 2	4- 5 M	12.7	19.4	26.4	34.3	43.2	52.6	1:02.3	1:12.6	1:23.2	1:44.9
90.0%	2- 3	4- 5 M	13.0	19.9	27.2	35.3	44.4	54.0	1:04.1	1:14.6	1:25.5	1:47.8
87.5%	3- 4	3- 4 M	13.4	20.5	27.9	36.3	45.6	55.6	1:05.9	1:16.7	1:28.0	1:50.8
85.0%	4- 5	3- 4 M	13.8	21.1	28.8	37.4	47.0	57.2	1:07.8	1:19.0	1:30.5	1:54.1
82.5%	6- 7	2- 3 M	14.2	21.7	29.6	38.5	48.4	58.9	1:09.9	1:21.4	1:33.3	1:57.6
80.0%	8- 9	2- 3 M	14.6	22.4	30.6	39.7	49.9	1:00.8	1:12.1	1:23.9	1:36.2	2:01.2
77.5%	10-12	1- 2 M	15.1	23.1	31.5	41.0	51.5	1:02.7	1:14.4	1:26.6	1:39.3	2:05.1
75.0%	13-15	1- 2 M	15.6	23.9	32.6	42.3	53.2	1:04.8	1:16.9	1:29.5	1:42.6	2:09.3
72.5%	16-18	60-90 S	16.1	24.7	33.7	43.8	55.1	1:07.1	1:19.5	1:32.6	1:46.2	2:13.8
70.0%	19-21	60-90 S	16.7	25.6	34.9	45.4	57.0	1:09.5	1:22.4	1:35.9	1:50.0	2:18.6
67.5%	22-24	45-75 S	17.3	26.6	36.2	47.1	59.1	1:12.0	1:25.4	1:39.5	1:54.0	2:23.7
65.0%	25-29	45-75 S	18.0	27.6	37.6	48.9	1:01.4	1:14.8	1:28.7	1:43.3	1:58.4	2:29.2
62.5%	30-35	30-60 S	18.7	28.7	39.1	50.8	1:03.9	1:17.8	1:32.3	1:47.4	2:03.1	-----
60.0%	36-40	30-60 S	19.5	29.9	40.7	52.9	1:06.5	1:21.0	1:36.1	1:51.9	-----	-----

SPEED	REPS	REST	700 MT	800 MT	1000 MT	1200 MT	1500 MT	1600 MT	2000 MT	2400 MT	2800 MT	3200 MT
95.0%	0- 1	---	2:03.4	2:24.7	3:09.4	3:54.8	5:04.4	5:28.1	7:03.3	8:40.1	10:17.7	11:55.7
92.5%	1- 2	4- 5 M	2:06.8	2:28.6	3:14.5	4:01.1	5:12.6	5:37.0	7:14.8	8:54.2	10:34.4	12:15.0
90.0%	2- 3	4- 5 M	2:10.3	2:32.7	3:19.9	4:07.8	5:21.3	5:46.3	7:26.8	9:09.0	10:52.0	12:35.4
87.5%	3- 4	3- 4 M	2:14.0	2:37.1	3:25.6	4:14.9	5:30.5	5:56.2	7:39.6	9:24.7	11:10.6	12:57.0
85.0%	4- 5	3- 4 M	2:18.0	2:41.7	3:31.7	4:22.4	5:40.2	6:06.7	7:53.1	9:41.3	11:30.3	13:19.9
32.5%	6- 7	2- 3 M	2:22.1	2:46.6	3:38.1	4:30.4	5:50.5	6:17.8	8:07.5	9:59.0	-----	-----
80.0%	8- 9	2- 3 M	2:26.6	2:51.8	3:44.9	4:38.8	6:01.5	6:29.6	-----	-----	-----	-----
77.5%	10-12	1- 2 M	2:31.3	2:57.3	3:52.2	4:47.8	6:13.1	-----	-----	-----	-----	-----
75.0%	13-15	1- 2 M	2:36.4	3:03.3	3:59.9	4:57.4	-----	-----	-----	-----	-----	-----
72.5%	16-18	60-90 S	2:41.8	3:09.6	4:08.2	-----	-----	-----	-----	-----	-----	-----
70.0%	19-21	60-90 S	2:47.5	3:16.3	-----	-----	-----	-----	-----	-----	-----	-----
67.5%	22-24	45-75 S	2:53.7	-----	-----	-----	-----	-----	-----	-----	-----	-----
65.0%	25-29	45-75 S	-----	-----	-----	-----	-----	-----	-----	-----	-----	-----
62.5%	30-35	30-60 S	-----	-----	-----	-----	-----	-----	-----	-----	-----	-----
60.0%	36-40	30-60 S	-----	-----	-----	-----	-----	-----	-----	-----	-----	-----

CH

Other books of interest from
Track & Field News and TAFNEWS PRESS

THE CONDITIONING OF DISTANCE RUNNERS. Tom Osler's useful training ideas, 6 miles and up. Very valuable.   **$1.25**
HIGH SCHOOL RUNNERS & Their Training Programs, Joe Mc-Neff. Workout programs of 110 recent prep stars, 440-10mi. **$3.00**
HOW THEY TRAIN. Training programs of top runners, 880-6 mi. Popular, much valued work. By Fred Wilt. Paper **$2.00**; Hard **$3.50**
LONG DISTANCE RUNNING. Excellent AAA instructional book by Martin Hyman & Bruce Tulloh. Training, theory, etc. **$1.50**
LONG SLOW DISTANCE: The Humane Way to Train. Joe Henderson's alternative to back-breaking interval training.   **$2.00**
LYDIARD'S RUNNING TRAINING SCHEDULES. Workout schedules devised by the famed New Zealand coach. New 2nd ed. **$1.50**
MIDDLE DISTANCE RUNNING. Percy Cerutty's best technique work: hill running, schedules, diet, training programs, etc. **$4.50**
MIDDLE DISTANCE RUNNING, A.P. Ward. British AAA instructional booklet: technique, tactics, rules, theory, training. **$1.50**
MODERN TRAINING FOR RUNNING. Ken Doherty. Definitive text covers all aspects of contemporary training concepts. **$10.95**
ROAD RACERS AND THEIR TRAINING, Joe Henderson. Comprehensive survey covers workout programs, philosophies, personalities of 60 road runners of every ability, age-group, etc. **$2.50**
RUN RUN RUN, Fred Wilt. Perhaps the most useful book ever on running training: all training methods, theory, pace, tactics, warm-up, etc.—sprinting thru marathon. 281pp. Paper **$3.50**; Hard **$5.00**
RUN TO THE TOP. Arthur Lydiard's premier technique work has schedules & training for middle & long distance runners, etc. **$4.95**
STAMPFL ON RUNNING. Theories and schedules of interval training by the coach of Roger Bannister, Ralph Doubell, etc. **$3.95**
TULLOH ON RUNNING. Training ideas and theory by ex-distance ace Bruce Tulloh. Excellent presentation, human approach. **$3.95**

WHAT RESEARCH TELLS THE COACH ABOUT DISTANCE RUNNING, D.L. Costill. Contemporary research findings. **$2.95**
MY RUN ACROSS THE U.S.A., Don Shepherd. Shepherd tells his incredible story of his 1964 solo run across America. **$3.50**
FOUR MILLION FOOTSTEPS, Bruce Tulloh. Tulloh "broke" the trans-America record in 1969. This is his fascinating account. **$3.95**
TRACK & FIELD: The Great Ones. Cordner Nelson tells of 13 of history's top tracksters, with 179 profiles on other stars. **$5.75**
THE JIM RYUN STORY. Biography of the Kansas phenom by Cordner Nelson, with 187 photos by Rich Clarkson. **$5.95**
THERE'S A HUMAN BEING IN THAT SWEAT SUIT, Marv Rothenstein. A 5000-mile-a-year "jogger" tells why and how. **$2.00**
RUN FOR YOUR LIFE: Jogging with Arthur Lydiard. Lydiard's program of fitness thru jogging. Must read. Paper **$2.50**; Hard **$4.50**
THE NEW AEROBICS, Dr. Kenneth Cooper. Updated, revised theories, point scores by the author of "Aerobics." **$5.95**
THE UNFORGIVING MINUTE. Outstanding autobiography of Ron Clarke, great Australian multi-record holder.   **$5.75**
NO BUGLES NO DRUMS. Peter Snell's autobiography makes lively, always interesting reading.   **$4.50**
SUPER FOOD FOR SUPER ATHLETES, A. Fleming. High protein, quick energy diets, etc. Bulk-up, weight reducing foods, etc. **$2.95**
TRACK & FIELD NEWS. News, features, photos, stats of men's track, h.s. thru Olympics, U.S. & international. 18 issues a yr. **$6.00**
TRACK TECHNIQUE. THE technical quarterly of track & field: articles on technique, training, psychology, injuries, etc. **$3.00** a year

Prices subject to change. Add 25¢ per book to cover postage and handling. Order from TRACK & FIELD NEWS, P.O. Box 296, Los Altos, Calif. 94022.